Legalines

Constitutional Law

by

JONATHAN NEVILLE
ATTORNEY AT LAW

D1407530

KEYED TO THE SEVENTH EDITION OF THE STONE CASEBOOK

GILBERT

Mat #41563490

Copyright © 2010 by Thomson/West
© 2014 LEG, Inc. d/b/a West Academic
    444 Cedar Street, Suite 700
    St. Paul, MN 55101
    1-877-888-1330

Printed in the United States of America

ISBN: 978-0-314-29126-4

Summary of Contents

Table of Contents

Constitutional Law

KEYED TO THE SEVENTH
EDITION OF THE STONE
CASEBOOK

Chapter I
Introduction to the Constitution

A. Basic Document

The Constitution of the United States currently consists of seven articles and 27 amendments. It was created in response to the inadequacies of the Articles of Confederation and was ratified by the nine states necessary in 1788. The Constitution separates the powers of the national government into three branches: executive, legislative, and judicial. Each branch was intended to remain independent yet subject to restraint by the other branches through a system of checks and balances. The Constitution also establishes the federal/state framework of government. The study of constitutional law is essentially an examination of the sources of governmental power and the limitations imposed on its exercise. Through the system of judicial review, the United States Supreme Court has the final say in interpreting the Constitution; hence the heavy reliance on studying decisions of that Court.

B. Significant Amendments

The articles of the Constitution contain important protections of individual liberty, including the writ of habeas corpus, prohibition of ex post facto laws, and the Privileges and Immunities Clause. Two groups of amendments, however, provide the majority of the civil liberties enjoyed in the United States today.

1. The Bill of Rights

Many of the states included a bill of rights in their constitutions, but none was included in the original Constitution. Adoption of the first 10 amendments, or Bill of Rights, was prompted largely by the concerns expressed during the state ratification conventions. These amendments did not affect state power; they were only limitations on the power of the federal government.

2. Civil War Amendments

The abolition of slavery during the Civil War presented serious social problems. The Thirteenth Amendment, which was ratified in 1865, provided legal support to eradicate slavery, which had been recognized in the original Constitution. In 1866, Congress enacted the Civil Rights Act to prohibit racial discrimination practiced by the states. The President vetoed the act on grounds that it was unconstitutional, and although Congress overrode the veto, the Fourteenth Amendment was proposed to overcome constitutional objections to the Civil Rights Act. It was ratified largely because Congress made ratification a condition for the rebel states to be represented in Congress. The Fifteenth Amendment prohibited denial of the right to vote for racial reasons.

C. The Process of Constitutional Interpretation

Effective study of the Constitution requires more than just learning what "the law is." Many of the currently prevailing constitutional doctrines are relative newcomers; some are even the exact opposite of the doctrines that prevailed in earlier times. To be an effective constitutional advocate, a lawyer must understand various approaches to an issue. Often there is no "correct" interpretation of the Constitution; the interpretation that persuades a majority of the Supreme Court Justices is the one which becomes the law.

Chapter II

The Role of the Supreme Court in the Constitutional Order

A. Judicial Review of the Constitutionality of Legislation

1. Origins of Judicial Review

Although there was some debate at the Constitutional Convention about the role of the judiciary in reviewing legislative acts, nothing in the Constitution expressly gives the Supreme Court power to rule on the constitutionality of acts of Congress or state statutes, nor the power to review decisions of state courts. Article III merely creates the Supreme Court and extends the judicial power to "all Cases, in Law and Equity, arising under this Constitution, the Laws of the United States, and Treaties made . . . under their authority." Section 2 spells out those cases in which the Supreme Court has original jurisdiction and specifies that in all other cases, the Court shall have appellate jurisdiction.

2. Judiciary Act of 1789

In the Judiciary Act of 1789, Congress created lower federal courts as permitted by the Constitution, but did not give them general jurisdiction in civil cases arising under federal law. The state courts were to exercise jurisdiction over such cases. The Supreme Court was authorized to hear three types of cases on appeal, all essentially involving state court rejection of claims made under federal law.

3. Review of Acts of Congress

The authority of the Supreme Court to review acts of Congress is not set forth in the Constitution. In the early days of the Marshall Court there was a considerable dispute about the propriety of this doctrine.

a. Hamilton

The Federalist No. 78, written by Alexander Hamilton, argues that the judiciary is the least powerful of the branches of government in that it controls neither public funds nor the military. The independence of the judiciary allows it to guard the Constitution and the rights of individuals from improper actions of the other branches. Judicial decisions must be governed by the Constitution rather than by any contrary statute.

b. Jefferson

Thomas Jefferson argued that each branch was responsible to determine for itself the constitutionality of its actions, and that the judges should not be the ultimate arbiters of all constitutional questions, although he recognized that the courts would face constitutional questions more often than the other branches.

c. The Judiciary Act

In the Judiciary Act of 1789, Congress also gave the Supreme Court power to issue writs of mandamus to United States officials. This grant of original jurisdiction arguably violated the specific provisions of Article III, section 2, setting the stage for the following case.

4. Assertion of Judicial Review Power

Marbury v. Madison
5 U.S. (1 Cranch) 137 (1803).

Facts. Marbury (P) and others were appointed justices of the peace for the District of Columbia by President Adams and confirmed by the Senate on Adams's last day in office. Their formal commissions were signed but not delivered. Madison (D), as Secretary of State, was directed by the new President, Thomas Jefferson, to withhold the commissions. P brought a writ of mandamus directly to the Supreme Court under the Judiciary Act of 1789, which established United States courts and authorized the Supreme Court to issue writs of mandamus to public officers.

Issue. Is the Supreme Court empowered to review acts of Congress and void those that it finds to be repugnant to the Constitution?

Held. Yes. P's action is discharged because the Court does not have original jurisdiction; section 13 of the Judiciary Act is unconstitutional.

♦ The facts demonstrate a plain case for mandamus action, and under the Judiciary Act this Court could so act.

♦ P claims that since the constitutional grant of jurisdiction is general and the clause assigning original jurisdiction to the Supreme Court (Article III, section 2, clause 2) contains no negative or restrictive words, the legislature may assign original jurisdiction to this Court in addition to that specified in the Constitution. But the clause specifies in what cases this Court is to have original jurisdiction, and that in all other cases its jurisdiction is appellate. P's contention would render the clause ineffectual, an impermissible construction. Therefore, the Judiciary Act's grant of original mandamus jurisdiction is unconstitutional and void.

♦ The grant of judicial power extends to all cases arising under the Constitution and laws of the United States. Since the Constitution is superior to any ordinary legislative act, it must govern a case to which both apply.

♦ The Supremacy Clause (Article VI, section 2) declares that the Constitution and those acts of Congress made in pursuance thereof shall be the supreme law of the land. Thus, the Court must determine when such acts are actually made in pursuance of the Constitution. The power of judicial review is implicit in the Constitution.

Comment. In more recent times, the Court has asserted a broad judicial review power, claiming the responsibility of being the ultimate interpreter of the Constitution. Once a law is declared unconstitutional, the courts simply decline to enforce it.

---

5. Review of State Legislation

Martin v. Hunter's Lessee
14 U.S. (1 Wheat.) 304 (1816).

Facts. British subject Martin (D) was heir to the Virginia estates of Lord Fairfax, who died in England in 1781. Through state legislation confiscating the property of British loyalists, Virginia had conveyed title to Hunter. Hunter's lessee (P) brought an action of ejectment. D defended his title by virtue of two treaties between the United States and Britain that protected such British-owned property. The Virginia Court of Appeals sustained P's claim but was reversed by the United States Supreme Court. The Virginia court refused to comply with the reversal, and D again appeals.

Issue. Does the United States Supreme Court have appellate jurisdiction over the highest state courts on issues involving the federal Constitution, laws, and treaties?

Held. Yes. The Virginia court must obey the United States Supreme Court's rulings.

♦   The Judiciary Act of 1789, section 25, provided for review by the United States Supreme Court of final state court decisions rejecting claims under the federal Constitution and laws. The outcome of this case depends on the constitutionality of that section.

♦   Appellate jurisdiction is given by the Constitution to the Supreme Court in all cases where it does not have original jurisdiction, subject to congressional regulations.

♦   All cases involving the Constitution, laws, and treaties of the United States are included in the judicial power granted by the Constitution to the Supreme Court; hence all such cases are properly subject to that Court's appellate jurisdiction, and section 25 of the Judiciary Act is valid.

♦   Such power is necessary for uniformity of decisions throughout the whole United States, upon all subjects within the purview of the Constitution.

Comments.

♦   In *Cohens v. Virginia*, 19 U.S. (6 Wheat.) 264 (1821), a case involving the illegal sale in Virginia of lottery tickets issued with congressional authority in the District of Columbia, the Court extended the *Martin* decision to permit review of state court criminal judgments.

♦   When the Supreme Court reverses a state court judgment, it normally remands for "proceedings not inconsistent with this opinion." This allows the state court to both review previously undecided issues and to reconsider its decision on matters of state law.

B. Sources of Constitutional Doctrine

1. Introduction

The Constitution itself is a relatively brief document and cannot include all the various legal doctrines a court must use to decide cases. The text of the Constitution is often merely the starting point for the court to determine what constitutional law is. Other sources of constitutional doctrine include concepts of natural law and natural rights, and notions about "public policy," or what would promote the principles and values behind our representative form of government.

2. The Necessary and Proper Clause

A good example of the need for constitutional doctrine to illuminate the text of the Constitution is the Necessary and Proper Clause. Article I, section 1 grants legislative powers to Congress. This is the power to make laws and to do all things that are necessary to enact them, such as to conduct investigations, hold hearings, etc. Because the federal government has only such power as is granted by the people, the powers of Congress are specifically enumerated in section 8; every federal statute must be based on one of the enumerated powers. The Necessary and Proper Clause, however, gives Congress authority to "make all laws which shall be necessary and proper for carrying into execution the foregoing powers." The interpretation of this clause was a critical issue because, if narrowly construed, it could severely limit the federal government's ability to function, while if broadly construed, it could undermine the notion of federalism by removing any limits on the power of the federal government vis-à-vis the states.

3. The Bank of the United States

The meaning of federalism was initially clarified by the outcome of the controversy over the Bank of the United States. Nothing in the Constitution specifically granted Congress power to organize a Bank of the United States. However, Congress did create such a bank, as proposed by Secretary of the Treasury Alexander Hamilton, despite the objections of Thomas Jefferson and James Madison that Congress lacked power to do so. The original bank's charter expired after 20 years. Four years later. Congress established a second Bank of the United States. Many of the states objected to the bank and imposed stiff taxes on it. Maryland's tax on the bank became the basis for the first important Supreme Court opinion on federalism.

a. Scope of federal authority

McCulloch v. Maryland
17 U.S. (4 Wheat.) 316 (1819).

Facts. The state of Maryland (P) imposed a tax requiring all banks chartered outside the state to print their bank notes on stamped paper if they established any branch or office within P's boundaries. The tax was similar to those passed in other states during a period of strong state sentiment against the Bank of the United States. The taxes were aimed at excluding the Bank of the United States from operating branches within those states. The bank fell within the statutory definition but issued notes on unstamped paper. Accordingly, P brought an action for debt collection against McCulloch (D), the cashier of the Baltimore branch of the Bank of the United States. The state courts imposed penalties on D, and D appeals.

Issue. Even though the Constitution does not expressly grant Congress the power to incorporate a bank, can it do so under a doctrine of implied powers?

Held. Yes. Judgment reversed.

♦ Under the Necessary and Proper Clause, any appropriate means that Congress uses to attain legitimate ends that are within the scope of the Constitution and not prohibited by it, but are consistent with the letter and spirit of the Constitution, are constitutional.

♦ The federal government is one of enumerated powers, which are found in the Constitution. However, the Constitution cannot contain an accurate detail of all the subdivisions of governmental powers and of all the means by which they may be carried into execution.

Otherwise, the Constitution would become nothing more than a legal code. The government must have the ability to execute the powers entrusted to it through the best available means.

♦ Any means that directly execute a power enumerated in the Constitution may be considered incidental to the enumerated power. The word "necessary" in the Necessary and Proper Clause does not limit Congress to indispensable means; rather, the term enlarges the powers vested in the federal government. Congress has discretion in choosing the best means to perform its duties in the manner most beneficial to the people.

♦ The creation of a corporation is one of those powers that can be implied as incidental to other powers or used as a means of executing them. The incorporation of the Bank of the United States is a convenient, useful, and essential instrument in the performance of the fiscal operations of the federal government. The United States is a sovereign and thus has the power to create a corporation.

♦ The states have no power to burden the constitutional acts of Congress by taxation.

Comment. This case is one of the most important in the history of the Court because it established the doctrine of implied powers and emphatically articulated the supremacy of the federal government. The opinion went far beyond the needs of the specific case to promote a powerful federal government. Many commentators at the time objected that the idea of the nation as a union of sovereign states was being undermined. Instead of giving Congress only those additional powers that were needful or indispensable, the Necessary and Proper Clause was now a grant of discretionary power. However, exercise of this discretion must be based on powers granted by the Constitution.

---

b. Subsequent history of the bank

In 1832, Congress extended the charter of the bank, but President Andrew Jackson vetoed the legislation. Among other things, he objected to the windfall that the original private stockholders would have received upon extension of the charter. He also objected that many of these stockholders were foreigners. He found insufficient precedent to sustain the Act, because Congress had been inconsistent over the years in its support and because the states were primarily against it. The Supreme Court's opinion was not determinative; President Jackson felt that each branch of the government had to determine for itself the constitutionality of a proposal, and he did not view the bank as necessary and proper.

4. Philosophical Limits on Governmental Power

In *Calder v. Bull*, 3 U.S. (3 Dall.) 386 (1798), the Court refused to set aside state legislative action that overrode a judicial probate proceeding. The case is known best for the differing views of Justices Chase and Iredell on the nature and origin of legislative power.

a. Justice Chase

Justice Chase expressed the view that legislative action is limited by the social compact that gave the legislature its power, *i.e.*, courts should be able to appeal to natural rights in making constitutional decisions.

b. Justice Iredell

Justice Iredell, on the other hand, argued that constitutional limitations were the only restraint on legislative action. There is no reason why the courts should be able to define and apply natural law better than the legislature.

c. Comment

The view expressed by Justice Chase is the approach generally taken today, partly by applying concepts of due process.

C. External Regulation of Judicial Power

1. Introduction

The power of judicial review gives the courts significant power over the other branches of government. By declaring what the Constitution means, the Supreme Court can establish the binding law for the entire government. This power is not unchecked, however.

2. Amendments

A decision of the Supreme Court may be overturned through the cumbersome and difficult constitutional amendment procedure. This procedure has been used in the past to overturn four Supreme Court decisions.

3. Appointment Power

Because the President appoints the Supreme Court Justices, subject to the advice and consent of the Senate, there is some political control over the court. Of course, the President has no control over the Justice after the appointment is approved.

4. Impeachment and Public Opinion

The Constitution provides for removal of Justices upon impeachment for and conviction of treason, bribery, or other high crimes and misdemeanors, but this procedure has never been successfully used against a Supreme Court Justice. Public opinion may have some influence on the Court, although the Court has made decisions in highly controversial areas.

5. Supreme Court Jurisdiction

The Supreme Court's original jurisdiction, codified in 28 U.S.C. section 1251, mainly concerns controversies between two or more states. Congress cannot alter this jurisdiction. However, under Article III, section 2, clause 2, Congress has the power to regulate and limit the appellate jurisdiction of the Supreme Court. This power arguably applies at any time and at any stage of proceedings and may even allow Congress to withdraw particular classes of cases from the Court's appellate review. Congress has codified the Court's appellate jurisdiction in 28 U.S.C. sections 1254 and 1257.

a. Review of courts of appeals

Under section 1254, the Court may review cases in the courts of appeals by writ of certiorari or by certification from a court of appeals.

b. Review of final judgments of the highest state courts

Under section 1257, the Court may review final judgments of the highest state courts by writ of certiorari where the validity of a federal treaty or statute is drawn in question or where the validity of a state statute is drawn in question on the grounds of its being repugnant to the federal Constitution, treaties, or laws; or where any title, right, privilege, or immunity is specially set up or claimed under the United States Constitution, laws, or treaties.

6. Withdrawal of Jurisdiction Daring Consideration of Case

Ex parte McCardle
74 U.S. (7 Wall.) 506 (1869).

Facts. After the Civil War, Congress imposed military government on many of the former Confederate states. McCardle (P), a newspaper editor in Mississippi, was held in military custody. P sought a writ of habeas corpus pursuant to an 1867 Act of Congress, but the federal court denied the petition. P appealed to the Supreme Court as provided by the 1867 Act. After a hearing but before the final decision, Congress repealed the portions of the Act that permitted the appeal.

Issue. Does congressional negation of previously granted jurisdiction preclude further consideration of matters brought to the Supreme Court based on that jurisdiction?

Held. Yes. Case dismissed.

♦ The Supreme Court's jurisdiction is conferred by the Constitution subject to such exceptions and under such regulations as Congress shall make. The First Congress established the federal courts and prescribed regulations for jurisdiction. Congressional affirmation of appellate jurisdiction implies the negation of all jurisdiction not so affirmed.

♦ Here, Congress has expressly removed jurisdiction previously granted. The Court may not inquire into the motives of Congress; without jurisdiction, the Court cannot proceed to consider the case.

♦ No judgment can be rendered in a suit after the repeal of the Act under which it was brought and prosecuted. Judicial duty requires rejection of ungranted jurisdiction as much as it requires exercise of valid jurisdiction.

Comment. This case represented the third major attempt to have the Court review the Reconstruction Acts, which had been passed over President Johnson's veto. The *McCardle* decision has never been directly reexamined by the Court, although Justice Douglas doubted that its rationale would prevail today.

---

7. Limits on Congress's Authority

There are two basic theoretical limits on congressional authority over the Court's jurisdiction. First, Congress should not be able to interfere with the essential role of the Court in the constitutional scheme. This would include interference with the Court's independence, as by altering appellate jurisdiction in response to specific Court opinions. Second, Congress should not curtail jurisdiction in a manner that impairs the rights of litigants, *i.e.*, limits on jurisdiction should not violate litigants' due process and equal protection rights.

8. Modern Attempts to Limit the Court's Jurisdiction

In modern times, legislation to limit the Court's jurisdiction has been introduced in response to particularly controversial decisions, such as the *Miranda* decision, the busing decisions, the school prayer decisions, and the abortion decisions. To date, these proposals have not succeeded.

9. Limitation of Jurisdiction of Lower Federal Courts

Because Congress has power to create lower federal courts, it can limit their jurisdiction. Only in 1875 did the lower federal courts receive general jurisdiction to decide federal questions. At various times, Congress has removed certain types of cases from the jurisdiction of these courts.

D. Case or Controversy

1. Introduction

In addition to the congressional power over Supreme Court jurisdiction, the Court has itself imposed certain limits on the exercise of federal jurisdiction to avoid nonessential interpretation of the Constitution.

a. Cases and controversies

Article III, section 2 limits the jurisdiction of all federal courts to "cases and controversies," requiring federal courts to deal only with real and substantial disputes that affect the legal rights and obligations of parties having adverse interests, and that allow specific relief through a conclusive judicial decree.

b. Justiciability

Justiciability is the term of art expressing the limitation placed on federal courts by the case and controversy doctrine. Justiciability is a highly flexible concept, construed narrowly by activist courts, broadly by more conservative courts. The limits of justiciability also preclude rendering advisory opinions (opinions based on assumed or hypothetical facts that are not part of an existing, actual controversy), deciding moot cases (ones already decided by circumstances) or collusive or friendly suits, or adjudicating purely political questions.

c. Common scenarios

Problems of case and controversy and justiciability arise most frequently when a plaintiff seeks an injunction or a declaratory judgment as to the constitutionality of a statute.

2. Advisory Opinions

The Supreme Court has an established policy against providing advisory opinions, even though some state supreme courts do provide such opinions. While it may appear that the use of advisory opinions would prevent considerable litigation, the Court has determined that preservation of the system of checks and balances, as well as the Court's status as the court of last resort in the nation, outweigh any advantages to be gained. This policy was first articulated when President George Washington requested advice pertaining to legal aspects of foreign relations.

3. Standing

The requirement of Article III that federal courts adjudicate actual cases and controversies has been interpreted to require that litigants have "standing." This means that each litigant must be entitled to have the court decide the merits of the dispute or of particular issues.

a. Aspects of standing

The concept of standing has two aspects—one constitutional, the other self-imposed.

1) Injury in fact

The court will not pass upon constitutional questions unless the party raising the claim is actually injured by the statute or act in question. If the claimant does not show such injury, she has no standing to raise the issue. Thus there is not a justiciable controversy as required by Article HI, and the appeal will be dismissed.

2) Injury likely to be redressed by the court

Even if the claimant is injured, the court must deem it prudent to resolve the issues presented by that party. This latter issue of judicial "self-governance" arises primarily when a litigant seeks to assert the constitutional rights of a third party (*e.g.*, a doctor asserting his patient's right to purchase contraceptives).

3) Framing the argument

Successfully satisfying the standing requirement often depends on framing the argument correctly. In *Regents of the University of California v. Bakke*, 438 U.S. 265 (1978), Bakke challenged an affirmative action program. If his claim had been that he had been denied admission, he would not have had standing. Instead, his claim was based on his being denied an opportunity to compete for admission because of his race, which gave him standing. Whether or not he was actually admitted was merely a matter of relief.

b. Direct personal injury required

Allen v. Wright
468 U.S. 737 (1984).

Facts. The Wrights (Ps) brought a class action on behalf of black school children, claiming that the failure of the IRS (D) to deny tax-exempt status to private schools that practice racial discrimination constituted federal support for such schools and interfered with efforts to desegregate public schools. Ps sought declaratory and injunctive relief to force D to deny tax exemptions to discriminatory private schools. The court of appeals held for Ps, and the Supreme Court granted certiorari.

Issue. Does a private person have standing to force the government to comply in accordance with law when the person can show no direct personal injury resulting from the alleged failure of the government to obey the law?

Held. No. Judgment reversed.

♦ Under Article III, Ps must have standing in order to obtain their requested relief. The standing requirement prevents a litigant from raising another person's legal rights, prevents adjudication in courts of generalized grievances better suited to representative branches, and precludes consideration of complaints that do not fall within the zone of interests protected by the law invoked.

♦ Although the standing doctrine may not be precisely defined, it fundamentally requires a plaintiff to allege personal injuries fairly traceable to the defendant's allegedly unlawful conduct and likely to be redressed by the requested relief. The plaintiff's injury must be distinct and palpable. It cannot be abstract or hypothetical.

♦ The first injury alleged by Ps is that of direct injury due to the mere fact of government financial assistance to racially discriminatory private schools. To the extent this claim is for a violation of the right to have the government abide by its laws, the claim is not sufficient to confer jurisdiction on the federal courts. To the extent the claim is for the stigma of being a member of a group that is discriminated against, the claim is cognizable only as to those persons who are personally discriminated against. However, Ps were not personally victims of discrimination.

♦ The second injury Ps alleged is that the federal tax exemptions granted to racially discriminatory private schools make desegregation of public schools more difficult and thus give their children a diminished ability to receive an education in a racially integrated school. This type of injury is serious. However, the injury is not fairly traceable to the government conduct that Ps challenge.

♦ The only way the tax exemptions could possibly cause the harm Ps complain of would be if there were enough racially discriminatory private schools receiving the exemptions in Ps' community that withdrawal of the exemptions would make an appreciable difference in public school integration. Ps have not alleged such a causal connection, and there is no evidence of the number of such schools in Ps' community. One can only speculate whether withdrawal of the exemption would cause a school to change its policies, or whether parents would transfer their children to public school as a result of those changes, or whether enough private schools and parents would react to make a difference. Because Ps' claimed injury cannot be fairly traced to the challenged action, Ps have no standing.

Dissent (Brennan, J.). Ps' injury is clear, and the causal connection they allege is sufficient. They have identified 14 elementary schools in their own community that receive the tax exemption despite racially discriminatory policies.

Dissent (Stevens, Blackmun, JJ.). The actual wrong Ps complain of is that the government subsidizes the exodus of white children from public schools that would otherwise be racially integrated. Clearly, D's tax exemption policy causes this wrong. The standing requirement measures the plaintiffs' stake in the outcome, not whether the court is authorized to provide the plaintiff with the outcome sought. The Court should examine the justiciability of Ps' case, not their standing.

----

c. Public interest not enough

Lujan v. Defenders of Wildlife
504 U.S. 555 (1992).

Facts. Section 7(a)(2) of the Endangered Species Act ("ESA") requires federal agencies to insure, in consultation with the Secretary of the Interior, that any action carried out by such agency is not likely to jeopardize the continued existence of any endangered or threatened species. The Fish and Wildlife Service and National Marine Fisheries Service promulgated a joint regulation providing that section 7(a)(2) extended to actions that were taken in foreign nations, but the regulation was later modified to require consultations only for actions taken in the United States or on the high seas. The ESA also provided that "any person may commence a civil suit on his behalf to enjoin a government agency who is alleged to be in violation of the Act. The Defenders of Wildlife (P) brought suit against Lujan (D), the Secretary of the Interior, seeking a declaratory judgment that the more recent regulation incorrectly interpreted the ESA. Both parties moved for summary judgment. The district court granted P's motion. The court of appeals affirmed, and the Supreme Court granted certiorari.

Issue. May Congress convert the public interest in proper administration of the laws into an individual right such that all citizens may have standing to sue?

Held. No. Judgment reversed.

♦ Neither P nor any of its members had any injury in fact. P's standing, if any, depends on the validity of the "citizen-suit" provision of the ESA. The court of appeals held that this provision created a "procedural right" to interagency consultation in all persons, so that anyone can file suit to challenge D's failure to follow the allegedly correct consultative procedure, even if there is no discrete injury resulting from that failure. In effect, the court held that the injury-in-fact requirement under Article III has been satisfied by congressional conferral upon all persons of an abstract, self-contained "right" to have the executive branch follow the procedures required by law.

♦ Article III confers jurisdiction on the federal courts only where there is a case or controversy. This requirement is not met by a plaintiff who merely raises a generally available grievance about the government, where the harm is only to the interest of all citizens in the proper application of the Constitution and laws. Hence, a taxpayer does not have standing to challenge alleged violations of the Constitution by the executive or legislative branch where the violations would adversely affect only the generalized interest of all citizens in constitutional governance. The federal courts may only decide on the rights of individuals. Vindicating the public interest is the responsibility of Congress and the President.

♦ If Congress could convert the undifferentiated public interest in an executive that complies with the law into an "individual right" to be vindicated in the courts, Congress could transfer from the President to the judicial branch his most important constitutional responsibility, to "take Care that the Laws be faithfully executed."

♦ The fact that Congress may not eliminate the requirement of a concrete personal injury does not preclude Congress from creating legal rights, the invasion of which creates standing.

Concurrence (Kennedy, Souter, JJ.). Congress may define injuries and establish chains of causation that give rise to cases or controversies where none existed before, but at a minimum, Congress must identify what injury it desires to vindicate and relate the injury to the class of persons who are entitled to bring suit. The citizen-suit provisions of the ESA do not provide that there is an injury in any person by virtue of any violation. The case and controversy requirement assures both that the parties have an actual stake in the outcome and that the legal questions presented will be resolved in a concrete factual context conducive to a realistic appreciation of the consequences of judicial action. The public is entitled to know what persons invoke the judicial power, their reasons, and whether their claims are vindicated or denied.

Concurrence (Stevens, J.). P does not lack standing, but Congress did not intend section 7(a)(2) to apply to activities in foreign countries.

Dissent (Blackmun, O'Connor, JJ.). Congress granted considerable discretion to the executive branch to determine how best to attain the goals of ESA, constrained by specific procedural requirements. This does not constitute a violation of the separation of powers, nor should the separation of powers be deemed violated when Congress requires the federal courts to enforce the procedures. The citizen-suit provisions of ESA were based on the same understanding that arose from earlier cases in which the Court justified a relaxed review of congressional delegation to the executive branch because Congress provided for judicial review of the exercise of that power. [*See* Immigration & Naturalization Service v. Chadha, *infra*]

---

d. Regulation of global warming

Massachusetts v. Environmental Protection Agency
549 U.S. 497 (2007).

Facts. Respected scientists believe there is a relationship between an increase in the concentration of atmospheric carbon dioxide and the rise in global temperatures—the greenhouse effect. A group of states (including Massachusetts), local governments, and private organizations (Ps) alleged in a petition for certiorari that the Environmental Protection Agency (D) abdicated its responsibility under the Clean Air Act to regulate greenhouse gas emissions. The Supreme Court granted certiorari.

Issue. Does a state have standing to contest the regulations of a federal agency?

Held. Yes. Judgment reversed and case remanded.

♦ The Clean Air Act requires that the EPA prescribe standards applicable to the emission of any air pollutant from any class of new motor vehicles that causes or contributes to air pollution that may reasonably be anticipated to endanger public health or welfare. Ps' dispute is based on the construction of a congressional statute and is properly addressed by the federal courts. Congress specifically authorized this type of challenge to EPA actions.

♦ D erroneously claims that because greenhouse gas emissions inflict widespread harm, the doctrine of standing presents an insuperable jurisdictional obstacle to Ps' claims.

♦ *Lujan, supra*, holds that a litigant must demonstrate that: it has suffered a concrete and particularized injury that is either actual or imminent; the injury is traceable to the defendant; and it is likely that a favorable decision will redress that injury. However, when Congress creates a procedural right, such as the right to challenge agency action unlawfully withheld, a litigant can assert the right without meeting all of the normal standing requirements. Pursuant to this procedural right, Ps have standing once they show some possibility that the requested relief will prompt D to reconsider the decision that allegedly harmed Ps.

♦ For this Court to consider the petition for review, only one of the petitioners needs to have standing. Massachusetts has a special position and interest because rising sea levels, associated with global warming, have already begun to swallow its coastal land. Unlike the party seeking review in *Lujan*, Massachusetts is a state rather than a private individual. Although states are not normal litigants for the purpose of invoking federal jurisdiction, we have recognized that a state may have an interest independent of its citizens that supports federal jurisdiction. Here, Massachusetts is entitled to standing. The risk of harm to Massachusetts is actual and imminent, it is traceable to D, and there is a substantial likelihood that the judicial relief requested will prompt D to redress that risk.

♦ D does not dispute the existence of a causal connection between man-made greenhouse gas emissions and global warming. Thus, D's refusal to regulate these emissions contributes to Massachusetts's injuries. However, D claims that there is no realistic possibility that the relief Ps seek would mitigate global climate change and remedy their injuries, especially since predicted increases in greenhouse gas emissions from developing countries will likely offset any domestic decrease. But agencies generally resolve extensive problems in steps, rather than in one fell swoop. Reducing emissions from automobiles would be a significant first step. Even if reducing automobile emissions will not reverse global warming, we have jurisdiction to decide whether D has a duty to take steps to reduce it.

♦ Massachusetts has been harmed by the rise in sea levels, and although the risk of catastrophic harm is remote, it is real. The risk would be reduced to some extent if Ps received their requested relief. Thus, Ps have standing.

Dissent (Roberts, C J., Scalia, Thomas, Alito, JJ.). Ps are apparently dissatisfied with the executive and legislative branches' progress on global climate change. However, Ps' challenges are not justiciable. To have standing, Ps must allege an injury that is fairly traceable to D's failure to regulate greenhouse gases. But Ps did not satisfy the basic standing requirements of an injury in fact, causation, and redressability. Global warming is harmful to humanity, not specific to Ps. The harm to Massachusetts from rising sea levels is pure conjecture. The connection between automobile emissions in new cars in the United States and the loss of Massachusetts coastland is far too speculative to establish causation.

---

e. Domestic relations exception

In *Elk Grove Unified School District v. Newdow*, 542 U.S. 1 (2004), Newdow challenged the school district's practice of requiring elementary school classes to recite the Pledge of

Allegiance each day. Newdow's daughter participated. Newdow objected that this was religious indoctrination by the state and that he had standing to sue on behalf of his daughter as her "next friend." The Ninth Circuit held that Newdow had standing as a parent. The girl's mother intervened, claiming she had exclusive custody under a state order. The Supreme Court reversed, holding that Newdow lacked standing because, under state law, he was not entitled to litigate as his daughter's next friend. The Court noted that there is a "domestic relations exception" that divests the federal courts of power to issue divorce, alimony, and child custody decrees and that the federal courts should not hear cases involving elements of the domestic relationship. The Court also held that Newdow's claims regarding his own standing were inadequate to overcome the prudential concerns.

4. Political Questions

a. Constitutional decisionmaking by other branches

The requirement of a justiciable Article III controversy is deemed to carry with it a limitation against the deciding of purely "political questions." Hence, the Court will leave the resolution of such questions to the other departments of government. In determining whether there is a political question, the primary criteria are:

1) A "textually demonstrable" constitutional commitment of the issue to the political branches for resolution;

2) The appropriateness of attributing finality to the action of the political branches;

3) The lack of adequate standards for judicial resolution of the issue; and

4) The lack of adequate judicial remedies.

b. Legislative districting

In early decisions, the Supreme Court consistently refused to review questions arising from a state's distribution of electoral strength among its political or geographical subdivisions. In *Baker v. Carr*, below, the Court decided that federal courts had jurisdiction over challenges to apportionment plans. The modern approach to federal elections requires that representation must reflect the total population as precisely as possible. More flexibility is permitted in apportionment of state legislatures, but grossly disproportionate districts are not allowed. State apportionment may not be used to further discrimination, but numerical deviations resulting from political considerations may be allowed.

c. Justiciability of apportionment challenges

Baker v. Carr
369 U.S. 186 (1962).

Facts. The state of Tennessee continued to base the apportionment of voting districts on the 1901 census. In the intervening years, the population had grown at different rates in different voting districts. Baker (P) sought to force reapportionment through the courts because the unequal representation was unconstitutional and because the legislature in its present composition would not pass a state constitutional amendment. The lower federal courts denied relief on grounds of nonjusticiability, and P appeals.

Issue. Do federal courts possess jurisdiction over a constitutional challenge to a legislative apportionment?

Held. Yes. Judgment reversed and case remanded.

♦ The relationship between the judiciary and the coordinate branches of the federal government gives rise to political questions, not the federal judiciary's relationship to the states. This case involves none of the types of problems normally identified as involving political questions.

♦ The issue here is whether the state's activity is consistent with the federal Constitution. Case remanded for consideration of that issue.

Dissent (Frankfurter, Harlan, JJ.). The Court improperly hears a hypothetical claim based on abstract assumptions. The Court now permits federal courts to devise what they feel to be the proper composition of state legislatures.

---

d. Justiciability of challenges to impeachment actions

In *Nixon v. United States*, 506 U.S. 224 (1993), Nixon, a former federal district court judge, was convicted of making false statements before a federal grand jury. The United States House of Representatives adopted articles of impeachment and presented them to the Senate. The Senate appointed a committee to hold evidentiary hearings. The committee made a report to the full Senate, which then convicted Nixon on the impeachment articles and removed him from his office. Nixon sued, claiming that the Senate's failure to participate in the evidentiary hearings as a full body violated the Senate's constitutional authority to "try" impeachments. The lower courts held that Nixon's claim was nonjusticiable. The Supreme Court affirmed, holding that the Senate had exclusive authority to try impeachments, the courts had no final reviewing authority, and thus the claim was nonjusticiable. The Court stated that the need for finality and the difficulty of fashioning relief demonstrated why judicial review was inappropriate in this case. The Court found that the use of the word "try" does not require a judicial trial; it is not an implied limitation on the Senate's method of trying impeachments.

e. Justiciability of political gerrymandering claims

Vieth v. Jubelirer
541 U.S. 267 (2004).

Facts. A map drawn by the Pennsylvania General Assembly (D) established districts for the election of congressional representatives. Vieth and other voters (Ps) challenged the redistricting, claiming that it was an unconstitutional political gerrymander. The United States District Court dismissed Ps' claim. Ps appeal.

Issue. Are political gerrymandering claims justiciable?

Held. No. Judgment affirmed.

♦ In *Davis v. Bandemer*, 478 U.S. 109 (1986), the Court held that political gerrymandering claims are justiciable, but the Court could not agree on a standard to adjudicate them. Eighteen years of experience with the *Bandemer* ruling has left courts without any judiciable standards to apply. *Bandemer* should be overruled because political gerrymandering claims are nonjusticiable; there are no judicially discernible and manageable standards for adjudicating such claims.

♦ The dissenters have come up with three different standards for adjudicating political gerrymandering claims, each with serious unresolved problems.

Concurrence (Kennedy, J.). Although there is no existing manageable standard for this case, the courts should continue to adjudicate such claims. If a limited and precise rationale were found to correct an established violation of the Constitution in some redistricting cases, an injured party should have the possibility of judicial relief.

Dissent (Stevens, J.). The plurality acknowledges that legislatures can fashion manageable standards to remedy political gerrymandering, and several standards for identifying impermissible partisan influence are available to judges. Today's decision is not driven by the unavailability of judicially manageable standards. It is driven by a failure of the judiciary to condemn even the most blatant violations of a state legislature's fundamental duty to govern impartially.

Dissent (Souter, Ginsburg, JJ.). A plaintiff should have a case if he is able to show: (i) his membership in a cohesive political group or party; (ii) a disregard for traditional districting principles in the district of his residence; (iii) specific correlations between that disregard and the distribution of the population of the plaintiff's group; (iv) the existence of a hypothetical district that deviates less from traditional districting principles; and (v) intentional action by the defendants to adversely affect the plaintiff's group.

Dissent (Breyer, J.). Courts can devise a workable test to determine whether purely political districting factors are being used unjustifiably to entrench a minority in power.

---

f. Federal supervision of presidential elections

Bush v. Gore
531 U.S. 98 (2000).

Facts. The 2000 United States presidential election was so close that the national decision depended on the outcome of the vote in Florida. The vote in Florida was also very close. The Florida secretary of state certified that Bush (P) was the winner, but Gore (D) challenged the certification in the Florida Supreme Court. On December 8, 2000, the Florida Supreme Court ordered a manual recount of the "undervotes" (ballots on which no vote had been registered during the machine count) in all counties that had not yet completed a recount. Election officials were left to determine the intent of voters who cast ballot cards that were not perforated with enough precision for the machine to count them. There was no uniform standard for determining how to ascertain such intent. P objected to the procedure. On December 9, the United States Supreme Court granted P's emergency application for a stay of the Florida court's mandate.

Issue. In a presidential election, may a state supreme court order standardless manual recounts of ballots that have not registered votes during the normal ballot counting procedures?

Held. No. Judgment reversed.

♦ The Constitution authorizes the state legislatures to determine the manner for appointing electors who vote for election of the President. Where a state legislature vests the right to vote for President in its people, the right to vote as the legislature has prescribed is fundamental. Equal protection applies not only to the initial allocation of the franchise, but also to the manner of its exercise.

♦ The state may not value one person's vote over that of another by arbitrary and disparate treatment. The Florida Supreme Court's recount order does not satisfy the minimum requirement for nonarbitrary treatment because there are no uniform standards to determine a voter's intent. Ballots in one county are evaluated more leniently than ballots in another county, which will lead to disproportionate results.

♦ Under 3 U.S.C. section 5, any controversy or contest designed to lead to a conclusive selection of electors must be completed by December 12. As there is no constitutionally adequate recount procedure in place in Florida, there is no time to develop and implement such a procedure before December 12.

Concurrence (Rehnquist, C.J., Scalia, Thomas, JJ.). A presidential election is unique because the President and Vice-President are the only elected officials who represent all the voters. The presidential election is one of the few areas in which the Constitution confers a power on a particular branch of state government, in this case the state legislature. A significant departure from a state's legislative scheme for appointing presidential electors presents a federal constitutional question. In this area, the state supreme court must be mindful of the legislature's role. Here, the Florida Supreme Court deviated from the legislature's directives by overriding the decisions of the designated state election officials. Nothing in Florida law requires the counting of improperly marked ballots.

Dissent (Stevens, Ginsburg, Breyer, JJ.). Under the Florida Constitution, the legislative power in Florida is subject to judicial review. The Florida legislature cannot act outside of that Constitution. P's challenge to Florida's election procedures, as set forth by the Florida Supreme Court, demonstrates a lack of confidence in the impartiality and capacity of the state judges involved. In this case, the loser is the Nation's confidence in the judge as an impartial guardian of the rule of law.

Dissent (Souter, Breyer, JJ.). There is still time for Florida to adopt uniform standards and apply them to the recount.

Dissent (Ginsburg, Stevens, Souter, Breyer, JJ.). The concurring opinion violates the basic principle that a state may organize itself as it sees fit.

Dissent (Breyer, Stevens, Ginsburg, Souter, JJ.). The constitutional procedure for resolving disputes about electors contemplates resolution by state courts, not by the United States Supreme Court. Congress alone has the authority and responsibility to count electoral votes. If disputes remain after the states have tried to resolve them, then Congress is the body designated to provide the ultimate resolution.

E. Jurisdiction

1. Discretionary Review

Most of the cases on the Court's docket are discretionary. Petitions for certiorari are granted on a discretionary basis. The Supreme Court accepts cases brought to it on a writ of certiorari if at least four of the Justices want to grant the writ. United States Supreme Court Rule 10 sets forth the type of cases the Court will likely hear by granting certiorari. These are:

a. Supervision of federal courts

When a federal court of appeals renders a decision in conflict with another circuit or a state court of last resort, or has departed from the usual course of judicial proceedings, the Court will likely exercise its supervisory power.

b. Control over federal law

When a state court of last resort decides a federal question in conflict with a federal circuit or another state court of last resort, the Court will likely review the decision.

c. Important cases

Whenever a lower court decides an important question that the Supreme Court has not settled, or whenever the lower court decides a federal question in conflict with a Supreme Court decision, the Court will likely review the decision.

2. Jurisdiction over State Courts

The Supreme Court's only power over state judgments is to correct them when they incorrectly adjudge federal rights. The Court will not review severable state issues also decided in the case. To avoid advisory opinions, review is denied when an adequate and independent state ground supports the judgment, since a reversal of the federal law interpretation would not change the outcome. Whether adequate and independent state grounds exist is a federal question, however. If a decision appears to rest primarily on federal law, the Court assumes that the state court felt bound by federal law unless it clearly states that its decision rests on an adequate and independent state ground. [Michigan v. Long, 463 U.S. 1032 (1983)]

Chapter III
Congress and the National Economy

A. Sources and Nature of National Legislative Power

Much of the Constitution deals with the allocation of governmental powers among the branches of government and between the federal and state governments. From an early date, the Supreme Court has had to determine the scope of these powers. It is useful to classify governmental powers as follows.

1. Exclusive Federal Powers

Certain federal powers specifically enumerated in the Constitution are exclusive by the terms of the granting provisions. Others are deemed exclusive because of the nature of the power itself, or because the power is denied to the states, *e.g.*, the powers to enter treaties, to coin money, and to collect duties on imports. Many of the early constitutional cases involved disputes over the scope of the enumerated powers, especially when Congress acted under the Necessary and Proper Clause of section 8, clause 18.

2. Exclusive State Powers

Under the Tenth Amendment, the federal government may not exercise power in a fashion that impairs the states' integrity or their ability to function effectively in the federal system. The states are sovereign within their spheres.

3. Concurrent Powers

Most of the enumerated federal powers do not specifically deny state power in the areas covered. Under the Supremacy Clause, however, federal law prevails over any conflicting or inconsistent state law. Hence, Congress may preempt an area when uniform national laws are deemed necessary. Many of the disputes between the states and the federal government arise from differing views as to the application of the Supremacy Clause.

4. Denied Powers

In addition to the specific limitations on state powers contained in Article I, section 10, the Bill of Rights and other amendments deny powers to the federal and state governments; *e.g.*, Congress cannot establish a religion or abridge the freedom of speech.

5. Necessary and Proper Powers

The Necessary and Proper Clause of Article I, section 8 gives Congress authority to make all laws necessary and proper to execute the enumerated powers and all other powers given by the Constitution to the federal government. The clause provoked controversy as the states met to ratify the Constitution. It allows Congress to take action not specifically authorized by the Constitution and has provided the basis for many decisions upholding federal laws. The Court has consistently held that this clause does not grant a new and independent power, however; it simply makes effective the enumerated powers.

6. Scope of the Federal Legislative Power

Article I, section 1 lodges all legislative power in Congress. This is the power to make laws and to do all things that are necessary to enact them, such as to conduct investigations and hold hearings. Article I enumerates many specific powers, but it also contains a broad provision in section 8, clause 18, which permits Congress to "make all laws which shall be necessary and proper for carrying into execution the foregoing powers, and all other powers vested by this Constitution in the government of the United States, or in any department or officer thereof." The scope of the Necessary and Proper Clause has been a subject of intense debate.

B. Federalism and Judicial Review

1. Relationship Between State and Federal Authority over "Commerce"

Gibbons v. Ogden
22 U.S. (9 Wheat.) 1 (1824).

Facts. A New York statute granted the exclusive right to navigate by steamboat between New York City and Elizabethtown, New Jersey, to Livingston and Fulton, who in turn conveyed the right to Ogden (P). Gibbons (D) also operated boats along P's route. D's boats were licensed in the coasting trade under the federal Coasting Act. P sought and obtained a state court injunction prohibiting D's operation. D appeals, claiming that the power of Congress to regulate interstate commerce under the Commerce Clause is exclusive.

Issue. Is state regulation of commercial navigation that excludes federally licensed operators constitutional?

Held. No. Judgment reversed.

♦ P admits that Congress has the power to regulate commerce with foreign nations and among the several states, but would limit the meaning of commerce to traffic (buying and selling) or the interchange of commodities, and would exclude navigation. But one of the primary objects of the creation of the federal government was to grant the power over commerce, including navigation.

♦ The commerce power of Congress must be exercised within the territorial jurisdiction of the states, even though it cannot reach solely intrastate commerce. The power of Congress does not stop at the boundary lines of a state; it follows interstate commerce into the territory of a state.

- P attempts to analogize between the taxing power and the commerce power, claiming that since the taxing power is concurrent, the commerce power should be. But regulation of interstate commerce is an exclusive federal power. When a state regulates commerce with foreign nations or among the several states, it exercises the very power granted to Congress, and the analogy fails.

- State inspection laws are recognized in the Constitution, but do not derive from a power to regulate commerce. They act upon the subject before it becomes an article of foreign commerce.

- D has been granted, through a federal license, the privilege of employment in the coasting trade. P would restrict such trade to property transport, excluding passengers. Such a narrow interpretation would eventually "explain away the Constitution." Instead, safe and fundamental principles must be followed, and the coasting trade includes transport of both property and persons for hire.

- For these reasons, the federal license must be recognized, and state laws prohibiting exercise of such licenses are void.

Comments.

- This case illustrates the difficulty in interpreting the language of the Constitution. The entire case revolved around the proper definition of the term "commerce." Some commentators look to the dictionary for definitions, others look to the context in which the term is used, and others attempt to determine the intent of the framers as expressed in letters and other writings. The most commonly used expression of the framers' intent is the Federalist Papers. In this case, Chief Justice Marshall stated that the only limits on congressional power to regulate interstate commerce are political, not judicial. His broad definition included as commerce any commercial intercourse among the states.

- Just five years after this case was decided, the Court decided *Willson v. Black Bird Creek Marsh Co.*, 27 U.S. (2 Pet.) 244 (1829). The state had permitted a private party to build a dam across a navigable creek, and Willson, whose vessel was licensed under federal law, broke *the* dam. The Court upheld the state law against Willson's challenge, emphasizing that the state regulation affected only a small, navigable creek concerning which Congress had not acted. The law was intended to preserve property values and protect the public health, and was therefore a permissible exercise of state police power.

---

2. Promotion of Social Values by Congress

Hammer v. Dagenhart (The Child Labor Case)
247 U.S. 251 (1918).

Facts. Dagenhart (P) sought to enjoin Hammer (D), the United States Attorney General, from enforcing the Child Labor Act, which prohibited the shipment in interstate commerce of any product produced or mined by child labor. P was the father of two children who were to be discharged in compliance with the law by the company for which they worked. The district court enjoined enforcement. D appeals.

Issue. May Congress prohibit the transportation in interstate commerce of goods manufactured by child labor?

Held. No. Judgment affirmed.

- Congress does not have general police power. Unlike *The Lottery Case, infra*, this case involves goods that are themselves harmless. Congress does not have power to prohibit movement of ordinary commodities.

- Manufacturing is purely a local activity, not subject to the congressional commerce power. The constitutional scheme must be respected; only the states may regulate purely local matters.

- Even though this result leaves those states without their own child labor laws with an advantage in interstate competition, Congress simply has no power to force states to exercise their police power or to equalize conditions among the states.

Dissent (Holmes, McKenna, Brandeis, Clarke, JJ.). The Child Labor Act does not meddle with state rights. When products are sent across state lines, the states are no longer within their rights. If there were no Constitution and no Congress, their power to cross the line would depend on their neighbors. Under the Constitution, control of such commerce belongs to Congress and not the states. Congress may carry out its views of public policy, whatever the indirect effect on the states. Instead of being encountered by a prohibitive tariff at its boundaries, the state encounters the public policy of the United States, which is for Congress to express.

Comment. This case illustrates the so-called geographic view of interstate commerce. This approach precluded congressional regulation over activity that begins and ends and at all times takes place within a single state. It was the first of many cases that frustrated attempts by Congress to deal with the social and economic problems created by the industrialization of America. The conflict between the legislative's and executive's broad view of congressional commerce power and the Court's narrow view of that power came to a peak during President Franklin D. Roosevelt's first term, when the Court struck down many of the programs of the New Deal.

---

3. Congressional Power over Local Activity

Wickard v. Filburn
317 U.S. 111 (1942).

Facts. Wickard (D), the Secretary of Agriculture, imposed a marketing penalty upon the portion of Filburn's (P's) crop grown in excess of his allotment under the Agricultural Adjustment Act of 1938. P sued to enjoin enforcement of the penalty, claiming that application of the marketing quota to him was beyond Congress's commerce power, because P used the wheat on his own farm. The trial court granted an injunction, and D appeals.

Issue. May Congress regulate individual home production of wheat and use of a major interstate commodity based on the substantial effect of the aggregate of such activity?

Held. Yes. Judgment reversed.

- The purpose of the Act is to restrict supply of wheat in order to maintain the price, and the power to regulate commerce includes the power to regulate the prices at which commodities are sold. Commerce among the states in wheat is large and important, so the subject is clearly within Congress's power.

- P's activity involved small-scale, local production of wheat, partly for home consumption. But even if the activity is local and not regarded as commerce, it may be reached by Congress if it exerts a "substantial economic effect on interstate commerce, and this irrespective of whether such effect is what might at some earlier time have been defined as 'direct' or 'indirect'."

- Home consumption of the wheat does not detract from the economic effect of the excess crop because it substitutes for purchases on the open market. That P's effect is trivial is irrelevant because, taken together with many others similarly situated, it is far from trivial.

- Therefore, Congress may properly include wheat consumed on the farm in its scheme of regulation if it determines that such inclusion is essential to achievement of its policy purposes.

C. The Evolution of Commerce Clause Doctrine

1. Basic Commerce Clause Concepts

Among the most important powers of government are its powers to regulate commerce and to tax goods and instrumentalities in commerce.

a. Overlapping nature of commercial regulation

The states granted power to Congress to regulate commerce with foreign nations, and among the several states, and with the Indian tribes; if they had not done so, they could have erected trade barriers among themselves that would have destroyed the political union. [*See* U.S. Const. art. I, § 8, cl. 3] In effect, the United States was intended to be a "common market," made up of individual states. The federal power to regulate commerce among the several states overlaps with each state's power to regulate commerce within its boundaries.

b. Development of Commerce Clause jurisprudence

Most early cases dealing with the Commerce Clause involved challenges against state action that allegedly discriminated against or burdened interstate commerce. The Commerce Clause acted primarily as a restraint upon state regulation. It was not until 1887 and the enactment of the first Interstate Commerce Act that the Commerce Clause was relied on as the basis for the affirmative exercise of federal power. This occurred when Congress attempted to solve certain national economic problems. After the Interstate Commerce Act, Congress enacted several other regulatory statutes, including the Sherman Antitrust Act of 1890. The primary issue faced by the Court in deciding commerce cases was the definition of "interstate commerce." Recall that states have power over commerce within their boundaries. Thus federal power is concurrent with state power to some extent.

c. Manufacturing not considered commerce

United States v. E. C. Knight Co.
156 U.S. 1 (1895).

Facts. When the American Sugar Refining Company (D) acquired four competing sugar refineries, effectively monopolizing the production of sugar, the United States (P) sought to break up the company under the Sherman Antitrust Act. D challenged the constitutionality of the antitrust laws.

Issue. May Congress suppress monopoly in the production of goods?

Held. No.

♦ The monopoly alleged here involves manufacturing. Manufacturing is not commerce, but precedes it. The commerce power is independent of the power to suppress monopoly. Production of an article intended for export to another state or country is not commerce.

Dissent (Harlan, J.). When manufacturing ends, the subject of the manufacturing becomes a subject of commerce. Whatever obstructs the free course of interstate trade may be reached by Congress.

---

d. Rate-setting as commerce

Houston, East & West Texas Railway v. United States
(The Shreveport Rate Case)
234 U.S. 342 (1914).

Facts. The Houston, East & West Texas Railway (P) charged proportionately higher rates for interstate hauls as compared to intrastate hauls. The Interstate Commerce Commission ("ICC") ordered P to desist from charging higher rates on its interstate lines. P appeals its unsuccessful challenge of the ICC order.

Issue. Does Congress have the power under the Commerce Clause to control intrastate charges of an interstate carrier in order to end injurious discrimination against interstate commerce?

Held. Yes. Judgment affirmed.

♦ Congressional authority over interstate carriers includes the right to control their operations in all matters having such a close and substantial relation to interstate traffic that the control is essential or appropriate to: (i) the security of that traffic; (ii) the efficiency of interstate service; and (iii) the maintenance of conditions under which interstate commerce may be conducted upon fair terms and without molestation or hindrance.

♦ When the interstate and intrastate transactions of carriers are closely interrelated, Congress, not the state, is entitled to prescribe the final and dominant rule.

---

e. Using the commerce power to regulate undesirable activity

Champion v. Ames (The Lottery Case)
188 U.S. 321 (1903).

Facts. Champion (D) was arrested for shipping a box of lottery tickets from Texas to California in violation of the Federal Lottery Act, which prohibited importation, mailing, or causing interstate carriage of lottery tickets. Claiming that the Act was unconstitutional, D obtained a writ of habeas corpus. D appeals from a dismissal of the writ.

Issue. Does Congress have power under the Commerce Clause to regulate undesirable activity?

Held. Yes. Judgment affirmed.

♦ This statute does not interfere with traffic or commerce carried on exclusively within the limits of a state. A state could prohibit sales of lottery tickets within its boundaries; so also Congress, for the purpose of guarding the people of the United States against the "widespread pestilence of lotteries," and to protect the commerce that concerns all the states, may prohibit the carrying of lottery tickets from one state to another.

♦ This does not mean that Congress may arbitrarily exclude from commerce among the states anything that it chooses. This case does not require that we declare the full extent of the power that Congress may exercise in the regulation of commerce among the states, but as we have said before, the power of Congress to regulate commerce among the states is subject to such limitations or restrictions as are prescribed by the Constitution.

Dissent (Fuller, C.J., Brewer, Shiras, Peckham, JJ.). The power to suppress lotteries belongs to the states and not to Congress. Use of the police power has been reserved to the states by the Tenth Amendment. Furthermore, lottery tickets are not objects of commerce. This decision attempts to transform a noncommercial article into a commercial one simply because it is transported.

---

2. Regulation of Economic Problems Through 1936

Industrialization and the Depression presented many new social and economic problems for the nation to address. Congress and the President initiated new kinds of legislative programs to deal with these problems, often bringing government into the private sector through increased economic regulation. Although the Commerce Clause was raised as the constitutional basis for many of these laws, the Court narrowly construed the clause through 1936.

3. The Court's Threat to the New Deal

Soon after President Roosevelt took office, a flood of new legislation was passed in an attempt to deal with the Depression, a national economic disaster. Much of this legislation was based on the Commerce Clause.

a. Relationship or nexus to interstate commerce

In the first test of New Deal Commerce Clause legislation, the Supreme Court invalidated the Railroad Retirement Act of 1934. [*See* Railroad Retirement Board v. Alton Railroad, 295 U.S. 330 (1935)] The Act established a compulsory retirement and pension plan for all carriers subject to the Interstate Commerce Act. The argument was that such a plan was necessary to the morale of the workers, and that this morale affected efficiency, which in turn affected interstate commerce. The Court held that the relationship of such legislation to interstate commerce was too remote.

b. The "indirect effect" theory

A.L.A. Schechter Poultry Corp. v. United States
295 U.S. 495 (1935).

Facts. Pursuant to the National Industrial Recovery Act of 1933, the federal government adopted a Live Poultry Code that imposed certain business standards on the live poultry industry in New York City. Among other things, the Code established a minimum wage and a 40-hour work week. The Schechters (Ds) operated a slaughterhouse in New York. Most of the poultry they purchased was shipped from other states to New York, but all of Ds' customers were local. Ds did not fully comply with the Code and were convicted. The court of appeals upheld the convictions, and Ds appeal.

Issue. May Congress regulate intrastate commerce that has only an indirect effect on interstate commerce?

Held. No. Judgment reversed.

♦ The conditions to which power is addressed, such as the grave national crisis that Congress faced here, should always be considered when the exercise of power is challenged. Extraordinary conditions may call for extraordinary remedies, but they do not create or enlarge constitutional power. Assertions of extraconstitutional authority were anticipated and precluded by the explicit terms of the Tenth Amendment.

♦ The poultry that Ds purchased and slaughtered may have come from out of state, but Ds' own dealings with the poultry were entirely in New York. The poultry was no longer in a current or flow of interstate commerce; the flow had ceased once it arrived in New York and was held for local disposition and use. There is no basis for applying the Commerce Clause to products that are no longer in the flow of interstate commerce.

♦ An alternative basis for regulation under the Commerce Clause is a finding that the transaction to be regulated "directly affects" interstate commerce. For this analysis, there must be a clear distinction between direct and indirect effects. To the extent that the Code sought to regulate the hours and wages of Ds' employees, who were engaged solely in local commerce, the violations could have no direct relation to interstate commerce. The fact that the Code could ultimately affect the prices involved in interstate commerce does not change the fact that such an effect would be indirect.

Concurrence (Cardozo, Stone, JJ.). Local activities do not become interstate because of distant repercussions.

---

c. Regulation of employment conditions

Carter v. Carter Coal Co.
298 U.S. 238 (1936).

Facts. Carter (P) was president and a stockholder of Carter Coal Company (D). P sued to enjoin D from paying a tax assessed against it under the Bituminous Coal Conservation Act, which sought to regulate hours and wages in coal mines and imposed a tax on the sales price or fair market value of all coal mined by any producer that did not comply with the regulations. The United States conceded that the tax was a penalty and that its validity depended on whether its regulatory aspects were within the federal commerce power. The district court held for D, and P appeals.

Issue. May Congress regulate the hours, wages, and other employment conditions of a national industry?

Held. No. Judgment reversed.

♦ Affirmations in the preamble to the Bituminous Coal Conservation Act constitute a recital of considerations, such as the health and comfort of the people and the general welfare of the nation, rather than legislation. The preamble demonstrates that Congress was exercising general powers to protect the general public interest, conserve privately owned coal, and maintain just relations between producers and employees, by controlling nationwide production and distribution of coal. Although these considerations are important, whether the end sought to be attained by an act of Congress is legitimate is a matter of constitutional power, and not a matter of legislative discretion.

♦ "Commerce" has been defined as "intercourse for the purposes of trade." The employment of men and the fixing of their wages, hours of labor, and working conditions constitute intercourse for purposes of production, not of trade. The local character of mining, manufacturing, or farming does not change merely because the products of those activities move into interstate commerce. The relations between employer and employee are local in nature and subject only to local regulation.

♦ The production of every commodity intended for interstate sale and transportation has some effect upon interstate commerce. However, activities relating to production have only an indirect effect on commerce. The distinction between direct and indirect effects turns not upon the magnitude of either the cause or the effect, but entirely upon the manner in which the effect has been brought about. Congress can regulate only those things that have a direct effect on commerce. Mining is not one of them.

Dissent (Cardozo, Brandeis, Stone, JJ.). Mining, agriculture, and manufacture are not interstate commerce if considered by themselves, yet their relation to interstate commerce may be such that for the protection of the one there is need to regulate the other. This language of direct/indirect relation to commerce has not been literally applied in past cases. The proximity or remoteness of activities to commerce is a more logical way to approach the subject.

Comment. This case illustrates the Court's movement, just prior to 1936, away from a geographic approach toward the direct/indirect analysis. Under this analysis, an activity that takes place entirely within a single state may be regulated by Congress if it has a direct effect on interstate commerce. This approach faded after 1936 as the Court broadened its view of the congressional commerce power.

---

d. The Court-packing plan

President Roosevelt felt that the Court was judging the public policy of the New Deal, rather than its constitutionality. He proposed legislation to allow him to appoint an extra Justice for every Justice over age 70 who did not resign. The legislation never passed, but some observers believe that it prompted a change in the Court's analysis of New Deal legislation.

4. Expansion of the Commerce Power After 1936

a. The affectation doctrine

Beginning in 1937, the Court abandoned the "geographical" and "direct vs. indirect" approaches to federal regulation under the Commerce Clause. The Court's position currently extends to Congress the power to regulate any activity, whether interstate or intrastate in nature, as long as it has any appreciable effect on interstate commerce. This approach is called the "affectation doctrine."

b. Steel production

NLRB v. Jones & Laughlin Steel Corp.
301 U.S. 1 (1937).

Facts. The National Labor Relations Act provided for union-employer collective bargaining in all industries affecting interstate commerce. Jones & Laughlin Steel Corporation (D), a steel manufacturer, had discharged certain employees who were union activists. D was ordered by the National Labor Relations Board (P) to comply with the Act's provisions, but D claimed that Congress had no power to regulate its industry. P went to federal court to have its order enforced, but the court refused on the ground that federal power did not extend so far. During the hearings, the evidence showed that D was an integrated company that owned subsidiaries all over the United States, that 75% of the product of the plant affected by P's order was shipped out of state, and that it received its raw materials from out of state. P appeals.

Issue. May Congress regulate a manufacturer if the manufacturer's activity significantly affects interstate commerce?

Held. Yes. Judgment reversed.

♦ The term "affecting commerce" means burdening or obstructing commerce or the free flow of commerce, or having led or tending to lead to a labor dispute burdening or obstructing commerce or the free flow of commerce.

♦ Labor strife at this plant could conceivably cripple the entire interstate operation of the company. Thus, interstate commerce was affected, and P may regulate D's activity.

---

c. Manufacturing

United States v. Darby
312 U.S. 100 (1941).

Facts. The Fair Labor Standards Act of 1938 prescribed maximum and minimum wages for workers who manufactured goods for interstate commerce and prohibited interstate shipment of goods made by workers not employed in compliance with the Act. Darby (D), a lumber manufacturer, was charged with violating the Act. The district court quashed the indictment, finding the Act inapplicable to D's employees, who were involved in manufacturing, not interstate commerce. The United States (P) appeals.

Issue. May Congress establish and enforce wage and hour standards for manufacture of goods for interstate commerce?

Held. Yes. Judgment reversed.

♦   The purposes of the Fair Labor Standards Act are to exclude from interstate commerce goods that are produced under substandard labor conditions and to prevent the use of interstate commerce as the means of competition in the distribution of goods so produced.

♦   Following its own conception of public policy as to the restrictions that may appropriately be imposed on interstate commerce, Congress is free to exclude from interstate commerce goods that it believes are injurious to the public health, morals, or welfare, even if the states of destination do not regulate their use. This is not a forbidden invasion of state power unless it is prohibited by other Constitutional provisions.

♦   Regulations of commerce that do not infringe on some constitutional prohibition are within the plenary power conferred on Congress by the Commerce Clause. Thus, the prohibition of the shipment interstate of goods produced under the forbidden substandard labor conditions is within the constitutional authority of Congress.

Comment. This opinion overruled *Hammer v. Dagenhart, supra. Darby* involved manufacturing prior to interstate shipment. Another case, *United States v. Sullivan*, 332 U.S. 689 (1948), upheld federal regulation extending to activity after interstate commerce had terminated. Sullivan, a druggist, had repackaged drugs he had received six months earlier from another state. He omitted certain directions and warnings required by federal law. The Court upheld Sullivan's conviction on the theory that the Commerce Clause allows Congress to regulate the branding of articles held for resale after being shipped interstate, and it did not matter that Sullivan repackaged them at the local level.

---

5. Modern Case Law

At one time, it appeared that the Court recognized few, if any, federalism constraints on the congressional power to regulate commerce. The federal commerce power appeared to embrace almost every phase of the economy, national or local, that taken separately or in the aggregate affects interstate commerce. With the Civil Rights Act of 1964, Congress used this extensive power to protect civil rights within the sphere of commerce. More recently, the Supreme Court has made it clear that the power of Congress to regulate commerce, although very broad, does have limits. To be within Congress's power under the Commerce Clause, a federal law must regulate either: (i) the channels of interstate commerce; (ii) the instrumentalities of interstate commerce; *or* (iii) activities that have a substantial effect on interstate commerce.

a. Protection of civil rights

1) Private motels

Heart of Atlanta Motel v. United States
379 U.S. 241 (1964).

Facts. The owner of the Heart of Atlanta Motel (P) refused to rent rooms to black persons. P sought a declaratory judgment that Title II of the Civil Rights Act of 1964 was unconstitutional. A three-judge federal court sustained the Act, and P appeals.

Issue. May Congress prohibit racial discrimination by private motels that accept out-of-state business?

Held. Yes. Judgment affirmed.

♦ The legislative history of the Civil Rights Act contains numerous examples of how racial discrimination places burdens upon interstate commerce, which comprehends the movement of persons through more than one state.

♦ Even though the operation of the motel was local, if it is interstate commerce that feels the pinch, then it does not matter how local the operation is that applies the squeeze.

---

2) Private restaurants

Katzenbach v. McClung
379 U.S. 294 (1964).

Facts. McClung (P), the owner of a restaurant that excluded black persons from its dining accommodations, challenged Title II of the Civil Rights Act. The lower court granted an injunction against enforcement by Katzenbach (D), the Assistant Attorney General, finding that P would lose a substantial amount of business if required to serve black persons.

Issue. May Congress use its commerce power to forbid racial discrimination by a restaurant on the sole ground that slightly under one-half of the food it serves originates from outside the state in which it operates?

Held. Yes. Judgment reversed.

♦ The fact that discrimination in restaurants resulted in sales of fewer interstate goods and that interstate travel was obstructed directly by it shows sufficient connection between the discrimination and the movement of interstate commerce to allow federal intervention.

♦ Once the court finds a rational basis for holding a chosen regulatory scheme necessary to the protection of interstate commerce, the only inquiry is whether the facts fit the scheme. Here the lower court found that P serves food, a substantial portion of which has moved in interstate commerce. Hence, P is covered by the regulation.

Concurrence (Black, J.). Every possible speculative effect on commerce should not be accepted as an adequate constitutional ground to uproot and discard all our traditional distinctions between what is purely local, and therefore controlled by state laws, and what affects the national interest, and therefore is subject to control by federal laws. The one isolated local event, however, when added to many other similar events, could impose a burden on interstate commerce.

---

b. Limits on Congressional power

1) Gun-Free School Zones Act

United States v. Lopez
514 U.S. 549 (1995).

Facts. In the Gun-Free School Zones Act, Congress made it illegal for any person knowingly to possess a firearm in a school zone. Lopez (D), a 12th grade student, carried a concealed gun to his high school. D was ultimately convicted under the Act. The court of appeals reversed on the ground that Congress did not have power under the Commerce Clause to regulate this type of activity. The Supreme Court granted certiorari.

Issue. May Congress prohibit the possession of firearms within a school zone?

Held. No. Judgment affirmed.

♦ As business enterprises expanded beyond local and regional territories and became national in scope, the scope of the Commerce Clause as interpreted by the Court also expanded. In cases such as *NLRB v. Jones & Laughlin Steel Corp., supra*, and *Maryland v. Wirtz*, 392 U.S. 183 (1968), the Court noted that while the power to regulate commerce is broad, it does have limits.

♦ There are three broad categories of activity that come within Congress's commerce power:

(i) Congress may regulate the use of the channels of interstate commerce;

(ii) Congress may regulate the instrumentalities of interstate commerce, as well as persons or things in interstate commerce; and

(iii) Congress can regulate activities that have a substantial relation to interstate commerce, meaning those that substantially affect interstate commerce.

♦ The Act in this case is a criminal statute that has nothing to do with commerce. Possessing a gun in a school zone does not arise out of a commercial transaction that substantially affects interstate commerce. Nor does the Act contain a requirement that the possession be connected in any way to interstate commerce.

♦ The government claims that possession of a firearm in a local school zone substantially affects interstate commerce because it might result in violent crime. This in turn imposes costs on society, which are borne throughout the country through insurance rates. The government also claims that guns disrupt the educational process, which leads to a less productive society, which ultimately affects interstate commerce. If either of these propositions were adopted, there would be no limitation on federal power. The only way to find an effect on interstate commerce in this case is to pile inference upon inference, and the result would be to uphold a general police power for Congress.

Concurrence (Kennedy, O'Connor, JJ.). In a sense, any conduct in the interdependent world has an ultimate commercial origin or consequence. However, the Court must still determine whether the exercise of national power intrudes upon an area of traditional state concerns. Education in particular is a traditional concern of the states.

Concurrence (Thomas, J.). The term "commerce" as used in the Constitution is much more limited than the Court's opinions have recognized. The term referred to buying, selling, and transporting goods, as distinguished from agriculture and manufacturing. Furthermore, the Constitution does not give Congress authority over all activities that "substantially affect" interstate commerce. If it did, there would be no need for specific constitutional provisions giving Congress power to enact bankruptcy laws, to establish post offices and post roads, to grant patents and copyrights, etc.

Dissent (Stevens, J.). Congress clearly has power to regulate the possession of guns to some degree. This power should include the ability to prohibit possession of guns at any location. The market for possession of handguns by persons covered by the Act is sufficiently substantial to justify congressional action.

Dissent (Souter, J.). The Court seeks to draw fine distinctions between what is patently commercial and what is not, which is basically the same distinction between what directly affects commerce and what affects it only indirectly. The Court should not be placed in a position to make these fine distinctions; Congress should have to make them. The majority approach of the last 60 years should prevail.

Dissent (Breyer, Stevens, Souter, Ginsburg, JJ.). Case law recognizes that Congress can regulate even local activity if it significantly affects interstate commerce. In determining whether a local activity will have such an effect, the court must consider the cumulative effect of all instances similar to the one in the specific case. The courts are required to defer to congressional determinations about the factual basis for making this determination. In this case, Congress could rationally find that violent crime in school areas affects the quality of education and thereby interstate commerce.

---

2) Violence Against Women Act

United States v. Morrison
529 U.S. 598 (2000).

Facts. Morrison (D), a member of a varsity football team at Virginia Tech, assaulted and repeatedly raped a female student and made vulgar remarks about women. The student brought suit in federal court based on the federal Violence Against Women Act. The Act provided a damage remedy for a victim of gender-motivated violence. The lower courts held that Congress lacked constitutional authority to enact this civil remedy, and the Supreme Court granted certiorari.

Issue. May Congress provide a civil remedy for gender-motivated crimes of violence?

Held. No. Judgment affirmed.

♦ Commerce Clause regulation of intrastate activity is permitted only if that activity is economic in nature. Gender-motivated crimes of violence are not economic activity, and therefore are beyond the scope of the Commerce Clause.

♦ The congressional findings relied on a method of reasoning that is unworkable because it would make it impossible to preserve a constitutional distinction between what is truly national and what is truly local. It would allow Congress to regulate any crime as long as the nationwide, aggregated impact of that crime had substantial effects on commerce.

Dissent (Souter, Stevens, Ginsburg, Breyer, JJ.). The relative powers of the federal and state systems have changed substantially since the framing of the Constitution. The Seventeenth Amendment was a major factor in this change, and the modern integrated national economy is a fact not reflected in the majority's notion of federalism.

Dissent (Breyer, Stevens, Souter, Ginsburg, JJ.). Congress could have approached the same problem with legislation that focused on acts of violence perpetrated at public accommodations or by those who have moved in interstate commerce. The majority's approach could lead to complex rules creating fine distinctions that achieve random results.

---

3) Health care mandate

National Federation of Independent Business v. Sebelius
__ U.S. __, 132 S.Ct. 2566 (2012).

Facts. The Patient Protection and Affordable Care Act (ACA) included a mandate for citizens and legal residents to maintain health insurance coverage. Those not covered through their employer or a government program had to buy insurance from a private company. Those who did not comply with the mandate had to pay a penalty to the Internal Revenue Service, based on a percentage of household income. The National Federation of Independent Business (P) challenged the law by suing Sebelius (D), Secretary of Health and Human Services. The District Court held the mandate unconstitutional. The Eleventh Circuit affirmed, although it severed the mandate from the rest of the ACA. The Supreme Court granted certiorari.

Issue. Does the Commerce Clause grant Congress authority to require people to purchase a product?

Held. No. Judgment reversed on other grounds.

- D claims the individual mandate is a valid exercise of Congressional power under the Commerce Clause. The health care market suffers from a cost-shifting problem because those who don't have insurance shift the cost of their care to hospitals that are required by law to provide services. The hospitals pass on the costs to insurers, who pass it along to policy holders through higher rates. Another problem is those who can't buy insurance because of preexisting conditions.

- The ACA addresses this problem partly by requiring insurance companies to cover those who could not previously obtain insurance because of preexisting conditions. However, that exacerbates the cost-shifting problem because it gives individuals an incentive not to buy insurance until they need it. To solve that problem, the ACA requires everyone to buy insurance, including healthy individuals whose premiums will be higher than their health care expenses, thereby subsidizing the costs of covering unhealthy individuals.

- Although the lack of a mandate would worsen the cost-shifting problem, Congress has never before relied on its commerce power to compel individuals not engaged in commerce to purchase an unwanted product. If the power to "regulate" something included the power to create it, many Constitutional provisions would be superfluous. Construing the Commerce Clause to give Congress power to regulate individuals because they are doing nothing would vastly expand congressional power.

- *Wickard v. Filburn* is the most far-reaching example of the commerce power, but even in that case, the farmer was actively engaged in producing wheat. The ACA would override that limitation under *Wickard*. It would allow Congress to use a mandatory purchase requirement to solve almost any problem. Congress could order everyone to buy vegetables to solve the problem of poor health resulting from poor diets. To allow Congress to solve problems by forcing people to purchase things they don't want would change the nature of our Government.

- D argues that because everyone will need health care at some point, the uninsured are active in the market. But Congress cannot anticipate activity to regulate individuals not currently engaged in commerce. The ACA's individual mandate forces individuals into commerce because they elected to refrain from commercial activity. That provision cannot be sustained under the power of Congress to "regulate commerce."

Concurrence and Dissent in part (Ginsburg, Breyer, Sotomayor, Kagan, JJ.).

- The Commerce Power allows Congress to enact the ACA's minimum coverage provision. The market for health care has the special attribute that everyone will eventually need health care, and often the need is unexpected and the costs unaffordable. Health insurance addresses the risks of cost, unpredictability and inevitability. But cost-shifting arises because not everyone gets insurance.

- States cannot resolve the problem of the uninsured because if any one state covered everyone, unhealthy people would migrate to that state, raising costs. Rising costs would lead healthy individuals to leave the state. Only the federal government can address the collective-action impasse.

- The mandate to buy insurance bears a reasonable connection to the goal of protecting the health-care market from the disruption caused by individuals who fail to obtain insurance. The commerce power reflects practical considerations, including actual experience such as that of Massachusetts, which the ACA was modeled after.

- Medical insurance is different in kind from other products; upholding the ACA's mandate would not justify Congress in mandating the purchase of other products and services that individuals will not inevitably buy. The Chief Justice uses the example of a mandate to buy broccoli. But such a mandate could not be upheld without piling inference upon inference regarding its substantial effect on the health-care costs borne by Americans. Political resistance is an adequate constraint on the power to impose mandates, since the States, which have such power, have rarely adopted mandates.

- ♦ No one disputes that Congress can ban the practice of charging higher prices or denying coverage to individuals with preexisting medical conditions. However, banning that practice by itself would not work because guaranteed-issue and community-rating requirements would trigger an adverse-selection death-spiral in the health insurance market. The minimum coverage and mandate provisions are necessary to attain the legitimate purpose under the commerce power. Therefore, the Necessary and Proper Clause allows Congress to enact this legislation.

Dissent (Scalia, Kennedy, Thomas, Alito, JJ.).

- ♦ The Commerce Clause cannot enable the Federal Government to regulate all private conduct and compel the States to function as administrators of federal programs. The ACA reaches beyond Wickard and would extend federal power to virtually all human activity.

- ♦ D claims that the ACA is a complicated regulatory scheme that increases costs on the health insurance industry that can only be offset by requiring healthy people to get insurance they wouldn't otherwise buy. But these healthy people are the furthest removed from an interstate market, and if Congress can force them to participate, Congress would have unlimited power. Gonzales v. Raich does not support D's position because in that case, Congress chose the only practicable way to prohibit interstate traffic in marijuana. Here, there are other ways to reduce insurance premiums and ensure the profitability of insurers.

- ♦ D claims that everyone will eventually need health care, but if the Commerce Clause includes the power to regulate every person because he or she will one day engage in commerce, there would be no limit to government power.

Dissent (Thomas, J.). This case demonstrates that the very notion of a "substantial effects" test under the Commerce Clause is inconsistent with the original understanding of Congress' powers.

D. State Regulation of Interstate Commerce

1. Introduction

The modern approach to the Commerce Clause gives Congress absolute power over interstate commerce. Congress may permit a state to exercise this power or may prohibit a state from so doing. Where Congress has in fact acted to prohibit state regulation, it has "preempted the field." Even when Congress has not acted, the very existence of the Commerce Clause forbids state regulation that places an unreasonable burden on interstate commerce. These areas have produced considerable litigation, partly because of the ambiguous nature of the standards involved and partly because of the large financial stakes affected. When Congress has not enacted legislation regarding the subject matter of commerce, the states may regulate local transactions even though they affect interstate commerce, subject to certain limitations. This principle applies to regulation of transportation as well.

a. Development of principles

1) Early approach

In *Gibbons v. Ogden, supra,* Chief Justice Marshall discussed the relationship between federal and state regulation. Ogden had argued that the commerce power was like the taxing power; since the taxing power is concurrent, the commerce power should be. Marshall noted that regulation of interstate commerce is an exclusively federal power. When a state regulates commerce with foreign nations or among the several states, it exercises the very power granted to Congress, and the analogy fails. The Constitution does recognize state power to inspect goods for health and safety, but such laws do not derive from a power to regulate commerce. Even though inspection laws may affect commerce, their existence does not imply that the states can directly regulate interstate commerce.

2) National vs. local issues

In *Cooley v. Board of Port Wardens,* 53 U.S. (12 How.) 299 (1851), the Supreme Court held that Congress may permit the states to regulate aspects of commerce that are primarily local in nature. Pennsylvania had passed a statute requiring vessels entering or leaving the Port of Philadelphia to accept local pilots while in the Delaware River. The penalty for disobedience was one-half the pilotage fees. Cooley, consignee of two violating vessels, was sued by the Board of Wardens of the Port based on a 1789 congressional statute that incorporated all then-existing state laws regulating pilots and that mandated conformity with subsequently enacted state regulation, such as the law in this case. Cooley contended that Congress could not delegate its powers in this manner. The Court found that the correct approach looks to the nature of the subjects of the power, rather than the nature of the power itself. Many subjects are national in nature, but some are local, like the one involved here. When a subject is national it is best governed by one uniform system and therefore requires exclusive legislation by Congress. But a local subject is best handled by the states, which can adapt regulation to the local peculiarities. The *Cooley* opinion was widely ignored at the time, although its approach was somewhat revived later on. After *Cooley,* the Court again applied the Marshall view that the states could not regulate interstate commerce. [*See, e.g.,* Paul v. Virginia, 75 U.S. (8 Wall.) 168 (1869)]

3) Negative implications

Congress may validate state laws regulating commerce that, in the absence of such consent, would violate the Commerce Clause.

a) The Wilson Act

In *Leisy v. Hardin,* 135 U.S. 100 (1890), the Court invalidated an Iowa law prohibiting the sale of liquors as applied to Illinois-brewed beer that was sold in the original package in Iowa. Later, however, after the passage of the federal Wilson Act, the Court held that a state may apply its prohibition laws to sales of intoxicating liquors in the original packages. In so ruling in *In re Rahrer,* 140 U.S. 545 (1891), the Court held that through the Wilson Act Congress had merely allowed certain designated subjects of interstate commerce to be divested of that character, so that the liquor, once imported, immediately fell within the local jurisdiction.

b) Insurance business and the McCarran Act

After passage of the McCarran Act of 1945, which deferred and limited the applicability of antitrust laws to the insurance business, the Court held that the Act validated state taxes that were discriminatory and invalid under Commerce Clause decisions. In *Prudential Insurance Co. v. Benjamin*, 328 U.S. 408 (1946), the plaintiff New Jersey company had objected to the continued collection of tax of 3% of the premiums received from business done in South Carolina, when South Carolina corporations were not similarly taxed.

b. Traditional state regulation of transportation

Where the subject matter is traditionally subject to local regulation, the Court is more likely to allow state regulation. Transportation has been one of the most highly regulated areas.

1) Basic principles

Over time, the Court has developed an approach to transportation problems that is fairly principled. To be constitutional, state regulation must not violate these principles:

a) Uniform national regulation not required

The subject matter must not inherently require uniform, national regulation. [*See* Wabash, St. Louis & Pacific Railway Co. v. Illinois, 118 U.S. 557 (1886)]

b) No discrimination

The state regulation must not discriminate against interstate commerce so as to "substantially impede" the free flow of commerce across state lines. [*See* Seaboard Air Line Railway Co. v. Blackwell, 244 U.S. 310 (1917)]

c) Balance of interests favors the state

The state interest underlying the regulation must not be outweighed by the burden on interstate commerce—*i.e.*, the "balance of interests" favors the state as opposed to the national interest.

(1) Public safety and welfare

A state's interest in the public safety and welfare, where such is the predominant purpose of the state law, may justify obstruction of interstate commerce. For example, in *Bradley v. Public Utilities Commission*, 289 U.S. 92 (1933), the Court held that a state could restrict interstate truckers where the highway was already so badly congested by traffic that the proposed service would create excessive traffic hazards.

(2) Controlling competition

While state interests in protecting public health and welfare are given considerable weight, a state's interest in controlling competition is not. For example, in *Buck v. Kuykendall*, 267 U.S. 307 (1925), the Court held that a state could not deny an interstate carrier a permit to use its highways simply because the state determined that the territory was already adequately served.

2. Protection Against Discrimination

a. Regulation of trade

Where Congress has not acted, the states have power to regulate any phase of local business (production, marketing, sales, etc.), even though such regulations may have some effect on interstate commerce, as long as they neither discriminate against, nor impose any unreasonable burden upon, interstate commerce.

1) Regulation of incoming commerce

One way to develop a state's economy is to require businesses to operate within the state. The Commerce Clause prohibits such legislation if it burdens interstate commerce and is not necessary to promote a valid state purpose. Protecting local business against out-of-state competition is not a valid state purpose per se, but there may be valid reasons for excluding out-of-state products.

2) Protection of health and safety

a) Quarantine and inspection laws

Quarantine and inspection laws enacted to protect health are upheld as long as they do not discriminate against or unreasonably burden interstate commerce. [*See* Hannibal & St. Joseph Railroad Co. v. Husen, 95 U.S. 465 (1877)]

(1) Permissible regulation

A local statute requiring that cattle or meat imported from other states be certified as free from disease by the state of origin has been upheld. The burden on interstate commerce caused by supplying such a certificate was outweighed by the public health objectives of the state law. [Mintz v. Baldwin, 289 U.S. 346 (1933)]

(2) Impermissible regulation

Although having a valid "public health" purpose, a state law requiring local inspection of slaughterhouses prior to slaughter of livestock destined for local consumption has been held unconstitutional because it discriminates against out-of-state slaughterhouses (*i.e.*, it prevents importation of sound meats from animals slaughtered in other states). [Minnesota v. Barber, 136 U.S. 313 (1890)]

b) Protection of reputation

State laws enacted to protect local, publicly owned natural resources are traditionally a proper exercise of a state's "police power," and will usually be upheld by the Court; *i.e.*, the Court often "balances the interests" in favor of such regulations.

b. Environmental protection and conservation

1) Introduction

Environmental problems are often difficult to solve, especially when the sources of pollution are out of state. States frequently impose environmental regulations, but the Court does not allow environmental concerns to override the Commerce Clause.

2) Importation of wastes

City of Philadelphia v. New Jersey
437 U.S. 617 (1978).

Facts. New Jersey (D) passed a law prohibiting importation into the state of solid or liquid wastes in order to protect the public health, safety, and welfare from the consequences of excessive landfill developments. Philadelphia (P) and other cities, as well as New Jersey landfill operators, challenged the law under the Commerce Clause. The New Jersey Supreme Court upheld the law, and P appeals.

Issue. May a state prohibit importation of environmentally destructive substances solely because of their source of origin?

Held. No. Judgment reversed.

♦ D's reason for passing the law may be legitimate, but the evils of protectionism can reside in the legislative means used as well as legislative ends sought. D's ultimate purpose may not be achieved by discriminating against out-of-state items solely because of their origin. D has failed to show any other valid reason for its discrimination.

♦ D's statute requires out-of-state commercial interests to carry the burden of conserving D's remaining landfill space in an attempt to isolate itself from a problem shared by all. Protection against such trade barriers serves the interest of all states, and may even work to the advantage of New Jersey in the future.

♦ D claims that this statute resembles quarantine laws, which are exceptions to the general Commerce Clause rules. But quarantine laws merely prevent traffic in noxious articles, regardless of their origin. D claims no harm from the mere movement of waste into its borders and concedes that when the harm is felt (upon disposal), there is no basis to distinguish out-of-state waste from domestic waste.

Dissent (Rehnquist, J., Burger, C.J.). Under the Court's decision, New Jersey must either prohibit all landfill operations or accept waste from every portion of the United States. The Commerce Clause should not present the state with this choice. New Jersey may legally exclude such things as infected rags or diseased cattle from its borders while out of necessity disposing of such items that originate within New Jersey; the same rationale should apply to solid waste.

---

3) Limits on local government control

C & A Carbone, Inc. v. Clarkstown
511 U.S. 383 (1994).

Facts. To finance construction of a "waste transfer station," Clarkstown (D) guaranteed the station a minimum flow of waste. D enacted a "flow control ordinance," which provided that all solid waste must be deposited at the station. C & A Carbone (P) was a private recycler who had a sorting facility in Clarkstown. D's ordinance increased P's costs, because P could obtain the necessary services out of state at a lower cost than D's station charged. P challenged D's ordinance. The lower courts upheld the ordinance, and P appeals.

Issue. May a local government require that all solid waste within its boundaries be processed by a specific local processor?

Held. No. Judgment reversed.

♦ Although the ordinance has the effect of directing local waste to a local facility, the economic effects reach interstate commerce. P's facility received waste from out of state. D's ordinance required P to send the nonrecycleable portion of the waste to D's local facility, which increased

P's costs and hence the costs to the out-of-state sources of solid waste. The ordinance also deprives out-of-state businesses access to D's local market.

♦ D claims that its ordinance does not discriminate against interstate commerce because it applies to all solid waste, regardless of origin, before it leaves the town. However, the ordinance does discriminate because it allows only the favored processor to process waste within D's town limits. It is an example of local processing requirements that this Court has held invalid, such as the local milk pasteurizing requirement in *Dean Milk Co. v. Madison*, 340 U.S. 349 (1951). In fact, D's ordinance is even more restrictive than the one in *Dean Milk* because it leaves no room for outside investment.

♦ Any discrimination "against interstate commerce in favor of local business or investment is per se invalid," unless the municipality has no other means to advance a legitimate local interest. D has a variety of nondiscriminatory means available to address its local waste disposal problems. The objective of fundraising is not adequate to justify discrimination against out-of-state businesses.

Concurrence (O'Connor, J.). D's ordinance is different than the ordinances the Court has previously held invalid because it does not give more favorable treatment to local interests as a group as compared to out-of-state economic interests. Thus, it does not discriminate against interstate commerce. However, the ordinance does impose an excessive burden on interstate commerce when compared with the local benefits it confers.

Dissent (Souter, J., Rehnquist, C.J., Blackmun, J.). There is no evidence in this case that any out-of-state trash processor has been injured by the ordinance. The ordinance subjects all out-of-town investors and facilities to the same constraints as local ones, so there is no economic protectionism. The only right to compete that the Commerce Clause protects is the right to compete on terms independent of one's location. The ordinance merely imposes a burden on the local citizens who adopted it, and local burdens are not the focus of the Commerce Clause.

---

4) Subsidies instead of regulation

West Lynn Creamery, Inc. v. Healy
512 U.S. 186 (1994).

Facts. Massachusetts adopted a milk pricing order that required every milk dealer in the state to make a monthly "premium payment" based on the amount of its sales. The funds generated by these payments were distributed to Massachusetts dairy farmers in proportion to their respective contributions to the state's total milk production. West Lynn Creamery, Inc. (P) challenged the milk order in state court. The lower courts upheld the milk order, and the United States Supreme Court granted certiorari.

Issue. May a state impose a tax on all sales of a particular product in order to subsidize in-state producers of that product?

Held. No. Judgment reversed.

♦ The clearest examples of laws that discriminate against interstate commerce are protective tariffs or customs duties, which tax only imported goods and thereby make the goods more expensive. Such a duty both raises revenue and benefits local producers at the expense of out-of-state producers.

♦ The purpose for the milk order is to allow higher-cost in-state producers to compete with lower-cost producers in other states. The effect of the milk pricing order is to make milk that is produced in other states more expensive.

♦ Even though the pricing order is imposed on milk produced in-state as well as milk produced out of state, its effect on in-state producers is more than offset by the subsidy. Consequently, it functions like a protective tariff or customs duty.

♦ The state may properly tax all milk dealers, and it may also subsidize in-state farmers (although the constitutionality of subsidies has never been squarely addressed). However, the combination of a tax and subsidy is "more dangerous to interstate commerce than either part alone." The combination impairs the state's political process because those in-state interests who would otherwise oppose the tax are mollified by the subsidy.

♦ The fact that the taxes are paid by in-state businesses and consumers is irrelevant. The impact of the order is to divert market share to dairy farmers in Massachusetts, which hurts out-of-state farmers.

Concurrence (Scalia, Thomas, JJ.). Nearly all subsidies, whether funded by taxes imposed on out-of-state products, in-state revenues, etc., "neutralize advantages possessed by out-of-state enterprises." Standing alone, this effect does not render a subsidy scheme unconstitutional. A state may subsidize its own industry provided that the subsidies are funded through nondiscriminatory taxes, the proceeds of which go into a general revenue fund rather than back to those in-state persons burdened by the tax.

Dissent (Rehnquist, C.J., Blackmun, J.). The political reality is that there are other groups, namely milk dealers and consumers, who could still oppose the tax even if the dairy farmers choose not to. No precedent justifies applying the negative Commerce Clause against a subsidy funded from a lawful neutral tax.

Comment. Both the majority and dissent (in the full opinion) cited *Bacchus Imports, Ltd. v. Dias*, 468 U.S. 263 (1984). That case involved a Hawaii liquor tax with exemptions for fruit wine manufactured in Hawaii and for a brandy distilled from a plant indigenous to Hawaii. The tax exemption was deemed a protective tariff. While the majority in *West Lynn Creamery* thought insignificant the fact that the Massachusetts milk order did not help those who paid the tax (the milk dealers), as compared to the Hawaii tax exemption, which directly helped in-state producers, the dissenters thought that was an important difference that justified upholding the Massachusetts tax.

---

c. The state as a market participant

1) Introduction

The Court has recognized an exception to the normal Commerce Clause restrictions on state regulation when the state itself becomes a participant in the market. The proper scope of this exception has been the subject of much debate.

2) Purchases

In *Hughes v. Alexandria Scrap Corp.*, 426 U.S. 794 (1976), the Court permitted Maryland to impose more exacting documentation requirements on out-of-state junk-car processors than it imposed on in-state processors. The documentation was required to receive a "bounty" from the state of Maryland, which made the payments for each junk car registered in Maryland that was recycled. The purpose of the bounty was to improve the environment in the state. The Court reasoned that Maryland did not attempt to prohibit the flow of junk cars, but merely entered the market to bid up the value of Maryland junk cars. The state was a market participant, not a market regulator, so the Commerce Clause was not applicable.

3) Postsale obligations imposed by the state selling its resources

In *South-Central Timber Development v. Wunnicke*, 467 U.S. 82 (1984), the Court held that when a state sells its own natural resources it may not impose postsale obligations on the purchaser. The state of Alaska had offered to sell its timber, but only with a contractual requirement that it be processed within the state before being exported. In return, the price for the timber was significantly reduced from what it otherwise would have been. The Supreme Court found the requirement unconstitutional despite a similar federal policy for timber taken from federal land in Alaska. There was no indication that Congress intended to give such power to Alaska. The Court stated that the existence of a federal program similar to the state's was insufficient evidence to support an inference that the state's action was authorized by Congress. In addition, the fact that the state acted through a contract was not enough. The market-participant doctrine is limited to allowing a state to impose burdens on commerce within the market in which it participates. Alaska went too far by imposing conditions that had a substantial regulatory effect outside of the market it had entered. The program did not fall within the market-participant exception. The protectionist nature of Alaska's program resulted in interference with interstate and foreign commerce and thus violated the Commerce Clause.

d. Privileges and immunities

1) Introduction

Article IV, section 2, the Privileges and Immunities Clause, states that the citizens of each state shall be entitled to all privileges and immunities of citizens in the several states. This prohibits discrimination by a state against noncitizens (or nonresidents) of the state with respect to "essential activities" or "basic rights," unless justified by a substantial reason. To justify an exception, the state must show that: (i) the nonresidents are a peculiar source of the evil sought to be avoided; and (ii) the discrimination bears a substantial relation to the problem.

2) Protection of basic activities

The clause protects activities such as pursuit of a livelihood, the transfer of property, access to the state's courts, etc. [Toomer v. Witsell, 334 U.S. 385 (1948)] The Court has held that sport hunting is not an essential activity, so that a state may discriminate against nonresidents in this area. [Baldwin v. Montana Fish & Game Commission, 436 U.S. 371 (1978)]

3) Justification

If the state's discriminatory scheme is overbroad, it will not withstand scrutiny under the Privileges and Immunities Clause. In *Hicklin v. Orbeck*, 437 U.S. 518 (1978), the Court determined that a state hiring preference for residents was an overbroad solution to the problem of unemployment, because the preference extended to highly skilled state residents who did not have the problem of unemployment.

4) Application to municipalities

The Privileges and Immunities Clause also applies to municipalities that require contractors to hire the municipality's own residents to work on the municipality's construction projects. [United Building & Construction Trades Council v. Camden, 465 U.S. 208 (1984)] An ordinance is not immune from attack because it discriminates against some in-state residents as well as out-of-state citizens.

3. Facially Neutral Statutes Affecting Interstate Commerce

a. Introduction

Where Congress has not enacted legislation regarding the subject matter of commerce, the states may regulate local transactions even though they affect interstate commerce, subject to certain limitations. To be constitutional, state regulation must satisfy these criteria:

1) Uniform national regulation not required

The subject matter must not be one that inherently requires uniform, national regulation.

2) Nondiscriminatory

The state regulation must not discriminate against interstate commerce so as to "substantially impede" the free flow of commerce across state lines.

3) Balance of interests favors the state

The state interest underlying the regulation must not be outweighed by the burden on interstate commerce; *i.e.*, the "balance of interests" favors the state as opposed to the national interests.

b. Early cases

Before Congress became more directly involved in regulating the means of interstate commerce, the states created their own safety regulations, which often differed significantly from one state to another.

1) Highway safety

In *South Carolina Highway Department* v. *Barnwell Brothers*, 303 U.S. 177 (1938), the Court held that where Congress has not acted, a state could impose highly restrictive width and weight limitations on all carriers, even if this had the effect of seriously impeding interstate travel. The use of the state highways was considered a subject of peculiarly local concern, and the regulations were supported by legislative fact findings.

2) Train safety

In *Southern Pacific Co. v. Arizona*, 325 U.S. 761 (1945), Arizona had restricted the number of cars permitted on any train operating within the state to only 14 passenger cars or 70 freight cars. The Court rejected the state regulation, concluding that the record demonstrated that the total effect of the law as a safety measure was so slight that it did not outweigh the national interest in keeping interstate commerce free from interference. Railroads were less of a local concern than the highways involved in *Barnwell*. Justice Black dissented on the ground that the Court should have deferred to the legislative findings rather than act as a super-legislature.

c. Precision

Hunt v. Washington State Apple Advertising Commission
432 U.S. 333 (1977).

Facts. A North Carolina statute required that all closed containers of apples sold, offered for sale, or shipped into the state bear "no grade other than the applicable United States grade or standard," and a related regulation required the USDA grade or none at all. The statute was intended to eliminate confusion resulting from a multiplicity of inconsistent state grades. The Washington State Apple Advertising Commission (P) brought an action against Hunt (D), a North Carolina official, challenging the statute as discriminating against interstate commerce. P had developed its own grades, widely recognized as superior to the USDA grades, and on which the reputation of its apples depended. The district court found for P, and D appeals.

Issue. Must a local statute that has a valid, good faith purpose but burdens interstate commerce actually achieve its stated purpose in order to be upheld against a Commerce Clause challenge?

Held. Yes. Judgment affirmed.

♦   When discrimination against interstate commerce is shown, the burden falls on the state to justify its regulation both in terms of the local benefits flowing from the statute and the unavailability of nondiscriminatory alternative ways to accomplish the same objectives.

♦   This statute is clearly discriminatory as it covers only closed containers of apples, the very means by which apples are transported in commerce. The record also discloses that feasible, effective, and less discriminatory alternatives are available.

♦   D recognizes that the statute burdens the interstate sale of Washington apples but claims that the burden is outweighed by the local benefits of protection of the public from fraud and deception. In reality, the statute does little to further D's goal, at least with respect to P's apples. It permits marketing under no grades at all; it directs its primary efforts at wholesalers and brokers, rather than the consuming public; and since P's grades are in all cases equal or superior to USDA grades, they could only "deceive" or "confuse" a consumer to his benefit. In light of the statute's ineffectiveness and the existence of reasonable regulatory alternatives, the statute is invalid.

----

d. Permissible state barriers to incoming trade

Exxon Corp. v. Governor of Maryland
437 U.S. 117 (1978).

Facts. The state of Maryland (D) prohibited producers or refiners of petroleum products from operating retail service stations in the state, as a result of evidence that such retail stations had, in the past, received preferential treatment from suppliers. There were no producers or refiners within the state. Exxon Corporation (P) appeals lower court decisions upholding the statute.

Issue. May a state discriminate against a certain type of out-of-state business if there are no corresponding intrastate businesses?

Held. Yes. Judgment affirmed.

♦   Since all the state's petroleum supplies come from outside the state, there was no discrimination against interstate goods.

♦   Although the statute dealt with retail outlets, it did not discriminate against interstate retailers per se, but only against a certain type of interstate retailer for which there was no intrastate equivalent. Interstate retailers that were not also producers or refiners remain unaffected by the statute.

♦   Although there may be some shifting of business among retailers, the Commerce Clause protects the interstate market, not particular interstate firms, from prohibitive or burdensome regulation.

Dissent (Blackmun, J.). The effect of this prohibition is to protect in-state retail stations from competition from out-of-state businesses. This protectionism is not justified by a legitimate state interest that cannot be served by more evenhanded regulation. Discrimination need not be universal to offend the Commerce Clause, otherwise states could just identify and target the most potent competition, allowing less effective out-of-state actors to remain. No petroleum is produced in Maryland, thus no inherent nexus exists between out-of-state producers and refiners and the distribution and retailing of gasoline in Maryland.

---

e. Modern approach to transportation regulation

Kassel v. Consolidated Freightways Corp.
450 U.S. 662 (1981).

Facts. Consolidated Freightways (P) challenged an Iowa statute mat, like Wisconsin's law in *Raymond Motor Transportation, Inc. v. Rice*, 434 U.S. 429 (1978), prohibited the use of 65-foot double trailers on Iowa highways, with certain exceptions. Kassel (D), an Iowa official, defended the law as a reasonable safety measure in light of the *Raymond* holding. The lower courts held the law unconstitutional as it seriously impeded interstate commerce while providing only slight, if any, safety. D appeals.

Issue. May the courts examine evidence to determine whether a state's purported interest in safety is real and substantial enough to justify applying its police power to burden interstate commerce?

Held. Yes. Judgment affirmed.

♦   A state cannot avoid a Commerce Clause attack merely by invoking public health or safety. The courts are required to balance the state's safety interest against the federal interest in free interstate commerce.

♦   Despite the "special deference" usually accorded to state highway safety regulations, and D's serious effort to support the safety rationale, the record here is no more favorable to D than was Wisconsin's evidence in *Raymond*. P has demonstrated that D's law substantially burdens interstate commerce. Therefore, D's law is unconstitutional.

Concurrence (Brennan, Marshall, JJ.). D's law is unconstitutional under *Raymond* since it is protectionist. The plurality and the dissent insist on considering the legislative purposes advanced by D's lawyers. Separation of powers, however, requires that we defer to the elected lawmakers' judgment, not that we defer to the arguments of lawyers. D's statute exists because the governor of Iowa vetoed legislation that would have permitted 65-foot doubles, giving an essentially protectionist rationale for his action. This is an improper purpose. Safety became a purpose for the law only in retrospect, to defeat P's challenge.

Dissent (Rehnquist, J., Burger, C.J., Stewart, J.). Both the plurality and concurring opinions have intruded upon the fundamental right of the states to pass laws to secure the safety of their citizens. D's law is rationally related to its safety objectives. We are essentially reweighing the state legislature's policy choice, and are forcing D to lower its safety standards merely because its sister states' standards are lower.

Comment. In *Raymond*, the Court also invalidated a prohibition against the use of double-trailer units on state highways because the state failed to show that the regulation contributed to highway safety, and because numerous exceptions to the regulation undercut the safety claims.

---

f. Burden of proof

When the challenged regulation significantly burdens interstate commerce, the state must meet a heavy burden of justification based on its interests. In *Bibb v. Navajo Freight Lines*, 359 U.S. 520 (1959), the Court held that a state may not impose even nondiscriminatory safety regulations that conflict with the regulations of most other states where the asserted safety advantages are at best negligible. That case involved mudguards on trucks: 45 states permitted the conventional straight mudguards, but Illinois required the use of contour mudguards. The substantial burden on interstate commerce could not be justified by any compelling state safety consideration.

4. Federal Preemption

a. Introduction

Because federal law is supreme over state law, states may not normally regulate areas already subject to federal regulation. The difficult issues arise when no federal regulation specifically preempts the state law, but the state law conflicts with federal policy. Federal law rarely occupies a legal field completely. It normally builds on legal relationships established by the states, altering or supplanting them only where necessary to accomplish a particular purpose. The Supreme Court has stated that the question of preemption is primarily one of congressional intent.

b. Types of preemption

Congress may preempt state regulation in three ways.

1) Express preemption

Many federal statutes clearly provide that they preempt state law. Even in these cases, however, the extent of the preemption may be in question.

2) Conflict preemption

When it is impossible to comply with both state and federal law, or when the state law prevents or frustrates the objectives of Congress, federal law must preempt the state law. [Hines v. Davidowitz, 312 U.S. 52 (1941)] In *Gade v. National Solid Wastes Management Association*, 505 U.S. 88 (1992), several state licensing provisions for hazardous waste workers were struck down even though the relevant OSHA regulations concerned only worker safety and the state regulations were aimed at both worker safety and public health. Conflict preemption was found present since the federal scheme was interpreted to forbid duplicative regulation. A strong dissent objected to the Court's approval of supersession of historic state powers absent clear congressional intent.

3) Field preemption

The scheme of federal regulation may be so pervasive as to make reasonable the inference that Congress left no room for the states to supplement it. [Rice v. Santa Fe Elevator Corp., 331 U.S. 218 (1947)]

c. Preemption over Immigration

Arizona v. United States
__ U.S. __, 132 S.Ct. 2492 (2012).

Facts. Arizona (D) enacted a law to address problems with illegal aliens. Section 3 made it a misdemeanor to fail to comply with federal alien-registration requirements. Under Section 5, it was a misdemeanor for an unauthorized alien to seek or engage in work in Arizona. The United States (P) brought suit, seeking to enjoin enforcement of the state law. The District Court issued a preliminary injunction. The Ninth Circuit affirmed. The Supreme Court granted certiorari.

Issue. Is a state law that prohibits unauthorized aliens from working preempted by federal immigration laws?

Held. Yes. Judgment affirmed.

◆ The federal government has broad, undoubted power over the subject of immigration and the status of aliens. Congress can preempt state laws in this area expressly, by determining that federal regulation is exclusive, or by enacting laws with which the state law conflicts.

◆ Section 3 creates a state-law penalty for conduct prohibited by federal law. Congress has occupied the entire field of alien registration, so the State cannot also regulate in this area, even if the state's regulation is complementary or parallel to federal regulations.

◆ Section 5 differs by created a criminal offense where no federal counterpart exists. Federal law prohibits employers from hiring unauthorized aliens, but does not sanction the workers. Arizona instead focuses on the aliens. Even though federal law is silent on whether penalties may be imposed against these employees, D's law stands as an obstacle to the accomplishment of the objectives of Congress. It creates a conflict in the method of enforcement of federal immigration laws. Congress decided not to impose criminal penalties on aliens who seek or engage in unauthorized employment, so the states are preempted from doing that.

Dissent (Scalia, J.). The Court has deprived the states of the defining characteristic of sovereignty: the power to exclude from the sovereign's territory people who have no right to be there. States have the inherent sovereign power to protect their borders against foreign nationals, regardless of whether the federal government is concerned about upsetting foreign powers.

Dissent (Thomas, J.). D's law should not be preempted because there is no conflict between the ordinary meaning of the federal law and the state law. The majority uses as "purposes and objectives" theory of implied pre-emption that is inconsistent with the Constitution. The Supremacy Clause applies to statutes, not judicially divined legislative purposes.

Dissent (Alito, J.). There is little evidence that Congress intended to pre-empt state laws such as Section 5. Congress specifically pre-empted state laws penalizing employers, but not laws penalizing employees. This leads to an inference that Congress did not intend to pre-empt laws such as Section 5.

Chapter IV

The Scope of Congress's Powers: Taxing and Spending, War Powers, Individual Rights, and State Autonomy

A. Regulation Through Taxing, Spending, and the War Power

1. The Taxing Power

a. Introduction

Article I, section 8 grants Congress power "to lay and collect taxes, duties, imposts and excises, to pay the debts and provide for the common defense and general welfare of the United States." Congress may exercise its taxing power as a means of promoting any objective that is within an enumerated power. If Congress has the power to regulate the activity taxed, the tax is valid even though clearly enacted for a regulatory, rather than a revenue-raising, purpose. If Congress has no power to regulate the activity taxed, the validity of the tax depends on its validity as a revenue-raising measure, although incidental regulatory effects are permissible. Congress generally does not rely on the taxing power to regulate because of its extensive regulatory powers under other provisions, but this is still an important federal power.

b. Purpose of tax

A few months after the *Hammer v. Dagenhart* decision, *supra*, as a means to circumvent that decision, Congress imposed an excise tax of 10% on the yearly net profits of any employer knowingly using child labor in his business without regard to whether goods produced were shipped in interstate commerce. The Supreme Court found the tax unconstitutional. [Bailey v. Drexel Furniture Co., 259 U.S. 20 (1922)] In *Bailey*, the Supreme Court indicated that the important factor is the motive of Congress. This means that the Court looks at the taxing statute to see its purpose, its intended effect, and its effect in normal operation (*i.e.*, the Court examines the statute on its face). If the true purpose is to raise revenue, then the tax is valid. In *United States v. Kahriger*, 345 U.S. 22 (1953), the Court upheld a tax on wagering, despite its indirect effect of penalizing professional gamblers. The legislative history showed an intent to raise revenue, and the tax actually did raise funds, although the legislative history also showed an intent to suppress wagering. The penalty on wagering was considered as merely an indirect effect. Unless the penalty provisions are extraneous to the tax need, courts cannot limit the exercise of the taxing power. (As noted *supra*, after 1936, the Court expanded its view of the commerce power, and it became less necessary for Congress to use its taxing power to regulate.)

c. The Individual Mandate Tax

National Federation of Independent Business v. Sebelius
__ U.S. __, 132 S.Ct. 2566 (2012).

Facts. The Patient Protection and Affordable Care Act (ACA) included a mandate for citizens and legal residents to maintain health insurance coverage. As an alternative to its Commerce Clause argument, the Government claimed the mandate imposed a tax on those who do not buy insurance. The Court considered this argument in this part of its opinion.

Issue. May Congress impose a tax on individuals who do not buy health insurance as required by the ACA?

Held. Yes. Judgment reversed.

♦ Because the Commerce Clause does not authorize Congress to mandate the purchase of insurance, an alternative ground for upholding the ACA is the enumerated power of Congress to "lay and collect Taxes" under Article I, section 8, clause 1. The ACA can, as the Government asserts, be read not as an order to buy insurance but as the imposition of a tax on those who do not buy insurance.

♦ The ACA mandate creates a condition—not owning health insurance—that triggers a tax. The payment must be made to the IRS, which also enforces and collects the payment in the same manner as taxes.

♦ The ACA refers to the payment as a "penalty" and not a "tax," but the label is not controlling. In Drexel Furniture, the Court held the imposition was a penalty instead of a tax because it was an exceedingly heavy burden triggered by the smallest infraction, because the law required scienter, and because the Department of Labor enforced the law. By contrast, under the ACA, the payment is small, there is no scienter requirement, and the IRS enforces the law. Consequently, the ACA imposes a tax, not a penalty.

♦ The payment in this case does affect individual conduct, but so do many taxes. Unlike taxes, penalties are punishment for unlawful acts or omissions, but the ACA does not make failure to buy health insurance unlawful. The only negative legal consequence is a required payment to the IRS. Because the payment required by the ACA is relatively small, the Court does not need to determine at what point an exaction is so punitive that it constitutes a penalty instead of a tax.

Dissent (Scalia, Kennedy, Thomas, Alito, JJ.). There is a clear distinction between a penalty and a tax. The ACA imposes a penalty for violation of the law's requirement to buy health insurance. Regardless of the magnitude of the payment, it is still a penalty, not a tax. The Court has not interpreted the ACA but has rewritten it. Courts have no authority to impose a tax; under the Constitution, only the House of Representatives can do that.

---

2. The Spending Power

a. Introduction

The "general welfare" power of Article I, section 8 is connected with the taxing and spending power. This clause can therefore be invoked only when there is an expenditure of money appropriated by Congress. Thus, Congress could not pass a law under the General Welfare Clause requiring seat belts in all cars. The rule is that Congress must tax for revenue and not merely regulatory purposes, and then it must spend for the general welfare. The spending must be for a national concern as opposed to a local one. However, the Supreme Court gives great deference to the determinations of Congress in deciding what is for the "common benefit."

b. Local vs. general welfare

United States v. Butler
297 U.S. 1 (1936).

Facts. The 1933 Agriculture Adjustment Act authorized the Secretary of Agriculture to extend benefit payments to farmers who agreed to reduce their planted acreage. Processors of the covered crops were to be taxed to provide a fund for the benefit payments. Butler (P) was receiver for a processor who had paid the tax. P brought suit to recover the tax paid on grounds that it was part of an unconstitutional program to control agricultural production. The court of appeals held the tax unconstitutional, and the United States (D) appeals.

Issue. May Congress use its taxing and spending powers to operate a self-contained program regulating agricultural production?

Held. No. Judgment affirmed.

♦ The power of Congress to authorize expenditures of public moneys for public purposes is not limited by the direct grants of legislative power found in the Constitution, but it does have limits. Appropriations cannot be made as a means to an unconstitutional end.

♦ Regulation of agricultural production is not a power granted to Congress; therefore it is left to the states. Attainment of such a prohibited end may not be accomplished through the use of granted powers (here the taxing powers).

♦ This scheme, purportedly voluntary, in reality involves purchasing, with federal funds, submission to federal regulation of a subject reserved to the states. Because the end is invalid, it may not be accomplished indirectly through the taxing and spending power.

Dissent (Stone, Brandeis, Cardozo, JJ.). Courts are concerned only with the power to enact statutes, not the wisdom of the legislature. The depressed state of agriculture is nationwide; therefore, the Act does provide for the "general welfare." There is no coercion involved, since threat of loss, not hope of gain, which is involved here, is the essence of economic coercion. Conditioning the receipt of federal funds on certain activity does not infringe on state power.

Comment. *Butler* was one of the last of the series of cases striking down parts of the New Deal. Subsequent Commerce Clause cases indicate that the area involved in *Butler* would not now be held to be one of purely local concern.

---

c. Inducement of states permitted

Steward Machine Co. v. Davis
301 U.S. 548 (1937).

Facts. The Social Security Act taxed employers of eight or more persons a certain percentage of the salaries of their employees; the funds were to go to the United States Treasury. If an employer contributed to a state plan, he got a 90% credit toward the contribution of his federal responsibility. All state plans had to be approved by the Secretary of the Treasury, however. Steward Machine Company (P) paid the tax and then sought a refund, claiming that the Act unconstitutionally sought to coerce the states to adopt state plans. P appeals lower court decisions upholding the Act.

Issue. May Congress reduce private employers' federal tax obligations by crediting payments made only to federally approved state plans?

Held. Yes. Judgment affirmed.

♦ In the economic crisis of a depression, the spending here was clearly for the general welfare.

♦ P claims the Act seeks to coerce the states. In reality, the Act merely provides for fairness by not permitting states with security plans to be penalized by the double taxation on their business that would result if there were no credit for payments to these state plans.

---

d. Spending for the general welfare

Congressional power to spend is limited by the general welfare clause. However, the determination of what is in the nation's general welfare is left to Congress, and the courts will defer to appropriate legislative findings. For example, the old age provisions of the Social Security Act were upheld, largely by ascribing wide latitude to congressional determination of the national interest. [*See* Helvering v. Davis, 301 U.S. 619 (1937)]

e. Limits on the Spending Power

National Federation of Independent Business v. Sebelius
__ U.S. __, 132 S.Ct. 2566 (2012).

Facts. The Patient Protection and Affordable Care Act (ACA) included a provision that expanded Medicaid by requiring state programs to provide Medicaid to any adult having income up to 133 percent of the federal poverty level. The federal government agreed to pay for most of the additional costs. However, if a State failed to comply with the new requirement, the federal government would terminate all Medicaid funding, including the portion paid prior to the expansion. The Court considered this argument in this part of its opinion.

Issue. May Congress require States to expand Medicaid by threatening to cut off all Medicaid funding if they don't agree to the expansion?

Held. No. Judgment reversed.

♦ Under the Spending Clause, Congress may establish conditions on grants of federal funds to the states to ensure that the funds are used by the States in the manner Congress intended. However, Congress cannot coerce the states. The relationship is in the nature of a contract, such that the States must be free to voluntarily and knowingly accept the terms Congress establishes.

♦ Spending Clause cases require the Court to make sure Congress does not use financial inducements to exert a power akin to undue influence. When pressure turns into compulsion, Congress has acted contrary to the system of federalism.

♦ The ACA crosses the line. Instead of simply refusing to grant the new funds to States who don't expand Medicaid as the ACA requires, Congress threatens to withhold those States' existing Medicaid funds. This goes beyond setting a condition to ensure the funds are used for the purpose Congress intends.

♦ Unlike the "relatively mild encouragement" addressed in South Dakota v. Dole, the ACA creates a "gun to the head." This is no mere modification of an existing program but a change in the program from one designed to care for the neediest people, but one folded into the comprehensive national plan to provide universal health insurance coverage.

♦ While the Medicaid expansion is unconstitutional, it can be severed from the rest of the ACA. The only remedy necessary is to restrict the federal government from withdrawing existing Medicaid funds from any State that does not comply with the expansion requirements.

Dissent (Scalia, Kennedy, Thomas, Alito, JJ.). The Medicaid expansion authorizes a severe sanction. A State that chooses not to participate in the expansion would have to either drastically reduce funding for other programs or significantly raise taxes—on top of the taxes paid by the State's citizens to fund Medicaid in other States. This eliminates the voluntary nature of the States' choice to accept or decline federal funds. Almost half of all federal funds granted to the States are for Medicaid, which itself amounts to almost twenty-two percent of all state expenditures. Medicaid is the largest item in every State's budget. By contrast, Dole involved the withholding of funds that equaled less than .2 percent of South Dakota's state spending. Congress has exceeded its power under the Spending Clause here. Because the ACA includes no alternative to the cut-off of States who don't expand Medicaid, this provision cannot be severed from the overall ACA and the entire statute is unconstitutional.

Dissent in part (Ginsburg, Sotomayor, JJ.). This is the first time the Court has found a congressional exercise of the Spending Power to be unconstitutionally coercive. Yet Medicaid is a program designed to recognize federalism by giving the States the opportunity to partner in the program's administration and development. The ACA is merely another of several expansions of Medicaid over the years. The States received plenty of notice of the new requirements. However, based on the majority's conclusion, we agree that the Medicaid expansion is severable from the rest of the ACA.

---

3. The "War" Power

Article I, section 8 gives Congress power to declare war and establish the military. Relying on these provisions, Congress has enacted rent control and restricted civil liberties

B. Congress's Enforcement Power under the Reconstruction Amendments

1. Introduction

Section 5 of the Fourteenth Amendment provides that "Congress shall have power to enforce, by appropriate legislation, the provisions of this article." Congress has enacted substantial legislation to enforce the Reconstruction amendments. The issues raised by this legislation include the question of whether Congress is limited to remedying what the Supreme Court finds unconstitutional, or whether Congress can remedy what Congress itself finds unconstitutional. In other words, does section 5 confer remedial or substantive powers?

2. Voting Rights

The right to vote for federal, state, and local officials is protected from both state and federal government infringement by the provisions of the Fifteenth and Nineteenth Amendments, as well as from state infringement of this right by the Fourteenth Amendment. In 1965, Congress passed the Voting Rights Act, which essentially created a rebuttable presumption that literacy tests in certain states were used to perpetrate racial discrimination.

3. Congressional Control over State Voting Requirements

Katzenbach v. Morgan
384 U.S. 641 (1966).

Facts. Morgan (P), a registered voter in the city of New York, challenged section 4(e) of the Voting Rights Act of 1965, which provides that any person who has successfully completed sixth grade in an accredited school in Puerto Rico cannot be denied the right to vote because of lack of English proficiency. P claims that the law pro tanto prohibits enforcement of New York election laws based on English proficiency. A three-judge district court granted P relief. Katzenbach (D), the United States Attorney General, appeals.

Issue. May Congress prohibit enforcement of a state English-literacy voting requirement by legislating under section 5 of the Fourteenth Amendment, regardless of whether the judiciary would find such a requirement unconstitutional?

Held. Yes. Judgment reversed.

♦ Congress need not wait for a judicial determination of unconstitutionality before prohibiting the enforcement of a state law. Congress may enact any legislation that is appropriate.

♦ The test for appropriateness is whether (i) the end is legitimate, and (ii) the means are not prohibited by and are consistent with the letter and spirit of the Constitution.

♦ Section 4(e) is plainly adapted to the legitimate end of assuring equal protection to all, including non-English-speaking citizens. P claims that section 4(e) works an invidious discrimination in violation of the Fifth Amendment by failing to include persons attending schools not covered by the law. But section 4(e) extends the franchise and does not restrict or deny P. The fact that Congress went no further than it did does not constitute a constitutional violation.

Dissent (Harlan, Stewart, JJ.). The Court has confused the issue of the extent of the section 5 enforcement power with the distinct issue of what questions are better resolved by the judiciary than by the legislature. Congress should not be permitted to enact remedial legislation when there is no constitutional infringement to be remedied, and the judiciary alone ultimately determines whether a practice or statute is unconstitutional. This Court has previously held that a state English-literacy test is permissible. Here, the Court grants Congress authority to override that judicial determination and define the substantive scope of the Fourteenth Amendment.

Comment. This is a far-reaching decision that may exempt the Fourteenth Amendment from the principle of Court and Congress relationships set forth in *Marbury* v. *Madison, supra, i.e.,* that the judiciary is the final arbiter of the Constitution. This would allow Congress to act independently. Another view is that Congress was merely acting to strengthen the judicially declared right of equal access to government services.

---

4. Limits on Congressional Enforcement Power

City of Boerne v. Flores
521 U.S. 507 (1997).

Facts. In *Employment Division, Department of Human Resources of Oregon v. Smith*, 494 U.S. 872 (1990), the Court held that, except in special circumstances, the Free Exercise Clause was not violated by a facially neutral and secular law, drafted without legislative animus, that had the effect of interfering with a given religious practice. In that case, Smith had been denied unemployment benefits because he had used peyote in a sacramental ceremony. The Court rejected application of the *Sherbert v. Verner, infra,* balancing test. In response, Congress passed the Religious Freedom Restoration Act of 1993 ("RFRA"), which required courts to apply the balancing test. Under RFRA, courts would have to determine whether a statute substantially burdened a religious practice, and if it did, whether the burden was justified by a compelling government interest. The city of Boerne (D) denied a building permit to enlarge a church, based on an ordinance governing historic preservation in the area. Flores (P), the Archbishop of San Antonio, challenged the denial under RFRA. The district court held that in enacting RFRA, Congress exceeded the scope of its section 5 enforcement power under the Fourteenth Amendment. The fifth circuit reversed. The Supreme Court granted certiorari.

Issue. May Congress impose a rule of constitutional interpretation on the Supreme Court through its enforcement of the Fourteenth Amendment?

Held. No. Judgment reversed.

♦ Congress relied on the Fourteenth Amendment to impose the RFRA requirements on the states. The Fourteenth Amendment gives Congress power to enforce the constitutional guarantee that no state shall deprive any person of "life, liberty, or property, without due process of law"; nor deny any person "equal protection of the laws." In enacting RFRA, Congress sought to protect the free exercise of religion.

♦ While congressional authority under the Fourteenth Amendment is broad, it is not unlimited. Congress does have power to enforce the constitutional right to the free exercise of religion, since the First Amendment liberties are included within the Due Process Clause of the Fourteenth Amendment. This power extends only to enforcement, however. It does not extend to changing or defining what the right of free exercise is. There is a distinction between enforcement and changing governing law.

♦ The power to interpret the Constitution in a case or controversy is in the Judiciary, not in Congress. Congress does not have a substantive, nonremedial power under the Fourteenth Amendment. If Congress could define its own powers by altering the meaning of the Fourteenth

Amendment, the Constitution would no longer be a superior paramount law that cannot be changed by ordinary means.

- Preventive rules may sometimes be appropriate remedial measures, but the means must be appropriate to the ends to be achieved. In this case, there was no record of generally applicable laws that were passed because of religious bigotry. The provisions of RFRA are so out of proportion to a supposed remedial objective that it cannot be treated as responsive to unconstitutional behavior. RFRA is applicable to all state and federal law, whenever enacted. The substantial costs RFRA imposes on government far exceed any pattern or practice of unconstitutional conduct under the Free Exercise Clause as interpreted by *Smith*.

- Each branch of the government must respect both the Constitution and the proper determination of the other branches. RFRA was designed to control cases and controversies, but it is the interpretation of the Constitution that must govern cases and controversies, not RFRA.

Concurrence (Stevens, J.). RFRA is actually a law respecting an establishment of religion in violation of the First Amendment. It gives churches a preference that other organizations do not enjoy.

Dissent (O'Connor, Breyer, JJ.). The Court should reexamine the *Smith* holding, which was incorrect. That holding allows the government to prohibit, without justification, conduct mandated by an individual's religious beliefs, so long as the prohibition is generally applicable. In so doing, *Smith* harmed religious liberty. If the Court corrected the misinterpretation of the Free Exercise Clause in *Smith*, we could then review RFRA in light of a proper interpretation. But the Court does correctly hold that Congress cannot independently define or expand the scope of constitutional rights by statute.

Dissent (Breyer, J.). It is not necessary to consider the question whether the Fourteenth Amendment would allow Congress to enact RFRA.

Dissent (Souter, J.). The Court cannot soundly decide this case without reexamining the free-exercise standard of *Smith*.

Comment. It could be argued that since Congress is specifically mentioned in the Fourteenth Amendment, it does have special authority to determine what rights to enforce. It has such authority under the Thirteenth Amendment.

---

5. Congressional Power and State Immunity

The Eleventh Amendment grants federal immunity to states from lawsuits filed by private parties. Section 1 of the Fourteenth Amendment prohibits the states from making or enforcing any law that abridges the privileges or immunities of United States citizens or that denies due process or equal protection. Section 5 of the Fourteenth Amendment gives Congress the right of enforcement by appropriate legislation. The Supreme Court has had to determine how Congress can enforce the Fourteenth Amendment without violating the Eleventh Amendment.

a. Abrogation of immunity

The Court has held that Congress may abrogate the states' Eleventh Amendment immunity (by subjecting nonconsenting states to suit in federal court) only when Congress both unequivocally intends to do so and acts pursuant to a valid grant of constitutional authority. Article I of the Constitution does not grant Congress this authority. Instead, Congress must rely on section 5 of the Fourteenth Amendment.

b. Limitation of authority

Because only the Supreme Court can define the substance of constitutional guarantees, Congress cannot unilaterally declare its authority under the Fourteenth Amendment. In *Boerne, supra*, the Court determined that if Congress enacts legislation under section 5 that is beyond the scope of section 1's actual guarantees, such legislation is valid only if it exhibits "congruence and proportionality between the injury to be prevented or remedied and the means adopted to that end."

c. State employees cannot recover for ADA Title I violations

Board of Trustees v. Garrett
531 U.S. 356 (2001).

Facts. Garrett (P) was a nurse employed as a director of nursing by the Board of Trustees (D). P was diagnosed with cancer and had to take substantial leave from work for her treatments. When she returned to work, she had lost her director position and was transferred to a lower-paying position. P sued D under the Americans with Disabilities Act ("ADA"), claiming that D did not accommodate her physical disabilities. Title I of the ADA protects against discrimination in employment. In a separate lawsuit, Ash, a security officer for the Alabama Department of Youth Services, requested a modification of his duties and reassignment to the day shift because of his chronic asthma and sleep apnea. Ash's requests were denied. The district court granted D summary judgment on the ground that the ADA cannot override the state's immunity under the Eleventh Amendment. The circuit court reversed. The Supreme Court granted certiorari.

Issue. May state employees recover damages for the state's failure to comply with Title I of the ADA?

Held. No. Judgment reversed.

♦ To apply the basic principles of Fourteenth Amendment analysis, the first step is identifying the scope of the constitutional right at issue. This case involves the limitations that section 1 of the Fourteenth Amendment places on state treatment of the disabled.

♦ Under *City of Cleburne v. Cleburne Living Center*, 473 U.S. 432 (1985), the Fourteenth Amendment does not require a state to make special accommodations for the disabled so long as the state's action toward these individuals is rational. Such action need only satisfy rational-basis scrutiny.

♦ Congress has authority under section 5 only to respond to state transgressions. Congress must identify a history and pattern of unconstitutional employment discrimination by the states against the disabled to legitimately make the ADA apply to the states. Despite the 4.5 million people employed by the states, Congress assembled only a few incidents of unconstitutional state discrimination in employment against the disabled. This does not rise to a pattern of unconstitutional state behavior. However, even if it did, the ADA creates rights and remedies that fail the *Boerne* test of congruence and proportionality.

Concurrence (Kennedy, O'Connor, JJ.). Congress has failed to establish patterns of constitutional violations committed by the states in their official capacity, which is a requirement for a federal statute that allows private persons to sue the states for money damages.

Dissent (Breyer, Stevens, Souter, Ginsberg, JJ.). The Constitution requires only that Congress determine that the remedy is an appropriate way to enforce basic equal protection. Congress assembled a vast record of massive, society-wide discrimination against persons with disabilities which satisfies the Constitutional requirements. The Court should not unduly restrict the power of Congress to remedy discrimination under section 5.

d. State employees can recover under FMLA

In *Nevada Department of Human Resources v. Hibbs*, 538 U.S. 721 (2003), the Court upheld the abrogation of state sovereign immunity under the Family Medical Leave Act ("FMLA"), which allows eligible employees to take up to 12 work weeks of unpaid leave to care for family members. The FMLA creates a private right of action against any employer, including a public agency, that interferes with FMLA rights. Congress enacted the FMLA in reliance on its power under section 5 of the Fourteenth Amendment, which authorizes Congress to abrogate the states' Eleventh Amendment sovereign immunity. The FMLA protects the right to be free from gender-based discrimination in the workplace. The Court stated that stereotypes about women's domestic roles created a cycle of discrimination that forced women to continue to assume the role of primary family caregiver and fostered employers' stereotypical views about women's commitment to work and their value as employees. The Court found that Congress had created a legislative record that demonstrated widespread gender-based unconstitutional discrimination by the states that justified a private damages remedy. Justice Kennedy, joined by Justices Scalia and Thomas, dissented. Justice Kennedy argued that there was insufficient evidence of a pattern of unlawful conduct that would warrant the remedy of opening state treasuries to private suits.

e. State employees can recover for ADA Title II violations

Tennessee v. Lane, 541 U.S. 509 (2004), concerned the abrogation of state sovereign immunity under Title II of the Americans with Disabilities Act. Title II prohibits a public entity from denying the benefits of its services, programs, or activities to disabled persons. Lane, a paraplegic who used a wheelchair, was required to answer a set of criminal charges. The courtroom was on the second floor, and the courthouse had no elevator. Lane had to crawl up two flights of stairs to get to the courtroom, but he refused to do so again for a subsequent appearance and was jailed for failure to appear. Lane sued Tennessee under Title II of the ADA. The Supreme Court held that Congress may abrogate state immunity from suits brought under Title II for denial of public services to disabled individuals. The Court noted that, unlike Title I, Title II involves rights of access to the courts that are protected by the Due Process Clause, as well as the Confrontation Clause of the Sixth Amendment. The Court concluded that Title II is an appropriate response to the history and pattern of unequal treatment because its requirement of program accessibility is congruent and proportional to its object of enforcing the right of access to the courts.

C. The Tenth Amendment as a Federalism-Based Limitation on Congressional Power

1. Treaty and War Powers

a. Introduction

The Tenth Amendment provides that "[t]he powers not delegated to the United States by the Constitution, nor prohibited by it to the States, are reserved to the States respectively, or to the people." However, the powers of the federal government concerning foreign or external affairs are different in origin and nature from those involving domestic or internal affairs. In external affairs, federal power is exclusive; the states may not conduct foreign affairs. There is no allocation of this power between the states and the federal government.

b. Treaties

Article II, section 2 grants the President the power to make treaties with foreign nations, provided two-thirds of the senators present concur. Such treaties become the supreme law of the land under the Supremacy Clause. The Tenth Amendment is not a limitation on the treaty power. Thus, pursuant to a treaty, Congress may legislate on matters over which it otherwise would have no power.

c. Not limited by the Tenth Amendment

Missouri v. Holland
252 U.S. 416 (1920).

Facts. The Migratory Bird Treaty Act of 1918 implemented a treaty between the United States and Great Britain and prohibited killing or interference with migratory birds, except as permitted by regulations made by the Secretary of Agriculture. Missouri (P) brought suit in equity to enjoin Holland (D), a United States game warden, from enforcing the Act. P claims the Act unconstitutionally interferes with state rights and that an earlier similar act of Congress, not pursuant to a treaty, was held invalid. The district court dismissed the action, and P appeals.

Issue. May an act of Congress implementing a United States treaty create regulations that would be unconstitutional if the act stood alone?

Held. Yes. Judgment affirmed.

♦ The Tenth Amendment is irrelevant since the power to make treaties is delegated expressly. Furthermore, if the treaty is valid, the statute is equally so, being necessary and proper.

♦ The important national interest here can be protected only by national action in concert with that of another nation. Such a joint effort is possible only through a treaty. Since there is no specific constitutional restriction, and the national interest requires it, the treaty and its implementing statute are valid.

♦ The state's interest, while sufficient to justify regulation in the absence of federal regulation, is too transitory to preempt specific national regulation, especially when the national action arises from exercise of the treaty power.

---

2. State Immunity from Federal Regulation

a. Introduction

The Tenth Amendment provides that the powers not delegated to the federal government by the Constitution, nor prohibited to the states, are reserved for the states. This reservation of power is often cited as a restriction on Congress's power to regulate the states via the Commerce Clause.

b. Recognition of state autonomy

In *National League of Cities v. Usery*, 426 U.S. 833 (1976), the Court struck down amendments to the Fair Labor Standards Act that would have extended minimum wage and maximum hour protections to state employees. The Court held that Congress, in exercising its powers under the Commerce Clause, had impermissibly interfered with the integral government functions of the states, because the amendments would have displaced state policies regarding the manner in which states chose to deliver the services their citizens required. This was seen as not comporting with the federal system. Four justices dissented. *National League of Cities* was overruled by *Garcia, infra*, nine years later.

c. Renewed supremacy of federal government—*National League of Cities* overruled

In *Garcia v. San Antonio Metropolitan Transit Authority*, 469 U.S. 528 (1985), the Court held that Congress may enforce minimum wage and overtime requirements against a local government's mass transit authority. The Court found that the term, "traditional governmental functions," used in decisions following *National League of Cities, supra,* produced confusion and a variety of interpretations. The Court stated that the fundamental problem was that no distinction that purports to separate out important governmental functions can be faithful to the role of federalism in a democratic society. The Court rejected a rule of state immunity from federal regulation that turns on an unelected judiciary's decision as to whether a particular governmental function is "integral" or "traditional." The Court reasoned that the political process ensures that laws that unduly burden the states will not be promulgated; the states have political influence in Congress, especially in the Senate, where each state is equally represented. The Court said that the effectiveness of the procedural limit is evident by the fact that the states are exempt from the operation of many federal statutes and receive significant federal aid for their own programs.

1) Opposing views

Justice Powell, joined by Chief Justice Burger, Justice Rehnquist, and Justice O'Connor, dissented, stating that the most effective democratic government is at the state and local levels, "where people with firsthand knowledge of local problems have more ready access to public officials responsible for dealing with them." In a separate dissent, Justice O'Connor asserted that the true essence of federalism is that the states, as states, have legitimate interests that the national government must respect even though its laws are supreme.

3. Limit on Congressional Regulatory Authority

New York v. United States
505 U.S. 144 (1992).

Facts. Low-level radioactive waste is generated in substantial quantities by various industries, including the medical and research industries, but in 1979, the only United States disposal site for radioactive waste was in South Carolina. In 1980, Congress enacted the Low-Level Radioactive Waste Policy Act. The Act authorized states to enter into regional compacts that, once ratified by Congress, could after 1985 restrict the use of their disposal facilities to waste generated within member states. By 1985, only three approved regional compacts had operational disposal facilities. Thirty-one states (the unsited states) were not members of these compacts. Congress amended the Act in 1985, based on a proposal submitted by the National Governors' Association, whereby sited states agreed to accept waste until 1992, collecting a graduated surcharge for waste from unsited states, and unsited states agreed not to rely on sited states after 1992. A portion of the surcharges would be collected by the Secretary of Energy, who in turn would pay the surcharges to unsited states that complied with a series of deadlines for joining a regional compact or creating their own disposal sites. States that failed to meet the deadlines could lose access to disposal sites. Finally, any state or regional compact that was unable to dispose of all waste generated within its borders by 1996 would, upon the request of the waste generator, take title to the waste and be liable for all damages incurred by such generator as a consequence of the state's failure to take possession of the waste once notified that it is available. New York (P) did not join a regional compact, but did enact legislation providing for the siting and financing of a disposal facility. The two target counties objected and joined P in suing the United States (D), seeking a declaratory judgment that the Act violates the Tenth Amendment. The district court dismissed the complaint. The court of appeals affirmed, and the Supreme Court granted certiorari.

Issue. May Congress direct the states to regulate in a particular field or a particular way, using them as implements of regulation?

Held. No. Judgment reversed in part.

♦ The power of Congress to legislate so as to impact state autonomy has been analyzed both by inquiring whether Congress has the power under Article I to so act and by determining whether Congress has invaded the province of state sovereignty reserved by the Tenth Amendment. But these inquiries may be mirror images, because where a power is delegated to Congress, the Tenth Amendment expressly disclaims any reservation of power to the states, and if a power is an attribute of state sovereignty reserved by the Tenth Amendment, it is necessarily one not conferred on Congress. The Tenth Amendment merely states the truism that all is retained by the states that has not been surrendered to the federal government: yet it requires the courts to determine whether an incident of state sovereignty is protected by a limitation on an Article I power.

♦ P claims that Congress exceeded its powers not by regulating radioactive waste, which is interstate in character and thus falls within the Commerce Clause, but by directing the states to regulate in this field in a particular way. The Court has long recognized that Congress cannot directly compel the states to enact and enforce a federal regulatory program. A key difference between the Constitution and the Articles of Confederation is that under the Constitution, the federal government can exercise its legislative authority directly over individuals rather than over states.

♦ Congress may create incentives for states to adopt a legislative program consistent with federal interests, however. Congress has done so by attaching conditions on the receipt of federal funds and by offering states the option of regulating private activity in interstate commerce according to federal standards or having state law preempted by federal regulation. Such incentives do not compel state action. This preserves the accountability of both federal and state officials to their respective constituencies.

♦ The Act in this case creates three sets of incentives. First, the surcharge provisions provide for imposition by sited states of surcharges that are partially remitted to the federal government and paid out to states that meet specified milestones. The burden on interstate commerce is within Congress's Commerce Clause authority, and the payments are within its Spending Clause authority.

♦ The second set of incentives allows states that have disposal sites to increase the cost of access to the sites and eventually to deny access altogether to waste that is generated in states that do not meet federal guidelines. This gives unsited states the choice of complying with federal standards for self-sufficiency or becoming subject to federal regulation that allows sited states to deny access to their disposal sites. The affected states are not thereby compelled by Congress to regulate; the incentives are a conditional exercise of Congress's commerce power, which is permissible.

♦ The third set of "incentives" requires states that do not regulate according to federal standards to take title to and possession of any waste produced within their borders and become liable for all damages waste generators suffer because of the states' failure to take title promptly. But the Constitution does not provide that Congress may simply transfer radioactive waste from generators to state governments, or force states to become liable for generators' damages, either of which would "commandeer" state governments into serving federal regulatory purposes. And Congress cannot require state governments to implement federal legislation. Since neither "option" is constitutional, a choice between them is not permissible either. However, this "take title" provision is severable from the rest of the Act.

♦ No matter how great the federal interest, the Constitution does not give Congress authority to require the states to regulate. Congress must legislate directly, not by conscripting state governments. State officials cannot give Congress this authority by consenting to the federal statute.

♦ P claims that the first two incentives violate the Guarantee Clause, but neither incentive denied any state a republican form of government.

Concurrence and Dissent (White, Blackmun, Stevens, JJ.). The Act is a result of the efforts of state governments seeking to achieve a state-based remedy for the waste problem. It is essentially a congressional sanction of interstate compromises, not federal preemption or intervention. New York in particular should be estopped from asserting the unconstitutionality of the Act after the state has derived substantial benefits under the Act. The Court's opinion that the take title provision is unconstitutional does not preclude Congress from adopting a similar measure through its powers under the Spending or Commerce Clause. Ironically, the Court gives Congress fewer incentives to defer to the wishes of state officials in achieving local solutions to local problems, all in the name of promoting federalism.

Concurrence and Dissent (Stevens, J.). The Constitution enhanced the power of the federal government, and there is no history to suggest that the federal government may not impose its will upon the states as it did under the Articles of Confederation.

---

4. Limit on Congressional Power to Use State Officers Directly

Printz v. United States
521 U.S. 898 (1997).

Facts. The federal Brady Handgun Act required the United States Attorney General to create a national system to instantly check the background of prospective handgun purchasers. Pending establishment of the national system, the Act also required the chief law enforcement officer ("CLEO") of each local jurisdiction to conduct the back-ground checks. Printz (P) and another sheriff challenged the statute under *New York v. United States, supra.* The lower courts upheld the statute. The Supreme Court granted certiorari.

Issue. May Congress compel state officers directly to enforce a federal regulatory program?

Held. No. Judgment reversed.

♦ There is no constitutional text that addresses the issue of congressional action compelling state officers to execute federal laws.

♦ Historical practice has required state judges to enforce federal prescriptions. But courts commonly apply the law of other sovereigns. The Full Faith and Credit Clause requires state courts to enforce obligations arising in other states. This practice does not mean that Congress can impress the state executive into its service. Other historical texts refer to the ability of the federal government to use state officers to execute federal laws, but none imply that this can be done without the consent of the states.

♦ The structure of the Constitution gives Congress the power to regulate individuals, but not states. The separation of the federal and state governments is one of the Constitution's structural protections of liberty. The power of the federal government would be augmented immeasurably if it could impress into its service state police officers.

♦ Federal control of state officers would also affect the balance of powers among the three branches. The President is responsible for executing the laws, but the Brady Act transfers this responsibility to the CLEOs in the 50 states, without Presidential control.

◆ Under *New York v. United States, supra,* Congress cannot compel the states to enact or enforce a federal regulatory program. Congress cannot circumvent that prohibition by conscripting the states' officers directly. Such a practice would be fundamentally incompatible with the constitutional system of dual sovereignty.

Dissent (Stevens, Souter, Ginsburg, Breyer, JJ.). Congress may impose affirmative obligations on executive and judicial officers of state and local governments as well as ordinary citizens. The basic difference between the Articles of Confederation and the Constitution was the ability of the federal government to govern individuals directly. Members of Congress are elected by the people of the states, and it is unlikely that they would ignore their constituents' sovereignty concerns. The problem of unfounded mandates has already been addressed by Congress. By limiting the federal government's ability to utilize state officials, the majority has created incentives for the federal government to create vast national bureaucracies.

Dissent (Souter, J.). The Federalist Papers would support D's position in this case, although Congress should not be allowed to require administrative support without also paying fair value for it.

––––––––

Chapter V
The Distribution of National Powers

A. Introduction

The Constitution provides for separation of powers among the executive, legislative, and judicial branches, but there are gray areas in which responsibilities are shared to some extent. For example, the President may establish the national agenda and propose legislation, but only Congress can enact law. Yet the executive power also includes some legislative authority, such as the power to veto legislation under Article I, Section 7. Congress also may delegate essentially legislative power to administrative agencies operated under the executive branch.

B. Executive Authority

1. Introduction

The Constitution, in Article II, Section 1, vests the whole executive power of the United States in the President. The Constitution also grants the President limited legislative powers.

a. Proposal of legislation

Article II, Section 3 grants the President power to report to Congress on the state of the union and to propose legislation he deems necessary and expedient.

b. Delegation by Congress

Congress may delegate some of its legislative power to the President (as well as to other government agencies, such as the Securities and Exchange Commission, etc.) as long as the delegation is pursuant to reasonably definite standards.

c. The veto power

Article I, Section 7 gives the President the power to veto any act of Congress. However, Congress may override a presidential veto by a two-thirds vote of both houses.

2. Emergency Lawmaking Power Denied to the President

Youngstown Sheet & Tube Co. v. Sawyer
(The Steel Seizure Case)
343 U.S. 579 (1952).

Facts. The steelworkers, after prolonged negotiations, went on a nationwide strike during the Korean War. Citing the serious national interest in steel production, President Truman ordered Sawyer (D), the Commerce Secretary, to seize the steel mills and keep them running. Youngstown Sheet & Tube (P) challenged the seizure as unconstitutional and unauthorized by Congress. Congress had earlier passed the Taft-Hartley Act, giving the President authority to seek an injunction against such strikes, but had rejected an amendment to permit government seizures to avoid serious shutdowns. The district court issued a preliminary injunction against D, which was stayed by the court of appeals. The Supreme Court granted certiorari.

Issue. May the President, acting under the aggregate of his constitutional powers, exercise a lawmaking power independent of Congress in order to protect serious national interests?

Held. No. Judgment of the district court affirmed.

♦ The President's power to issue the order must stem either from an act of Congress or from the Constitution itself. Congress clearly gave no such power. In fact, it specifically rejected the means used by D.

♦ The President's authority as Commander in Chief does not warrant the seizure, as it is too far removed from the "theater of war." His general executive power is inapplicable since there is no relevant law to execute.

♦ The order does not direct that a congressional policy be executed in a manner prescribed by Congress but that a presidential policy be executed in a manner prescribed by the President. Such presidential usurpation of the lawmaking power is unauthorized and invalid.

Concurrence (Frankfurter, J.). Congress specifically expressed its will on the subject, which is that the President ought not have the powers he has here attempted to exercise.

Concurrence (Jackson, J.). There are three categories of circumstances in which the President may act:

(i) First, he may act pursuant to the authorization of Congress. This situation gives him maximum authority because he acts under the powers granted to him by the Constitution plus all the authority delegated by Congress.

(ii) Second, the President may act on the strength of his independent powers, absent any authorization by Congress.

(iii) Third, he may act in ways contrary to *the* expressed will of Congress. In such a situation, his power is at its lowest ebb.

This case clearly falls under the third category, and the President's action can be sustained only if it was entirely within his constitutional domain and beyond the control of Congress. However, this action was not within his constitutional domain. The President cannot use his powers as Commander in Chief or his powers to control the nation's foreign policy to enlarge his mastery over the internal affairs of the nation.

Concurrence (Douglas, J.). The President may seize but it is up to Congress to ratify the seizure making it lawful. This is the price of our system of checks and balances.

Dissent (Vinson, Reed, Minton, JJ.). The President has a duty to execute the legislative programs of supporting the armed forces in Korea. The President's action was an effective means of performing his duty, and was clearly temporary and subject to congressional direction.

Comment. Two of the majority Justices were willing to agree with the dissent that the President had inherent legislative powers to act in preserving the nation, but only when there was an absence of any provision passed by Congress purporting to deal with the situation. Here these Justices pointed to the fact that Congress had passed the National Labor Relations Act, which set forth specific provisions to be followed by the President in case of strikes that threatened the national security.

C. Foreign Affairs

1. Executive Authority

a. Inherent powers in foreign affairs

The President has special powers in foreign affairs due to the need for decisive action and a uniform policy with regard to sensitive foreign relations. Congress, however, retains certain powers over foreign affairs, including the power to declare war, appropriate funds, and ratify treaties.

b. Scope of federal power in foreign affairs

United States v. Curtiss-Wright Corp.
299 U.S. 304 (1936).

Facts. Congress, by a joint resolution, provided that if the President found that a prohibition of the sale of arms from the United States to those countries involved in conflict in the Chaco would contribute to peace, then he could issue such a prohibition. Penalties for violation were prescribed. Curtiss-Wright (D) was indicted for conspiracy to violate the prescription; D appealed on the basis that the resolution was an invalid delegation of legislative power to the President. The lower court held that the delegation was unconstitutional, and the government appeals.

Issue. May Congress delegate legislative-type power to the President to conduct foreign affairs?

Held. Yes. Judgment reversed.

♦ The power of the federal government in regard to external affairs is not delegated by the Constitution, but it is derived as a necessary concomitant of sovereignty. Thus, these powers are as broad as the powers held by any other nation.

♦ Furthermore, federal power is exclusive in this realm. The states have no concurrent powers. Congress may delegate to the President much broader powers in this area than it could in internal affairs.

---

c. Authority to enter executive agreements

Dames & Moore v. Regan
453 U.S. 654 (1981).

Facts. On November 4, 1979, American diplomatic personnel in Iran were captured and held hostage. On November 14, President Carter declared a national emergency and froze all Iranian assets in the United States. The next day, the Treasury Department issued regulations requiring licensing of any judicial process against Iranian interests and specifying that any such licenses could be revoked at any time. Dames & Moore (P) sued Iranian defendants for $3.5 million and attached Iranian assets pending the outcome of the litigation. On January 19, 1981, the United States, through Algeria, agreed to terminate all legal proceedings in United States courts against Iran, to nullify all attachments and judgments obtained therein, and to terminate such claims through binding arbitration. This agreement was implemented through executive order. On January 27, P obtained a judgment against the Iranian defendants and attempted to execute the judgment on the attached property. The district court nullified the prejudgment attachments and stayed all further proceedings against the Iranian defendants in light of the executive order. P then sued Regan (D), the Treasury Secretary, for declaratory and injunctive relief against enforcement of the executive order and regulations on grounds that they were unconstitutional and that the President had exceeded his authority in implementing the agreement with Iran. The district court denied P's claim, and P appeals.

Issue. May the President, in response to a national emergency, suspend outstanding claims in American courts?

Held. Yes. Judgment affirmed.

♦ The questions presented by this case touch fundamentally upon the manner in which our republic is to be governed. Although little authority exists that is relevant to concrete problems of executive power, much relevant analysis is contained in *Youngstown Sheet & Tube Co. (supra)*. There the Court observed that exercise of executive power is closely related to congressional action; executive power is greatest when exercised pursuant to congressional authorization and weakest when exercised in contravention of the will of Congress.

♦ The International Emergency Economic Powers Act ("IEEPA"), by its terms, permits the President to "regulate and nullify any acquisition of any right to any property in which any foreign country or a national thereof has any interest." In essence, IEEPA was intended to permit freezing of assets to serve as "bargaining chips." P's attachment and judgment were obtained after the President had acted pursuant to this specific statutory authority. We conclude that IEEPA authorized the nullification of the attachments.

♦ IEEPA does not directly authorize the suspension of in personam lawsuits, which merely establish liability and fix damages and do not in themselves involve Iranian property- Nor does the Hostage Act of 1868 authorize such action. However, the general tenor of these enactments, combined with the International Claims Settlement Act of 1949, which created the International Claims Commission, indicates congressional approval of, or at least acquiescence in, executive agreements settling the claims of United States nationals against foreign countries.

♦ P can resort to the International Claims Commission as an alternative forum.

♦ This holding is limited to the narrow facts at hand, where the settlement is a necessary element of a resolution of a major foreign policy dispute between our country and another and where Congress has acquiesced in the President's action.

---

d. Executive implementation of treaty

Medellin, a Mexican national, was convicted of murder in a Texas state court and was sentenced to death. In 2004, the International Court of Justice held that the United States had to review the case because Medellin had not been informed of his right to request assistance from the Mexican consul. President Bush issued a memorandum to the Attorney General, requiring the state court to comply. In *Medellin v. Texas*, 128 S.Ct. 1346 (2008), the Supreme Court held that because the treaty involved was not self-executing, the President's

Memorandum could not displace state procedural rules. The Court pointed out that the President's authority to act must stem either from an act of Congress or from the Constitution itself. The Court noted that the power to make the necessary laws is in Congress, and the power to execute is in the President. The President cannot unilaterally convert a non-self-executing treaty into a self-executing one.

e. Constitutional provisions

Article II, Section 2 provides that the President shall be the Commander in Chief to the Army and Navy and the state militias when they are called into the service of the United States.

1) The use of armed forces

Although the Constitution specifies that the President is the Commander in Chief of the Army and Navy, only Congress has the power to initiate or declare war. The interplay of these powers was not made clear in the Constitution.

2) Deployment

However, in the event of insurrection or invasion, the President may deploy our military forces against any enemy, foreign or domestic, without waiting for congressional declaration of war. [The Prize Cases, 67 U.S. (2 Black) 635 (1863)]

f. Executive detention of enemy combatants

The Constitution does not contain any general "state of emergency" exception to its provisions that would suspend constitutional rights in the event of a national emergency. The Fifth Amendment does relax the requirement for a grand jury indictment for military cases in actual service in time of war or public danger. The Supreme Court has held that the constitutional protections apply even in time of war, such as in *Youngstown Sheet & Tube Co. v. Sawyer, supra.* In *Ex Parte Milligan*, 71 U.S. 2 (1866), the Court held that President Lincoln could not suspend the writ of habeas corpus during the Civil War and could not try civilians in military tribunals. In 1948, Congress enacted the Non-Detention Act, 18 U.S.C. Section 4001(a), which provides that no citizen shall be imprisoned or otherwise detained by the United States except pursuant to an Act of Congress.

1) Enemy combatants in military tribunals

In *Ex parte Quirin,* 317 U.S. 1 (1942), the Court upheld the conviction before a military tribunal of eight Nazi saboteurs, including a United States citizen, who landed in the United States armed with explosives. The Court stated that *the* capture, detention, and trial of unlawful combatants were important incidents of war. Congress authorized detention to prevent enemies from returning to the battlefield. The Court found that American citizenship of a captive enemy does not limit the government's power to deal with him under the usages of war.

2) Joint resolution authorizing the use of military force

In response to the attack on September 11, 2001, Congress passed a joint resolution titled "Authorization for Use of Military Force" that gave the President broad authority to use force against nations, organizations, or persons that the President determines aided the terrorist attacks. No particular enemy was defined. President Bush committed the United States military to combat in Afghanistan and Iraq and detained alleged enemy combatants inside the United States and at Guantanamo Bay, Cuba.

3) Detention of enemy combatants at Guantanamo Bay

The United States military captured several hundred foreign fighters in Afghanistan and held them as "enemy combatants" at Guantanamo Bay, a territory leased by the United States from Cuba since 1903. Under the lease, the territory remains under the "ultimate sovereignty" of Cuba. Some of the prisoners sought writs of habeas corpus in the federal district court for the District of Columbia. In *Rasul v. Bush*. 542 U.S. 466 (2004), the Court held that federal judges do have jurisdiction to consider such habeas petitions from Guantanamo detainees. The Court reasoned that although technically Cuba has sovereignty over the territory, under the lease, the United States exercises "complete jurisdiction and control" over the base and may continue to exercise such control permanently if it chooses. As such, Guantanamo Bay is in every practical respect a territory of the United States. Another consideration is the indefinite status of the detention and the lack of any legal procedure to determine the detainees' status. The dissenters argued that the decision extends the habeas statute to aliens beyond the sovereign territory of the United States to anywhere in the world and that Congress could have changed the habeas jurisdiction of federal judges if it wanted to.

4) Detention of United States citizens

Hamdi v. Rumsfeld
542 U.S. 507 (2004).

Facts. Hamdi (P), an American citizen, was captured in an active combat zone abroad, detained by the United States military as an "enemy combatant," and held in a naval brig in South Carolina. P sought habeas corpus relief against Rumsfeld (D), Secretary of Defense, claiming that the Non-Detention Act barred indefinite detention. The Fourth Circuit held that P was not entitled to habeas relief, despite being a United States citizen, because of military needs. The court held that the Authorization for Use of Military Force ("AUMF") satisfied the requirement in the Non-Detention Act for an Act of Congress authorizing detention. P appeals.

Issue. Does the President have the authority to detain citizens who qualify as "enemy combatants" for an indefinite period of time with no opportunity for an impartial hearing?

Held. No. Judgment vacated and case remanded.

♦ D claims that the Executive has plenary authority to detain pursuant to Article II of the Constitution, but that question need not be addressed because Congress authorized detention through the AUMF. The detention of individuals falling into the limited category of combatants, for the duration of the particular conflict in which they were captured, is a fundamental incident of war and falls within the AUMF.

♦ There is no reason that the government cannot hold one of its own citizens as an enemy combatant. *Quirin, supra*, held that citizenship does not preclude detention for the duration of hostilities.

♦ P claims that Congress did not authorize indefinite detention. He also claims that he faces the prospect of perpetual detention because the "war on terror" is an unconventional war that does not fit within normal law-of-war principles. While indefinite detention is not authorized by Congress, there are active combat operations in Afghanistan against Taliban combatants, and the United States may lawfully detain Taliban combatants during these hostilities.

♦ Although the AUMF did authorize the detention of combatants such as P in the narrow circumstances of this case, the writ of habeas corpus remains available to every person detained within the United States. The writ has not been suspended. P may properly seek a habeas determination on the issue of whether he falls within the category of hostile forces subject to detention. Due process demands that a citizen held in the United States as an enemy combatant be given a meaningful opportunity to contest the factual basis for that detention before a neutral decisionmaker.

♦ To satisfy the minimum requirements for such a hearing, the citizen-detainee must receive notice of the factual basis for his classification and a fair opportunity to rebut the government's factual assertions before a neutral decisionmaker. Evidentiary standards may be relaxed so that the government may use hearsay to support the classification. There may be a rebuttable presumption in favor of the government's evidence.

Concurrence and dissent (Souter, Ginsburg, JJ.). To the extent that the plurality rejects the government's proposed limit on the exercise of habeas jurisdiction, it is correct. However, the plurality goes too far when it agrees that P can be detained if his designation as an enemy combatant is correct. The AUMF does not refer to detention, so it cannot provide a basis for P's detention. The government has failed to justify holding P in the absence of an Act of Congress, criminal charges, a showing that P's detention conforms to the law of war, or a showing that section 4001(a) is unconstitutional. Without a showing of something more, P should be released. In a moment of genuine emergency, the President can detain a citizen if there is a reason to fear he is an imminent threat to the safety of the Nation and its people, but such emergency power must be limited by the emergency. P has been held for over two years, so that exception does not apply here.

Dissent (Scalia, Stevens, JJ.). A citizen who wages war against the United States may be prosecuted for treason, but unless Congress suspends the usual protections under the Suspension Clause, a citizen cannot be detained without charge. The lower court decision should be reversed. The traditional treatment of enemy aliens that includes detention until the cessation of hostilities does not apply to American citizens. The criminal law process is the only means for punishing and incapacitating traitors. Unless the writ of habeas corpus is suspended, a citizen is entitled either to a criminal trial or a judicial decree requiring his release. The AUMF is not a suspension of the writ. The Court's opinion establishes a procedure that makes P's detention legal, but that is an incorrect application of the writ.

Dissent (Thomas, J.). The detention of P falls within the government's war powers, and the courts have no expertise or capacity to second-guess the decision to detain P. The President has constitutional authority to protect the national security and has broad discretion to exercise that authority. The courts should not interfere in these matters. Due process requires only a good-faith executive determination.

Comment. In *Rumsfeld v. Padilla*, 542 U.S. 426 (2004), Padilla, a United States citizen, was arrested in the United States on a material witness warrant in connection with a federal grand jury investigation of al-Qaeda-sponsored terrorism. Padilla was later taken into military custody after the President declared him to be an enemy combatant. Padilla filed a habeas corpus petition. After the circuit court held that the President did not have authority to detain Padilla, the Supreme Court remanded, holding that there was no reason to reach the merits of the case because Padilla had filed the petition in the wrong venue. Justice Stevens, joined by three other Justices, wanted to reach the merits of the case. Justice Stevens asserted that Padilla's protracted, incommunicado detention for purposes of interrogation was like the Star Chamber and was a violation of due process.

---

2. Legislative Authority

a. Constitutional provisions

Under Article I, Section 8, Congress has the power to declare war, to raise and support armies, to maintain a navy, to make rules for the regulation of the land and naval forces, and to provide for organizing, arming, disciplining, and calling forth the militia.

b. War powers

The Vietnam War called into question the whole matter of the relationship between Congress and the President in the conduct of war. Some commentators argued that the President had acquired more power in this area than was originally intended by the Constitution. Until President Theodore Roosevelt unilaterally sent troops into Panama in 1903, the Presidents did not initiate military action against foreign states without congressional approval. After World War II, troops were sent to several locations without congressional action, including Korea and Lebanon. The exact scope of executive and congressional powers in this area is not clearly defined by the Constitution. Consequently, each branch has been free to take initiatives to make national policy in this area. The basic issue is whether the President has the power to use armed forces against a foreign nation without the authorization of Congress.

c. The War Powers Resolution

In 1973, Congress adopted the joint War Powers Resolution [50 U.S.C. §§1541–48], which spells out the President's authority to use the armed forces. If the President uses the armed forces in foreign nations under specified conditions, without a congressional declaration of war, he must formally report to Congress. In the absence of any congressional action, the forces must (in most cases) be removed within 60 days. The constitutionality of the resolution has not been considered by the courts.

d. The Boland Amendments

In response to an alleged "secret war" carried on by the Administration against the government in Nicaragua, Congress added the "Boland Amendments" to appropriations bills. The Boland Amendments basically forbid any agency of the United States involved in intelligence activities from spending funds in support of military or paramilitary operations in Nicaragua. Despite these amendments, certain members of the Administration assisted in raising non-government funds to assist the Contra troops. There was a significant divergence of views regarding the constitutionality of the amendments to the extent that they interfered with the President's ability to conduct foreign affairs.

D. Domestic Affairs

1. Executive Authority

a. Impoundment

Impoundment refers to the President's power to refuse to spend funds appropriated by Congress. Congress passed the Congressional Budget and Impoundment Control Act to limit the President's power to defer spending (he cannot do so if one house passes a resolution requiring him to spend the money) or to terminate a program or cut spending authorized by Congress. The statutory scheme contemplates a congressional response to a presidential proposal to defer or rescind a budget program. Both the President and Congress have generally followed the framework of this Act.

b. Executive immunity

1) Introduction

Executive officials are not given any express immunity in the Constitution. The case law seems to reject any implied immunity under the separation of powers doctrine.

2) Immunity from civil damages

In *Nixon v. Fitzgerald,* 457 U.S. 731 (1982), the Court held that absent explicit affirmative action by Congress, the President is absolutely, rather than qualifiedly, immune from civil liability for his official acts. In this action brought by a whistleblower who charged violation of his First Amendment and statutory rights when he lost his job with the Department of Defense, the Court stated that absolute presidential immunity is a functionally mandated incident of the President's office that is rooted in the doctrine of separation of powers. Just as with judges and prosecutors, who have absolute immunity, the President must make decisions on matters likely to arouse the most intense feelings. The public interest in his ability to deal fearlessly and impartially with these duties is a compelling one. The President's prominence would make him a target for numerous suits for civil damages. The President could not function if he were subject to inquiry about his motives and subject to trial on virtually every allegation of unlawful conduct. The proper protection against presidential misconduct is the constitutional remedy of impeachment. The dissenting Justices argued that this holding put the President above the law and that the better approach would make the scope of immunity depend on the function, not the office.

3) Qualified immunity for presidential aides

The Court held in *Harlow v. Fitzgerald,* 457 U.S. 800 (1982), that presidential aides are entitled to only qualified immunity. This is the normal type of immunity for executive officials, and it balances the interests of those citizens who suffer damages against the public need to protect officials who must exercise their discretion in an official capacity. Absolute immunity is available to such aides when the responsibilities of their offices include such a sensitive function that such immunity is required and the liability claim is based on performance of that protected function.

c. Executive privilege

Although not mentioned in the Constitution, a privilege has been recognized to protect against the disclosure of presidential communications made in the exercise of executive power. This privilege derives from both the doctrine of separation of powers and the inherent need to protect the confidentiality of high level communications.

d. Military, diplomatic, or national security secrets

When presidential communications relate to military, diplomatic, or sensitive national security secrets, the claim of privilege is given the utmost deference by the courts. However, other presidential communications are only presumptively privileged.

e. Evidence in a criminal trial

United States v. Nixon
418 U.S. 683 (1974).

Facts. The special prosecutor, acting for the United States (P) in the Watergate investigation, sought and received a subpoena ordering President Nixon (D) to produce various tapes and other records relating to presidential conversations and meetings, despite D's motion to quash and motions to expunge and for protective orders. The Supreme Court granted certiorari.

Issue. Does executive immunity give the President an absolute, unqualified general privilege of immunity from judicial process under all circumstances?

Held. No. Judgment affirmed.

- D contends that the case is merely an intra-branch dispute between officers of the executive branch and thus lacks the requisite justiciability. However, the special prosecutor has been given special authority to pursue the criminal prosecution and has standing to bring this action in the courts.

- The doctrine of separation of powers does not preclude judicial review of a President's claim of privilege, because it is the duty of the courts to say what the law is with respect to that claim of privilege, even if the judicial interpretation varies from the President's.

- The President's need for and the public interest in the confidentiality of communications is accorded great deference. But absent a need to protect military, diplomatic, or sensitive national security interests, in camera inspection of presidential communications will not significantly diminish the interest in confidentiality. Legitimate judicial needs may therefore outweigh a blanket presidential privilege.

- Applying a balancing test to the interests involved supports the district court's order. P sought the subpoena to assure fair and complete presentation of evidence in a criminal proceeding, pursuant to the fundamental demands of due process. The generalized assertion of privilege must yield to the demonstrated, specific need for evidence in a pending criminal trial.

---

2. Legislative Authority

Congress has pursued two basic approaches to controlling executive power. One has been the enactment of quasi-constitutional statutes intended to set forth guidelines or a framework for interaction between the legislative and executive branches. An example of this is the Gramm-Rudman-Hollings Deficit Control Act, which attempts to control aspects of the budgeting process. Another example is the War Powers Resolution, discussed above. The other approach has been to preserve legislative authority in specific cases, such as through the legislative veto, discussed in *INS v. Chadha, infra.*

a. Legislative vetoes

1) Introduction

Congress has occasionally included provisions in legislation that leave it some power to override executive action taken pursuant to the legislation. This device, called the legislative veto, had been praised for bringing greater efficiency to the government, but it raised potential conflicts with the principle of separation of powers among the branches of government.

2) Rejection of legislative veto

INS v. Chadha
462 U.S. 919 (1983).

Facts. Chadha (P) was an East Indian who lawfully entered the United States on a nonimmigrant student visa. After his visa expired, the Immigration and Naturalization Service (D) held a deportation hearing. The immigration judge suspended P's deportation and sent a report to Congress as required by section 244(c)(1) of the Immigration and Naturalization Act. Section 244(c)(2) provided that either House of Congress could veto a suspension of deportation. The House of Representatives adopted a unilateral resolution opposing P's permanent residence, and P was ordered deported. P sought review in the Ninth Circuit, which held section 244(c)(2) unconstitutional. The Supreme Court granted certiorari.

Issue. May Congress employ the legislative veto device to oversee delegation of its constitutional authority to the executive branch?

Held. No. Judgment affirmed.

♦ Although this case has political ramifications, it is primarily a constitutional challenge presenting a bona fide controversy, properly subject to judicial action.

♦ Article I of the Constitution vests all legislative powers in both Houses of Congress. Every bill or resolution must be passed by both Houses and approved by the President (or his veto overridden) before it takes effect. These provisions are intended to secure liberty through separation of powers. The bicameral nature of Congress similarly insures careful consideration of all legislation.

♦ The action taken by the House in this case was essentially legislative in purpose and effect. The legislative veto replaced the constitutional procedure of enacting legislation requiring P's deportation (a private bill). Yet the Constitution enumerates only four instances in which either House may act alone—impeachment, trial after impeachment, ratification of treaties, and confirmation of presidential appointments. The legislative veto is not enumerated.

♦ Although the legislative veto may be efficient, efficiency is not the overriding value behind the Constitution. Separation of powers, as set up by the Constitution, may not be eroded for convenience. Therefore, the legislative veto is unconstitutional. Once Congress delegates authority, it must abide by that delegation until it legislatively alters or revokes it.

Concurrence (Powell, J.). There is no need to invalidate all legislative vetoes. This one is an unconstitutional exercise of the judicial function by the House because it decided the specific rights of P.

Dissent (White, J.). The legislative veto is a valid response to the dilemma of choosing between no delegation (and hence no lawmaking because of the vast amount of regulation necessary under our system) and abdication of the lawmaking function to the executive branch and administrative agencies. The legislative veto has been included in nearly 200 statutes and accepted by Presidents for 50 years. It allows resolution of major constitutional and policy differences between Congress and the President. Because the underlying legislation was properly enacted, and because the Constitution does not prohibit it, the legislative veto is constitutional.

Dissent (Rehnquist, White, JJ.). Section 244(c)(2) is not severable from the rest of the Act, so the judgment below should be reversed.

---

b. Appointments power

1) Basic rule

Article II, Section 2 indicates that the President may appoint, with the consent of the Senate, ambassadors, consuls, Justices of the Supreme Court, and all other officers of the United States whose appointments are not otherwise provided for. In addition, Congress may vest the power to appoint "inferior officers" in the President alone.

2) No appointment of officers by Congress alone

In *Buckley v. Valeo,* 424 U.S. 1 (1976), the Court relied upon this provision in holding that the composition of the Federal Election Commission established by the Federal Election Campaign Act was unconstitutional. Because of the enforcement powers of the commissioners, who were appointed by Congress, the Court held that they exercised executive powers, thus making them officers of the United States whose appointment was subject to the Appointments Clause.

c. Delegation of spending power

Bowsher v. Synar
478 U.S. 714 (1986).

Facts. The Deficit Control Act of 1985 (Gramm-Rudman-Hollings Act) was enacted to reduce the federal budget deficit to zero over a period of years. Automatic reductions in federal spending were to take place in any fiscal year for which the deficit exceeded the statutory target. The reductions would take effect after the directors of the Office of Management and Budget and the Congressional Budget Office independently calculated the necessary budget reductions. These directors would then report their findings to the Comptroller General, who would make conclusions as to the necessary spending reductions. The President was then required to issue a "sequestration" order mandating the Comptroller General's conclusions. This order would become effective unless Congress reduced spending by legislation. An alternative procedure was also established in case the primary procedure was invalidated. The alternative procedure provided for an expedited congressional joint resolution that would become a sequestration order when the President signed it. Synar and others (Ps) challenged the statute. The district court held the reporting provisions unconstitutional. Comptroller General Bowsher (D) appeals.

Issue. May Congress assign to the Comptroller General the function of determining which accounts of the federal budget must be cut to meet deficit targets?

Held. No. Judgment affirmed.

♦ Standing in this case lies in one plaintiff, an employees' union whose members would not receive a scheduled increase in benefits if the Act is sustained.

♦ Although the Constitution gives Congress a role in appointment of executive officers, it does not give Congress an active role in supervising such officers. It has the power of removal only upon impeachment. Although Congress may limit the President's powers of removal, it cannot reserve for itself the removal power. Otherwise, Congress would have control over the execution of the laws in violation of the separation of powers.

♦ Because Congress may not execute the laws, it cannot grant to an officer under its control the power to execute the laws. D argues that the Comptroller General performs his duties independently of Congress, but in fact Congress is the sole removal authority for the Comptroller General. Accordingly, the Comptroller General may not possess executive powers.

♦ Under the Act, the Comptroller General prepares a report by exercising his independent judgment. This is more than a mechanical function; it requires interpretation of the Act and application of judgment concerning a set of facts. This constitutes execution of the law. In fact, the President is required to comply with the report in ordering the reductions.

♦ Because the reporting procedures are unconstitutional, the fallback provisions are effective.

Concurrence (Stevens, Marshall, JJ.). Labeling the Comptroller General's functions "executive powers" is uninformative. Under the fallback provisions, the congressional report based on the Comptroller General's report has the same legal consequences and could not be considered "executive." In fact, the infirmity of this Act is that Congress has delegated its exclusive power to make policy that will bind the nation to an individual agent of Congress, bypassing the constitutional processes.

Dissent (White, J.). Whether Congress or the Comptroller General determines the level of funding available to the President to carry out the Act's duties, the effect on the President is the same. The President has no authority to establish spending levels. Congress has not granted policymaking discretion; it has specified a detailed procedure based on specific criteria. The Act is an effective response to a serious national crisis and presents no real threat to separation of powers.

---

d. Creation of independent counsel

Morrison v. Olson

487 U.S. 654 (1988).

Facts. The Ethics in Government Act of 1978, 28 U.S.C. sections 591 *et seq.,* provides for the appointment of an "independent counsel" to investigate and prosecute specified government officials for violations of federal criminal law. Under the Act, the Attorney General conducts a preliminary investigation of possible violations, and then reports to the Special Division, a court created by the Act. If the Attorney General determines that there are reasonable grounds to believe further investigation or a prosecution is warranted, then he applies for appointment of independent counsel. The Special Division then appoints such counsel and defines the counsel's prosecutorial jurisdiction. The independent prosecutor is required to comply with Department of Justice policies to the extent possible. The Attorney General may remove an independent prosecutor for cause; otherwise, the counsel's tenure expires upon completion of the specified investigations or prosecutions. The counsel notifies the Attorney General of the completion; alternatively, the Special Division may find the task completed. Certain congressional committees have oversight jurisdiction regarding the independent counsel's conduct. Pursuant to this Act, the Special Division appointed Morrison (D) to investigate allegations that Olson (P), an assistant attorney general, had lied in testimony to Congress. D obtained a grand jury subpoena against P. P moved to quash the subpoena, claiming that D had no authority to proceed because the Act was unconstitutional. The trial court upheld the Act, but the court of appeals reversed. D appeals.

Issue. May Congress provide for the judicial appointment of independent counsel for purposes of investigating and prosecuting federal criminal offenses?

Held. Yes. Judgment reversed.

♦ Under the Appointments Clause, there are two classes of officers: (i) principal officers, who are selected by the President with the advice and consent of the Senate; and (ii) inferior officers, whom Congress may allow to be appointed by the President alone, by the heads of departments, or by the Judiciary. Thus, if D is a principal officer, the Act violates the Constitution.

♦ The difference between principal and inferior officers is not always clear. However, D is clearly an inferior officer because D may be removed by the Attorney General, D's authority is limited to performing certain, limited duties, and D's office is limited in jurisdiction and tenure. Evaluation of these factors leads to the conclusion that an independent counsel is an inferior officer.

♦ P claims that Congress may not provide that an officer of one branch be appointed by officers of another branch. However, the clause itself does not forbid interbranch appointments, but instead gives Congress discretion to determine the propriety of vesting the appointment of executive officials in the courts. The limitation on this power is where it implicates the separation of powers or impairs the constitutional functions assigned to one of the branches. The very reason for the Act was to remove the appointment power from the executive branch, and the judicial branch is the most logical alternative. By making members of the Special Division ineligible to participate in any matters relating to an independent counsel they have appointed, Congress has protected the separation of powers.

♦ Article III limits the judicial power to cases and controversies. However, if the Appointments Clause gives Congress the power to authorize the courts to appoint officials such as an independent counsel, which it does, the appointment power is a source of authority independent of Article III. The additional powers granted to the Special Division, such as defining the counsel's authority and tenure of office, are incidental to the exercise of the appointment power itself.

◆ The Special Division also has power to terminate an independent counsel's office, which is an administrative power. This power must be narrowly construed to avoid constitutional problems. It is thus limited to removing an independent counsel who has served her purpose, but does not acknowledge that fact and remains on the payroll.

◆ P also asserts a separation of powers problem because the Attorney General can remove an independent counsel only by showing "good cause." In *Bowsher, supra,* for example, Congress could not involve itself in the removal of an executive officer. Under the Act in this case, however, Congress did not acquire a removal power over executive officials beyond Congress's power of impeachment and conviction.

◆ The Attorney General retains the removal power, subject to the good cause requirement. But the Constitution does not give the President unbridled discretion to remove officials of independent agencies. Prior cases have distinguished purely executive officials from quasi-legislative and quasi-judicial officials, but this is an inappropriate distinction for analyzing removal powers. The proper question is whether the removal restrictions impede the President's ability to perform his constitutional duty. Because the independent counsel has a limited function, and because the Attorney General has removal authority for good cause, the good cause restriction does not unconstitutionally impede the President.

◆ The second separation of powers issue is based on interference with the role of the executive branch. However, the Act does not permit either congressional or judicial usurpation of executive functions. It also leaves the executive branch with the ability to supervise the counsel's prosecutorial powers.

Dissent (Scalia, J.). The power to conduct a criminal prosecution is a purely executive power, and the Act deprives the President of the exclusive control over the exercise of that power. It does not matter to what extent the Act reduces presidential control; the Act violates the separation of powers doctrine. In addition, D's appointment could only be constitutional if she is an "inferior" officer, but she is not inferior because she is not subordinate to another officer. The final infirmity of the Act is that it improperly imposes restrictions on the removal of the independent counsel.

Comment. In a different case, the Court held that Congress can delegate the power to establish sentencing guidelines for criminal cases to a sentencing commission located in the federal courts and made up, in part, of federal judges, as long as the tasks delegated do not undermine the integrity of the judiciary or usurp the powers of the other branches. [Mistretta v. United States, 488 U.S. 361 (1989)]

––––––––––

e. Veto power over administrative actions

In *Metropolitan Washington Airports Authority v. Citizens for the Abatement of Aircraft Noise,* 501 U.S. 252 (1991), Congress had transferred operation of Washington, D.C., airports from the federal government to a new airport authority. Congress conditioned the transfer on the creation of a board of review, consisting of nine members of Congress, with power to veto major decisions made by the authority. The Court held that the statute authorizing the transfer was unconstitutional. The Court observed that it did not need to decide whether the power exercised by the board of review was legislative or executive in nature. If the board exercised executive power, Congress could not be a participant. If the board exercised legislative power, congressional power would be invalid because it did not comply with the bicameralism and presentment requirements of Article I, Section 7.

Chapter VI
Equality and the Constitution

A. Introduction to Equal Protection Analysis

1. Basic Principles

The Fourteenth Amendment provides that no state may deny to any person within its jurisdiction the equal protection of the laws. Although no comparable provision expressly limits acts by the federal government, the guarantee of equal protection is implicit in the concept of Fifth Amendment due process. Basically, "equal protection" is a limitation on the exercise of government power that means that government regulation cannot be "arbitrarily discriminatory." All laws are to some extent inherently unequal, because part of the purpose of legislation is to distinguish among citizens. For example, tax laws vary depending on the individual's sources and uses of income, and criminal sanctions apply only to those convicted of crimes. Thus, equal protection does not require that all persons be treated equally under the law at all times, but that whatever classifications are made in a statute must be reasonable.

2. Standards of Review

a. Development of equal protection doctrine

1) Traditional approach

At one time, courts used equal protection only to insure that the legislative means were reasonably related to the legislative purpose; *i.e.,* that the regulation had a rational basis. This approach supported only minimal judicial intervention. This traditional approach is characterized by the following three requirements:

a) The first requirement that must be established under the traditional equal protection test is that any statutory classification be "rational," or based on factors (economic, social, historic, geographic, etc.) that justify disparate treatment. This requirement is generally satisfied as long as the classifications are not patently arbitrary.

b) The second requirement is that the classification (the disparate treatment) rationally promote a proper governmental purpose.

c) Assuming that the classification drawn in the statute meets the first two requirements, it is also required that all persons affected by the classification be treated equally.

2) The Warren Court's "new" equal protection

The Warren Court utilized the traditional equal protection analysis in most areas of economic and social regulation. However, it also articulated a new, higher level of scrutiny applicable when legislation affected one of two areas: a "suspect classification" or a "fundamental right" or interest.

a) Old standard

In the absence of a suspect classification or fundamental right, equal protection requires that the legislative means must be "reasonably" related to "legitimate" state ends. This is also called the "rational basis" standard.

b) New standard

When a suspect classification such as race or a fundamental interest such as voting is involved, the legislative means must be "necessary" to achieve "compelling" state interests. This standard of review—also called "strict scrutiny"—has resulted in significant judicial intervention in assessing the constitutionality of legislation.

c) Characteristics

Common to most classifications that demand heightened scrutiny are the following characteristics: historical lack of political power; history of discrimination; immutableness of classification; irrelevance to performance; and obviousness (the basis for classification acts as a badge).

3) The Burger and Rehnquist Courts

The Burger and Rehnquist Courts have generally accepted the old and new standards of equal protection, although they have given greater effect to the old standard than the Warren Court did. The Court has also added a third, intermediate tier of scrutiny for certain classifications, including those based on sex, alienage, and illegitimacy. The new intermediate standard requires that the legislative means be "substantially related" to "important" governmental objectives. In actuality, the whole equal protection jurisprudence is confusing and at times inconsistent. The Court has never expressly adopted the "sliding scale" approach suggested by Justice Marshall, but clearly there are no rigid guidelines with which to decide every equal protection case.

3. Types of Classifications

If [ ] represents the evil being proscribed, ////// represents people that threaten the evil, and xxxxx represents people who do not threaten the evil, then the following types of classifications are possible:

a. [//////] The statute covers all of those that threaten the evil.

b. [ ] ////// The statute covers none of those that threaten the evil.

c. [///] // The statute covers only a few. This is an under-inclusive classification.

d. [xxx///] The statute covers the target population but also innocent persons. This is an over-inclusive classification.

e. [xxx//]// The statute is both under- and over-inclusive.

B. Race, the Constitution, and Changing Conceptions of Equality

1. Slavery

Because the participation of the southern states was critical to adoption of the Constitution, the terms of the Constitution tacitly recognized and even condoned slavery. The federal government was not empowered to regulate slavery, but the Constitution did not preclude emancipation. Article IV, Section 2, Clause 3 did require states to deliver up escaped slaves, however.

a. State constitutional law

State v. Post
20 NJ.L. 368 (1845).

Facts. The constitution of New Jersey contained a clause that made "all men" "free and independent," having certain natural rights including those of life, liberty, the possession of property, and the pursuit of happiness. A demurrer to a lawsuit was based on the claim that slavery was illegal under the state constitution.

Issue. May slavery exist under a state constitution that makes all men free and independent?

Held. Yes.

♦ The language of the constitution must be understood in the context of the society that adopted it. In reality, no man is absolutely free and independent; all are subject to the rights of others and the laws of the government. Each person yields a portion of his natural rights to the government in order to secure the remainder of those rights.

♦ If the constitutional convention really meant to abolish slavery as it existed when the convention assembled, it would have clearly stated so in the Constitution. This matter is too important to be resolved through construction of abstract political propositions. Even the Declaration of Independence declares that all men are created equal, yet the United States Constitution recognizes the existence of slavery.

---

b. Status of slaves and former slaves under United States Constitution

Dred Scott v. Sandford
60 U.S. (19 How.) 393 (1857).

Facts. Dred Scott (P) was born as a slave in Virginia. His owner took him from Missouri (a slave state), where he was sold to Emerson. Emerson took him to Illinois, a nonslave state, and then to Wisconsin Territory, which was free under the Missouri Compromise. Later they moved to Louisiana, but P did not seek freedom there. They moved back to Missouri. Emerson died and P sued the widow for freedom but lost. P was then sold to Sandford (D), the widow's brother and a resident of New York. P sued D for trespass in federal court, claiming diversity jurisdiction. The Circuit Court directed the jury to apply Missouri law, and because the Missouri Supreme Court had previously ruled that P was a slave, the jury found for D. P appeals.

Issue. May a person of African descent be a citizen of a State?

Held. No. Judgment affirmed.

◆ Under the Constitution, the citizens of the United States have the power to conduct the government through their representatives and are thus the sovereign people. This status was not accorded to persons imported as slaves, or their descendants, whether free or not. The federal government has exclusive authority to naturalize aliens; even if P was deemed a citizen of Missouri under state law, that status cannot confer federal citizenship. For this reason, P could not sue in federal court.

◆ Even though Congress has declared that slavery is prohibited in the Louisiana Territory, Congress does not have power under the Constitution to deprive a citizen of his liberty or property merely because he brings the property into a particular Territory of the United States. The Constitution expressly upholds the right of property in a slave. Accordingly, the law that prohibits a slave owner from owning slaves in the Louisiana Territory is unconstitutional, and P was not made free by virtue of being taken to the territory by his owner.

◆ Although P was taken to Illinois, a nonslave state, his current status is governed by Missouri law, not Illinois law. Under Missouri law, P is still a slave.

———————————

2. Reconstruction

a. Introduction

The first eight amendments to the Constitution were originally intended to protect individual rights against the action of the federal government, which was perceived as the greatest threat to those rights. It was generally assumed that the states would protect individual liberty. By the end of the Civil War, however, it was obvious that the southern states would not protect the rights of the emancipated slaves. As a result, the Reconstruction Congress adopted three amendments to the Constitution.

1) Thirteenth Amendment

The Thirteenth Amendment made the Emancipation Proclamation constitutional by prohibiting slavery throughout the United States. It also gave Congress power to enforce its provisions through appropriate legislation. However, it did not prohibit the states from discriminating against blacks, which many states did through enactment of so-called "Black Codes" that restricted the rights of blacks.

2) Fourteenth Amendment

In response to the Black Codes, Congress enacted the Civil Rights Act of 1866, which made all persons born in the United States citizens, and gave citizens full civil rights. The constitutionality of the Act was disputed, however, so Congress adopted the Fourteenth Amendment to provide a constitutional basis for the Civil Rights Act, which was subsequently reenacted.

3) Fifteenth Amendment

The final reconstruction amendment assured the right to vote to all persons.

4) Impact

These amendments made an immediate impact, but the meaning they have today was developed only after many years of litigation. At first, the Court limited the application of the Thirteenth and Fourteenth Amendments to the racial context. [*See* The Slaughter-House Cases, *infra*] Although the amendments were applied to protect the rights of blacks, they were not construed to apply to private discrimination in public accommodations. [*See* The Civil Rights Cases, *infra*] Early cases also recognized an exception to the equal protection requirement that permitted racial discrimination in public where separate but equal facilities were provided. The interpretation of these amendments over the years has given progressively expansive meaning and power to the amendments.

b. Separate but equal doctrine

Plessy v. Ferguson
163 U.S. 537 (1896).

Facts. Plessy (P), who was seven-eighths white and one-eighth black, refused to comply with a demand that he sit in the black railway carriage rather than the one for whites. P was convicted of violation of a state statute providing for separate railway carriages for the white and black races. P challenged the law but lost, and he appeals.

Issue. May a state require that separate railway carriages be provided for black citizens and white citizens?

Held. Yes. Judgment affirmed.

♦ The law does not imply the inferiority of one race or the other. The only proper restraint on the exercise of state police power is that it be reasonable and intended for the promotion of the general good. The state legislature may properly have concluded that the law would preserve the public peace and good order.

♦ It certainly is no more obnoxious to the Fourteenth Amendment than laws requiring separate schools, which are universally accepted. Legislation cannot overcome social prejudices; the attempt to do so can only result in accentuating difficulties. The Constitution can act to equate civil and political rights of the two races, but cannot affect social standing.

Dissent (Harlan, J.). No legislature or court may properly regard the race of citizens where civil rights are involved. Every citizen, regardless of color, has a right to occupy the public transportation of his choice; governmental infringement of that right is unconstitutional. Our Constitution is color-blind, and neither knows nor tolerates classes among citizens. Any evils resulting from commingling of the races are less than those resulting from curtailment of civil rights upon the basis of race.

---

3. School Desegregation and Repudiation of the Separate but Equal Doctrine

Even after the Thirteenth Amendment was ratified, several southern states adopted racially discriminatory statutes, referred to as the Black Codes. These were designed to keep blacks in an inferior position, socially, politically, and economically. The Civil Rights Act of 1866 and the Fourteenth Amendment were intended to counter this official discrimination, although apparently they were not originally supposed to insure full protection of civil rights for all races. For nearly 100 years, states followed a "separate but equal" doctrine, whereby state facilities, including public schools, could be racially segregated as long as they provided "equal" services. The doctrine was successfully challenged beginning in 1938 in cases involving state law schools. The most significant case, however, involved secondary and primary schools.

a. Application to secondary and primary schools

Brown v. Board of Education (Brown I)
347 U.S. 483 (1954).

Facts. Brown and other black schoolchildren (Ps) (the opinion consolidates appeals from four states) were denied admission to schools attended by white children under laws requiring or permitting segregation based on race. Ps challenged the law but were denied relief under the "separate but equal" doctrine. (In the Delaware case, the plaintiff was admitted solely because the white school was superior; *i.e.,* separate was not equal.) Ps appeal.

Issue. May children be segregated in essentially "equal" public schools solely on the basis of race?

Held. No. Judgments vacated and reargument on the issue of appropriate relief ordered.

♦ The circumstances surrounding adoption of the Fourteenth Amendment are not determinative, especially here where public education, which barely existed then, is at issue. The effect of segregation on public education in its current setting is therefore determinative.

♦ Granted that black and white schools are substantially "equal" in tangible factors, there yet exists an invidious effect when black and white children are segregated. Namely, segregation creates a feeling of inferiority, which may significantly affect a child's motivation to learn. Separate educational facilities are therefore inherently unequal, and their maintenance by government authority denies equal protection of the law.

---

b. Implementation of desegregation

Brown v. Board of Education (Brown II)
349 U.S. 294 (1955).

Facts. *See Brown v. Board of Education (Brown I)* above. The Court initially permitted gradual integration of public schools in recognition of the difficulties inherent in school desegregation. This opinion addresses the relief granted in *Brown I.*

Issue. In what manner is relief to be accorded?

Held.

♦ The full implementation of the constitutional principles requires solution of various local school problems, to be solved by school authorities and reviewed by the courts to assure good faith compliance.

♦ The cases are remanded to the lower courts, who are to be guided by equitable principles in fashioning decrees. The competing interests involve Ps' rights to admission at the earliest date and the need for systematic, effective, and orderly removal of obstacles to full integration.

Comment. The Court emphasized its determination that all public schools be integrated by holding that threats of violence resulting from state actions against desegregation would not justify failure to integrate. [Cooper v. Aaron, 358 U.S. 1 (1958)] All nine Justices delivered the opinion to emphasize their unity.

---

4. Remedying Segregation

a. Introduction

The significance of disproportionate impact has been articulated most fully in school desegregation cases. The Court has adopted a bifurcated approach to school desegregation problems. "De facto" segregation is nondeliberate segregation. If an official segregation policy existed as of 1954, there could not be de facto segregation in the school system. Thus, in the south, most school systems were characterized by "de jure" or deliberate segregation. The Court faced three alternatives in fashioning guidelines for remedying segregation:

1) Prohibit only activity that results in segregation; *i.e.*, require desegregation only (the emphasis is on process).

2) Hold that any racially imbalanced school system is by itself a violation; *i.e.*, require integration (the emphasis is on results).

3) Hold that once de jure segregation is shown (process), integration is required (results). This is the approach that the Court currently applies.

b. Early judicial remedies

After *Brown, supra,* the Court decided several cases involving judicial responses to segregation.

1) Public schools

In *Griffin v. County School Board,* 377 U.S. 218 (1964), the Court ordered the reopening of a public school system that the school board closed because of court-ordered integration. The record showed that the schools were closed to perpetuate segregation; the state and county were providing financial assistance to the remaining private schools, which were segregated.

2) Transfer plans

In *Goss v. Board of Education,* 373 U.S. 683 (1963), a transfer plan (allowing a student in a school where he was in a racial minority to transfer to a school where he would be in the racial majority) was struck down. The Court also stated that what was "deliberate speed" in 1955 might not be deliberate speed in 1963.

3) Acceleration of desegregation

In *Green v. New Kent County School Board,* 391 U.S. 430 (1968), the Court held that school boards had an affirmative duty to take immediate steps to desegregate schools.

4) Authority of district courts to order desegregation

In *Swann v. Charlotte-Mecklenburg Board of Education,* 402 U.S. 1 (1971), the Supreme Court held that district courts are justified in ordering compliance with their own desegregation plans when local school authorities fail to desegregate voluntarily. The Court found four categories of problems involving student assignment. The first is the extent to which racial quotas may be used to correct a segregation system. According to the Court, a remedial plan is judged by its effectiveness. Awareness of the racial composition of a school system is a useful starting point in shaping an effective remedy, and limited use of mathematical ratios is permissible. The guiding principle is that no pupil should be excluded from any school on account of race, but every school need not always reflect the racial composition of the school system as a whole. The remaining categories discussed by the Court included elimination of one-race schools, remedial altering of attendance zones, and transportation of students in order to dismantle the dual school system. Demographic factors may result in virtually or completely one-race schools; these are not certain indications of imposed segregation. However, gerrymandering of school districts and attendance zones and provision for optional transfer of students to other schools are useful techniques. To be effective, such plans must grant free transportation and assurance of a place in the desired school.

c. Judicial remedies for northern schools

1) All minorities

In determining whether a school is "segregated," the courts must consider the number of all minority groups (not just blacks) who have suffered unequal treatment in education.

2) Presumption

A finding that school authorities intentionally segregated—or delayed integrating—any significant portion of the school district creates a presumption that the entire school district is being operated on a segregated basis. This is because of the "substantial reciprocal effect" that segregation of some schools may have on others.

a) This presumption is not rebutted or satisfactorily explained merely by showing that the board had adopted a "neighborhood school policy" (assigning students to the schools closest to their homes), even though such policy on its face appears to be racially neutral.

b) But the presumption may be rebutted by a showing that because of natural geographic boundaries, the school district is in fact divided into clearly unrelated areas, which require separate treatment. But the burden of proving this is on the school board.

3) Prima facie case

Keyes v. School District No. 1, 413 U.S. 189 (1973), concerned the lawfulness of school segregation in Denver, Colorado, where segregated education had never been mandated by statute. The plaintiffs, who alleged that the school district deliberately created or maintained segregated schools, bore the burden of establishing that there was unlawful intentional segregation. However, once the plaintiffs established this with regard to a substantial portion of the system, they were not required to show deliberate segregation as to each school within the school system. Justice Powell, the only white southerner men on the Court, concurred in part and dissented in part. He advocated for the formulation of constitutional principles of national, rather than merely regional, application.

C. Rational Basis Review

1. Introduction

As indicated *supra,* the equal protection doctrine is not limited to issues of race. The Court has adopted various standards of review for different types of classifications. Racial and other suspect classifications merit a stringent standard of review, while other classifications are upheld as long as they pass a rational basis review. A statute's legislative purpose usually may be defined so that the statutory classification is rationally related to it. The classification will necessarily be rationally related to such a purpose because the reach of the purpose is derived from the classification itself. The courts may still find that the purpose was illegitimate, or that while the purpose was legitimate, the classification did not rationally further the specified purpose.

2. Classification Based on Drug Usage

New York City Transit Authority v. Beazer
440 U.S. 568 (1979).

Facts. The New York City Transit Authority (D) refused to hire persons who used narcotic drugs. Pursuant to its rule, D refused to hire Beazer (P) because he was using methadone. Methadone was used to treat heroin addiction. P brought a class action. The trial court found that many methadone users are as employable as nonmethadone users and that D could use normal personnel-screening procedures to eliminate unqualified applicants. Accordingly, the court held that the methadone-use blanket exclusion policy was unconstitutional, but that D could impose limited restrictions for safety reasons. The court of appeals upheld the decision, and the Supreme Court granted certiorari.

Issue. May a city refuse to employ all persons who use a particular substance because it is used for treatment of drug addiction?

Held. Yes. Judgment reversed.

♦ Essentially, the district court held that D's rule was broader than it had to be to exclude those methadone users who are actually not qualified as employees. Even if this conclusion is correct, and D's policy is unwise, the personnel policy does not violate equal protection interests.

♦ D's rule promotes D's objectives of safety and efficiency. The rule is not directed against any particular individual or category of persons, but instead is a policy choice. The classification is not based on an unpopular trait or affiliation, but has some rational basis. The courts are not authorized to interfere with the policy decision.

Dissent (White, Marshall, JJ.). It is not rational to place successfully recovering drug addicts in the same category as those merely attempting to recover. P and members of his class should be included with the general population because they are no more likely to prove unsatisfactory employees than persons chosen from the general population. In addition, D has singled out this one group out of many groups that could be considered to be more likely to contain individuals not suitable as employees.

---

3. Exclusion of Unrelated Households

United States Department of Agriculture v. Moreno, 413 U.S. 528 (1973), concerned a provision in the food stamp program that excluded any household containing an individual who was unrelated to any other members of the household. In finding the provision unconstitutional, the Court stated that a legislative classification must be sustained if it is rationally related to a legitimate government interest. However, the purposes of the Food Stamp Act were to "raise levels of nutrition among low-income households," and to increase utilization of food to "strengthen [the] agricultural economy." The Court found that the classification excluding households with nonrelatives was clearly irrelevant to the statute's purposes. The Court further observed that there were no other legitimate governmental interests that the classification rationally furthered. The legislative history indicated that the rule was intended to prevent "hippies" and "hippie communes" from receiving food stamps. Intent to harm a politically unpopular group cannot constitute a legitimate governmental interest.

4. Mental Retardation

In *City of Cleburne v. Cleburne Living Center,* 473 U.S. 432 (1985), under a city zoning ordinance, a wide variety of structures were permitted to be built on a particular site, but certain uses were not allowed. Pursuant to the ordinance, the applicants for a group home for the mentally retarded were denied a special use permit. The Supreme Court found that the ordinance was not rationally related to a legitimate governmental purpose. Rather, the permit requirement was based on an irrational prejudice against the mentally retarded and violated the Equal Protection Clause. In his concurring opinion, Justice Stevens stated that the mentally retarded have historically been subject to unfair mistreatment. This ordinance reflects the irrational fears of neighboring property owners, not a concern for the welfare of the mentally retarded.

5. Prohibition of Antidiscrimination Measures

In *Romer v. Evans, infra,* Colorado voters had adopted an amendment to the Colorado Constitution that prohibited all legislative, executive, or judicial action at any level of state or local government designed to confer a protected status upon, or to allow claims of discrimination by, any person based on homosexual, lesbian, or bisexual orientation. The Supreme Court held that the amendment defied conventional rational basis analysis. It imposed an undifferentiated disability on a single named group (an invalid form of legislation), and its breadth so far exceeded the reasons claimed that the amendment could only be explained by animus toward the class. A bare desire to harm a politically unpopular group cannot constitute a legitimate state interest. The dissent noted that the state can consider certain conduct reprehensible, such as murder or polygamy, and can prohibit that conduct. The animus is not toward any human being or class, but toward the conduct.

6. Environmental Protection

Minnesota v. Clover Leaf Creamery Co., 449 U.S. 456 (1981), involved the constitutionality of a Minnesota law that banned the retail sale of milk in plastic nonreturnable, nonrefillable containers but allowed such sale in nonreturnable paperboard milk cartons. A state court found that the actual basis for the law was to promote the economic interests of local dairy and pulpwood industries. On appeal, the Minnesota Supreme Court concluded that although the law was designed to serve environmental interests, the ban on plastic containers was not rationally related to these purposes. The United States Supreme Court upheld the law, stating that the standard of review was the rational basis test and that the purposes of the law were legitimate. The Court found that even if there was a question as to the environmental consequences of the law, states are not required to convince the courts of the correctness of their legislative judgments.

7. Safety Regulation

Railway Express Agency, Inc. v. New York, 336 U.S. 106 (1949), involved a New York City traffic regulation that prohibited advertising on vehicles, except for "business notices upon business delivery vehicles" or other owner-advertising. Railway Express Agency, a nationwide express business, sold the space on its truck for advertising by other businesses and was convicted for violation of the regulation. Railway Express's equal protection argument was based on the allegedly irrational distinction between allowing owner advertising but banning advertising-for-hire. The Supreme Court ultimately upheld the conviction, reasoning that New York City may have concluded that the former type of advertising was less distracting and possibly necessary for business. In a concurring opinion, Justice Jackson opined that the Court should use equal protection analysis more often than due process analysis in evaluating governmental action. He maintained that the best practical guarantee against arbitrary and unreasonable governmental action is the requirement that laws imposed on a minority must be imposed generally.

8. Deference to State Legislature

Williamson v. Lee Optical, 348 U.S. 483 (1955), concerned a challenge to a state law that, among other things, forbade an optician from fitting or duplicating lenses or even replacements without a prescription from an ophthalmologist or optometrist. The Court held that the legislature could take one step at a time in solving problems, as long as it made no invidious discrimination. Thus, the state could regulate opticians, while exempting sellers of ready-to-wear glasses.

D. Heightened Scrutiny and the Problem of Race

1. Discrimination Against Racial and Ethnic Minorities

Because racial discrimination prompted adoption of the Fourteenth Amendment, racial classifications are "suspect," meaning they invite the strictest judicial scrutiny. There are numerous types of discrimination based on race. The government may place unequal burdens on persons because of their race, or it may restrict interaction among people of different races, or it may gather and disseminate racial information. Discrimination may be expressly stated, or it may consist in discriminatory enforcement of an ostensibly neutral law. It may arise when the adoption of a neutral law is motivated by racial considerations. These situations present difficult issues for the courts.

a. Discrimination on the face of the law

Strauder v. West Virginia
100 U.S. 303 (1880).

Facts. Strauder (D), a black person, was tried and convicted of murder. The jury that had indicted him was composed only of whites because, under state law, blacks were ineligible to serve on grand juries. D appeals, claiming that the state law is unconstitutional.

Issue. May a state forbid all persons of a particular race from serving on a grand jury?

Held. No. Judgment reversed.

♦   No one has a right to have persons of his own race serve on the grand jury that indicted him, but the Fourteenth Amendment prevents the states from withholding equal protection from blacks. In other words, the law must be the same for blacks as it is for whites.

♦   The law excluding blacks from grand jury service is unconstitutional discrimination. States may establish qualifications for jurors, but not racial qualifications.

---

b. Proper distinction based on race

Korematsu v. United States
323 U.S. 214 (1944).

Facts. Korematsu (D) was convicted of remaining in a "military area" in violation of an Army command that all persons of Japanese ancestry be excluded from certain areas for national defense reasons. D was not accused of disloyalty. D appeals, claiming denial of equal protection.

Issue. May race be used as a criterion for curtailing civil rights in a time of grave threats to national security?

Held. Yes. Judgment affirmed.

♦   Legal restrictions that curtail the civil rights of a single racial group are subject to the most rigid judicial scrutiny, but are not per se unconstitutional. Although never justified by racial antagonism, they may be permitted in times of pressing public necessity.

♦   Here, military authorities determined that the existence of Japanese sympathizers was a threat. Espionage and sabotage must be deterred even at great cost. Under war emergency, nothing less than exclusion of the entire group would solve the problem of guarding against disloyalty. The power to protect must be commensurate with the threatened danger.

♦ In light of the totality of the circumstances, the exclusion order cannot be held to be unjustified.

Dissent (Murphy, J.). The exclusion exceeds the brink of constitutional power. The exigencies were not so great as to preclude hearings for the persons involved, and there is no basis for the assumption that this racial group had distinct dangerous tendencies toward disloyalty.

Dissent (Jackson, J.). The Court permits an inference of inheritable guilt, contrary to the fundamental assumption of our system. A civil court is not competent to determine whether a military command is reasonable, and should not attempt to justify one as the Court has done here.

Comment. *Korematsu* was the Court's last decision upholding overt racial discrimination.

———————

c. Facially neutral, race-based classifications

1) Introduction

A statute may provide for racial classifications and yet not, on its face, disadvantage members of any particular classification. However, such statutes have the potential to authorize or encourage actual discrimination.

2) Equal application to all races

An early case, *Pace v. Alabama,* 106 U.S. 583 (1883), upheld a theory of "equal application," whereby a statute that created racial classes was upheld as long as it applied to all races equally.

3) Equal protection is more than equal application

Loving v. Virginia
388 U.S. 1 (1967).

Facts. The Lovings (Ds), an interracial married couple, were convicted of violating a Virginia antimiscegenation statute. The state courts upheld the conviction. Ds appeal, claiming that the statute violates the Equal Protection and Due Process Clauses of the Fourteenth Amendment.

Issue. May a state prevent marriages between persons solely because they are of different races?

Held. No. Judgment reversed.

♦ The state claims that equal protection is afforded when any penalties due to interracial elements of an offense are applied equally to members of both races. However, equal protection means more than mere "equal application."

♦ The court must consider whether statutory classifications constitute arbitrary and invidious discrimination. Racial classifications, especially in criminal statutes, are subject to the most rigid scrutiny and must be essential to the accomplishment of some permissible state objective to be constitutional.

♦ The state has failed to show any legitimate overriding purpose for the distinction between one-race and interracial marriages other than invidious discrimination. Thus, the statute cannot be upheld.

Concurrence (Stewart, J.). A state law that makes the criminality of an act dependent on the race of the actor cannot be constitutional.

———————

4) Private bias cannot be used in making child custody determination

In *Palmore v. Sidoti,* 466 U.S. 429 (1984), upon divorce, a mother was awarded custody of her three-year-old daughter. After the mother, who was white, married a black man, the court determined that the best interests of the child required that the father obtain custody. The court stated that the child would suffer from social stigmatization because of the racially mixed household. However, the Supreme Court reversed the decision, stating that although the state has a duty to protect the interests of minor children, and racial prejudices may subject a child to pressures and stresses she would not face if her stepfather were of the same race, such private biases are not permissible considerations under the Constitution. Private biases may be beyond the reach of the law, but the law cannot give them effect.

a) Permissible distinctions

The Court has never adopted a per se rule of unconstitutionality for all governmental distinctions based on race. For example, it is permissible to require racial data in certain government records, but race may not be used as a basis for separating files.

5) Racial identification and classification

In invalidating a state requirement that a candidate's race appear on the ballot, the Court held that even though the requirement applied to all candidates, by directing the citizen's attention to the single consideration of race or color, the state indicated that race or color was an important consideration that may influence the citizen to cast his ballot along color lines. [Anderson v. Martin, 375 U.S. 399 (1964)] In *Hunter v. Erickson,* 393 U.S. 385 (1969), the Court struck down a city's charter amendment, adopted by citizen initiative, requiring an automatic majority-vote referendum procedure before ordinances regulating real estate transactions on the basis of race, color, religion, national origin, or ancestry became effective. The initiative suspended enforcement of a fair housing ordinance. The Court held that the amendment made an explicitly racial classification because it treated racial housing matters different from other housing matters. The impact of the initiative fell on the minority groups because the majority did not need protection against discrimination. Consequently, it placed special burdens on racial minorities within the governmental process.

2. Classifications that Disadvantage Racial Minorities

a. Introduction

A statute may create classifications that are not explicitly based on race, but have disparate impacts on particular groups, including racial groups. Such statutes create difficult analysis problems.

b. Relevance of discriminatory impact in finding discriminatory purpose

1) General rule

Laws or other official actions that are racially neutral on their face and that rationally serve a permissible government end do not violate equal protection simply because they have a racially discriminatory impact (*i.e.,* affect minorities more adversely than whites). A violation requires that the government action have a discriminatory purpose (intentional or deliberate discrimination).

2) Qualification test

Washington v. Davis
426 U.S. 229 (1976).

Facts. Black applicants for positions on the police force (Ps) challenged the promotion policies and recruiting practices of the District of Columbia Police Department. Ps filed for partial summary judgment on the recruiting question, specifically challenging a qualification test that allegedly discriminated against blacks in violation of the Fifth Amendment Due Process Clause. The district court denied Ps' motion, and the court of appeals reversed. Washington (D) appeals.

Issue. Does a qualification test that has not been established as a reliable measure of job performance and that fails a higher percentage of blacks than whites violate the Fifth Amendment Due Process Clause?

Held. No. Judgment reversed.

♦ A disproportionate impact on different races resulting from a general qualification test does not, by itself and independent of any discriminatory purpose, establish a constitutional violation. Government action is not unconstitutional solely because it has a racially disproportionate impact; there must be a racially discriminatory purpose to justify invalidation. The purpose need not be express, but it must exist, whether on the face of the statute or in its application.

♦ When a disproportionate racial impact is proven, the government must show that the law is neutral on its face and serves proper governmental ends, but the burden is not high. The test involved here has a reasonable relation to the need for competent police officers. Additionally, D has made affirmative efforts to recruit black officers, indicating a lack of intent to discriminate.

♦ Even though the test was not shown to relate directly to eventual job performance, it is closely related to the requirements of the training program for new recruits.

Concurrence (Stevens, J.). The line between discriminatory purpose and impact is not bright and not determinative, since dramatic discriminatory impact is unacceptable.

---

c. De jure and de facto discrimination

1) Introduction

"De jure" discrimination exists where the statute explicitly discriminates or where the law, although neutral on its face, is deliberately administered in a discriminatory way. "De facto" discrimination exists where an otherwise neutral law and administration nevertheless results in discrimination. Also, if the law was enacted with a discriminatory motive, it is de jure discrimination.

2) Discriminatory administration of law

In *Yick Wo v. Hopkins,* 118 U.S. 351 (1886), the Supreme Court held that discriminatory application of a statute that is fair and impartial on its face constitutes denial of equal protection under the Fourteenth Amendment. San Francisco had passed an ordinance requiring that all laundries housed in wooden buildings be licensed before operating. Yick Wo, a Chinese citizen, was convicted and imprisoned for violation of the ordinance. He petitioned for a writ of habeas corpus, proving that his equipment was not a fire hazard and that, while he and 200 other Chinese laundrymen had been denied permits, virtually all non-Chinese who made application received permits. The Court found that although the statute appeared fair and impartial on its face, its administration made illegal and unjust discriminations of a material character among people in similar circumstances. Discriminatory application such as this denies equal protection of the law and cannot be sanctioned.

d. Statistical evidence of disproportionate impact

McCleskey v. Kemp
481 U.S. 279 (1987).

Facts. McCleskey, a black man, was sentenced to death after being convicted in Georgia state court of the murder of a white person. He petitioned for habeas corpus, citing the Baldus study, which, through statistical analysis, concluded that defendants who kill whites were 4.3 times more likely to receive the death penalty than defendants who killed blacks. The district court dismissed the petition, and the court of appeals affirmed.

Issue. Does the Georgia capital punishment statute deny defendants who kill whites equal protection?

Held. No. Judgment affirmed.

♦ The Baldus study alone is not enough to prove an equal protection violation. The Court cannot rely solely on statistics to prove discrimination in criminal sentencing, since capital sentencing is fundamentally different from jury selection or Title VII issues. The inferences drawn from the statistics are not as comparable, and, unlike venire selection and Title VII, the prosecutor has no opportunity to rebut the statistics.

♦ The defendant has not shown that the Georgia legislature maintains the capital punishment statute because of the racially disproportionate impact suggested by the study. The discretion used in sentencing is critical to the criminal justice system. Lack of predictability does not warrant condemnation of discretion. The risk of racial bias is not significant due to safeguards already in place and the benefits of discretion to defendants. The legislature should determine the appropriate punishment for crimes.

Dissent (Brennan, Marshall, Blackmun, Stevens, JJ.). Georgia has a long history of distinguishing between crimes committed by blacks and whites. Racial bias is antithetical to the justice system. Allowing criminal sentencing to be solely in the legislature's province would disrupt the separation of powers. The Constitution directs the judiciary to protect the voice of the minority, which may not be heard if left to majoritarian rule.

---

3. Classifications Favoring Racial Minorities

a. Background

Attempts to remedy adverse effects of past discrimination have resulted in various means such as affirmative action, quotas, and minority preferences, which in effect discriminate in favor of minorities. In the 1970s, responding to social trends, some schools and employers began voluntary use of racial criteria to benefit racial minorities.

1) *Bakke*

The Court evaluated the constitutionality of a voluntary affirmative action program in *Regents of the University of California v. Bakke,* 438 U.S. 265 (1978). The Regents had established a special admissions program for the Davis Medical School that reserved 16 out of 100 places for minorities. Bakke, a white applicant, was denied admission for two consecutive years. He sued to be included in the special admissions program. The Court held that a state school could use race as a factor in its admissions process, but that the specific program in tins case was unlawful. There was no majority opinion. Four

Justices held that the program was unconstitutional and that the states cannot consider race as a factor, even for a "benign" preference for minorities. Four Justices held that the program was not unconstitutional and that the states can consider race as a factor. Justice Powell agreed that the program was unconstitutional because it set aside seats specifically for minorities, but he also concluded that the states can constitutionally consider race as a factor in pursuit of a goal of assembling a diverse student body.

2) *Fullilove*

Congress included a Minority Business Enterprise provision in the Public Works Employment Act of 1977, which denied applications for grants to receive public funding if the application did not include assurances that at least 10% of the grant would be spent with minority-owned businesses. In *Fullilove v. Klutznick,* 448 U.S. 448 (1980), the Court upheld the statute by finding that it was narrowly tailored to the achievement of the goal of remedying the present effects of past discrimination.

3) Collective bargaining agreement found unconstitutional

In *Wygant v. Jackson Board of Education,* 476 U.S. 267 (1986), the Court considered a collective bargaining agreement that limited the percentage of minority personnel laid off to the percentage of minorities employed at the time of the layoff. The effect was to protect recently-hired minority teachers at the expense of more senior white teachers. The Court held that the provision was unconstitutional because it was not related to specific prior discrimination by the government unit involved and did not necessarily bear a relationship to the harm caused by prior discriminatory hiring practices.

b. Rejection of state and local set-aside programs absent evidence of direct discrimination

In *City of Richmond v. J.A. Croson Co.,* 488 U.S. 469 (1989), the city of Richmond, citing the authority of *Fullilove, supra,* required prime contractors on city projects to set aside at least 30% of their subcontracts to minority business enterprises, using the *Fullilove* definition of minority group members. The program was adopted based on evidence that minority businesses had received a significantly lower percentage of contracts (.67%) than the percentage of minorities living in the city (50%). However, there was no evidence of racial discrimination on the city's part or on the part of any of its prime contractors. Richmond noted that under *Fullilove,* Congress was not required to make specific findings of discrimination to engage in race-conscious relief. Richmond asserted that if the federal government could do this, a city could as well. However, the Court pointed out that unlike the states and their subdivisions, Congress has a specific constitutional mandate to enforce the Fourteenth Amendment. Furthermore, the Richmond plan denied certain citizens the opportunity to compete for a fixed percentage of public contracts based solely on their race, and thereby implicated the personal rights of the excluded persons. The Court found that such race-based regulations are subject to strict scrutiny, regardless of the race of those burdened or benefited by the classification. Richmond's program failed both prongs of the strict scrutiny inquiry. First, remedying the effects of "past societal discrimination" by using a rigid racial quota did not serve a compelling state interest. Second, the plan was not narrowly tailored—there had been no consideration of the use of race-neutral means to increase minority business participation in city contracting. Justice Scalia, concurring, added that the federal government is uniquely capable of dealing with past racial discrimination because racial discrimination finds more ready expression at the state and local levels than it does at the federal level.

c. Strict scrutiny of affirmative action

Adarand Constructors, Inc. v. Pena
515 U.S. 200 (1995).

Facts. Adarand Constructors, Inc. (P) submitted the low bid for a guardrail subcontract on a federal road project. The prime contract's terms provided for additional compensation if subcontractors were hired who were certified as small businesses controlled by "socially and economically disadvantaged individuals." P's competitor, Gonzales Construction Company, certified as such a business and received the subcontract, although its bid was higher than P's. Under federal law, general contractors must presume that "socially and economically disadvantaged individuals" include specified racial minorities. P sued Pena (D), the Secretary of Transportation, claiming that he was deprived of property without due process of law under the Fifth Amendment. The court of appeals upheld the law, and P appeals.

Issue. Is the federal government's use of race-based classifications subject to strict scrutiny even for affirmative action?

Held. Yes. Judgment reversed and remanded.

♦ The Fifth Amendment protects against arbitrary treatment by the federal government, but it does not guarantee equal treatment.

♦ In *Croson, supra,* the Court held that the Fourteenth Amendment requires strict scrutiny of all race-based action by state and local governments. Thus, any person, of whatever race, has the right to demand that the government justify any racial classification subjecting that person to unequal treatment under the strictest judicial scrutiny.

♦ In *Metro Broadcasting, Inc. v. FCC,* 497 U.S. 549 (1990), the Court held that "benign" racial classifications required only intermediate scrutiny. This holding undermined the basic principle that the Fifth and Fourteenth Amendments protect persons, not groups. Group classifications must be subject to detailed inquiry to assure that the personal right to equal protection has not been infringed. Therefore, it is inconsistent to treat "benign" racial classifications differently from other types of racial classifications, and all racial classifications shall now be subject to strict scrutiny.

♦ This holding does not preclude the government from acting in response to the lingering effects of racial discrimination. When race-based action is necessary to further a compelling interest, it is permitted as long as it satisfies the "narrow tailoring" test of strict scrutiny.

Concurrence (Scalia, J.). There can never be a compelling interest in discriminating on the basis of race to compensate for past racial discrimination in the opposite direction. Under the Constitution, there can be neither a creditor nor a debtor race.

Concurrence (Thomas, J.). The government may not make distinctions on the basis of race, whether the objectives are to oppress a race or to help a race. Affirmative action programs undermine the moral basis of the equal protection principle and arouse resentment by those not benefited. The targeted minorities are stamped with a badge of inferiority and are prompted to develop dependencies or an attitude that they are "entitled" to preferences.

Dissent (Stevens, Ginsburg, JJ.). There is a clear distinction between policies designed to oppress minorities and policies designed to eradicate racial subordination.

Dissent (Ginsburg, Breyer, JJ.). The judiciary should defer to Congress, as the political branches are better suited to respond to changing conditions.

———————————

d. Race as a factor for law school admission

Grutter v. Bollinger
539 U.S. 306 (2003).

Facts. Grutter (P), who was white, applied for admission to the University of Michigan Law School but was denied admission. P brought suit against school officials (Ds), claiming their admissions policy discriminated against her on the basis of race. D's admissions policy sought to achieve diversity in the student body and therefore enrolled a critical mass of minority students, including African-Americans, Hispanics, and Native Americans. The district court found that D's use of race as a factor in admissions decisions was unlawful, but the court of appeals reversed. The Supreme Court granted certiorari.

Issue. Does a state university have a compelling state interest in obtaining the educational benefits that flow from a diverse student body, sufficient to justify the use of race as a factor in admissions criteria?

Held. Yes. Judgment affirmed. . . .

♦ Under the Equal Protection Clause, a racial classification must survive strict scrutiny review. Justice Powell's decision in *Bakke* recognized that student body diversity is a compelling state interest that can justify the use of race in university admissions.

♦ The Court has never held that only remedial objectives can provide a basis for consideration of race. D in this case was not seeking to remedy past discrimination, but was seeking diversity in its student body, which D considers essential to its educational mission.

♦ Given the important purpose of public education and the expansive freedoms of speech and thought associated with the university environment, universities have a special niche under the Constitution. D's consideration of race is not simply to assure racial balancing, which is patently unconstitutional, but instead focuses on the educational benefits that diversity produces. In addition, law schools are the training ground for a large number of civil leaders. To cultivate a set of leaders that the citizens deem legitimate, the path to leadership must be open to talented and qualified individuals of every race and ethnicity.

♦ D's admissions policy is narrowly tailored to further the compelling state interest. There is no quota. Admissions decisions are based on individual considerations. Race is considered as a "plus" factor during consideration of each individual candidate. Race is not the defining feature of an application. There are many other diversity considerations, including living or traveling abroad, speaking other languages, etc. At the same time, D's program does not unduly burden individuals who are not members of the favored racial and ethnic groups.

♦ D's race-conscious admissions program must be limited in time, however. In 25 years, racial preferences will likely be unnecessary to further the diversity interest.

Concurrence (Ginsburg, Breyer, JJ.). Minority students still encounter inadequate and unequal educational opportunities, which hopefully will be remedied within the next generation.

Dissent (Rehnquist, C.J., Scalia, Kennedy, Thomas, JJ.). D's admissions program is not narrowly tailored to the interest D asserts. Over five years, D has admitted 91 to 108 African-Americans to achieve "critical mass," so that members of that race would not feel isolated or like spokespersons for their race. During the same time, D admitted 13 to 19 Native Americans and between 47 and 56 Hispanics. D offers no explanation why fewer Hispanics and Native Americans are needed to achieve "critical mass." It turns out that the percentage of students admitted in each of these groups corresponds very closely to the percentage of applicants who were in the same groups. This is the type of racial balancing that is not permissible.

Dissent (Kennedy, J.). Without an admissions program that meaningfully satisfies the strict scrutiny test, the talents and resources of the law school faculties and administrators will not be used to devise fairer ways to ensure individual consideration. Constant judicial review is required to make sure that these faculties and administrators undertake their responsibilities as state employees with utmost fidelity to the mandate of the Constitution.

Concurrence and Dissent (Scalia, Thomas, JJ.). The Court invites further litigation about the scope of a "good faith effort" and the extent of the permissible "critical mass." The government should simply not discriminate on the basis of race.

Concurrence and Dissent (Thomas, Scalia, JJ.). Minorities can achieve in every avenue of American life without the meddling of university administrators. The Court has deferred to D in an unprecedented way that is inconsistent with the concept of "strict scrutiny." "Selective" admissions should not be protected by the Constitution. If D wants to use the LSAT test, on which D knows blacks perform poorly, D should not also be allowed to "correct" for black underperformance by using racial discrimination. Racial classifications are per se harmful and are not necessary to remedy general societal ills. The Court is correct in holding that racial discrimination that does not help a university to enroll a "critical mass" of underrepresented minority students is unconstitutional. However, the Court should not uphold discrimination even to achieve the critical mass.

Comment. In response to *Bakke,* state schools modified their admissions policies to avoid racial quotas. This did not eliminate the use of race as a factor in deciding whether to admit individual students, however. The Court has recognized that diversity is a legitimate basis for considering race, but not if the admissions policy is in effect a quota.

---

e. Race as a preferential factor for undergraduate admission

In *Gratz v. Bollinger,* 539 U.S. 244 (2003), the Court held that the University of Michigan's policy for admissions to its undergraduate college of liberal arts and sciences was unconstitutional. Under the admissions policy, college applicants were ranked according to a 150 point scale. Applicants who were members of an underrepresented minority group automatically received 20 points. The Court stated that under the *Bakke* opinion, each applicant should be assessed as an individual. However, the University of Michigan's policy granted preferences to minority applicants, solely on the basis of race, and did not include sufficient individualized consideration. The Court recognized that the admissions policy may be easier to administer than an individualized consideration process but asserted that administrative challenges cannot make constitutional an otherwise problematic system.

f. Indigenousness as a factor

In *Rice v. Cayetano,* 528 U.S. 495 (2000), the Court held that the state of Hawaii could not limit the election of the trustees of the Office of Hawaiian Affairs ("OHA") to descendants of the aboriginal inhabitants of Hawaii. While the Court had recognized the quasi-sovereign nature of American Indian tribes, including the right to exclude non-Indians from voting in tribal elections, the OHA was a state agency. A state may not use racial classifications to exclude classes of citizens from decisionmaking in crucial state affairs.

g. Race as a factor in K-12 school assignments

Parents Involved in Community Schools v. Seattle School District
551 U.S. 701 (2007).

Facts. The Seattle school district and the Jefferson County school district in Louisville, Kentucky, (Ds) voluntarily adopted student assignment plans that used race as a factor in determining which public school certain children could attend. The Seattle school district classified children as "white" or "nonwhite," and used its plan to allocate slots in oversubscribed high schools. The Jefferson

County school district classified children as "black" or "other," and used its plan to make certain elementary school assignments. Both school districts sought to maintain a racial balance within a predetermined range based on the racial composition of the school district as a whole. Seattle used a series of tiebreakers when its schools were oversubscribed by students. The first tiebreaker was whether the student had a sibling at the school. The second tiebreaker was based on race. If an oversubscribed school was not within 10 percentage points of the district's overall white/nonwhite racial balance, it selected students who would bring the school into balance. Seattle had never operated segregated schools. Although the Jefferson County district had maintained a segregated school system in the past, it achieved unitary status in 2000. Still, in 2001, the county adopted a voluntary assignment plan that required nonmagnet schools to maintain black enrollment between 15% and 50%. Parents whose children were denied assignments to desired schools solely because of race (Ps) sued. The appellate courts upheld the plans. The Supreme Court granted certiorari.

Issue. May a public school that has not operated legally segregated schools or that has been found to have achieved unitary status choose to classify students by race and rely upon that classification in making school assignments?

Held. No. Judgment reversed.

♦ Government action that distributes benefits or burdens on the basis of individual racial classification is subject to strict scrutiny. Thus, Ds' use of racial classifications in this case must be narrowly tailored to achieve a compelling government interest.

♦ In the school context, one compelling interest is remedying the effects of past intentional discrimination, but that interest does not apply to either D in this case. The other compelling interest is diversity in higher education, as upheld in *Grutter*. But *Grutter* approved the use of racial classifications as part of a broader assessment of diversity, not merely as an effort to achieve racial balance. And since *Grutter* applied to higher education, it does not govern cases involving Ds.

♦ In this case, Ds' plans are directed only to racial balance and are not narrowly tailored to achieve educational and social benefits that allegedly flow from racial diversity. The plans are tied solely to racial demographics. Racial balancing is unconstitutional and may not be sought for its own sake. If racial balancing was a compelling state interest, it could be imposed throughout American society.

♦ Ds claim that they have to use these classifications to achieve their stated ends, but in fact they have used the racial classifications to shift only a small number of students. This suggests that the racial classifications are not really necessary.

♦ Both parties have debated the *Brown* case, but the plaintiffs in *Brown* asserted that "[t]he Fourteenth Amendment prevents states from according differential treatment to American children on the basis of their color or race." The Equal Protection Clause prohibits states from using race as a factor in providing educational opportunities.

Concurrence (Thomas, J.).

♦ Racial imbalance is not segregation, and these districts are not threatened with resegregation. Neither of their plans can survive strict scrutiny because neither serves a genuinely compelling state interest.

♦ Contrary to the dissent's assertion, it has not been shown that coerced racial mixing has any educational benefits or that black achievement depends on integration. The dissent contends that weight must be given to a local school board's knowledge, expertise, and concerns and that the districts' plans embody the results of local experience. Like the segregationists in *Brown,* the dissent argues for deference to local authorities. However, the school boards are the very government entities whose race-based practices we must strictly scrutinize. The dissent marginalizes the notion that our Constitution is colorblind.

Concurrence in part (Kennedy, J.).

♦ The government has a legitimate interest in ensuring that all people have equal opportunity regardless of race. School districts cannot ignore the problem of de facto resegregation. To the extent the plurality opinion suggests that the Constitution mandates that state and local school authorities must accept the status quo of racial isolation in schools, it is mistaken.

♦ State and local authorities should be able to consider the racial makeup of schools and adopt general policies to encourage a diverse student body. However, the small number of students affected by Ds' plans suggests that they could have achieved their stated ends through different means, without treating students differently based solely on race.

♦ This country has a compelling interest in avoiding racial isolation, and a school district may consider it a compelling interest to achieve a diverse student population. Race may be one component of that diversity, along with others, such as special talents and needs. However, if, as here, there is no showing of necessity, the government may not classify students on the basis of race and assign each of them to schools based on that classification.

Dissent (Stevens, J.). *Brown* applied to situations in which only black children were told where to go; white children were not striving to get into black schools.

Dissent (Breyer, Stevens, Souter, Ginsburg, JJ.).

♦ Because of the evident risk of a return to school systems that are resegregated, many school districts have maintained or extended their integration efforts. Seattle and Louisville are typical of the numerous districts that have devised various plans, often with race-conscious elements, to eradicate earlier school segregation, bring about integration, or prevent de facto resegregation.

♦ We have approved of narrowly tailored plans that are no less race-conscious than these plans. And the Constitution permits local communities to adopt desegregation plans even where it does not require them to. History has required special administrative remedies to advance or to maintain racial integration in primary and secondary schools.

♦ There is a compelling interest in promoting or preserving racial integration of public schools. The three essential elements to the interest at stake are: (i) an interest in setting right the consequences of prior conditions of segregation; (ii) an interest in overcoming the adverse educational effects of highly segregated schools; and (iii) an interest in producing an educational environment that reflects the pluralistic society in which our children will live. Ds' plans reflect narrow tailoring and satisfy strict scrutiny. The strict scrutiny test forbids racial classifications that harmfully exclude, not those that include.

♦ As measured against the Constitution's objectives, the plurality's approach is legally unsound. School districts use different integration plans throughout the country. The fact that many of these plans have used racial criteria suggests that such criteria are important. The controlling opinion would make a school district's use of racial criteria often unlawful, and the plurality's "colorblind" view would make such use always unlawful. Today's opinion will require setting aside the laws of several states and many local communities and threatens a surge of race-based litigation.

E. Heightened Scrutiny and the Problem of Gender

1. Introduction

Although early decisions dealt with sex-based classifications under the traditional equal protection tests, more recent cases have judged sex-based classifications under a higher standard, but not so high a test as would apply to the inherently suspect classes.

a. Rational basis standard applied

In *Reed v. Reed,* 404 U.S. 71 (1971), Reed, a minor, died intestate after his parents separated. Each of the parents sought to administer his estate. The probate court ordered that Reed's father be appointed administrator, because a state statute required that when equally entitled persons sought to administer an estate, males were to be preferred over females. The state claimed that this preference served its objective of eliminating an area of controversy and thus reducing the probate workload. However, the Court asserted that the gender classification was an arbitrary legislative choice that was forbidden by the Equal Protection Clause.

b. Comment

The Court declined to make sex a suspect classification, but this was the first decision to hold that sex discrimination violated the Equal Protection Clause.

2. Development of the Intermediate Standard

As late as 1961, the Court based a decision that generally excluded women from jury duty on the role of the woman as the center of home and family life. [Hoyt v. Florida, 368 U.S. 57 (1961)] After *Reed,* the Court began developing an intermediate standard of review for sex classifications.

a. Military benefits

Frontiero v. Richardson, 411 U.S. 677 (1973), concerned a federal law under which male members of the armed forces could claim wives as dependents without any showing, but women in the service had to show that their spouses were actually dependent on them for over one-half of their support. The government claimed that the differential treatment of men and women served the purpose of administrative convenience. Writing for four justices, Justice Brennan argued that classifications based on gender are suspect and, therefore, are subject to close scrutiny. Justice Powell, joined by two other justices, concurred, but asserted that since the statute was unconstitutional under *Reed, supra,* there was no need to go further and characterize sex as a suspect classification. He contended that to do so would unnecessarily preempt the prescribed constitutional processes of amending the Constitution, which he said were being utilized on that very issue in the guise of the Equal Rights Amendment.

b. Social Security survivors' benefits

The Court struck down a provision in the Social Security Act that granted "survivors' benefits" to widows, but not widowers, while they care for minor children of the deceased wage earner. The disqualification of widowers was held "irrational," since the purpose of the benefits was to enable the surviving parent to stay at home and care for the children. The classification thus discriminated against the children based on the gender of the surviving parent. [Weinberger v. Wiesenfeld, 420 U.S. 636 (1975)]

c. Widows' tax benefits

In *Kahn v. Shevin,* 416 U.S. 351 (1974), the Court upheld a property tax exemption for widows that did not apply to widowers. The law was reasonably designed to assist the sex for whom the loss of a spouse is a disproportionately heavy burden. The classification was not a mere administrative convenience as in *Frontiero.*

d. Military career regulations

The Court upheld a federal law that gave women more time to get promoted in the Navy because of the restricted sea and combat duty available to women. [Schlesinger v. Ballard, 419 U.S. 498 (1975)]

e. Classifications favoring women

Craig v. Boren
429 U.S. 190 (1976).

Facts. Craig (P), a male, challenged an Oklahoma statute that denied beer sales to males under 21 and females under 18. The three-judge district court dismissed P's action, and P appeals.

Issue. May a state properly impose gender-based differentials in regulating sales of alcoholic drinks?

Held. No. Judgment reversed.

♦ To withstand constitutional challenge, classifications by gender must serve important governmental objectives and must be substantially related to the achievement of those objectives. The state objective here—enhancement of traffic safety—is clearly important. However, the relation between this objective and the challenged statute is based on statistical evidence fraught with shortcomings and is inadequate to show that sex represents a legitimate, accurate proxy for the regulation of drinking and driving.

♦ Failure to show a substantial relation between the gender-based classification and achievement of the state's objectives requires that the statute be invalidated as unconstitutional. The operation of the Twenty-First Amendment, limited as it is when applied outside Commerce Clause issues, does not alter application of the equal protection standards that govern here.

Concurrence (Powell, J.). The Court has added confusion to the appropriate standard for equal protection analysis. The statistics do tend to support the state's view but are inadequate to support the classification.

Concurrence (Stevens, J.). The classification here is not totally irrational, but it is unacceptable because it has little relation to traffic safety. It prohibits only sales of beer, not consumption, which is the real threat to traffic. The law punishes all males for the abuses of only 2% of their class.

Dissent (Rehnquist, J.).

♦ Men challenging a gender-based statute unfavorable to themselves should not be able to invoke a more stringent standard of review than normally pertains to most other types of classifications, since men, as a group, have not suffered the type of prior discrimination that has always supported a standard of special scrutiny. Nor is the interest involved here—beer purchasing—"fundamental" in the constitutional sense of invoking strict scrutiny.

♦ The Court has added a new standard to the norm of "rational basis" and the "compelling state interest" required where a "suspect classification" is involved—that of the "important governmental objectives" and "substantial relation to achievement of those objectives." This new standard is unnecessary and invites judicial confusion and interference into the proper roles of the legislature.

♦ The correct standard here is the rational basis test, under which a classification is invalid only if it rests on grounds wholly irrelevant to the achievement of the state's objective. The state has provided sufficient evidence to show a rational basis, and the statute should be upheld.

---

3. Real Differences vs. Generalizations

Some sex-based classifications are based on generalizations derived from long-held perceptions about the respective roles of men and women. Others are based on the objective differences between men and women. The Court has distinguished between the two types of classifications.

a. Single-sex military school

United States v. Virginia
518 U.S. 515 (1996).

Facts. The Virginia Military Institute ("VMI") was founded in 1839 and at the time of the litigation was the only single-sex school among Virginia's (D's) public schools of higher learning. VMI's mission was to produce "citizen-soldiers" who were prepared for leadership in civilian and military life. The school's training used an "adversative method" designed to instill physical and mental discipline in its cadets. This involved complete lack of privacy, wearing uniforms, and eating and living together, all in a high-pressure environment comparable to Marine Corps boot camp. VMI excluded women from its program, although neither the school's goals nor teaching methodologies were inherently unsuitable to women. When one woman complained about being denied admission, the United States (P) sued, alleging that D's single-sex policy violated equal protection. In response to an earlier remand from the federal court of appeals, D proposed a separate but parallel program for women, called Virginia Women's Institute for Leadership ("VWIL"), which would have a goal of producing "citizen-soldiers" but still differed significantly from VMI's program. The court of appeals approved this approach, and the Supreme Court granted both parties' petitions for certiorari.

Issue. If a state-sponsored single-sex school denies equal protection, may the state offer a parallel program for the opposite sex while retaining the single-sex status of the school?

Held. No. Judgment reversed.

♦ Those who seek to defend gender-based government action must demonstrate an "exceedingly persuasive justification" for that action. Gender classifications have not been equated with racial or national origin classifications for all purposes, but official action that denies opportunities to an individual because of gender must be carefully inspected by the courts. Gender is not a proscribed classification; physical differences between men and women are enduring. These differences may not be used to denigrate the members of either sex or to artificially constrain their opportunities.

♦ To prevail against a challenge, D must show that the classification serves "important governmental objectives" and that the discriminatory means used are "substantially related" to the achievement of those objectives. In this case, D has shown no "exceedingly persuasive justification" for its exclusion of all women from VMI. D claims the single-sex education contributes to diversity in education. While that may be true, diversity was not the reason VMI excluded women. D's plan to provide a unique educational benefit only to males is not equal protection when there is no corresponding plan for females.

♦ D also claims that VMI's adversative method of training provides educational benefits that cannot be made available to women without modification. To accommodate women, VMI claims it would have to "destroy" its program. In fact, the VMI methodology could be used for some women, and the only accommodation necessary would be in housing assignments and physical training programs for female cadets. But while most women may not choose VMI's adversative method, many men would also not choose it. D simply cannot constitutionally deny entrance to women who have the will and capacity to attend VMI.

♦ Establishment of a comparable school for women would not remedy the constitutional problem. D's separate program does not include the rigorous military training found at VMI. D claims that the methodological differences between the institutions are based on "real" differences between men and women, but again this is based on estimates of what is appropriate for most women. Such generalizations fail to recognize that some women do well under the adversative method and want to attend VMI. D's alternative program for women is simply not the equal of VMI.

Concurrence (Rehnquist, C.J.). The Court should continue to follow the *Craig* approach, and not introduce new terminology such as "exceedingly persuasive justification." The true constitutional violation was not the exclusion of women, but the maintenance of an all-men school without providing a comparable institution for women. D might have cured the violation if VWIL was truly comparable to VMI.

Dissent (Scalia, J). VMI existed for over 150 years. The tradition of having government-funded military schools for men has not been unconstitutional over those years. Changes such as the one the Court imposes should be brought about through democratic means, not by the courts. The Court now holds that a sex-based classification is invalid unless it relates to characteristics that hold true in every instance. In so doing, it has executed a *de facto* abandonment of the intermediate scrutiny that should be applied to gender-based classifications. The facts in this case show that D's real options were an adversative method that excludes women or no adversative method at all. The courts below found that VMI would be fundamentally changed if it admitted women.

----

b. Other applications

In *J.E.B. v. Alabama ex rel. T.B.*, 511 U.S. 127 (1994), the Court held that gender-based peremptory challenges were unconstitutional. The concurring opinions noted the reality of different live experiences and perceptions affected by gender, so that while gender makes no difference as a matter of law, it may make a difference as a matter of fact. In *Rostker v. Goldberg,* 453 U.S. 57 (1981), the Court upheld a statute that required only men to register for the draft. The rationale was that registration was a preparation for a draft that would focus on a need for combat troops, and that since women as a group were not eligible for combat, the exclusion of women from registration was permissible. In *Michael M. v. Sonoma County Superior Court,* 450 U.S. 464 (1981), the Court upheld a statutory rape provision that defined the offense as sexual intercourse where the unmarried female is under 18 years of age. The statute's purpose was to prevent nonmarital pregnancies.

c. Family relations

Nguyen v. Immigration and Naturalization Service
533 U.S. 53 (2001).

Facts. Nguyen (D) was a nonmarital child, born in Vietnam to a Vietnamese mother and a father who was a United States citizen. D entered the United States at age six, when he became a lawful permanent resident, and he was thereafter raised by his father. When D was 22, he was convicted of sexual assault, and the Immigration and Naturalization Service (P) started deportation proceedings against D. The Immigration Judge ordered D deportable. D appealed the order to the Board of Immigration Appeals. While that appeal was pending, D's father got an order of parentage from a state court based on a DNA test, and D sought to claim United States citizenship. Federal law, 8 U.S.C. section 1409(a), granted automatic United States citizenship to a child born abroad whose unmarried mother was a United States citizen who had lived in the United States for a continuous period of at least one year. If only the child's unmarried father is a United States citizen, the child can become a citizen only if, once paternity is clearly established, the father agrees in writing to support the child and the child or father obtains a paternity determination before the child turns 18. The Board dismissed D's appeal for failure to comply with the statute. D appealed to the Fifth Circuit, claiming the statute denied him equal protection. The Fifth Circuit rejected D's appeal. The Supreme Court granted certiorari.

Issue. May federal law establish a different presumption of citizenship for foreign-born children of unmarried mothers who are United States citizens than they do for foreign-born children of unmarried fathers who are United States citizens?

Held. Yes. Judgment affirmed.

♦ The first governmental objective served by the statute is the importance of assuring that a biological parent-child relationship exists. In the case of the mother, the fact of birth establishes this relationship. In the case of the father, clear and convincing evidence of parentage is necessary.

♦ To require Congress to legislate without reference to the parent's gender with regard to establishing a blood tie between parent and child would be to insist on a hollow neutrality because the mother's relationship is established at birth. The use of gender specific terms takes into account this biological difference between the parents.

♦ The government also has an important interest in ensuring that the child and citizen parent have an opportunity to develop a personal relationship in addition to their legal one. Birth alone is such an opportunity with respect to the mother. Additional facts must be shown to establish that the father has such an opportunity.

♦ The means that Congress chose to further its objectives substantially relate to the purpose of the statute. Congress can require that the opportunity for a father-child relationship occur during the child's formative years. The means chosen are easily administered yet effective to demonstrate whether or not the opportunity has existed.

Dissent (O'Connor, Souter, Ginsburg, Breyer, JJ.). The Court invokes heightened scrutiny, but does not really apply it. The statute's 18-year limitation on the time allowed for proof does not substantially further the assurance of a blood relationship. The statute could be facially neutral and yet have a disparate impact due to the differences in the sexes, but a law that specifically provides for disparate treatment should not be upheld when the only justification is to prove the existence of an opportunity for a parent-child relationship in the first 18 months of the child's life. This is not an "important" governmental interest.

---

4. Discrimination Against Men

a. Proof of dependency requirement

Califano v. Goldfarb
430 U.S. 199 (1977).

Facts. Hannah Goldfarb worked for 25 years before she passed away. She had fully paid her Social Security taxes, but her husband (P) was told that he was not entitled to a widower's benefit because he had not been receiving at least one-half of his support from his wife. Under federal law, survivors' benefits based on a husband's earnings were payable to his widow, but a widower had to satisfy the "one-half support" requirement to collect benefits based on his wife's earnings. P challenged the law. The district court held the requirement unconstitutional. The Supreme Court granted certiorari.

Issue. May Congress impose a gender-based distinction if it is intended to benefit widows as compared with widowers?

Held. No. Judgment affirmed.

♦ A gender-based distinction that deprives women of protection for their families which men receive as a result of their employment is not permitted under the Constitution. In this case, Hannah Goldfarb did not receive the same protection for her husband that a similarly situated male worker would have received for his wife. The only justification for this distinction is the overbroad generalization and assumption regarding a wife's dependency on her husband, which is inadequate under the Constitution.

♦ While in a sense the distinction is between widows and widowers based on a finding that widowers as a class were less likely to have been dependent upon their wives than were widows on their husbands, the gender-based distinction against wage-earning female workers is determinative.

♦ The objective of the statute is not to provide for those who are more needy, but for those who are presumed to have been dependent on their deceased spouses. The statute is not intended to remedy the arguably greater needs of widows, but to aid dependent spouses of deceased wage earners, based on a presumption that wives are usually dependent. This assumption does not justify the gender-based discrimination against women.

Concurrence (Stevens, J.). P raised a claim for benefits, which is the focus of this case, and not P's wife's tax obligation. A classification that treats widows more favorably than widowers is not "invidious" discrimination. However, the discrimination against males in this case is an accidental byproduct of traditional ways of thinking about females. The discrimination can only be upheld if there is a "legitimate basis for presuming that the rule was actually intended to serve the interest" asserted by the government, and that test is not satisfied in this case.

Dissent (Rehnquist, J., Burger, C.J., Stewart, Blackmun, JJ.). The effect of the federal law "is to make it easier for widows to obtain benefits than it is for widowers." This requirement does not perpetuate the economic disadvantage that has previously led the Court to apply "heightened scrutiny" to gender-based distinctions. The majority incorrectly focuses on the wage earner because P's claim to benefits is not contractual. The statute simply benefits widows over widowers, and is supported by legislative judgments that widows are more likely to have greater needs than widowers. P would have had no claim had Congress required proof of dependency by widows as well as widowers. The statute is not exclusive, but overinclusive for reasons of administrative convenience. The classification merely favors aged widows and should be allowed.

----

b. Calculation of Social Security benefits

In *Califano v. Webster,* 430 U.S. 313 (1977), involved a statutory scheme for computing Social Security old-age benefits, which effectively gave women fewer elapsed years from which to exclude lower earning years in order to increase the average monthly wage. As a result, women generally were able to compute a higher average monthly wage than similarly situated men. The Court recognized that reduction of the disparity in economic condition between men and women was an important governmental objective and found the scheme to be substantially related to achievement of that proper objective.

F. The Problem of Sexual Orientation

1. Introduction

The legal treatment of sexual orientation has raised many issues. The courts have reached a variety of conclusions about what is appropriate and what is required under the Constitution. In *Lawrence v. Texas, infra,* the Supreme Court overruled *Bowers v. Hardwick, infra,* which had held that there is no constitutionally protected right to commit consensual homosexual sodomy.

2. States Cannot Prohibit Protection of Homosexuals

Romer v. Evans
517 U.S. 620 (1996).

Facts. Colorado voters adopted an amendment to the Colorado Constitution that prohibited all legislative, executive, or judicial action at any level of state or local government designed to confer a protected status upon, or to allow claims of discrimination by, any person based on homosexual, lesbian, or bisexual orientation. Evans (P) initiated litigation to have the amendment declared unconstitutional. The Colorado Supreme Court held that the amendment was subject to strict scrutiny because it infringed the fundamental right of homosexuals to participate in the political process, and, after remand to the trial court, held the amendment unconstitutional. The Supreme Court granted certiorari.

Issue. May a state prohibit governmental action that confers a protected status upon, or allows claims of discrimination by, any person based on homosexual, lesbian, or bisexual orientation?

Held. No. Judgment affirmed.

♦ D claims that the amendment simply puts homosexuals in the same position as all other persons; *i.e.,* it does no more man deny homosexuals special rights. However, the actual effect of the amendment is to put homosexuals in a solitary class with respect to transactions and relations in both the private and governmental spheres. It imposes a special disability upon these persons by forbidding them to seek or enjoy the safeguards against discrimination that other groups can enjoy.

♦ To reconcile the Equal Protection Clause with the reality that most legislation creates classes, the Court has held that legislation that neither burdens a fundamental right nor targets a suspect class will be upheld so long as the classification bears a rational relation to some legitimate end. The amendment in this case has the peculiar property of imposing a broad and undifferentiated disability on a single named group, and its breadth is so discontinuous with the purported reasons for it that it cannot be explained by anything but animus toward homosexuals. As such, it lacks a rational relationship to legitimate state interests.

♦ Animus toward a politically unpopular group cannot constitute a legitimate state interest. The interest asserted is respect for other citizens' freedom of association, such as the liberties of employers or landlords who oppose homosexuality. But the breadth of the amendment is so far removed from these justifications that they cannot reasonably be deemed the true legitimate purpose of the amendment.

Dissent (Scalia, J., Rehnquist, C.J., Thomas, J.). This amendment is a modest attempt to preserve traditional sexual mores against the efforts of a politically powerful minority to revise those mores through the use of the laws. The majority has made the Court accept the proposition that opposition to homosexuality is as reprehensible as racial or religious bias. But the Constitution says nothing about the subject, and the resolution of such public values should be left to the democratic processes, not the courts. The only denial of equal treatment articulated by the Court is that homosexuals may not obtain preferential treatment without modifying the state constitution. Furthermore, there was a legitimate rational basis for the amendment. In *Bowers v. Hardwick,* 478 U.S. 186 (1986), the Court held that the Constitution does not prohibit making homosexual conduct a crime. If a state may make homosexual conduct criminal, it should be allowed to enact laws disfavoring homosexual conduct; and if so, it should certainly be allowed to adopt a provision that does not even disfavor homosexual conduct but merely prohibits special protections for homosexuals. The animus toward homosexuals—moral disapproval of homosexual conduct—is the same "animus" that for centuries led to criminalization of homosexual conduct. Congress itself required the states of Arizona, New Mexico, Oklahoma, and Utah to adopt, as a condition of statehood, a ban against polygamy. The Court has approved tins criminalization of polygamy; thus the Court has today concluded that the perceived social harm of polygamy is a legitimate concern of government, and the perceived social harm of homosexuality is not. The amendment is simply designed to prevent piecemeal deterioration of the sexual morality favored by a majority of Coloradans, and should be upheld.

G. Other Candidates for Heightened Scrutiny

1. Introduction

Because racial discrimination prompted adoption of the Fourteenth Amendment, racial classifications are clearly "suspect," meaning that they invite the strictest judicial scrutiny. The Fourteenth Amendment was not phrased solely in terms of race, however. Other classifications may invite heightened scrutiny not reaching the strictest levels. Common to most of these classifications are the following characteristics: historical lack of political power; history of discrimination; immutability of the basis for classification; irrelevance to performance; and obviousness (the basis for classification acts as a badge).

2. Alienage

a. Introduction

Under the Constitution, Congress has plenary power over admission or exclusion of aliens, so the courts normally defer to federal law even when it draws distinctions based on alienage. State laws discriminating against aliens once admitted are inherently suspect, however. Most such laws are not upheld. The only significant exception permits such discrimination in situations involving state government functions. For example, a state may categorically exclude aliens from its police force [Foley v. Connelie, 435 U.S. 291 (1978)], but it cannot make citizenship a requirement for the practice of law [*In re* Griffiths, 413 U.S. 717 (1973)].

b. General exclusion from state government

Sugarman v. Dougall
413 U.S. 634 (1973).

Facts. The state of New York refused to accept aliens as civil servants, from menial labor jobs to policymaking positions. The exclusion did not extend to higher executive or elected positions, however. Sugarman (P) challenged the statute. The district court held the state statute unconstitutional. Dougall (D) appeals.

Issue. May a state prohibit all aliens from all competitive state civil service positions?

Held. No. Judgment affirmed.

♦ The issue in this case does not involve any particular alien or any particular basis for a refusal of employment; it is only a general question of a flat prohibition on all aliens. Aliens are clearly entitled to equal protection under the law.

♦ The state claims that its generic classification based on alienage is justified because of the identity between a government and its citizens, and the need for undivided loyalty in civil servants. The problem with this assertion is that the prohibition extends to jobs that have no relation to the state's interest in loyalty, yet does not cover high-level jobs where the state's interest is greatest. Equal protection requires greater precision than this.

♦ When properly and carefully formulated, a state may adopt guidelines requiring citizenship as a condition of employment for certain positions, especially those that include direct participation in the creation, execution, or review of public policy. The statute challenged by P here is not sufficiently precise.

Dissent (Rehnquist, J.). P and the other aliens could have become citizens if they wanted to, so there is no reason to apply strict scrutiny to the classification. Nor does anything in the Equal Protection Clause justify the treatment of alienage as a "suspect classification."

---

3. Wealth Classifications

For many years, the Court suggested that the government could not discriminate on account of poverty any more than it could on grounds of religion or race. In more recent years, the Court has deferred to state rules that withhold benefits because of inability to pay. In *Maker* v. *Roe,* 432 U.S. 464 (1977), the Court stated that it had never held that financial need alone identifies a suspect class for purposes of equal protection analysis. In areas of criminal law, however, the Court has held that the Equal Protection Clause requires the states to provide trial transcripts for appeals by indigents [Griffin v. Illinois, 351 U.S. 12 (1956)], and that states must provide indigents with appellate counsel for an initial appeal [Douglas v. California, 372 U.S. 353 (1963)]. The Court has also required states to pass strict scrutiny for regulations that prevent indigents from getting necessities such as welfare aid. In *San Antonio Independent School District v. Rodriguez,* 411 U.S. 1 (1973), the Court held that a state could finance its schools by property taxes on the property located within each school district, which meant that schools in the wealthier areas would have more resources. The Court applied a low-level scrutiny and stated that the Equal Protection Clause does not require absolute equality or precisely equal advantages.

4. Other Disadvantaged Groups

a. Mental retardation

In *City of Cleburne v. Cleburne Living Center, supra,* the Court held that heightened scrutiny should not be applied to equal protection challenges to regulations involving mentally retarded persons. For one thing, these issues require a variety of solutions best addressed by the legislatures, with the input of qualified professionals. Another reason for lower scrutiny is that, in modern times, the legislative bodies have been responsive to the needs of this group.

b. Age classifications

In *Massachusetts Board of Retirement v. Murgia,* 427 U.S. 307 (1976), the Court held that the aged are not entitled to special judicial protection through heightened scrutiny.

Chapter VII
Implied Fundamental Rights

A. Meaning of Due Process

The Fourteenth Amendment Due Process Clause prevents any state from depriving any person of life, liberty, or property without "due process" of law. Today, the clause is probably most meaningful as a protection of individual rights. The scope of the clause in this area has changed greatly over the years.

B. Privileges and Immunities

1. Fourteenth Amendment Considerations

a. Substantive due process under the Fourteenth Amendment

The concept of due process under the Fifth Amendment merely assured fair legal procedures. It applied only to the federal government. The Fourteenth Amendment Due Process Clause specifically prevents any state from depriving any person of life, liberty, or property without due process of law. Of course, the Fourteenth Amendment was adopted to prevent racial discrimination. However, the broad language used encouraged lawyers to try using it as a restriction on state regulation of business, not merely to attack the procedures used, but also to attack the substantive fairness of the regulations.

b. First look at the Civil War amendments

The Slaughter-House Cases
83 U.S. (16 Wall.) 36 (1873).

Facts. The state of Louisiana granted a state corporation the exclusive right to operate facilities in New Orleans for the landing, keeping, and slaughter of livestock. The Butchers' Benevolent Association (Ps), a group of excluded butchers, sought an injunction against the monopoly on the grounds that they were prevented from practicing their trade unless they worked at the monopolist corporation and paid its fees. The state courts upheld the law. Ps appeal, based on four main grounds: (i) that the statute creates an involuntary servitude forbidden by the Thirteenth Amendment; (ii) that it abridges the privileges and immunities of citizens of the United States; (iii) that it denies Ps the equal protection of the laws; and (iv) that it deprives Ps of their property without due process of law, all under the Fourteenth Amendment.

Issue. Do the Civil War amendments grant United States citizens broad protection against the actions of state governments?

Held. No. Judgment affirmed.

♦ The proper interpretation of the Civil War amendments must reflect their historical setting. Thus, the meaning of "involuntary servitude" as used in the Thirteenth Amendment is restricted to personal servitude, not a servitude attached to property as Ps claim.

♦ The Fourteenth Amendment clearly distinguishes between citizenship of the states and citizenship of the United States. Only those privileges and immunities of United States citizens are protected by the Fourteenth Amendment. Privileges and immunities of state citizens upon which Ps rely here are unaffected, and rest for their security and protection in the power of the several states as recognized in Article IV. The Constitution does not control the power of the state governments over the rights of their own citizens except to require that a state grant equal rights to its own citizens and citizens of other states within its jurisdiction. Therefore, Ps, as citizens of the United States, have no privilege or immunity that has been infringed by the state law.

♦ The Equal Protection Clause of the Fourteenth Amendment is intended primarily to prevent state discrimination against blacks, although Congress may extend its scope to other areas. But Ps have not claimed a denial of equal justice in the state courts and therefore have no reason to have a remedy under the Equal Protection Clause.

♦ The restraint imposed by Louisiana upon the exercise of Ps' trade simply cannot be held to be a deprivation of property within the meaning of the Fourteenth Amendment. That clause should not be construed to cover such state restraint upon trade.

Dissent (Field, J., Chase, C.J., Swayne, Bradley, JJ.). These amendments were intended to protect the citizens of the United States against the deprivation of their common rights by state legislation. The majority holding as to the Privileges and Immunities Clause would add no more protection than existed prior to adoption of the amendment, making it meaningless. A distinguishing privilege of citizens of the United States is equality of right to the lawful pursuits of life throughout the whole country. To permit a state to interfere with such a basic privilege is to ignore the true purpose of the Fourteenth Amendment.

Dissent (Bradley, J.). A state infringes personal liberty when it grants a monopoly to individuals or corporations. A law that prohibits a large class of citizens from pursuing a lawful employment deprives them of liberty as well as property without due process of law. The citizens' occupation is their property, and their choice is their liberty. The law also deprives the citizens of equal protection.

Comment. This case, the first requiring interpretation of these amendments, rendered the Privileges and Immunities Clause ineffective in protecting individual rights against invasion by state governments. Instead, the Court looked to the Due Process and Equal Protection Clauses. The plaintiffs in this case were not attacking the procedure used, but the actual fairness of the state-approved monopoly. Although the Court rejected the notion of substantive due process in this case, the scope of the clause was unclear for many years. Gradually, the Court began to examine the substantive reasonableness of state legislation.

C. The Incorporation Controversy

1. Introduction

Whether the Due Process Clause incorporates rights guaranteed at the federal level by the Bill of Rights is an important question. Some commentators and judges argued for total incorporation; *i.e.,* the Bill of Rights should apply fully to state action. Others argued that "due process" includes only "fundamental" principles of liberty. The Supreme Court has consistently held that the Fourteenth

Amendment only incorporates the Bill of Rights on a selective basis, although to date all provisions of the Bill of Rights have been incorporated except the Second, Third, and Seventh Amendments and the Grand Jury Clause of the Fifth Amendment. The concept of due process is not limited to the protections in the Bill of Rights, however.

2. Effect of Civil War Amendments

The Civil War amendments changed the relationship between the federal and state governments. Application of these amendments was based largely on due process principles. Prior to the adoption of the Fourteenth Amendment, in *Murray v. Hoboken Land & Improvement Co.,* 59 U.S. (18 How.) 272 (1856), the Court noted that the Due Process Clause of the Fifth Amendment was not further explained in the Constitution itself. Instead, the framers intended that the courts look to the settled usages and procedures existing in the common and statute law of England.

3. Privilege Against Self-incrimination Not Part of Due Process

In *Twining v. New Jersey,* 211 U.S. 78 (1908), the Court held that the privilege against self-incrimination was not a necessary part of due process. The Court noted that the privilege is specifically established in the Fifth Amendment and was not deemed fundamental in due process by the states or even the Magna Carta. The Court held that if some of the personal rights safeguarded in the Bill of Rights were also safeguarded against state action, it would be because a denial of these rights would be a denial of due process itself.

4. Double Jeopardy Provision Not Incorporated

Palko v. Connecticut, 302 U.S. 319 (1937), concerned a Connecticut statute permitting appeals by the prosecution. The Court held that the Fourteenth Amendment does not prevent a state from enacting a statute permitting the state to appeal in criminal cases. The Court noted that, while it is true that the Fifth Amendment prohibits retrial against the will of a defendant once convicted, no such protection extends to prosecution by a state. There is no general rule applying all of the protections of the original Bill of Rights to state action. The Court further explained that some immunities, such as those found in the First Amendment, have been extended to state action, but solely because of their indispensability to the concept of ordered liberty. Absorption of any of the Bill of Rights by the Fourteenth Amendment Due Process Clause is due solely to the belief that neither liberty nor justice would exist without them. The double jeopardy provision is not such an essential privilege; some would even say it is a mischief rather than a benefit.

5. Total Incorporation Rejected

It has been argued that the Fourteenth Amendment Due Process Clause incorporates all of the Bill of Rights in full, but this view has been consistently rejected by the Court. [*See* Adamson v. California, 332 U.S. 46 (1947)] In *Adamson,* the Court decided that due process did not require reversal of a state criminal conviction where the prosecution had commented on the defendant's refusal to testify, although such a comment would be reversible error at the federal level because of the Fifth Amendment. Justices Black and Douglas dissented, arguing that the original purpose of the Fourteenth Amendment was to incorporate fully all of the Bill of Rights guarantees. They argued that failure to incorporate those specific guarantees would leave citizens without assured rights and would at the same time grant the Court an unauthorized broad power to expand or contract the scope of due process virtually at will. They also indicated a preference for selective incorporation over no incorporation at all.

6. Right to Trial by Jury Incorporated

In *Duncan v. Louisiana,* 391 U.S. 145 (1968), the Court stated that the right of trial by jury in serious criminal cases is fundamental to the American scheme of justice and qualifies for protection under the Due Process Clause of the Fourteenth Amendment against violation by the states. After discussing the increase in the selective incorporation of other guarantees of the Bill of Rights into the Due Process Clause, the Court held the Sixth Amendment guarantee of a right to jury trial applicable through the Fourteenth Amendment to state criminal cases which, if tried in a federal court, would be covered.

D. Substantive Due Process

1. Increased Judicial Intervention in Economic Regulation

a. State constitutional law

Most state constitutions contain a clause referring to "due process" or the "law of the land." Although these phrases originally were intended to establish a method of legal procedure, lawyers and state judges began to use them as a means of invalidating legislation. For example, in *Wynehamer v. People,* 13 N.Y. 378 (1856), the New York court held a state prohibition statute unconstitutional on due process grounds as applied to liquor already owned when the statute was enacted.

b. Development of substantive due process

As noted above, the state courts were the first to accept arguments in favor of some type of substantive due process. Then, in *Munn v. Illinois,* 94 U.S. 113 (1877), the Court held that the Due Process Clause does protect private property, but a state may control such property if it is "affected with a public interest," so that a state could set maximum storage charges at central warehouses. Eventually, the Court began to scrutinize the substantive rights affected by legislation because there existed "fundamental rights," which were entitled to judicial protection. For example, in *Allgeyer* v. *Louisiana,* 165 U.S. 578 (1897), the Court invalidated a state law that prohibited the insuring of Louisiana property by any company not licensed to do business in Louisiana. Allgeyer had insured his property with a New York insurer in violation of the state law. The Court held that this statute deprived Allgeyer of his liberty to contract, without due process of law.

c. Concept of substantive due process

With the *Lochner* case that follows, the Court applied the following concepts of due process:

1) Ends or purposes

The Court examined the purposes of the legislation, asking whether the object was legitimate, appropriate, or necessary. Did the law promote in some way the health, safety, welfare, or morals of the people? These questions were answered from the language of the statute, the legislative record, and the history behind the passage of the statute. These were considered questions of law for the court.

2) Means

The Court also determined whether the means used to accomplish the legislation's purpose were reasonable and appropriate. That is, was there a real and substantial relationship between the means used and the legitimate end?

3) Effect

Finally, the Court inquired into the effect of the law on the liberty and property of the parties involved. If the effect was too drastic, then the law violated due process.

d. Pivotal case

Lochner v. New York
198 U.S. 45 (1905).

Facts. Lochner (D) was convicted of permitting an employee to work for him more than the statutory maximum of 60 hours per week. D appeals, claiming the law violated his freedom to contract under the Fourteenth Amendment Due Process Clause.

Issue. May a state generally prohibit private agreements to work more than a specified number of hours?

Held. No. Judgment reversed.

♦ The general right to contract in business is clearly part of the individual liberty protected by the Fourteenth Amendment. However, both liberty and the right to hold property are subject to such reasonable conditions as may be imposed by a government pursuant to its police powers.

♦ An earlier law restricting the work hours in certain dangerous occupations was upheld. The law here challenged, however, has no reference whatsoever to the health, safety, morals, or welfare of the public. The state claims an interest in the individual worker's health, but this goes too far; the individual's liberty must impose some restraint on the police power.

♦ This is not a substitution of the Court's judgment for the legislature's but merely a determination of whether the attempted regulation is within the state's police power.

Dissent (Harlan, White, Day, JJ.). There is room for debate about the validity of the state's interest in preventing more than 10 hours' work per day. Excessive work could impair the ability of workers to serve the state and provide for their dependents. The Court should not go further than to determine that such reasons for the law exist.

Dissent (Holmes, J.). Many comparably restrictive uses of the police power have been upheld by the Court. The Constitution was not intended to embody a particular economic view but was framed to permit expression of dominant opinions, *i.e.,* that the laws freely reflect the people's choices. The law is not clearly unrelated to public health and ought to be upheld.

Comment. In *Lochner,* the Court applied principles of general constitutional law that formerly had been applied only in diversity cases. The Court began to define the limits of the police power when it excessively imposed upon individual freedoms, the scope of which the Court in turn was broadening. The Court began inquiring as to the propriety and reasonableness of the objectives sought through exercise of the police power.

---

2. Judicial Control over Legislative Policy

a. Introduction

After *Lochner,* the Court began substituting its judgment for legislative judgments in a variety of cases involving economic regulation. Most legislation held unconstitutional involved regulation of labor, prices, and entry into business.

b. Maximum working hours

The Court upheld a law fixing maximum work hours for women, distinguishing *Lochner* by the special state interest in healthy women. [Muller v. Oregon, 208 U.S. 412 (1908)] The Court later effectively overruled *Lochner by* upholding a general maximum work hour law in *Bunting v. Oregon,* 243 U.S. 426 (1917). In that case, the Court did not refer to *Lochner,* and substantive due process survived.

c. "Yellow dog" contracts

In *Coppage v. Kansas,* 236 U.S. 1 (1915), the Court held that a state law that prohibited employers from requiring employees to agree not to join a labor union ("yellow dog" contracts) violated due process because it interfered with the right to make contracts. *Adair v. United States,* 208 U.S. 161 (1908), invalidated a similar federal law.

d. Minimum wages

The Court invalidated a federal minimum wage law applicable only to the District of Columbia *in Adkins v. Children's Hospital,* 261 U.S. 525 (1923), again finding that interference with freedom to contract violated due process.

3. Decline of Substantive Due Process

a. Introduction

Some time after *Lochner,* the Court changed its earlier view and began to apply less strict scrutiny to economic regulation. Instead it granted deference to legislative determinations of need and reasonableness.

b. Regulation of prices

Nebbia v. New York
291 U.S. 502 (1934).

Facts. New York (P) passed a law establishing minimum and maximum retail prices for milk. The purpose was to aid the dairy industry, which was in a desperate situation because the prices received by farmers for milk were below the cost of production. Nebbia (D), a retail grocer, sold milk below the minimum price and was convicted of violating the statute. D challenges the statute as a violation of due process.

Issue. May a state strictly control retail prices, even if such control inhibits the use of private property and the making of contracts?

Held. Yes. Judgment affirmed.

♦ As long as the law has a reasonable relationship to a proper legislative purpose, is not arbitrary or discriminatory, and the means chosen are reasonably related to the ends sought, due process is not offended.

♦ No area is outside the province of state regulation for police power purposes, including the direct regulation of prices.

----

c. Regulation of minimum wage

The Court overruled *Adkins, supra,* in *West Coast Hotel Co. v. Parrish,* 300 U.S. 379 (1937), by upholding a state minimum wage law for women. The Court found that the only issue for consideration was whether the legislative act was arbitrary or capricious and concluded that the legislature had the right to consider minimum wage requirements as an important means of implementing its policy of protecting abused workers.

d. Regulation of labor

In *Lincoln Federal Union v. Northwestern Iron & Metal Co.*, 335 U.S. 525 (1949), the Court upheld a statute prohibiting employers from entering into "closed shop" contracts so as to exclude nonunion workers. It also upheld a law requiring employers to give employees paid time off for voting. [Day-Brite Lighting, Inc. v. Missouri, 342 U.S. 421 (1952)]

e. Regulation of food

United States v. Carotene Products Co., 304 U.S. 144 (1938), concerned the "Filled Milk Act," which was enacted by Congress and which provided that filled milk (skimmed milk combined with nondairy fats) was an adulterated article of food, the sale of which was a fraud upon the public. The Act prohibited the shipment of filled milk in interstate commerce. The Court held that the Act was supported by sufficient evidence to sustain it and that even if there had not been any hearings, the existence of facts supporting the legislative judgment must be presumed. The Court asserted that, when the existence of a rational basis for legislation depends on facts outside the sphere of judicial notice, the court may inquire into those facts, but, in this case, the evidence was sufficient to support the Act.

1) Comment

Footnote 4 of the opinion sets forth principles regarding this varying presumption of constitutionality. It noted that the scope of the presumption may be narrower when the legislation appears on its face to be within a specific prohibition of the Constitution, such as those of the Bill of Rights. Another area that may invoke a narrower presumption is when the legislation may restrict the political process that could lead to repeal of undesirable legislation. The third general area is legislation directed at particular religions or minorities.

f. Regulation of business entry

1) Deference to state legislature

Williamson v. Lee Optical Co., 348 U.S. 483 (1955), involved a state law that, among other things, forbade an optician from fitting or duplicating lenses, without a prescription from an ophthalmologist or optometrist. The Court upheld the law, stating that although the law may exact a needless, wasteful requirement in many cases, the legislature, not the courts, must balance the advantages and disadvantages of a new requirement. The law need not be logically consistent with its aims in every respect to be constitutional. The Court asserted that it would no longer strike down state laws regulating business and industrial conditions merely because they may be unwise, improvident, or out of harmony with a particular school of thought.

2) Prohibitory vs. regulatory state laws

In *Ferguson v. Skrupa*, 372 U.S. 726 (1963), the Court upheld a Kansas law that prohibited the business of "debt adjusting" except as incident to "the lawful practice of law" in Kansas. The Court acknowledged that it once relied on the Due Process Clause to strike down laws that were thought to be unwise or incompatible with a particular economic or social philosophy. However, the Court explained that, in time, it recognized that states have the power to legislate against injurious practices in their internal commercial and business affairs if the legislation does not defy a federal constitutional prohibition.

E. Fundamental Interests and the Equal Protection Clause

1. Introduction

In addition to the suspect classifications that merit strict scrutiny, the Court has also applied heightened review when a classification impinges on a "fundamental" interest. Such fundamental interests include voting, access to the courts, and welfare.

2. Procreation

Skinner v. Oklahoma
316 U.S. 535 (1942).

Facts. Oklahoma provided for sterilization of habitual criminals, defined as people who, having been convicted two or more times in the United States for felonies involving moral turpitude, are then convicted in Oklahoma of such a felony and sentenced to an Oklahoma prison. The procedure requires a court or jury finding that the person is a habitual criminal and that sterilization would not harm the person's general health. However, the law does not apply to offenses arising out of the violation of the prohibitory laws, revenue acts, embezzlement, or political offenses. Skinner (D) was convicted of stealing chickens, then of armed robbery, and again of armed robbery. Williamson (P), the state attorney general, instituted the sterilization proceeding against D. The state courts rejected D's Fourteenth Amendment challenge. The Supreme Court granted certiorari.

Issue. May a state sterilize habitual criminals if it distinguishes among the types of crimes that satisfy the definition of "habitual criminal"?

Held. No. Judgment reversed.

♦ There are several inequities in this act that render it invalid under the Equal Protection Clause. For example, a stranger who steals more than $20 from a cash register is subject to sterilization, but a clerk who takes the same amount is not, because embezzlement is not covered.

♦ Because marriage and procreation are such fundamental interests, classifications made in a state's sterilization scheme are subject to strict judicial scrutiny. The classifications in P's scheme cannot withstand such scrutiny.

Concurrence (Stone, C.J.). If the state knows habitual criminals transmit their tendencies genetically, it may also know that some classes of offenders have a greater propensity to transmit. Hence, equal protection analysis is inappropriate. Due process, however, requires that before such an invasion of personal liberty, the individual be given the opportunity to show that his case does not justify resort to so drastic a measure.

---

3. Voting

a. The right to vote

Several constitutional provisions relate to voting and elections. The Fourteenth Amendment Equal Protection Clause has been applied to the right to vote. The Fifteenth Amendment forbids denial or abridgment of the right to vote on account of race, color, or previous condition of servitude, and the Nineteenth Amendment granted the franchise to women. The

Twenty-Fourth Amendment abolished the poll tax for federal elections. The Twenty-Sixth Amendment granted the right to vote in state and federal elections to 18-year-olds.

b. Denial or qualification of the right to vote

1) Impact of a poll tax

Harper v. Virginia State Board of Elections
383 U.S. 663 (1966).

Facts. Harper (P) and other Virginia residents brought suit to have Virginia's poll tax declared unconstitutional. The district court, under *Breedlove v. Suttles,* 302 U.S. 277 (1937), dismissed P's complaint. P appeals.

Issue. May a state exact a poll tax as a condition for exercise of the right to vote?

Held. No. Judgment reversed.

♦ Once the franchise is granted to the electorate, lines may not be drawn that are inconsistent with the Equal Protection Clause of the Fourteenth Amendment.

♦ Lines drawn by the affluence of the voter or by the payment of any fee violate equal protection. Undoubtedly, states may impose reasonable voter qualifications, but these must pass careful scrutiny because the franchise is preservative of other basic civil and political rights. Wealth or payment of a fee is an irrelevant factor in measuring a voter's qualifications.

♦ Notions of what constitutes equal treatment for purposes of the Equal Protection Clause do change, and *Breedlove* is overruled.

Dissent (Black, J.). The Court has ignored the original meaning of the Constitution and has instead given the Equal Protection Clause a new meaning according to the Court's idea of a better governmental policy. Such changes are unjustifiable; they should be made only through the proper amendment procedure.

Dissent (Harlan, Stewart, JJ.). The decision to abolish state poll taxes for state elections ought to be made by the states, not by the United States Supreme Court.

---

2) Voter qualifications not based on wealth

Kramer v. Union Free School District
395 U.S. 621 (1969).

Facts. Kramer (P) challenged a state law that restricted eligibility to vote in certain school district elections to those who either own or lease taxable real property within the district, or who are parents (or have custody of) children enrolled in the local public schools. The lower courts upheld the law, and P appeals.

Issue. May a state restrict the franchise for limited purpose elections merely on a showing of a rational basis for the restrictions?

Held. No. Judgment reversed.

♦ Statutes denying some residents the right to vote impinge on one of the most fundamental rights of a democratic society. Accordingly, such exclusions must be necessary to promote a compelling state interest.

♦ Even if the state interests here are substantial enough to justify limiting the exercise of the franchise to those "primarily interested" or "primarily affected" (which is not decided), this statute is not narrowly drawn to effectuate that purpose. It is both underinclusive and overinclusive. Therefore, it cannot stand.

Dissent (Stewart, Black, Harlan, JJ.). If a state may impose valid restrictions based on residence, literacy, and age, it ought to be able to impose these requirements, which are rational. The Court should apply only the traditional equal protection standard.

---

3) Additional restrictions on the franchise

a) Special purpose elections

In *Cipriano v. City of Houma,* 395 U.S. 701 (1969), a state law granted only property taxpayers the right to vote in elections to approve municipal utility bonds. The Court held the restriction invalid since all citizens have an interest in the quality of utility services and rates. In *Phoenix v. Kolodziejski,* 399 U.S. 204 (1970), the Court held that a statute limiting the vote for the issuance of general obligation bonds to real property owners was unconstitutional even though only property taxes would pay for the improvements, since all residents were said to have a substantial interest in the municipal improvements to be made. But in *Salyer Land Co. v. Tulare Lake Basin Water Storage District,* 410 U.S. 719 (1973), the Court upheld an election scheme in which only landowners could vote for the members of the district board, because costs were assessed against land benefitted. The board had a special limited purpose, and its activities disproportionately affected landowners as a group. In *Ball* v. *James,* 451 U.S. 355 (1981), the Court applied *Salyer* to the Salt River District in Arizona, which delivers 40% of its water to urban users and is a major generator and supplier of hydroelectric power.

b) Durational residence requirements

State residence requirements have been held to violate equal protection because they divide voters into two classes—old and new residents—and discriminate against the latter. The principal case was *Dunn v. Blumstein,* 405 U.S. 330 (1972), which used the burden on the right to travel, as well as the burden on the right to vote, to invalidate such state residence requirements. However, the Court has recognized the need for some registration requirements, and upheld a 50-day residency and registration requirement where necessary to prepare voters' lists, etc. [*See* Marston v. Lewis, 410 U.S. 679 (1973)] And in *Rosario* v. *Rockefeller,* 410 U.S. 752 (1973), the Court upheld a law requiring voters to enroll in the party of their choice at least 30 days before the November general election in order to vote in the next party primary. There was held to be no violation of equal protection— the lengthy time period was said to be connected with the important state goal of preventing "raiding," whereby one party's members register with another party to influence the result of the latter's primary. Distinguishing *Rosario,* the Court in *Kusper v. Pontikes,* 414 U.S. 51 (1973), invalidated an Illinois law restricting the voting in a primary by anyone who had voted in another party's primary in the preceding 23 months, because the provision restricted the voter's First Amendment associational freedom to change political party affiliation.

c) Disenfranchisement of felons

In *Richardson v. Ramirez,* 418 U.S. 24 (1974), the Court held that the states may disenfranchise convicted felons because section 2 of the Fourteenth Amendment specifically permits such a limitation on the right to vote.

c. Dilution through apportionment

1) Federal vs. state apportionment

In early decisions, the Supreme Court consistently refused to review questions arising from a state's distribution of electoral strength among its political or geographical subdivisions. In *Baker v. Carr, supra,* the Court decided that federal courts had jurisdiction over challenges to apportionment plans. The modern approach to federal elections requires that representation must reflect the total population as precisely as possible. More flexibility is permitted in apportionment of state legislatures, but grossly disproportionate districts are not allowed. State apportionment may not be used to further discrimination, but numerical deviations resulting from political considerations may be allowed.

2) Constitutional standards

Reynolds v. Sims
377 U.S. 533 (1964).

Facts. Sims (P) and others challenged the apportionment of the Alabama legislature, which was based on the 1900 federal census and thus seriously discriminated against voters who lived in an area where the population had grown disproportionately in the intervening years. The district court ordered temporary reapportionment; Reynolds (D) and other state officials appeal.

Issue. Must a state apportion its legislative districts on the basis of population?

Held. Yes. Judgment affirmed.

♦ The right to vote is essential to a democratic society and is denied by abasement or dilution of a citizen's vote just as effectively as by wholly prohibiting the free exercise of the franchise. The fundamental principle of representative government is one of equal representation for equal numbers of people, regardless of race, sex, economic status, or place of residence within a state.

♦ The Equal Protection Clause guarantees the opportunity for equal participation by all voters in the election of state legislators. Therefore, votes cannot be weighed differently on the basis of where the voters happen to reside. This applies whether the state legislature is unicameral or bicameral.

♦ The federal Congress cannot be taken as a guide for state legislative district apportionment because it arose from unique historical circumstances and represents a union of sovereigns. Political subdivisions of states never have been sovereign entities in that sense.

♦ Each state district must contain as nearly an equal population as possible, although precision, being impossible, is not required. Substantial equality of population must be the overriding objective. States need not perpetually update their apportionment plans, but there must be a reasonable plan for periodic readjustment.

Dissent (Harlan, J.). The history of the adoption of the Fourteenth Amendment shows that the Equal Protection Clause was not meant to limit the power of the states to apportion their legislatures as they saw fit.

Dissent (Stewart, Clark, JJ.). A state's plan for legislative apportionment must be rational and not permit the systematic frustration of the will of a majority of the electorate. So long as a plan achieves effective and balanced representation of the variety of social and economic interests of the state, it cannot be considered irrational.

Comment. In one of the five companion cases to *Reynolds, Lucas v. Forty-Fourth General Assembly,* 377 U.S. 713 (1964), involving the Colorado apportionment scheme, the Court held that the fact that a scheme had been approved by the state's voters is without constitutional significance.

3) Local government

a) The principles of *Reynolds v. Sims, supra,* were extended to legislators in local government [Avery v. Midland County, 390 U.S. 474 (1968)] but not to nonlegislative officers [Sailors v. Board of Education, 387 U.S. 105 (1967)]. The Supreme Court held that "general governmental powers over an entire geographical area need not be apportioned among single-member districts of substantially unequal population." [Dusch v. Davis, 387 U.S. 112 (1967)]

b) *Hadley v. Junior College District,* 397 U.S. 50 (1970), extended the "one person-one vote" rule to all instances where a state or local government decides to select persons by popular election to perform governmental functions. No distinctions are to be made for "legislative officers" versus "administrative officers." However, there might be some cases in which a state elects certain functionaries whose duties are so far removed from normal governmental activities and so disproportionately affect different groups that a popular election according to the one person-one vote principle might not be required.

4) At-large system

City of Mobile v. Bolden
446 U.S. 55 (1980).

Facts. The city of Mobile (D) was governed by a three-member city commission, elected at large. Bolden (P), a black Mobile voter, challenged this system as unfairly diluting the black vote. The district court found for P and ordered D to institute a mayor-council system elected from single-member districts. The court of appeals affirmed, and D appeals.

Issue. Does an at-large system of municipal elections not motivated by a discriminatory purpose violate the rights of a minority group constituting about one-third of the population?

Held. No. Judgment reversed.

♦ D's system is a common one in our nation. State action that is neutral on its face, like D's, violates the Fifteenth Amendment only if motivated by a discriminatory purpose. There is no right to have black or other minority candidates elected. The amendment prohibits only the denial or abridgment of the freedom to vote, which P does not allege here.

♦ At-large electoral schemes are subject to challenge under the Fourteenth Amendment Equal Protection Clause when they are intended to result in a lack of representation of racial or ethnic minorities. There must be proof of official discrimination. [*See* White v. Regester, 412 U.S. 755 (1973)] Failure to elect proportional numbers of minority representatives is not sufficient proof. Here, P has failed to show the fatal purpose. D's system is readily explained on grounds apart from race.

♦ The dissent would find a substantive right of proportional representation, but no such right exists.

Concurrence (Blackmun, J.). The relief accorded was excessive; the case should be remanded for reconsideration of an appropriate remedy.

Concurrence (Stevens, J.). There is a distinction between state action that inhibits the right to vote, which is subject to strict scrutiny, and action affecting group political strength, which is judged by a standard that allows effective functioning of the political process. The proper test is the objective results of the state action, not the subjective motivation behind it. Under that test, D's plan is permissible.

Dissent (Brennan, J.). Proof of discretionary impact is sufficient. Even if it were not, P has adequately proven discriminatory purpose.

Dissent (White, J.). Invidious discriminatory purpose can be inferred from objective factors. The lower courts' findings were based on such a reasonable inference and should not be discarded.

Dissent (Marshall, J.). The plurality concludes that, absent proof of intentional state discrimination, the right to vote is meaningless for the politically impotent. There is a substantive constitutional right to equal participation in the electoral process that D denies P. There is no right to proportional representation per se, but the Court must affirmatively protect minorities such as P from vote dilution.

---

d. Ballot access

The Court has looked closely at attempts to impede ballot access by independent candidates and fringe political parties. Most of these are defended as attempts to maintain the integrity of the political process, and this is a legitimate state interest. But the states may not be unduly restrictive.

1) Denial of access

Williams v. Rhodes
393 U.S. 23 (1968).

Facts. Under Ohio law, established political parties had to receive just 10% of the vote in the gubernatorial election to receive a ballot position in the next presidential election, while new parties had to petition for ballot access with signatures totaling 15% of the ballots cast in the prior election, and also had to meet state organizational standards and hold a primary. Two parties (Ps) brought suit to challenge the validity of the law on the ground that it denied Ps and the voters who might wish to vote for them equal protection. The district court found the requirements unconstitutional but refused to grant Ps the relief they sought. All parties appeal.

Issue. May a state give a preference to established political parties by placing a higher burden on new parties than on the established parties to gain ballot access?

Held. No. Judgment affirmed.

♦ This law burdens the right to association and the right to vote. It gives Republicans and Democrats a monopoly and places unequal burdens on minority groups. The risk that the ballot will be overcome with large numbers of parties is too remote to justify this law.

Comment. In *Jenness v. Fortson*, 403 U.S. 431 (1971), the Court upheld a less restrictive ballot access scheme, which permitted access by independent candidates who filed petitions with signatures of only 5% of those eligible for the previous election. Later, the Court invalidated an Illinois system requiring new political parties and independent candidates to gather more voter signatures to appear on the Chicago city ballot than on the statewide ballot. [Illinois State Board of Elections v. Socialist Workers Party, 440 U.S. 173 (1979)] Justice Marshall emphasized the less drastic means available to the state in screening out frivolous candidates and the overbroad restriction on ballot access of the provision.

---

2) Party loyalty

In *Storer v. Brown*, 415 U.S. 724 (1974), the Court applied strict scrutiny but upheld a California law prohibiting a person from running as an independent if she had registered as a party member within a year prior to the primary election immediately preceding the election in which she was running.

3) First Amendment approach

In *Anderson v. Celebrezze,* 460 U.S. 780 (1983), the Court specifically relied on the First Amendment instead of equal protection to invalidate an early filing deadline that applied to independents but not the nominees of political parties. The Court articulated a balancing test, comparing the restriction's injury to First Amendment rights with the justifications asserted by the state.

4. Access to Courts

a. Administration of criminal justice

The Court has shown sensitivity to burdens placed on the access of litigants, especially criminal defendants, to the courts. Both procedural due process and equal protection have been invoked for analysis.

1) Right to record on appeal

In *Griffin v. Illinois,* 351 U.S. 12 (1956), the Court held that due process requires that a state furnish an indigent defendant a free transcript of his trial to permit appellate review. The Court reasoned that a defendant's inability to pay court costs before trial could affect his rights to plead not guilty and to defend himself. Indigency cannot justify deprivation of a fair trial. A state is not required by the Constitution to provide appellate review, but all of the states have so provided. A substantial proportion of criminal convictions are reversed by state appellate courts. This appellate review having become such an integral part of the trial system, a state may not discriminate against indigents by foreclosing review if they cannot buy a transcript.

2) Right to counsel on appeal

Douglas v. California, 372 U.S. 353 (1963), concerned a California rule that required that, when an indigent criminal defendant requested counsel for his appeal, the state appellate court was to make an independent investigation of the record and appoint counsel only if it would likely be helpful to the defendant or to the court. The Court held the rule to be unconstitutional, stating that denial of counsel in this situation is the same kind of invidious discrimination against indigents as was involved in *Griffin (supra).* The Court explained that, while absolute equality between rich and poor may not be required, the merits of the one and only appeal a person is entitled to are too important to allow a decision without the benefit of counsel just because the appellant is indigent. Justice Harlan, joined by Justice Stewart, dissented. Justice Harlan argued that, although the states are prohibited from discriminating between rich and poor in the formulation and application of their laws, equal protection does not impose on the states an affirmative duty to lift the handicaps flowing from differences in economic circumstances. In *Ross v. Moffit,* 417 U.S. 600 (1974), the Court refused to extend the *Douglas* approach to discretionary appeals. In *Fuller v. Oregon,* 417 U.S. 40 (1974), the Court sustained a recoupment law through which the state sought recoupment of legal expenses from convicted defendants and conditioned probation on reimbursement of expenses incurred when a now-solvent defendant was indigent. In so ruling, the Court rejected the argument that the obligation to repay might indirectly chill a defendant's right to counsel.

b. Civil litigation

In many of the cases dealing with civil litigation there is disagreement whether due process or equal protection should apply.

1) Divorce filing fee

Boddie v. Connecticut
401 U.S. 371 (1971).

Facts. A Connecticut law required a filing fee of $45 and a service fee of $15 from people wanting a divorce in that state. Boddie (P) was indigent and unsuccessfully sought from Connecticut (D) a waiver of the fees.

Issue. May a state require indigents to pay court fees as a condition for judicial dissolution of marriage?

Held. No. Judgment reversed.

♦ The state holds a monopoly on the legal binding and dissolution of the marriage relationship. It denies indigents due process when it requires payment of a fee for legally dissolving a marriage.

♦ Absent a countervailing state interest of overriding significance, persons forced to settle their claims through the judicial process must be given a meaningful opportunity to be heard.

Dissent (Black, J.). This is different than *Griffin*. Civil lawsuits are not like government prosecutions for crime.

Comment. The Court limited the scope of the decision by noting (i) the basic position of the "marriage relationship" in society, and (ii) the "state monopolization of the means for legally dissolving this relationship." It reasoned that due process requires that "absent a countervailing state interest of overriding significance, persons forced to settle their claims . . . through the judicial process must be given a meaningful opportunity to be heard."

---

2) Bankruptcy

The Court has given *Boddie* a narrow construction in other contexts. In *United States v. Kras,* 409 U.S. 434 (1973), the Court held that the Bankruptcy Act filing fee requirement as a condition for discharge is "rational" and does not violate equal protection as applied to indigent persons who seek voluntary bankruptcy. The right to bankruptcy is not a "fundamental" interest but is in the "area of economics and social welfare."

3) Termination of parental rights

In *M.L.B. v. S.L.J.,* 519 U.S. 102 (1996), the Court held that, under the Due Process and Equal Protection Clauses, a state may not preclude a person from appealing a decree terminating parental rights solely because the person cannot pay the fees for preparing a transcript. The Court asserted that cases involving state controls or intrusions on family relationships are within a narrow category of civil cases in which a state must provide access to judicial process without regard to a party's ability to pay fees. The Court noted that, in this case, the termination order described no evidence as to why M.L.B. was found to be unfit and that only a transcript could reveal the sufficiency or insufficiency of the evidence. The Court concluded that the state could not justify the record payment requirement because the parent-child relationship was at stake.

5. The Right to Travel

a. Interstate mobility

A citizen has a constitutional right to travel freely from state to state. State durational residence requirements that would impair this right must be justified by a "compelling" state interest, at least where they affect the citizen's right to receive some vital government benefit or service. However, states may apply a requirement of residency at the time of (and during) receipt of governmental benefits, subject only to the "traditional" test. For example, *McCarthy v. Philadelphia Civil Service Commission,* 424 U.S. 645 (1976), held that requiring personal residence at the place of governmental employment does not violate the right to travel.

b. State welfare denied

Shapiro v. Thompson
394 U.S. 618 (1969).

Facts. The Thompsons (Ps) were denied welfare benefits solely because they had not been residents of Connecticut for a full year prior to their applications. Two similar cases were joined before the Supreme Court. In all three instances, the district courts found that the state's denial of benefits to otherwise eligible residents of less than a year constituted an invidious discrimination denying Ps equal protection of the laws. Shapiro (D), representing Connecticut, appeals.

Issue. May a state create a one-year residency requirement as a condition for receiving state welfare assistance?

Held. No. Judgment affirmed.

♦ D argues that the statute preserves the fiscal integrity of state public assistance programs, which it clearly does, but only by discouraging the influx of poor families needing assistance. However, a state purpose of inhibiting immigration by needy persons is constitutionally impermissible as a burden on the right to travel. Any law whose sole purpose is the chilling of the exercise of constitutional rights is invalid. D's argument that the statute intends to discourage immigration of needy people seeking solely to obtain larger benefits does not save it from this constitutional defect, since in such circumstances it still infringes on those persons' right to travel.

♦ States may not withhold welfare benefits from short-term residents who have contributed through taxes any more than they may withhold state services such as fire and police protection from short-term residents.

♦ Because the classification here touches on a fundamental constitutional right, it must be judged under the strict standard of whether it promotes a compelling state interest. D's assertion that other administrative objectives are served by the one-year requirement falls short of satisfying this standard. D claims that the statutes are approved by federal legislation. Even if true, it is the state statutes, by themselves, that must be examined for constitutional defects. Congress cannot authorize the states to deny equal protection.

♦ The state statutes violate the Equal Protection Clause and are therefore invalid.

Concurrence (Stewart, J.). The Court has simply recognized and protected an established constitutional right.

Dissent (Warren, C.J., Black, J.). Congress has the power both to impose minimal nationwide residence requirements and to authorize the states to do so. Since the states here acted pursuant to congressional authorization, the statutes should be upheld.

Dissent (Harlan, J.). The compelling interest doctrine should be applied only to racial classifications and not to the enlarged list of suspect criteria that includes classifications based upon recent interstate movement and perhaps the exercise of any constitutional right. In addition, when a statute affects only matters not mentioned in the Constitution and is not arbitrary or irrational, then the Court should not characterize these matters as affecting fundamental rights, thereby giving them the added protection of an unusually stringent equal protection test. Applying the rationality standard, a welfare residence requirement has valid governmental objectives and has advantages not shared by other methods.

---

c. State welfare limited

Saenz v. Roe
526 U.S. 489 (1999).

Facts. In response to high welfare benefit payments, California began limiting welfare benefits, for the first 12 months of a new citizen's residency in the state, to the level received by the individual in his previous state of residence. This change was permitted by Congress. Roe and others (Ps) challenged the California statute. The lower courts held the California statute unconstitutional. The Supreme Court granted certiorari.

Issue. May a state limit the welfare benefits of a new citizen to the amount the new citizen would have received in his previous state of residency?

Held. No. Judgment affirmed.

♦ The right to travel includes at least three components:

   (i)   The right to enter and leave another state;

   (ii) The right to be treated as a welcome visitor; and

   (iii) The right to elect to become a permanent resident and to be treated like other citizens of the new state.

♦ This case involves the third aspect of the right to travel, since Ps became residents of the state. The Privileges and Immunities Clause of the Fourteenth Amendment protects the third element of the right to travel. Under that clause, a United States citizen can become a citizen of any state by a bona fide residence therein, with the same rights as other citizens of that state. The right to travel includes the citizen's right to be treated equally in the new state of residence so the discriminatory classification is itself a penalty.

♦ D claims that the statute will save the state approximately $11 million per year, but the state's legitimate interest in saving money does not justify discrimination among equally eligible citizens.

♦ The fact that Congress approved the durational residence requirements is not sufficient to make the law valid because Congress cannot authorize the states to violate the Fourteenth Amendment. The Citizenship Clause is a limitation on the powers of the federal government as well as the state governments.

Dissent (Rehnquist, C.J., Thomas, J.). The right to travel is distinct from the right to become a citizen. In fact, Ps had to stop traveling to become citizens of California. The Court has ignored the state's need to assure that only persons who establish a bona fide residence receive the benefits provided to current residents of the state. States can impose durational residence requirements for college eligibility and divorce, and they should be able to do the same for welfare benefits.

Dissent (Thomas, J., Rehnquist, C.J.). The Court should investigate the original meaning of the Privileges and Immunities Clause, which is quite limited. Privileges or immunities are fundamental rights, not every public benefit.

---

6. Limit of Fundamental Rights

a. Introduction

The Court has limited the fundamental rights approach by refusing to extend it to certain areas. Certain opinions written by the Warren Court indicated that classifications based on wealth might be suspect, and hence that there may be a fundamental right to economic benefits. Since then the Court has held that there is no constitutional right to receive public welfare. Welfare classifications are subject only to the traditional equal protection test, unless they affect a "fundamental" right other than mere receipt of public assistance.

b. Family size and public assistance

Dandridge v. Williams
397 U.S. 471 (1970).

Facts. Maryland imposed an upper limit of $250 per month per family for Federal Aid to Families with Dependent Children ("AFDC"). Williams (P) challenged the statute as denying equal protection since large families received less aid per child than small families. The lower court held the statute invalid. Dandridge (D) appeals.

Issue. Does imposition of a ceiling on welfare benefits deny equal protection to large families, which receive less assistance per family member than do smaller families?

Held. No. Judgment reversed.

♦ No fundamental right is at stake here. In areas of economics and social welfare, a state does not deny equal protection merely because the classifications made by its laws are imperfect.

♦ The Fourteenth Amendment does not grant federal courts power to set economic or social policy on the states. It is enough that the state's action be rationally based and free from invidious discrimination. This statute, intended to encourage gainful employment, meets that test.

Dissent (Marshall, Brennan, JJ.). A state may not, in the provision of important services or the distribution of governmental payments, supply benefits to some individuals while denying them to others who are similarly situated. This case illustrates the impropriety of the abstract dichotomy between the "mere rationality test" and the "strict scrutiny test." The Court equates the interests of these needy children with the interests of utilities and other corporations by classifying their interests as "economic."

---

c. Housing

The right to housing is not guaranteed by the Constitution. State classifications in housing laws are subject only to the traditional test of reasonableness. Thus, a state may permit landlords to bring summary actions to evict tenants from rented premises but cannot require posting of a bond for twice the amount of rent in order to appeal. [Lindsey v. Normet, 405 U.S. 56 (1972)]

d. Education

Because there is no constitutional right to education, regulation of education is judged only by the traditional (rational basis) test.

1) State spending for education

San Antonio Independent School District v. Rodriguez
411 U.S. 1 (1973).

Facts. Rodriguez (P), a Mexican-American, challenged the Texas system of financing public education. The system involved a combination of state, local, and federal funding, and was operated so that state and local expenditures per pupil varied according to the market value of taxable property per pupil within the various districts. P claimed that the system denied equal protection by invidiously discriminating against the poor. The district court found the system unconstitutional. The San Antonio Independent School District (D) appeals.

Issue. Is a state system of financing public education that closely correlates spending per pupil and the value of local taxable property subject to strict judicial scrutiny?

Held. No. Judgment reversed.

♦ D's system might be regarded as discriminating against functionally indigent persons, against persons relatively poorer than others, or against all who, regardless of their personal incomes, happen to reside in relatively poorer school districts. However, there is no evidence to support a finding that any persons in the first two groups are discriminated against, and the third group clearly cannot fit the traditional definition of a suspect class.

♦ Although the system does not operate to the peculiar disadvantage of any suspect class, strict review is still required if the state's action impermissibly interferes with the exercise of a "fundamental" right, which P claims includes education. Although education is an important state service, that importance is not determinative of equal protection examination. Only those rights explicitly or implicitly guaranteed by the Constitution are "fundamental" for purposes of equal protection.

♦ Education is neither explicitly nor implicitly guaranteed. Additionally, D's system was implemented to extend public education, not to interfere with any rights. Finally, courts should not interfere with state fiscal policies if not necessary. Therefore, D's system is not subject to strict judicial scrutiny.

Dissent (White, Douglas, Brennan, JJ.). The Court merely requires D to establish that unequal treatment is in furtherance of a permissible goal, but it should also require D to show that the means chosen to effectuate that goal are rationally related to its achievement.

Dissent (Marshall, Douglas, JJ.). The Court appears to find only two standards of equal protection review—strict scrutiny or mere rationality. In reality, there is a wide spectrum of review, depending on the constitutional and societal importance of the interest adversely affected and the recognized invidiousness of the classification. The amount of review accorded to nonconstitutional rights or interests varies according to the nexus between those rights and specific constitutional guarantees. Discrimination on the basis of group wealth in this case calls for careful judicial scrutiny.

———————

2) Education of children of illegal aliens

Plyler v. Doe
457 U.S. 202 (1982).

Facts. Texas enacted a statute that withheld state funds for the education of illegal alien children and that allowed local school districts to deny enrollment to such children. Doe (P) challenged the constitutionality of the statute. The lower courts found the law unconstitutional. Plyler (D) appeals.

Issue. May a state deny to undocumented school-age children the free public education that it provides to citizens and legally admitted aliens?

Held. No. Judgment affirmed.

♦ The Fourteenth Amendment guarantees equal protection and due process to "any person within [a state's] jurisdiction." Even illegal aliens are entitled to this protection.

♦ Equal protection analysis does not require that illegal aliens be treated as a suspect class just because their illegal presence is not a constitutional irrelevancy. Education is not a fundamental right, although it is more than a mere government benefit. However, this case presents another consideration. The statute imposes a lifetime stigma on children who are not accountable for their disabling status. Therefore, the discrimination cannot be allowed unless it fulfills a substantial state purpose.

♦ Although national policy does not support unrestricted immigration, no policy exists that would deny these children an elementary education. The state interests—protection against excessive illegal immigration, avoidance of the special burden of educating such children, and the likelihood that the children will not remain in the state—are not furthered by the means chosen, even assuming that the policies are legitimate. Because no showing of furthering a state interest was made, the statutory discrimination is unconstitutional.

Concurrence (Marshall, J.). I concur without retreating from *Rodriguez*.

Concurrence (Blackmun, J.). This case is consistent with *Rodriguez,* which reserved judgment on the constitutionality of a system that absolutely denied education to any children.

Concurrence (Powell, J.). Like nonmarital children, the children discriminated against here are innocent with respect to their status. The legislative classification threatens the creation of an underclass of future residents. Therefore, the state must show a fair and substantial relation to substantial interests. This D has failed to do.

Dissent (Burger, C.J., White, Rehnquist, O'Connor, JJ.). The only issue here is whether Texas has a legitimate reason to distinguish between legal and illegal residents. The state purpose of preserving its limited resources for school financing is rationally related to the legislative classification. The majority admits that traditional equal protection analysis does not require a different result. Instead, the majority decided what the best result should be and then created an analysis to reach that result.

———————

F. Privacy and Family

1. Introduction

Although substantive due process no longer imposes any serious restraints on economic regulations, the Court has revived the notion as a means of protecting certain fundamental personal rights not specifically enumerated in the Constitution, including the right of privacy. Early cases began to recognize privileges recognized at common law but not specifically mentioned in the Constitution.

a. Family

In *Meyer v. Nebraska*, 262 U.S. 390 (1923), the Court recognized the rights to marry, raise children, and acquire useful knowledge as essential to the liberty protected by due process.

b. Education

In *Pierce v. Society of Sisters*, 268 U.S. 510 (1925), the Court invalidated a state law requiring attendance at public school as violative of parents' liberty to direct the education of their children.

2. Fundamental Privacy Rights

The right of privacy is nowhere mentioned in the Constitution. However, the Fourth and Fifth Amendments protect against invasion of privacy by search and seizure. The right of personal choice in matters of marriage and the bearing and raising of children is so fundamental to society that it is afforded protection. Some consider this right to be protected by the Ninth Amendment, others by the "penumbra" of the Bill of Rights.

a. Marital privacy within the Bill of Rights

Griswold v. Connecticut
381 U.S. 479 (1965).

Facts. Griswold, the Executive Director of Planned Parenthood in Connecticut, and the organization's Medical Director for New Haven (Ds) gave information, instruction, and medical advice about contraception to married persons. Ds were convicted as accessories to the crime of using contraceptives in violation of a Connecticut (P) statute prohibiting all such use. The conviction was upheld in all the state courts. Ds appeal.

Issue. Does a constitutional right of privacy exist that prohibits states from making use of contraceptives by a married couple a crime?

Held. Yes. Conviction reversed.

♦ The specific guarantees in the Bill of Rights have penumbras, or peripheral rights, that make the specific rights more secure. A right of educational choice has been noted in earlier cases, such as *Pierce* and *Meyer, supra,* even though it is not mentioned in the Constitution, because it is a peripheral right without which the specific First Amendment rights would be less secure.

♦ Various guarantees in the Bill of Rights create zones of privacy. The First Amendment protects the right of association with the related privacy. The Third Amendment protects the privacy of the home against quartering of soldiers. The Fourth and Fifth Amendments protect other facets of privacy, including the sanctity of the home. The Ninth Amendment protects rights retained by the people.

♦ This case involves a relationship lying within the zone of privacy created by several fundamental constitutional guarantees. The law at issue has a maximum destructive impact on that relationship. The privacy of marriage is older than the Bill of Rights. The association of marriage is for as noble a purpose as any involved in prior decisions protecting the right of association.

Concurrence (Goldberg, J., Warren, C.J., Brennan, J.). The Ninth Amendment expressly recognized fundamental personal rights not specifically mentioned in the United States Constitution. In determining which rights are fundamental, judges must look to the traditions and collective conscience of the people. Privacy in the marital relation is clearly one of these basic personal rights "retained by the people." The Court's holding does not interfere with a state's proper regulation of sexual promiscuity or misconduct, such as adultery and fornication.

Concurrence (Harlan, J.). The Fourteenth Amendment's Due Process Clause independently requires rejection of the Connecticut statute without reference to the Bill of Rights. The incorporation doctrine should not be used to restrict the reach of the Due Process Clause. (*Note:* Dissenting in *Poe v. Ullman,* 367 U.S. 497 (1961), Justice Harlan argued that if the Due Process Clause were merely a procedural safeguard, it would be no protection against legislation that could destroy the enjoyment of life, liberty, and property, even though the fairest procedures. He argued that the meaning of due process is based on a balance between the demands of organized society and respect for individual liberty, guided by tradition, good judgment, and restraint.)

Concurrence (White, J.). The state's ban on the use of contraceptives by married persons in no way reinforces the state's ban on illicit sexual relationships.

Dissent (Black, Stewart, JJ.). While the law is offensive, it is not prohibited by any specific constitutional provision and therefore must be upheld. Constitutional amendments, not judge-made alterations, are the correct means of modernizing the Constitution.

Dissent (Stewart, Black, JJ.). The law is silly, but there is no general right of privacy found in the Constitution, so we cannot hold that it violates the Constitution.

Comment. More recently, the Court has simply held that the right of personal privacy is implicit in the concept of "liberty" within the protection of the Fourteenth Amendment Due Process Clause— *i.e.,* it is one of those basic human rights that are of "fundamental" importance in our society. [Roe v. Wade, *infra*]

---

b. Further development of substantive due process

Regardless of its source, the right of privacy is regarded as a fundamental right for due process purposes, which means that regulation in these areas can only be justified by a compelling state interest. The right of privacy protects the individual interest in avoiding disclosure of personal matters and the interest in independently making certain kinds of important decisions.

c. Contraceptives

In *Eisenstadt v. Baird,* 405 U.S. 438 (1972), the Court held that the decision whether to use contraceptives was one of individual privacy; thus, the right belongs to single as well as married persons. In *Carey v. Population Services International,* 431 U.S. 678 (1977), the Court held that a state could not prohibit distribution of nonmedical contraceptives to adults except through licensed pharmacists, nor prohibit sales of such contraceptives to persons under 16 who did not have approval of a licensed physician.

3. Abortion

a. Introduction

A woman's decision to terminate her pregnancy is within her constitutionally protected right of privacy, and cannot be made conditional on parental or spousal consent. However, at some point during pregnancy, the state's interests in protecting the mother's life and in protecting prenatal life become sufficiently "compelling" to justify state regulation of abortion.

b. Basic constitutional rule on abortion

Roe v. Wade
410 U.S. 113 (1973).

Facts. Roe (P), unmarried and pregnant, sought declaratory and injunctive relief against Wade (D), a county district attorney, to prevent enforcement of the Texas criminal abortion statute. The district court invalidated the statute but declined to grant injunctive relief. P appeals.

Issue. May a state constitutionally make it a crime to procure an abortion except to save the mother's life?

Held. No. Judgment affirmed.

♦ P claims a constitutional right to terminate her pregnancy, based on the Fourteenth Amendment concept of personal "liberty," the Bill of Rights penumbras, and the Ninth Amendment. D claims a state interest in regulating medical procedures to insure patient safety and in protecting prenatal life.

♦ The right of privacy generally relates to marriage, procreation, and contraception, and includes the abortion decision, but is not without restraint based on the state's compelling interests. The state's interest in prenatal life cannot be based on the fetus's right to life, for a fetus cannot be considered a "person" in the constitutional sense. Unborn children have never been recognized in any area of the law as persons in the whole sense. However, the pregnant woman cannot be isolated in her privacy. The state may decide that at some point in time another interest, that of health of the mother or that of potential human life, becomes significantly involved. The woman's right of privacy must be measured accordingly.

♦ The state's interest in the health of the mother becomes "compelling" at approximately the end of the first trimester, prior to which mortality in abortion is less than mortality in normal childbirth. Only from this point forward may the state regulate the abortion procedure as needed to preserve and protect maternal health.

♦ The state's interest in potential life becomes "compelling" at viability. A state interested in protecting fetal life after viability may proscribe abortion except when necessary to preserve the life or health of the mother.

♦ The Texas statute challenged here is overbroad and cannot be upheld.

Concurrence (Stewart, J.). The Court has generally recognized freedom of personal choice in matters of marriage and family life as a liberty protected by the Fourteenth Amendment. The Texas statute directly infringes on that right and is correctly invalidated.

Concurrence (Douglas, J.). The Ninth Amendment does not create federally enforceable rights, but many rights come within the meaning of "liberty" in the Fourteenth Amendment. The state is justified in treating abortion as a medical concern.

Dissent (White, Rehnquist, JJ.). There is nothing in the language or history of the Constitution to support the Court's judgment. This issue should be left with the people and to the political processes.

Dissent (Rehnquist, White, JJ.). An abortion is not "private" in the ordinary use of this word. The Court seems to define "privacy" as a claim of liberty from unwanted state regulation of consensual transactions, protected by the Fourteenth Amendment. But that liberty is not guaranteed absolutely against deprivation, only against deprivation without due process of law. The traditional test is whether the law has a rational relation to a valid state objective, but this test could not justify the Court's outcome. Instead, the Court adopts the "compelling state interest test," which is more appropriate to a legislative judgment than to a judicial one. The Court's conclusions are more like judicial legislation than determination of the intent of the drafters of the Fourteenth Amendment.

Further, the fact that most states have had restrictions on abortion for over a century indicates that the asserted right to an abortion is not so universally accepted as P claims.

---

c. Government refusal to pay for abortions

Despite its strict scrutiny of regulation of abortion, the Court has held that the government may choose not to fund abortions.

1) Elective abortion

Maher v. Roe
432 U.S. 464 (1977).

Facts. Roe (P), a pregnant, indigent woman who was unable to get a physician's certificate of medical necessity for an abortion, sued Maher (D), a state official, challenging a state regulation that granted Medicaid benefits only for medically necessary abortions. The state granted benefits for all costs of childbirth. P claimed that the regulation's different treatment of abortion and childbirth violated her constitutional rights of due process and equal protection. D appeals a district court decision invalidating the law.

Issue. Is there an unqualified right to an abortion, interference with which must pass strict scrutiny?

Held. No. Judgment reversed.

♦   Financial need alone is not a suspect class for purposes of equal protection analysis. To subject D's regulation to strict scrutiny, therefore, a fundamental right to abortion must exist. There is no such right, however. The only fundamental right established by *Roe v. Wade* is a woman's freedom to decide whether to terminate her pregnancy. Interference with that particular freedom would be subject to strict scrutiny. D has not interfered with that freedom by favoring childbirth, so the regulation is permissible if rationally related to a constitutionally permissible purpose.

♦   The state's interest in protecting the potential life of the fetus is clear. Subsidizing the costs of childbirth is a rational means of protecting that interest. Therefore, the regulation is valid.

Dissent (Brennan, Marshall, Blackmun, JJ.). The effect of this regulation is to coerce indigent pregnant women to bear children they would not otherwise choose to have. It therefore infringes on P's fundamental right to choose and should be subject to strict equal protection scrutiny.

Dissent (Marshall, J.). The challenged regulation is an attempt to impose a moral viewpoint that no state may constitutionally enforce. Since attempts to overturn *Roe* have been unsuccessful, abortion opponents have tried every imaginable means to circumvent the Constitution and impose their moral choices on the rest of society. This is the most vicious yet.

---

2) Public funding of medically necessary abortions

Harris v. *McRae,* 448 U.S. 297 (1980), involved the Hyde Amendment, which denied public funding for most medically necessary abortions. The Court held that Congress may, consistent with the Due Process Clause, deny public funding for certain medically necessary abortions while funding substantially all other medical costs. The Court explained that the government may not place obstacles in the path of a woman's exercise of her freedom of choice to terminate her pregnancy, but it need not remove those not of its own creation, such as indigency. The Court stated that a woman's freedom of choice does not confer an entitlement to such funds as may be necessary to realize all the advantages of that freedom.

d. Permissible state regulation of abortion

Planned Parenthood of Southeastern Pennsylvania v. Casey
505 U.S. 833 (1992).

Facts. Pennsylvania adopted an Abortion Control Act requiring that a woman seeking an abortion must be given certain information at least 24 hours before the abortion; that the woman give informed consent prior to the abortion; that, if a minor, the woman obtain the informed consent of her parents unless a judicial bypass option is followed; that, if married, the woman certify she informed her husband; and that facilities providing abortion services must make certain reports about each abortion, including the woman's age, gestational age, type of abortion procedure, medical conditions and results, and the weight of the aborted fetus. Compliance with the requirements is not required in certain medical emergencies. Planned Parenthood of Southeastern Pennsylvania (P) challenged the Act on its face by suing Casey (D), the Governor of Pennsylvania. The district court held all the provisions unconstitutional, but the court of appeals upheld everything except the husband notification requirement. The Supreme Court granted certiorari.

Issue. May a state impose notification and consent requirements as prerequisites for obtaining an abortion?

Held, Yes. Judgment reversed in part.

♦ The three parts of the essential *Roe v. Wade, supra,* holding are reaffirmed. These are: (i) the woman's right to have an abortion before viability without undue state interference; (ii) the state's power to restrict abortions after fetal viability, as long as there are exceptions to protect a woman's life or health; and (iii) the state's legitimate interest from the outset of the pregnancy in protecting the health of the woman and the life of the fetus that may become a child.

♦ Substantive due process claims require courts to exercise reasoned judgment, and the Court must define the liberty of all, not mandate a moral code. The Constitution has been interpreted to protect personal decisions regarding marriage, procreation, and contraception. Defining one's own concept of existence, meaning, and the mystery of human life is at the heart of liberty. At the same time, abortion has consequences for persons other than the woman who is pregnant.

♦ *Roe* should be upheld under the principle of stare decisis because it has not proven unworkable, because people have relied on the availability of abortion, because under *Roe* women have been better able to participate equally in the economic and social life of the country, because no evolution of legal principle has left *Roe's* doctrinal footings weaker than they were in 1973 when the decision was announced, and because there have been no changed circumstances or new factual understandings. Even if *Roe* is wrong, the error involves only the strength of the state interest in fetal protection, not the liberty of women. Overruling *Roe* simply because of a change in philosophical disposition would undermine the Court's legitimacy.

♦ Although *Roe* has been criticized for drawing lines, the Court must draw specific rules from the general standards in the Constitution. The trimester approach was not part of the essential holding in *Roe* and it both misconceived the nature of the pregnant woman's interest and undervalued the state's interest in potential life. It is therefore overruled and replaced with a line drawn only at viability. Under this approach, a law that serves a valid purpose not designed to strike at the right of abortion itself may be sustained even if it makes it more difficult or more expensive to obtain an abortion, unless the law imposes an undue burden on a woman's ability to make an abortion decision. Thus, the state may further its interest in potential life but cannot place a substantial obstacle in the path of a woman's choice.

♦ The state may adopt health regulations to promote the health or safety of a woman seeking an abortion. It may not prohibit any woman from making the ultimate decision to terminate her pregnancy before viability. After viability, the state may promote its interest in the potentiality of human life by regulating and even proscribing abortion except where it is necessary to preserve the life or health of the mother.

♦ With regard to the specific provisions of the Act, the definition of medical emergency does not impose an undue burden on a woman's abortion right. The informed consent requirement is also permissible because it furthers the legitimate purpose of reducing the risk that a woman may elect an abortion, only to discover later, with devastating psychological consequences, that her decision was not fully informed. The 24-hour waiting period does not impose substantial obstacles, and it is not unreasonable to conclude that important decisions will be more informed and deliberate if they follow some period of reflection. The exception for cases in which a physician reasonably believes that furnishing the information would have a severely adverse effect on the woman's physical or mental health accommodates the interest in allowing physicians to exercise their medical judgment.

♦ The spousal notification requirement does, however, impose an undue burden on a woman's choice to undergo an abortion and cannot be sustained. In well-functioning marriages, the spouses discuss important intimate decisions such as whether to bear a child, and the notification requirement adds nothing in such situations. However, millions of women are the victims of physical and psychological abuse from their husbands, and requiring spousal notification in these situations can be tantamount to preventing the woman from getting an abortion. The husband's interest in the life of the child his wife is carrying does not permit the state to empower him with a veto over the abortion decision. Men do not have the kind of dominion over their wives that parents have over their children.

♦ The parental consent provision has been sustained before, and provided there is an adequate judicial bypass procedure, its constitutionality is reaffirmed. The recordkeeping and reporting requirements are also permissible, with the exception of whether the spouse was notified of the abortion.

Concurrence and Dissent (Blackmun, J.). The Court's decision preserves the liberty of women that is one vote away from being extinguished. The Court also leaves open the possibility that the regulations it now approves may in the future be shown to impose an unconstitutional burden.

Concurrence and Dissent (Stevens, J.). The Court properly follows the principle that a developing organism that is not yet a "person" does not have a "right to life." The state's interest in protecting potential life is not grounded in the Constitution, but reflects humanitarian and pragmatic concerns, including the offense taken by a large segment of the population at the number of abortions performed in this country and third-trimester abortions specifically. But the woman's interest in liberty is constitutional; the Constitution would be violated as much by a requirement that all women undergo abortion as by an absolute ban on abortions. The 24-hour delay requirement should not be upheld because it presumes that the abortion decision is wrong and must be reconsidered. The state may properly require physicians to inform women of the nature and risks of the abortion procedure and the medical risks of carrying to term, but it should not be allowed to require that the woman be provided with materials designed to persuade her to choose not to undergo the abortion.

Concurrence and Dissent (Rehnquist, C.J., White, Scalia, Thomas, JJ.). *Roe* was wrongly decided, and it can and should be overruled consistent with the traditional approach to stare decisis in constitutional cases. Stare decisis is not a reason to retain *Roe;* the Court's legitimacy is enhanced by faithful interpretation of the Constitution. The Court's revised "undue burden" standard is an unjustified constitutional compromise that allows the Court to closely scrutinize all types of abortion regulations despite the lack of any constitutional authority to do so. The new "undue burden" approach is still an imposition on the states by the Court of a complex abortion code. Abortion involves the purposeful termination of potential life and is thus different in kind from the other areas of privacy recognized by the Court, including marriage, procreation, and contraception. Prohibitions on abortion have been part of the law of many of the states since before the Fourteenth Amendment was adopted; there is no deeply rooted tradition of unrestricted abortion in our history that justifies characterizing the right as "fundamental." A woman's interest in having an abortion is a form of liberty protected by the Due Process Clause, but states may regulate abortion procedures in ways rationally related to a legitimate state interest. The Act should be upheld in its entirety.

Concurrence and Dissent (Scalia, J., Rehnquist, C.J., White, Thomas, JJ.). The states may permit abortion-on-demand, but the Constitution does not require that they do so. It is a legislative decision. The issue is not whether the right to an abortion is an absolute liberty or whether it is an important liberty to many women, but whether it is a liberty protected by the Constitution. It is not, because the Constitution says nothing about it and because longstanding traditions of American society have permitted it to be prohibited. Under the rational basis test, D's statute should be upheld. Instead, the Court perpetuates the premise of *Roe,* which is a value judgment, not a legal matter. The "undue burden" standard lacks meaningful content, and may be summed up by concluding that a state may regulate abortion only in such a way as to not reduce significantly its incidence. *Roe* nourished the deeply divisive issue of abortion by elevating it to the national level where it is much more difficult to resolve than it was at the state level. Political compromise is now impossible, and *Roe* has been a major factor in selecting Justices to the Court. The Court should not be concerned with predicting public perceptions but should do what is legally right by asking whether *Roe* was correctly decided and whether it has succeeded in producing a settled body of law. The answer to both questions is no, and *Roe* should therefore be overruled. The Court's reliance on value judgments instead of interpreting text has created political pressure directed to the Court, whereby various groups of people demonstrate to protest that the Court has not implemented the respective group's values.

---

e. Ban on partial birth abortion struck down

In *Stenberg v. Carhart,* 530 U.S. 914 (2000), the Court struck down a Nebraska statute that prohibited partial birth abortions and that lacked an exception for the preservation of the health of the woman. The Court found that partial birth abortions significantly prevent health risks in certain circumstances and that a statute forbidding partial birth abortions could endanger women's health. Also, the statute did not distinguish between partial birth abortions and "dilation and evacuation" ("D & E"), the most commonly used method for performing previability second trimester abortions. The Court reasoned that the statute imposed an undue burden on a woman's right to make an abortion decision, because those who perform abortion procedures using the D & E method would fear prosecution, conviction, and imprisonment.

f. Ban on partial birth abortion upheld

Gonzales v. Carhart
550 U.S. 124 (2007).

Facts. Most of the 1.3 million abortions performed annually in the United States occur during the first trimester. Of the remaining 10% to 15%, most occur in the second trimester, usually by a procedure called "dilation and evacuation" or "D & E." The doctor grabs the fetus in the womb and tears it apart, removing it piece by piece. In a variation of D & E, called "intact D & E" or "partial birth abortion," the fetus is extracted intact before it is killed. In response to *Stenberg, supra,* Congress enacted the Partial-Birth Abortion Ban Act of 2003. The Act prohibits anyone from knowingly performing this type of abortion, which is specifically defined in the statute in terms of how much of the fetus's body can be removed before the procedure constitutes a partial birth abortion. Carhart and other abortion doctors (Ps) challenged the constitutionality of the Act on its face. The lower courts held the Act unconstitutional. The Supreme Court granted certiorari.

Issue. May Congress prohibit a specific form of abortion as long as it does not impose a substantial obstacle to late-term, but previability, abortions?

Held. Yes. Judgment reversed.

♦ The Act is materially different from the statute in *Stenberg*. The Act is more specific regarding the instances to which it applies and more precise in its coverage. It punishes knowingly performing a partial birth abortion. To fall within the Act, the doctor performing the abortion must vaginally deliver a living fetus. The Act's definition of partial birth abortion requires the fetus to be delivered "until, in the case of a head-first presentation, the entire fetal head is outside the body of the mother, or, in the case of breech presentation, any part of the fetal trunk past *the* navel is outside the body of the mother." The doctor must perform an overt act that kills the partially delivered living ferns.

♦ As a facial matter, the Act does not impose an undue burden. It does not prohibit the D & E procedure in which the fetus is removed in parts. Ps contend that D & Es could sometimes result in the delivery of a living fetus beyond the Act's anatomical landmarks. Thus, they assert that any D & E has the potential to violate the Act and that a doctor will not know beforehand whether the abortion will proceed in a prohibited manner. However, the Act's intent requirements preclude liability from attaching to an accidental intact D & E.

♦ *Casey* held that the government may use its authority to show profound respect for the life within the woman; the state has a regulatory interest in protecting the life of the fetus that may become a child.

♦ A woman's decision to have an abortion is fraught with emotional consequences, and some doctors may prefer not to disclose details of the means that will be used. However, this lack of information concerning the way in which the fetus will be killed is of legitimate concern to the state, which has an interest in ensuring that such a serious decision is well-informed.

♦ It is argued that the standard D & E is as brutal, if not more, than the intact D & E. However, it was reasonable for Congress to think that partial birth abortion, more than the standard D&E, undermines the public's perception of the appropriate role of a physician during the delivery process.

♦ There is medical uncertainty as to whether the Act creates significant health risks for women. The evidence presented demonstrates that both sides have medical support for their position. The Court has traditionally given state and federal legislatures wide discretion to pass legislation in areas where there is medical and scientific uncertainty. This Act is not invalid on its face because of uncertainty over whether the barred procedure is ever necessary to preserve a woman's health, since there are other abortion procedures that are considered to be safe alternatives.

♦ The Act does not on its face impose a substantial obstacle to late-term, previability abortions. It may, however, be challenged on an as-applied basis.

Concurrence (Thomas, Scalia, JJ.). The Court's opinion accurately applies current jurisprudence. However, the Court's abortion jurisprudence has no basis in the Constitution.

Dissent (Ginsburg, Stevens, Souter, Breyer, JJ.).

♦ The majority opinion does not take *Casey* and *Stenberg* seriously. Instead, it encourages federal intervention to ban a procedure that medical experts find necessary and proper in certain cases. It blurs the line between previability and postviability abortions, and does not include an exception for a woman's health. Instead, it bans intact D & E, which provides safety benefits over D & E by dismemberment.

♦ In *Stenberg,* we expressly held that a statute banning intact D & E was unconstitutional, in part because it lacked a health exception. We made clear that as long as "substantial medical authority supports the proposition that banning a particular abortion procedure could endanger women's health," a health exception is required.

♦ Congress claimed that there was no credible medical evidence that partial birth abortions are safer than other abortion procedures. But during the district court trials, many accomplished and experienced medical experts explained that, in certain circumstances and for women with certain medical conditions, intact D & E is safer than alternative procedures and is necessary to protect women's health. Each of the district courts to consider the issue rejected Congress's findings as unreasonable and not supported by the evidence.

♦ The notion that the Partial-Birth Abortion Ban Act furthers any legitimate governmental interest is irrational. The Act does not save a single fetus from destruction; it merely requires doctors to use a brutal and more risky method. The Court is simply chipping away at the right to abortion.

---

4. Family and Other "Privacy" Interests

a. Housing

Moore v. City of East Cleveland
431 U.S. 494 (1977).

Facts. Moore (D) lived with her son and two grandsons, who were cousins. D was convicted of violating an East Cleveland (P) city ordinance restricting occupancy of a dwelling unit to members of a single family, defined by certain categories, none of which included D's arrangement. The state courts upheld the conviction. D appeals.

Issue. May a local ordinance restrict occupation of dwelling units to certain specified categories of related individuals?

Held. No. Judgment reversed.

♦ The state courts based their decision on *Village of Belle Terre v. Boraas,* 416 U.S. 1 (1974). That case involved restrictions only on unrelated individuals.

♦ When the government intrudes on choices of family living arrangements, the legitimacy of the governmental interests and the effectiveness of the regulations must be carefully examined. This statute cannot stand such scrutiny. The city's asserted justifications (preventing overcrowding, minimizing traffic and parking congestion, and avoiding undue financial burdens on school systems) are legitimate, but the ordinance serves them marginally, at best. The extended family has a strong tradition in our history, and the United States Constitution prohibits P from forcing all of its people to live in certain narrowly defined family patterns.

Concurrence (Stevens, J.). The ordinance constitutes a taking of property without due process and without just compensation.

Dissent (Stewart, Rehnquist, JJ.). The constitutionally protected freedom of association relates to promotion of speech, assembly, the press, or religion, not to an interest in the gratification, convenience, and economy of sharing the same residence. D's interest in sharing the dwelling cannot be equated with the fundamental decisions to marry and to bear and raise children, as the majority has done.

Dissent (White, J.). The ordinance merely denies D the opportunity to live with her grandchildren in this particular location.

---

b. The right to marry

Zablocki v. Redhail
434 U.S. 374 (1978).

Facts. Redhail (P), a Wisconsin resident, was denied a marriage license for failure to comply with a Wisconsin statute requiring that an applicant who has a support obligation for a child not in his custody prove that the child is not a public charge and that he has complied with the support obligation. P challenged the statute and obtained declaratory and injunctive relief. Zablocki (D), the county clerk, appeals.

Issue. May a state protect the welfare of out-of-custody children by denying a marriage license to persons not fulfilling their support obligations to such children?

Held. No. Judgment affirmed.

♦ Marriage is a fundamental right, and significant interference with its exercise cannot be upheld unless closely tailored to effectuate sufficiently important state interests. Assuming that the state's interests of protecting out-of-custody children and motivating applicants to fulfill prior support obligations are valid, the means used by the state unnecessarily impinge on the right to marry. The state has numerous other effective means for exacting compliance with support obligations that do not restrict the right to marry.

Concurrence (Stewart, J.). The problem here is not discriminatory classifications but unwarranted encroachment on liberty protected by the Due Process Clause.

Concurrence (Powell, J.). The Constitution does not bar a state from conditioning the right to marry on satisfaction of existing support obligations if this condition applies to persons who are able to make the support payments but merely shirk their obligations. The problem with the statute is that it fails to provide for those without the means to comply with child support obligations.

Concurrence (Stevens, J.). This statute is different from laws prohibiting marriage to a child, a relative, or a person with a venereal disease because a person's economic status is at issue. Although strict scrutiny is not justified, this distinction between the rich and the poor is irrational.

Dissent (Rehnquist, J.). Under the traditional presumption of validity, the statute is permissible to assure the support of minor children.

---

c. Restrictions on homosexual conduct upheld

In *Bowers v. Hardwick,* 478 U.S. 186 (1986), the Court upheld a Georgia law forbidding sodomy by any person. The Court defined the issue narrowly, as applying only to homosexuals. The Court noted that prior cases had recognized a right of privacy in matters of child rearing, family relationships, procreation, contraception, and abortion. But the Court stated that none of those rights bore any resemblance to the right to engage in homosexual sodomy. Concurring, Chief Justice Burger stated that there is no such thing as a fundamental right to commit homosexual sodomy, and to hold that homosexual sodomy is protected as a fundamental right would be to cast aside firmly rooted moral teaching. Justice Powell also concurred but noted that a long prison sentence for such conduct would create an Eighth Amendment issue. Justices Brennan, Marshall, and Stevens joined in Justice Blackmun's dissent.

d. Liberty interest in homosexual conduct

Lawrence v. Texas
539 U.S. 558 (2003).

Facts. Police officers responding to a reported weapons disturbance entered an apartment where Lawrence resided. The officers found Lawrence and another man (Ds) engaging in a sexual act. Ds were arrested and convicted of "deviate sexual intercourse with a member of the same sex." Ds claimed the statute was unconstitutional under the Due Process Clause of the Fourteenth Amendment. The Texas state courts upheld the statute. The Supreme Court granted certiorari.

Issue. May a state criminalize private and consensual sexual activity between two adults of the same sex?

Held. No. Judgment reversed.

♦ In *Bowers v. Hardwick, supra,* the Court held that there was no fundamental right for homosexuals to engage in sodomy, so the Constitution did not prevent the states from making such activity illegal. This framing of the issue, however, limited the claim to the right to engage in certain sexual conduct. In reality, criminal statutes prohibiting certain sexual activity have more far-reaching consequences because they control a personal relationship that is within the liberty of persons to choose without being punished as criminals.

♦ The *Bowers* Court based its decision in part on proscriptions against homosexual conduct that have ancient roots. The historical premises relied on by the Court, however, have been reevaluated by scholars. The concept of the homosexual as being in a distinct category did not actually emerge until the late 19th century. Before that, sodomy laws were designed to prohibit non-procreative sexual activity, regardless of gender. Laws against same-sex couples were not enacted until the last third of the 20th century.

♦ The *Bowers* Court noted that societies have condemned homosexual conduct as immoral for many centuries. While many people may consider this a moral issue, the legal issue is whether the majority may use the power of the state to enforce these views on the whole society through the operation of the criminal law.

♦ In recent years, society has recognized that liberty gives substantial protection to adults in deciding how to conduct their private sex lives. The European Convention on Human Rights has been interpreted to preclude laws against consensual homosexual conduct in Europe, for example. Since the *Bowers* decision, 12 states have abandoned their laws against sodomy, and the remaining 13 states have a pattern of nonenforcement against consenting adults acting in private.

♦ *Rower v. Evans, supra,* recognized that class-based legislation directed at homosexuals violates the Equal Protection Clause. This undermines the central holding of *Bowers* because the continued validity of *Bowers* demeans the lives of homosexual persons.

♦ The erosion of *Bowers* under *Romer,* the invalidity of many of the premises upon which *Bowers* was based, and the substantial criticism of *Bowers* by the states and the European Court of Human Rights suggest that *Bowers* should be overruled. Despite the importance of stare decisis, it is time to recognize that *Bowers* was incorrectly decided and it is hereby overruled.

Concurrence (O'Connor, J.). I do not join the Court in overruling *Bowers,* but I agree that the Texas statute here is unconstitutional under the Equal Protection Clause instead of the Due Process Clause. The Texas statute prohibits sodomy between homosexual partners, but not between opposite-sex partners. This makes homosexuals unequal in the eyes of the law. Thus, the law runs contrary to the values of the Constitution and the Equal Protection Clause.

Dissent (Scalia, J., Rehnquist, C.J., Thomas, J.). The Court has strongly rejected overruling *Roe v. Wade* out of stare decisis concerns, but the very conditions the Court finds applicable to *Bowers* also apply to *Roe*. The Court now allows us to overrule precedent if: (i) its foundations have been "eroded" by subsequent decisions; (ii) it has been subject to substantial and continuing criticism; and (iii) it has not induced individual or societal reliance that counsels against overturning. The Court's reasoning in this case calls into question laws against bigamy, prostitution, adultery, and related conduct. Until today, only fundamental rights qualify for heightened scrutiny protection, and all others may be abridged if the law is rationally related to a legitimate state interest. Homosexual sodomy is not such a fundamental right. The Court today effectively decrees the end of all morals legislation by holding that majoritarian sexual morality is not even a legitimate state interest.

Dissent (Thomas, J.). The Texas law is uncommonly silly and a waste of law enforcement resources, but there is no constitutional right of privacy that invalidates such laws.

Comment. The *Lawrence* opinion is the first Supreme Court majority opinion to cite an authority from European law as a factor in the decision. The Court took judicial notice of the laws in Europe, apparently concluding that it was useful to determine the extent of the governmental interest in proscribing such conduct.

---

5. The Right to Die

a. Incompetent patient

Cruzan v. Director, Missouri Department of Health
497 U.S. 261 (1990).

Facts. Nancy Cruzan was injured in an automobile accident and entered a persistent vegetative state, her body kept functioning by artificial nutrition and hydration procedures. Her parents (Ps) asked that the medical procedures be terminated, which would cause Nancy's death. When the hospital employees refused to do so without a court order, Ps sued the Director of the Missouri Department of Health (D) on Nancy's behalf. At the trial, one of Nancy's friends testified that Nancy had said, prior to her accident, that she would not want to live if she became a vegetable. Based on this evidence, the trial court granted Ps relief. The Missouri Supreme Court reversed on the ground that the evidence was insufficient to constitute clear and convincing proof of Nancy's desire to have hydration and nutrition withdrawn. The Supreme Court granted certiorari.

Issue. May a state require proof by clear and convincing evidence of an incompetent patient's wishes as to the withdrawal of life-sustaining medical treatment?

Held. Yes. Judgment affirmed.

◆ The common law doctrine of informed consent to medical procedures, developed out of the law of battery, includes the right of a competent individual to refuse medical treatment. This right is a constitutionally protected liberty interest, and it may be assumed that a competent person has a constitutionally protected right to refuse lifesaving hydration and nutrition, but this right must be balanced against the relevant state interests.

◆ Ps assert that an incompetent person should have the same right as a competent person to refuse lifesaving medical procedures. However, the incompetent person cannot by definition exercise this right; it must be exercised on her behalf by someone else. Missouri has determined that a surrogate may act on behalf of an incompetent patient, but only if there is clear and convincing evidence of the incompetent's wishes as to the withdrawal of the treatment.

◆ Missouri has an important interest in the protection and preservation of human life. In this case, the choice between life and death is a deeply personal decision, and the state may safeguard the personal element by requiring a high standard of proof. The state has placed the increased risk of an erroneous decision on those seeking to terminate the incompetent patient's life, and this does not violate the Constitution.

♦ Nor is the state required by the Constitution to defer to the "substituted judgment" of Ps, even though in other cases the Court has permitted state schemes in which parents make decisions for minors.

Concurrence (O'Connor, J.). The Constitution may require a state to give effect to the decisions of a surrogate decisionmaker, but that issue is not decided in this case.

Concurrence (Scalia, J.). The states, not the Constitution or the Supreme Court, have the power to prevent suicide, and the citizens of Missouri must decide whether to honor the wishes of a patient who wants life-sustaining medical procedures to be withdrawn. The Due Process Clause only protects against deprivation of liberty without due process of law. The Constitution says nothing about the alleged desire to die. The limits that ought not to be exceeded in requiring an individual to preserve her own life are not set forth in the Due Process Clause, but are to be determined by the democratic majority. The Equal Protection Clause, which requires the majority to accept for themselves what they impose on others, assures that the appropriate limits are not exceeded, whatever those limits are.

Dissent (Brennan, Marshall, Blackmun, JJ.). The liberty interest in being free of unwanted medical treatment is fundamental, and no state interest can outweigh the rights of a person in Nancy's position. Missouri does have a general interest in preserving life, but this does not outweigh an individual's choice to avoid medical treatment. Missouri, as parens patriae for the incompetent Nancy Cruzan, also has an interest in safeguarding the accuracy of the determination of her wishes. But by imposing a heightened evidentiary standard, Missouri has excluded relevant evidence and moved away from an accurate determination. Instead of protecting life, Missouri has defined life as the biological persistence of Nancy's bodily functions. There is no reasonable ground to believe that she has any personal interest in the perpetuation of what Missouri has decided is her life. In cases such as this, the best interests of all related third parties should prevail over Missouri's general state policy that ignores those interests.

---

b. Assisted suicide

In most states, patients may refuse even lifesaving medical treatment, or accept pain medication that can hasten death, but it is a crime to aid another to commit or attempt suicide. Many physicians assert that the assisted suicide ban prevents them from providing lethal medication for mentally competent, terminally ill patients who are suffering great pain and desire a doctor's help in taking their own lives, although it would be consistent with the standards of their medical practices to provide this type of service.

1) Due process analysis

Washington v. Glucksberg
521 U.S. 702 (1997).

Facts. Washington (D) enacted a statute that prohibited assisting suicide. Glucksberg and other physicians (Ps) occasionally treated terminally ill, suffering patients and would assist these patients in ending their lives if not for D's ban on assisted suicide. Ps brought suit seeking a declaration that the statute violates the Fourteenth Amendment, because Ps' patients have a liberty interest in a personal choice to commit physician-assisted suicide. The district court held the statute unconstitutional. The court of appeals initially reversed, but after an en banc hearing, affirmed the district court. The Supreme Court granted certiorari.

Issue. Is there a constitutional right to assistance in committing suicide?

Held. No. Judgment reversed.

♦ It is a crime to assist a suicide in almost every state and almost every western democracy. This reflects the states' commitment to protect and preserve all human life. For over 700 years, the Anglo-American common law tradition has punished both suicide and assisting suicide.

♦ In modern times, the states' bans on assisted suicide have been reexamined and mostly reaffirmed. There have been modifications to reflect current medical technology, which can prolong life. For example, states permit "living wills," surrogate health care decisionmaking, and withdrawal or refusal of life-sustaining medical treatment. However, the states continue to prohibit assisted suicide. D's voters rejected a ballot initiative that would have permitted a form of physician-assisted suicide.

♦ The Court has previously applied the Due Process Clause so as to protect the right to marry, have children, educate one's children, enjoy marital privacy, use contraception, and have abortions. Under *Cruzan,* the Clause protects the traditional right to refuse unwanted lifesaving medical treatment. However, the extension of constitutional protection to an asserted right or liberty interest is only appropriate for those areas that are rooted in the nation's history and tradition, and even then only where there is a careful description of the asserted fundamental liberty interest.

♦ To recognize the right asserted by Ps, the Court would have to reverse centuries of legal doctrine and practice, including the policy choices of almost every state. In contrast, the right to refuse medication recognized in *Cruzan* reflected a long legal tradition. Forced medication was a battery at common law.

♦ Given that the right to assisted suicide is not a fundamental liberty interest, the Constitution still requires that D's ban be rationally related to legitimate government interests. That is satisfied here, where D has an interest in the preservation of human life, an interest in protecting the integrity and ethics of the medical profession, an interest in protecting vulnerable groups, and an interest in not opening the door to euthanasia, both voluntary and involuntary.

Concurrence (O'Connor, J.). There is no generalized right to "commit suicide." However, a terminal patient who suffers great pain may obtain medication to alleviate that suffering, even to the point of hastening death. The state's interest in protecting those who are not truly competent or facing imminent death is sufficiently weighty to justify a prohibition against physician-assisted suicide. The democratic process will strike the proper balance in this area.

Concurrence (Stevens, J.). The value to others of a person's life is far too precious to allow the individual to claim a constitutional entitlement to complete autonomy in making a decision to end that life. But there may be situations where the individual's interest in choosing how to die might be paramount.

Concurrence (Souter, J.). The appropriate test would be to determine whether D's statute sets up an arbitrary imposition or a purposeless restraint contrary to the Due Process Clause. Substantive due process analysis requires a court to assess the relative weights of the contending interests. Statutes must give way when the legislation's justifying principle is so far from being commensurate with the individual interest as to be arbitrary or pointless. This case involves the right of a narrow class to help others in a narrow class under a set of limited circumstances. Ps note that D has largely repudiated the common law of suicide by decriminalizing suicide. A right to physician assistance in committing suicide is analogous to the right to physician assistance in abortion. D already allows doctors to administer pain relief medication that may hasten death. D could address its legitimate interests through a regulatory system. Ps propose state regulation "with teeth" to avoid some of the problems with assisted suicide; however, the Netherlands already uses such guidelines and there is evidence that there have been cases of involuntary euthanasia in that country.

Concurrence (Ginsburg, J.). I concur for the same reasons as Justice O'Connor.

Concurrence (Breyer, J.). Justice O'Connor's approach is persuasive. There may be a right to die with dignity, or a right to personal control over the manner of death, professional medical assistance, and the avoidance of unnecessary and severe physical suffering. Changes in medical technology may affect these types of cases in the future.

Comment. The Court noted that, at one time, Oregon voters enacted a ballot initiative that legalized physician-assisted suicide. This prompted proposals in many other states. The Court specifically noted that its decision would allow the debate about physician-assisted suicide to continue. In *Vacco v. Quill,* 521 U.S. 793 (1997), decided the same time as *Glucksberg,* the Court held that a ban on physician-assisted suicide does not violate the Equal Protection Clause.

G. Procedural Due Process

1. Due Process and Entitlements

a. Introduction

Both the Fifth and Fourteenth Amendments protect against the deprivation of "life, liberty, or property" without due process of law. Although due process was traditionally used most often to provide procedural safeguards for criminal defendants, it also protects a range of liberty and property interests outside the criminal context. The liberty and property interests of which persons cannot be deprived without due process do not turn upon whether the interest involved is a "right" rather than a "privilege." Such a definitional approach has been rejected by the Court. The scope of liberty and property rights protected by due process, however, has not always been easy to describe.

1) Liberty

It is clear that "liberty" connotes more than freedom from the bodily restraints imposed by the criminal process. It includes at least the right to contract, to engage in gainful employment, and "generally to enjoy those privileges long recognized at common law as essential to the orderly pursuit of happiness by free men."

2) Property

Similarly, "property" includes more than just actual ownership of realty, chattels, or money. It includes "interests already acquired in specific benefits." However, there must be more than a mere abstract need or desire for, or unilateral expectation of, the benefit. The Constitution does not create property interests; there must be a legitimate claim to an existing interest already derived from state or federal law. Thus there is a property interest in public education when school attendance is required [Goss v. Lopez, 419 U.S. 565 (1975)], in retention of a driver's license under prevailing statutory standards [Bell v. Burson, 402 U.S. 535 (1971)], and in having continued utility service where state law permits a municipal utility company to terminate service only "for cause" [Memphis Light, Gas & Water Division v. Craft, 436 U.S. 1 (1978)].

b. Procedural due process requirements

Procedural safeguards against invasion of private liberty and property rights have gained increased attention in recent years. The Court applies a two-pronged test. The first question is whether the implicated right is a constitutionally protected interest in life, liberty, or property. If so, the courts must examine the procedural safeguards to determine their constitutional adequacy.

c. Welfare benefits

In *Goldberg v. Kelly,* 397 U.S. 254 (1970), the Court held that welfare benefits are an entitlement. By definition, a person entitled to receive welfare needs welfare assistance for essentials such as food, clothing, housing, and medical care. Termination of benefits despite a controversy over eligibility may deprive an eligible recipient of the necessities of life. The same governmental interests behind the welfare program also support its continuation to eligible recipients. These interests are not outweighed by the need to conserve governmental fiscal and administrative resources; the latter interests are not overriding in the welfare context. Thus, welfare benefits may not be terminated without due process.

d. Public employment

Whether there is a "property" interest in continued public employment is determined by state (or federal) law. A statute (or ordinance), the employment contract, or some clear practice or understanding must provide that the employee can be terminated only for "cause." [Arnett v. Kennedy, 416 U.S. 134 (1974)] There is no "property" interest if the position is held "at the will of the public employer. [Bishop v. Wood, 426 U.S. 341 (1976)]

1) No right to be rehired

Board of Regents of State Colleges v. Roth
408 U.S. 564 (1972).

Facts. Roth (P) was hired as a teacher in a public university for a fixed term of one academic year. He was not rehired and was given no reason for the decision. State law allows tenure only after four years' employment and leaves hiring decisions for nontenured teachers to the discretion of university officials. P sued the Board of Regents (D), claiming that he was deprived of liberty and property without a constitutionally required hearing. The lower courts held for P, and D appeals.

Issue. Does a government employee have a constitutional right to a statement of reasons and a hearing on his employer's decision not to rehire him?

Held. No. Judgment reversed.

♦ Liberty and property interests protected by the Fourteenth Amendment are broadly construed, but not infinite. To have a property interest in a benefit, a person must have more man a unilateral expectation of it. He must have a legitimate claim of entitlement to it. For example, a person receiving welfare benefits under statutory and administrative standards defining eligibility for them has an interest in continued receipt of those benefits that is safeguarded by procedural due process.

♦ Property interests are not created by the Constitution but by independent sources, such as state law, that also define their dimensions. P here was given no specific contractual interest in being rehired, nor did state law recognize any such property interest. P has only an abstract concern in being rehired, which cannot be considered a property interest to be protected by the Fourteenth Amendment. Therefore the Constitution does not require that P be given a hearing before not being rehired.

Dissent (Marshall, J.). Every citizen is entitled to every government job he applies for unless the government can establish a reason for denying employment. This entitlement is a property right protected by the Fourteenth Amendment. It is also liberty to work, which is likewise protected.

Comment. A plaintiff can establish a prima facie case by showing that the government had an improper purpose that was a motivating factor in its decision not to rehire, which the government can rebut only by showing it would have made the same decision even were the improper purpose not present.

---

2) Implied contractual rights

In *Perry v. Sindermann,* 408 U.S. 593 (1972), the contract of a professor at a state junior college had not been renewed. The professor, who had worked at the college for several years, claimed that the college had a de facto tenure program. The Court held that the college's lack of a formal contractual tenure provision did not foreclose the possibility that the professor had a property interest that could not be taken away without due process.

3) Property interest in public job

Cleveland Board of Education v. Loudermill
470 U.S. 532 (1985).

Facts. Loudermill (P) was hired as a security guard by the Cleveland Board of Education (D). He had indicated on his application that he had never been convicted of a felony, but 11 months later D discovered that he had been convicted of grand larceny. D fired P by letter, citing his dishonesty. Under state law, P could only be fired for cause. P claimed the manner of his dismissal violated his due process rights. The lower courts agreed, and the Supreme Court granted certiorari.

Issue. Is a public employee who may only be terminated for cause entitled to a hearing before being terminated?

Held. Yes. Judgment affirmed.

♦ Property interests are protected by, but not created by, the Constitution. P clearly had a property interest here because under state law he could not be dismissed except for cause.

♦ D claims that because state law created the property interest, P's property right is conditioned on the legislature's choice of procedure for the termination of the right. While this notion once was accepted by the Court in *Arnett v. Kennedy, supra,* it is no longer the law. Instead, under the Due Process Clause, once a property right exists, it cannot be taken away except pursuant to constitutionally adequate procedures.

Dissent (Rehnquist, J.). The state created a limited right in employment, a type of tenure, and set forth the procedure for termination of the tenure. The majority is disregarding this limitation on P's property interest.

---

e. Liberty

In *Paul v. Davis,* 424 U.S. 693 (1976), the Court held that the plaintiff suffered no deprivation of liberty as a result of his identification as an active shoplifter in a flyer produced by the local police and distributed to local merchants. Defamation resulting only in damage to one's reputation was held not to be a denial of protected "liberty." As a result, the definition of liberty was assumed to depend on state determinations.

f. Use of rational basis standard

In an unusual set of concurring opinions, the majority of the Court held that a state scheme that permitted a hearing on an employment discrimination complaint only if processed within 120 days violated equal protection because the limitation was not rationally related to any legitimate governmental objective. [Logan v. Zimmerman Brush Co., 455 U.S. 422 (1982)]

2. Determination of What Process is Due

a. Introduction

In recent years, the courts have given increased attention to the actual procedural safeguards against invasion of private liberty and property rights. Once the existence of a constitutionally protected interest in life, liberty, or property is established, the courts must examine the adequacy of the procedures afforded. The courts must weigh the following factors to determine the extent of the procedures required:

1) The importance of the individual interest involved;

2) The value of specific procedural safeguards to that interest; and

3) The governmental interest in fiscal and administrative efficiency.

b. Weighing test

Mathews v. Eldridge
424 U.S. 319 (1976).

Facts. Eldridge (P) was awarded Social Security disability insurance benefits in 1968. About four years later the state agency that administered the benefits determined, based on medical reports, that P's disability terminated. The agency so notified P by letter, and after receiving a written rebuttal from P, terminated P's benefits. Rather than seek reconsideration, P sued, seeking an immediate reinstatement of benefits pending a hearing on the issue of his disability. The lower courts, relying on *Goldberg v. Kelly, supra,* upheld P's claim. The Supreme Court granted certiorari.

Issue. Is a recipient of disability insurance benefits entitled to an evidentiary hearing prior to the initial termination of benefits?

Held. No. Judgment reversed.

♦ The requirements of due process vary depending on the particular circumstances involved. In setting forth the constitutional requirements, courts must balance the private interest affected, together with the risk of an erroneous deprivation and the added value of additional procedural safeguards, against the government's interest.

♦ P's sole interest is in continuing payments, because if upon reconsideration he prevails, he will receive full retroactive relief. Unlike in *Goldberg,* a disabled person has other sources of income; disability payments are not based on financial need. Welfare benefits are available if the termination of disability places P below the subsistence level. Thus, P's interest is significant, but less than was at issue in *Goldberg,*

♦ The administrative pretermination procedures are less likely to err in disability cases as opposed to welfare cases because in the former, only medical records are involved. Welfare cases require consideration of a variety of factors. P was notified and given a chance to respond before benefits were terminated. An oral evidentiary hearing would add little.

♦ Finally, the government's interest in conserving resources must be considered, even though financial cost is not the controlling factor. Weight must be given to the good-faith judgments of those who administer the disability programs.

Dissent (Brennan, Marshall, JJ.). The legislative decision to provide disability benefits assumes a financial need the majority ignores. In fact, after his benefits were terminated, P's home and furniture were repossessed; P and his entire family had to sleep in one bed.

———————

c. Irrebuttable presumptions

The use of irrebuttable presumptions as to membership in a class may deny equal protection to individuals who meet the class qualifications but whose particular situations are divergent from the legislative purpose for the classification. Such persons have a right to a hearing to rebut the presumption of class membership.

H. The Contracts and Takings Clauses

1. The Contracts Clause

Article I, Section 10 of the Constitution provides that "no state shall pass any law impairing the obligation of contracts." Note that the Contracts Clause applies only to the states; there is no mention in the Constitution of a similar prohibition against the federal government. However, the Court has held that the Due Process Clause of the Fifth Amendment is broad enough to extend a similar prohibition to federal action. [Lynch v. United States, 292 U.S. 571 (1934)] The term "impairs" includes a substantial invalidation, release, or extinguishment of the obligation of a contract. "Obligation" includes the existing legal rules as well as the terms of the contract itself. This does not mean that the law can never change, but legitimate expectations of the parties cannot be impaired.

a. Development of Contracts Clause doctrine

The Contracts Clause was a major restraint on state economic regulation in the 19th century. It applied to both private and public contracts. More recently, the Court has applied a balancing test. Not all substantial impairments of contracts are unconstitutional. Private parties may not claim immunity from state regulation through private contractual arrangements. Rights and duties may be modified by legislation necessary to an important and legitimate public interest as long as the impairment of the contract is reasonable.

b. Basic requirements for a valid impairment

Home Building & Loan Association v. Blaisdell
290 U.S. 398 (1934).

Facts. Minnesota passed a law that permitted extensions of the period of redemption from a foreclosure and sale of real property under a mortgage. The Blaisdells (Ds) obtained such an extension. Home Building & Loan (P) challenged the extension as improper state interference in a private contract. The state defended the law as needed emergency legislation to deal with the Depression. The state courts upheld the law, and P appeals.

Issue. May a state alter existing contractual obligations in order to respond to emergency conditions?

Held. Yes. Judgment affirmed.

♦ An emergency does not create power, but it may justify the exercise of existing power. As maintenance of government is essential to having enforceable contracts, circumstances may arise when exercise of the police power to alter contracts is justified in order to maintain effective government.

♦ Legislation impairing contracts may be upheld when:

(i) The state legislature declares that an emergency exists;

(ii) The state law is enacted to protect a basic societal interest, not a favored group;

(iii) The relief is appropriately tailored to the declared emergency;

(iv) The imposed conditions are reasonable; and

(v) The legislation is limited to the duration of the emergency.

♦ The statute at issue here meets all five of the requirements and is therefore constitutional.

Dissent (Sutherland, Van Devanter, McReynolds, Butler, JJ.). The history of the Contracts Clause is clear: no state may act to impair the obligation of contracts, even where such action is to give relief to debtors, especially during a time of emergency.

———————

c. State obligations

United States Trust Co. v. New Jersey
431 U.S. 1 (1977).

Facts. New York and New Jersey (Ds) formed the New York and New Jersey Port Authority by interstate compact. In 1962, both states passed statutes prohibiting financing of passenger railroad facilities with revenues pledged to pay the authority's bonds, unless the facility was self-supporting. In 1974, the states retroactively repealed the 1962 covenant in order to permit greater subsidizing of mass transit. United States Trust Company (P), trustee and holder of Authority bonds, challenged the 1974 law on Contracts Clause grounds. The state courts upheld the 1974 law, and P appeals.

Issue. May a state impair the obligation of its own contracts, based on its own determination of reasonableness and necessity?

Held. No. Judgment reversed.

♦ Complete deference to a legislative assessment of reasonableness and necessity is not appropriate if the state's self-interest is at stake. Allowing a state to reduce its financial obligations whenever it wants to spend *the* money for what it regards as an important public purpose would negate all Contract Clause protection.

♦ Although mass transit, energy conservation, and environmental protection are important goals of legitimate public concern, we will not engage in a utilitarian comparison of public benefit and private loss to bondholders from the repeal of the covenant. A state cannot refuse to meet its legitimate financial obligations just because it would rather spend the money to promote the public good rather than the private welfare of its creditors.

♦ Total repeal of the covenant was not necessary; a less drastic modification would have served Ds' twin goals of discouraging automobile use and improving mass transit. And without even modifying the covenant at all, Ds could have adopted alternative means of achieving their goals.

Dissent (Brennan, White, Marshall, JJ.). Each generation of representatives is responsive to the needs and desires of those whom they represent. The Contract Clause is primarily a protection for economic transactions entered into by private parties. This does not mean that states should repudiate their obligations, financial or otherwise. But here P's financial welfare is being adequately policed by the political processes and the bond marketplace itself.

———————

d. Private obligations

Allied Structural Steel Co. v. Spannaus
438 U.S. 234 (1978).

Facts. Allied Structural Steel Company (P) established a pension plan, pursuant to IRS regulations, which provided that qualifying employees would acquire pension rights, but which gave no assurance that any employee would not be dismissed at any time. P had an office in Minnesota that it began to close. A few months previously, Minnesota had passed a law that subjected employers to a "pension funding charge" upon termination of a pension plan or closing of a Minnesota office. The law had the effect of making several of P's otherwise unqualified employees pension obligees, resulting in a charge to P of $185,000. P sued Spannaus (D), a Minnesota official, for injunctive and declaratory relief. The federal district court held the act valid. P appeals, claiming that the law violates the Contracts Clause.

Issue. Does the Contracts Clause preclude state legislation that significantly expands duties created by private contract?

Held. Yes. Judgment reversed.

♦ The Contracts Clause limits a state's ability to abridge existing contractual relationships. The first query is whether the state law has substantially impaired a contractual relationship. The challenged law nullifies express terms of P's contractual obligations and imposes a completely unexpected liability in potentially disabling amounts. Such severe impairment may be condoned only if justified by the need for the law.

♦ Unlike the law challenged in *Home Building & Loan Association v. Blaisdell, supra,* the law here is directed at a narrow class—those employers with voluntary private pension plans who either terminate the plan or close the Minnesota office. Nor was the law intended to deal with a broad and desperate economic emergency. It did not just temporarily change the contractual rights and duties, but imposed a permanent and immediate change.

Dissent (Brennan, White, Marshall, JJ.). The Act creates an additional, supplemental duty of the employer but does not relieve either the employer or his employees of any existing contract obligation. Thus, the Act does not implicate the Contract Clause in any way.

---

e. Modern trend

Despite the apparent revival of the Contracts Clause in *United States Trust Co. v. New Jersey* and *Allied Structural Steel Co. v. Spannaus, supra,* the Court has at times deferred to state power. In *Energy Reserves Group v. Kansas Power & Light,* 459 U.S. 400 (1983), the Court applied a three-part test. If the state substantially impairs a contractual relationship, it must have a significant and legitimate public purpose for so doing. If it does, and the contractual adjustment is reasonable and appropriate, the courts will defer to the state unless the state itself is a party to the contract. In *Exxon Corp. v. Eagerton,* 462 U.S. 176 (1983), the Court rejected a Contracts Clause challenge to a law that prohibited oil and gas producers from passing through to purchasers an increase in the severance tax, thereby preventing producers from taking advantage of existing contract provisions for such a pass-through. The Court held that the alleged impairment of contractual obligations was incidental to a generally applicable rule of conduct and not a direct attack on the original contracts. The law applied to all producers, not just those with pass-through provisions in their contracts. The law was not constitutionally different from laws regulating rates, which override contractual prices.

2. The Eminent Domain Clause

The governmental power to require a private landowner to convey his land to the government for public purposes is referred to as the power of "eminent domain." Although the Constitution does not specifically grant a power of eminent domain to the federal government, the power is implied. The Fifth Amendment provides in part that private property may not be "taken" for "public use" without just compensation. This clause is a restriction on both the federal and state power of eminent domain. Property rights may include tangible and intangible interests.

a. Meanings of terms

The two most troublesome constitutional issues here are the meanings of the terms "public use" and "taking."

1) Public use

The government may exercise its power of eminent domain only for a public use. This term is broadly defined by the Court. If the asserted use of the property is rationally related to a conceivable, articulated public purpose, the Court will defer to the legislative findings.

a) Scope of "public use"

In *Berman v. Parker,* 348 U.S. 26 (1954), the Supreme Court upheld the use of eminent domain by Congress to redevelop a slum area in the District of Columbia. State legislatures have used the eminent domain power to assist in commercial and industrial development as well, finding public use in the need to provide employment and tax bases for the localities involved. In *Hawaii Housing Authority v. Midkiff,* 467 U.S. 229 (1984), the Court upheld Hawaii's statute authorizing it to take title (with compensation) to large estates of land, of which ownership was concentrated in a few owners. The state then transferred title to the tenants living on smaller individual lots on the estates. A rational relationship to a conceivable public purpose is all the state need show. Federal courts may not second-guess legislative determinations in this area as long as the power is not used for a purely private purpose. In *Midkiff,* the state was attempting to reduce social and economic evils of a land oligopoly that interfered with the normal functioning of its residential land market.

2) Taking

Government action may affect property rights without constituting a taking. Mere regulation that limits the use of the property, such as zoning laws, is not normally considered a taking under the Fifth Amendment. The Court merely determines whether justice and fairness require that the public compensate the private owner for the loss. The particular facts of each case are determinative.

b. Compensation requirement

Pennsylvania Coal Co. v. Mahon
260 U.S. 393 (1922).

Facts. In 1878, Mahon (P) received title to the surface rights of a parcel of land from Pennsylvania Coal Company (D), which reserved the right to remove the coal under the surface. P also waived all claims for damages resulting from removal of the coal. D gave notice of intent to mine. P, knowing that D's activity would cause a subsidence of the surface and of P's house, sought an injunction based on a state statute that forbids coal mining in such a way as to cause subsidence of any human habitation. The lower court denied an injunction. The state supreme court held the statute a valid exercise of police power and granted an injunction. D appeals.

Issue. May a state exercise its police power to destroy previously existing property and contract rights without paying compensation?

Held. No. Judgment reversed.

♦ The general rule is that while the use of property may be regulated to a certain extent, if regulation goes too far it will be recognized as a "taking." One factor is the extent of the diminution in value of the property. Here, the statute would totally divest D of its properly reserved right to mine coal. Another factor is the extent of the public interest. Here, a single private house is involved, with no threat to personal safety since adequate notice was given.

♦ While there may be no doubt as to the need for the statute, the question is, who should pay for the changes initiated by the law? D's loss should not go uncompensated. The state may achieve its objectives properly only through eminent domain procedures. When private persons or communities take the risk of acquiring only surface rights, they ought not be given greater rights than they bought merely because their risk has become an actuality.

Dissent (Brandeis, J.). Every restriction abridges property rights. Here, D is merely prohibited from a noxious use. Future events may render the use harmless; it is merely a temporary restriction and need not be compensated for by the government.

---

c. Taking without compensation

Miller v. Schoene
276 U.S. 272 (1928).

Facts. A Virginia statute provided for the condemnation and destruction of red cedar trees infected by cedar rust, and made it illegal for any person to "own, plant or keep alive and standing" on his premises any red cedar tree that is or may be the source or "host plant" of the communicable plant disease known as cedar rust, and any such tree growing within a certain radius of any apple orchard is declared to be a public nuisance, subject to destruction. The statute also required the state entomologist, upon determining that red cedar trees are located within two miles of an apple orchard, to direct the owner to destroy the trees. Schoene (P), the state entomologist, required Miller (D) to destroy his cedar trees. D refused, and P obtained a court order requiring D to destroy them. The court did award D $100 to cover the expense of removal, but did not allow compensation for the value of the standing cedars or the decrease in the market value of the realty caused by their destruction. The state appellate courts upheld the judgment. D appealed.

Issue. May a state require the destruction of private trees without compensation if the trees present a danger of infection of nearby commercial orchards?

Held. Yes. Judgment affirmed.

♦ Presented with the threat of cedar rust, the state had to make a choice between preserving one class of property or another. If the state had done nothing, it would have permitted serious injury to the apple orchards. In such a situation, the state may properly exercise its power to require the destruction of one class of property to save another class of property that has greater value to the public.

♦ When the public interest is involved, it is a common exercise of the police power to prefer the public interest over the private interest. The statute in this case does not deny D due process.

---

d. Taking through regulation

Penn Central Transportation Co. v. New York City
438 U.S. 104 (1978).

Facts. Penn Central (P) owned the Grand Central Terminal in New York City (D). The terminal was designated a "landmark" under the City Landmarks Preservation Law, which prohibited destruction of designated landmarks. P was denied permission to alter the terminal solely because of the landmarks law, which P then challenged as an unconstitutional taking. The trial court granted P relief, but the higher state courts all held for D. P appeals.

Issue. May a city restrict development of individual historic landmarks, beyond applicable zoning regulations, without a "taking" requiring payment of just compensation?

Held. Yes. Judgment affirmed.

♦ The question here revolves around two basic considerations: the nature and extent of the impact on P and the character of the governmental action.

♦ The taking may not be established merely by showing a government-imposed inability to further develop a property, nor solely by a diminution in property value. Zoning laws have these effects yet are constitutional because they are part of a comprehensive plan for achieving a significant public purpose, as is D's law.

♦ P claims the law is discriminatory and arbitrary. Yet numerous other structures are likewise under the landmark regulations. Even if P does not receive benefits to completely offset its burdens, valid zoning laws may have a similar effect. If P finds application of the law to be arbitrary, it may obtain judicial review of any commission decision.

♦ The government has not taken P's airspace for its own purpose, but for the benefit of the entire public. It has done so pursuant to a legitimate interest in preserving special buildings.

♦ Finally, the impact on P is mitigated by the existence of transferable development rights and by the fact that P has not been prohibited from making any improvements, but only the two drastic proposals that were rejected by D. Thus, P may be permitted the use of at least some portion of its airspace.

Dissent (Rehnquist, J., Burger, C.J., Stevens, J.). A literal interpretation of the Fifth Amendment would clearly favor P. Even the Court's more relaxed view should result in a decision for P. Clearly valuable property rights have been destroyed. A taking need not be a physical seizure. Destruction of rights is a taking, except in two instances: prohibition of nuisances and prohibitions covering broad areas that secure an average reciprocity of advantage, such as zoning laws. Neither exception applies here. The people generally, not P individually, ought to pay the cost of the recognized public benefit of having P's property preserved.

Comment. In *Loretto v. Teleprompter Manhattan CATV Corp.*, 458 U.S. 419 (1982), the Court held that any permanent physical intrusion by the government is a taking requiring compensation. This rule applies regardless of the state's interest or the economic impact on the owner. The *Loretto* case involved a New York statute authorizing permanent cable TV installations for tenants of privately owned apartment houses. The tenant merely had to pay a one-time fee to the landlord of $1. The dissenting Justices noted that nonphysical government intrusions often diminish the value of property more than minor physical intrusions, and that therefore a per se rule for physical intrusion was inappropriate.

---

e. Extensive limitation on mining rights

Keystone Bituminous Coal Association v. DeBenedictis
480 U.S. 470 (1987).

Facts. A Pennsylvania statute intended to prevent or minimize subsidence of surface land caused by coal mining required 50% of the coal under specified structures to remain in place for surface support. The Keystone Bituminous Coal Association (P) challenged the statute as an unconstitutional taking. P's members had acquired the mineral rights and support estates from landowners who retained only the surface estate. The statute would significantly reduce the amount of coal that could be mined. The district court found for DeBenedictis (D), and the court of appeals affirmed. The Supreme Court granted certiorari.

Issue. May a state prohibit, without compensation, the mining of coal that would have the effect of causing subsidence of surface land?

Held. Yes. Judgment affirmed.

♦ A land use regulation will be deemed a taking if it: (i) does not substantially advance legitimate state interests, or (ii) denies an owner economically viable use of his land. For example, *Pennsylvania Coal Co. v. Mahon, supra,* relied on the premise that the act protected only private interests and made it commercially impracticable to mine coal in the affected areas. The statute in this case does not suffer from these deficiencies.

♦ The statute has a clear public purpose—the protection of health, environment, and fiscal integrity to support the tax base. Also, P has not claimed or shown that the statute makes it commercially impracticable for its members to continue mining their coal.

---

f. Public access to property through private property

Nollan v. California Coastal Commission
483 U.S. 825 (1987).

Facts. The Nollans (Ps) purchased a beachfront lot in southern California on the condition that they replace the existing structure with a new one. Ps applied to the California Coastal Commission (D) for permission to build a home like the others in the neighborhood, but D required Ps to grant a public easement across their property along the ocean. Ps sued and won a judgment. D appealed, but meanwhile Ps built the house. The state court of appeals reversed, and Ps appeal.

Issue. If a state may not require uncompensated conveyance of an easement over private property, may it require the conveyance as a condition to its approval of a land use permit for the property?

Held. No. Judgment reversed.

♦ It is clear that if D had simply required Ps to grant a public easement across their property, there would have been a taking. Such an easement constitutes a permanent physical occupation, and the right to exclude others is an essential stick in the bundle of rights that constitutes property.

♦ A land use regulation is permissible if it substantially advances legitimate state interests and does not deny an owner economically viable use of his land. If a condition is imposed short of an outright ban on construction, it must serve the same governmental purpose as the ban would. Otherwise, the condition is not a valid land use regulation but extortion.

Dissent (Brennan, Marshall, JJ.). The Court should defer to the state as long as the state rationally could have decided that the control used might achieve the state's objective. Instead, the majority has applied an inappropriately narrow concept of rationality. In fact, there is a reasonable relationship between the condition and the specific burden Ps' development imposes on public access. At any rate, the restriction is a minimal burden and the development increased the value of Ps' property much more than any diminution attributable to the easement.

Comment. Local governments have traditionally required developers to dedicate streets and utility easements within subdivisions, and frequently also require certain improvements that benefit the subdivision exclusively, such as paved streets or on-site utility facilities. In addition, some governments have required dedication of land for parks and schools, or a payment of money to develop parks and schools. Some courts disallow such requirements as not sufficiently attributable to the developer's activity to remove public responsibility for such improvements.

---

g. Complete destruction of property value

Lucas v. South Carolina Coastal Council
505 U.S. 1003 (1992).

Facts. Lucas (P) purchased two residential lots near the seashore, intending to build single-family homes. Two years later, South Carolina passed the Beachfront Management Act, which required P to obtain a permit from the South Carolina Coastal Council (D) before changing the use of his land. This effectively barred P from building homes on his land. P sued, and the trial court found that he was entitled to compensation because his property was now valueless. The South Carolina Supreme Court reversed, and the United States Supreme Court granted certiorari.

Issue. Must the government compensate a private landowner if the government's regulation prohibits all economically productive or beneficial uses of the land?

Held. Yes. Judgment reversed.

♦ In *Pennsylvania Coal Co. v. Mahon, supra,* the Court held that the Takings Clause extended beyond direct appropriations of property to regulations that go "too far." There are at least two categories of regulatory action that are compensable: (i) physical invasions, *e.g.,* requiring landlords to allow television cable companies to put cable in their apartment buildings [*see* Loretto v. Teleprompter Manhattan CATV Corp., *supra*]; and (ii) denial of all economically beneficial or productive use of land.

♦ The functional basis for allowing the government, without making compensation, to affect property values through regulation is the recognition that the government could not operate if it had to pay for every change in the law that affected property values, but this basis does not apply when the government deprives a landowner of all economically beneficial uses. Such regulation really presses the private property into a form of public service under the guise of mitigating serious public harm.

♦ P claims that the finding that his property has been rendered valueless requires compensation, regardless of the reason for the regulation. Prior opinions held that harmful or noxious uses of property may be proscribed by government regulation without compensation, but this really means that land-use regulation does not effect a taking if it "substantially advances legitimate state interests." But D cannot take land without compensation merely by reciting a noxious-use or benefit-conferring rationale. D could avoid paying compensation only if the nature of P's estate shows that the proscribed use interests were not part of his title to begin with; *i.e.,* that his bundle of rights did not include an expectation that the state would not eliminate all economically valuable use.

♦ Confiscatory regulations cannot be newly legislated without compensation; they must inhere in the title itself, in the restrictions that background principles of the state's law of property and nuisance already place on land ownership. The fact that a particular use has long been engaged in by similarly situated owners, or that other landowners similarly situated are permitted to continue the use denied to P, demonstrates a lack of any common law prohibition on the use. In this case, it is unlikely that common law principles would have prevented P from building a house on the land, but this must be determined on remand.

Concurrence (Kennedy, J.). Where a regulation deprives the property of all value, whether it is a taking depends on whether the deprivation is contrary to reasonable, investment-backed expectations. The state supreme court erred in not evaluating P's reasonable expectations. And D did not act until after the property had been zoned for residential development and other parcels had been built on, so that the remaining lots have to bear the entire burden of the regulation.

Dissent (Blackmun, J.). The state may prevent any use of property it finds to be harmful to its citizens, and a state statute is entitled to a presumption of constitutionality. The record supports D's assessment that the building restriction is necessary to protect people and property, and the Court has departed from traditional rules by creating a new scheme for regulations that eliminate all economic value.

Dissent (Stevens, J.). The Court's new categorical rule is arbitrary since it distinguishes between a landowner whose property is diminished in value 95% and who recovers nothing, and a landowner whose property is diminished in value 100% and recovers its full value. The reliance on a common law exception prevents the states from developing the common law in response to new learning, such as the significance of endangered species and wetlands.

---

h. Preexisting regulations

Palazzolo v. Rhode Island
533 U.S. 606 (2001).

Facts. In 1959, Palazzolo (P) formed a corporation with some associates and purchased a parcel of waterfront property. P later became the sole shareholder. He submitted a subdivision plat and made attempts to develop the property, all of which were rejected by the governing agencies. In 1971, Rhode Island (D) created a Coastal Resources Management Council that promulgated regulations for development of coastal wetlands, including salt marshes such as those on P's property. In 1978, *the* property passed to P from the corporation. In 1983, P began submitting new proposals for development. The applicable regulations required a "special exception" for a landowner wanting to fill salt marsh, which required that the activity serve a compelling public purpose. P's applications were not approved. P sued for inverse condemnation, claiming that he had been deprived of all economically beneficial use of his property. The trial court found for D. The Rhode Island Supreme Court affirmed, holding that P's takings claim was not ripe, that he could not challenge regulations that predated 1978 when he became the owner, and that the fact that one parcel of his property had a development value of $200,000 defeated his claim of deprivation of all economically beneficial use. The court also held that P's *Penn Central* claim, *supra,* was barred because he obtained the land after the regulation had been in effect. The Supreme Court granted certiorari.

Issue. Is a landowner barred from challenging land use regulations that were adopted before he acquired the property?

Held. No. Judgment reversed in part and case remanded.

♦ A takings claim is not ripe unless the government entity charged with implementing the regulations has reached a final decision regarding the application of the regulations to the property at issue. Only when a claim is ripe can the courts evaluate it under *Lucas, supra* (deprivation of all economically beneficial use), or *Penn Central* (taking by defeat of reasonable investment-backed expectation).

♦ In this case, the council rejected P's plan to fill all of the wetlands, as well as his proposal to fill only 11 of the wetland acres. These decisions make it clear that P would be prohibited from engaging in any filling or development activity on the wetlands. P's property also included a parcel that was not protected wetlands. None of the parties disputed that the development value of this parcel was $200,000. Because there was no uncertainty about this parcel, P was not required to explore other development opportunities. Thus, there were no development issues to be resolved before trial and P's claim was ripe.

♦ The state courts held that P's post-regulation acquisition of title was fatal to his *Lucas* and *Penn Central* claims. The rationale is that a purchaser is deemed to have notice of an earlier-enacted restriction and cannot claim that it effects a taking. This approach would allow a state to avoid its obligation to defend its actions restricting land use, no matter how extreme or unreasonable. D could effectively put an expiration date on the Takings Clause. An unreasonable land regulation does not become reasonable through passage of time or title.

♦ The ripeness requirement may take years to satisfy, and D's rule would prevent a successor in interest from asserting a right to compensation even when the claim does become ripe. A newly regulated landowner should not be stripped of the ability to transfer an interest that was possessed before the regulation. This is not like direct condemnation, whereby the state pays compensation to the owner and thereby terminates any future right of compensation. A regulation that otherwise would be unconstitutional without compensation does not become a background principle of state law by mere virtue of the passage of title to a new owner.

♦ The court's holding that P was not deprived of all economically beneficial use because the uplands portion of P's property can still be developed is supported in the record. While a state may not evade a compensation duty by leaving a landowner with a token interest, the $200,000 value of P's parcel is substantial enough to defeat P's *Lucas* claim. P's claim that this parcel is distinct from his wetlands parcel was not presented to the lower courts and so cannot be addressed.

♦ Because P's claims were ripe and were not barred by his acquisition of the property after the regulation was adopted, on remand, the courts must consider P's *Perm Central* claim.

Concurrence (O'Connor, J.). The timing of a regulation relative to the acquisition of title is not irrelevant to a *Penn Central* analysis. Interference with investment-backed expectations is a critical factor that may be affected by what regulations were in effect when the investment was made.

Concurrence (Scalia, J.). Investment-backed expectations do not include the assumed validity of a restriction that is actually unconstitutional.

Concurrence and dissent (Stevens, J.). P is the wrong party to bring this action. If D's regulations imposed an injury on anyone, it was whoever owned the property when the regulations became effective. P could only have acquired the net value that remained after the alleged diminishment occurred.

Comment—temporary restriction. *Tahoe-Sierra Preservation Council, Inc. v. Tahoe Regional Planning Agency,* 535 U.S. 302 (2002), involved a temporary moratorium on development. The Court held that the question whether a temporary moratorium was a taking depended on the particular circumstances of the case. In some circumstances, it might be a per se taking under *Lucas;* in others, it would require case-by-case evaluation under *Penn Central.* The duration of the restriction is one of several factors for the courts to consider. The dissent noted that the moratoria in the case had lasted six years, a duration long enough to constitute a per se taking under *Lucas.*

———————

Chapter VIII

Freedom of Expression

A. Introduction

1. Constitutional Provision

The First Amendment provides that "Congress shall make no law ... abridging the freedom of speech, or of the press; or the right of the people peaceably to assemble, and to petition the Government for a redress of grievances."

2. Balancing Interests

The right to freedom of expression is not an absolute right to say or do anything that one desires. Rather, the interests of the government in regulating such expression must be balanced against the very strong interests on which this right is based.

a. Rationale

The rationale behind freedom of speech is that such freedom will lead to the discovery of truth and better ideas through the competition of differing viewpoints. Such speech and action is a necessity for a free society that is to be governed by democratic principles. It allows the people to bring about changes through nonviolent expression.

b. Presumption of validity

Legislation is normally presumed valid. This rule also applies for restrictions on expression, although freedom of speech is an important interest that cannot be restricted unless the government has a clear overriding interest. A statute may be invalid on its face, which means that it is unconstitutional in all of its applications. More commonly, however, a statute is held unconstitutional only as applied to the particular fact situation presented by the case.

c. Special scrutiny

There is a general consensus that First Amendment rights are special. The issue in most cases involves the proper balance between the free speech interest and the countervailing government interest that is being asserted. In some areas involving expression, the law is clear. In other areas, the law remains unsettled.

B. Restrictions on Dangerous Ideas and Information

1. Advocacy of Illegal Action

a. Development of basic principles

Certain types of expression may be punished as criminal acts. For example, a riot may constitute an expression of dissent, but damaging property is a criminal act. Speech that is likely to produce illegal activity may itself be illegal. World War I prompted a series of cases in which the Court dealt with advocacy of illegal action. For example, in *Shaffer v. United States,* 255 F. 886 (9th Cir. 1919), the court of appeals upheld a conviction based on mailing a book that contained a passage stating that "patriotism is murder and the spirit of the devil," because the purpose of the book was to weaken patriotism and enlistment into military service.

1) Incitement

Masses Publishing Co. v. Patten
244 F. 535 (S.D.N.Y. 1917).

Facts. Patten (D), the New York postmaster, refused to accept for mailing a magazine published by Masses Publishing (P). D claimed that the publication violates the Espionage Act. P seeks an injunction.

Issue. May the government refuse to permit use of the mails by private magazines that criticize public policy?

Held. No. Injunction granted.

♦   The Act prohibits false statements that interfere with the military or aid its enemies. P has not made such false rumors but has published political arguments.

♦   The Act forbids anyone from willfully causing disloyalty among the military. Although anyone who adopts P's views would be more prone to insubordination than one having faith in the existing policies, such an interpretation of causation would prohibit any expression of views counter to those currently prevailing, an impermissible restriction in a democratic society. Of course, one may not counsel or advise violation of the law as it now stands, but everyone is free to advocate changing the law.

♦   The Act also forbids willful obstruction of the enlistment service. But here only direct advocacy of resistance, or actual incitement, is prohibited. P has not done such an incitement.

Comment. The decision by Judge Learned Hand was reversed on appeal. The circuit court did not agree with the incitement test and deferred to the Postmaster General's discretion.

---

2) Clear and present danger test

Schenck v. United States
249 U.S. 47 (1919).

Facts. The Espionage Act of 1917 made it a crime to cause or attempt to cause insubordination in the military forces or to obstruct recruitment. Schenck (D) published a pamphlet that attacked the

Conscription Act and encouraged disobedience to it. D distributed the pamphlet directly to draftees. D was convicted of attempting to cause insubordination. D appeals.

Issue. May Congress outlaw speech that presents a clear and present danger to an important government interest?

Held. Yes. Judgment affirmed.

♦ The right of free expression is not absolute but varies with the circumstances; *e.g.,* a man is not free to falsely yell "fire" in a crowded theater.

♦ The first question is whether Congress is pursuing a proper end or purpose in the legislation. Here it is. Congress has the right to prohibit the evils at which this statute is aimed, especially in time of war.

♦ The next question is to what extent Congress can go in seeking to effectuate its purposes; *i.e.,* how far can it go before it violates the First Amendment? Congress cannot make speech a crime unless there is a "clear and present danger" of action resulting from the accused's words that would lead to the legitimately proscribed evil.

♦ The evidence in this case supports the conviction.

Comment. The Court seemed to set up some sort of a scale concerning types of speech. At one end, receiving a low degree of judicial protection, is highly emotional speech, commands that do not appeal to reason or logic but that have the effect of force and advocacy of action ("Strike!"). At the other end, receiving a high degree of protection, is speech that has a high degree of ideological content (political ideas, debate, etc.).

---

3) Newspapers

Frohwerk v. United States
249 U.S. 204 (1919).

Facts. Frohwerk (D) prepared and circulated in a newspaper several articles attacking the position of the United States in World War I. The articles tended to attack the recruitment effort. D was convicted under the Espionage Act, and appeals.

Issue. May newspaper articles create a clear and present danger?

Held. Yes. Judgment affirmed.

♦ The expressions in the articles were basically like those involved in *Schenck.* Although the articles were further removed than the pamphlets that Schenck distributed directly to draftees, it is possible that these articles could kindle a larger flame and therefore endanger the war effort.

---

4) Public speech

Debs v. United States
249 U.S. 211(1919).

Facts. Debs (D) made two public speeches promoting socialism and denouncing capitalism and the war. He was convicted under the Espionage Act and appeals.

Issue. May a political speech denouncing public policy and advocating an alternative be made a criminal act?

Held. Yes. Judgment affirmed.

♦   D addressed potential draftees, encouraging them to resist the recruiting services as a way to oppose the war. His speech created a clear and present danger that his listeners would actually resist the draft, which is an illegal activity.

----

5) Intent element

Abrams v. United States
250 U.S. 616 (1919).

Facts. When the United States sent the Marines to Vladivostok and Murmansk in response to Russia signing a peace treaty with Germany during World War I, Abrams and other Russian immigrants (Ds) protested by distributing leaflets calling for a general strike. Ds were arrested, tried, and convicted of conspiracy to violate the Espionage Act. Specifically, they were convicted of conspiracy to urge a strike "with intent [to] cripple or hinder the United States in the prosecution of the war." Ds appeal.

Issue. May persons be convicted of criminal conspiracy as a result of urging a general strike to protest war activity?

Held. Yes. Judgment affirmed.

♦   The convictions are sustainable under Schenck v. United States, supra, and Frohwerk v. United States, supra.

Dissent (Holmes, Brandeis, JJ.). While the law may punish speech that produces or is intended to produce a clear and imminent danger that the speech will bring about specific evils that the United States may constitutionally seek to prevent, there must be a present danger of immediate evil. Congress cannot simply prohibit any effort to influence public opinion. Ds' publishing of pamphlets does not present any imminent danger of Ds' opinions hindering the success of the government's war efforts. Ds' intent was to help Russia and stop American involvement in Russia, where the United States was not at war. Under the Constitution, freedom of speech must be protected unless the speech so imminently threatens immediate interference with the lawful and pressing purposes of the law that an immediate check is required to save the country. The common law doctrine of seditious libel does not survive the First Amendment.

Comment. The "clear and present danger" doctrine became highly protective of free speech as a result of Justice Holmes's dissent in this case.

----

b. State sedition laws

After World War I, several states enacted what became known as sedition laws.

1) Legislative facts

Gitlow v. New York
268 U.S. 652 (1925).

Facts. Gitlow (D) was convicted and imprisoned for violating a New York law that prohibited language advocating, advising, or teaching the overthrow of organized government by unlawful means. D appeals. There was no evidence of any effect resulting from D's actions.

Issue. May states prohibit advocacy of criminal anarchy when there is no concrete result, or likelihood of such a result, flowing from such advocacy?

Held. Yes. Judgment affirmed.

- The state has penalized not doctrinal exposition or academic discussion, but language urging criminal action to overthrow the government. D's expressions clearly fit the statutory prohibition; his words were the language of direct incitement.

- The state has determined that such activity is so inimical to the general welfare that it must be controlled through use of the police power and suppressed in its incipiency. Because the statute is not arbitrary or unreasonable, it must be upheld.

- If the statute itself is constitutional and D's use of language falls within its reach, absence of actual results is irrelevant. The state's determination that these utterances involve sufficient likelihood of causing harm is not clearly erroneous.

Dissent (Holmes, Brandeis, JJ.). D's words did not constitute a present danger of an actual attempt to overthrow the government; they were too indefinite and ineffective. To say D's words were an incitement proves nothing, for every idea is an incitement, and may move the recipient to action depending on outside circumstances.

---

2) Rationale for free speech

Whitney v. California
274 U.S. 357 (1927).

Facts. Whitney (D) helped organize and became a member of the Communist Labor Party of California, an organization that advocated, taught, and aided criminal syndicalism as defined by the Criminal Syndication Act of California. She was convicted. D appeals, claiming that although she remained a member she did not intend that the Party be an instrument of terrorism or violence.

Issue. May the state outlaw mere membership in a criminal organization even if the individual member intends no criminal acts?

Held. Yes. Judgment affirmed.

- The Act is not void for vagueness, and its purpose is clearly proper. The state may exercise its police power to outlaw organizations menacing the peace and welfare of the state.

- A person who abuses the right of association by joining such an organization is not protected by the Due Process Clause from punishment.

Concurrence (Brandeis, J.). Freedom of expression is an end in itself. It is a safety valve for frustration, and it is a means for finding the truth through the competition of ideas. Suppression of free speech can be justified only if there exist reasonable grounds to fear that a serious evil would otherwise result, and here reasonable grounds exist for believing that there is imminent danger that the serious evil will occur.

---

c. Communism and illegal advocacy

1) Development of the clear and present danger approach

The clear and present danger test was kept alive by dissenting opinions until it was finally adopted, in modified form, by later opinions. In effect, it is a rule of evidence; *i.e.*, the government must show facts indicating a clear and present danger in order to be able to regulate expression. Evidence of the following is relevant:

a) Any actual effect from the speech;

b) The type of language used, *e.g.,* advocacy of action;

c) The circumstances in which the words were spoken; or

d) The intent of the speaker.

2) The Smith Act

The Smith Act, 18 U.S.C. section 2385, makes it unlawful for any person: (i) to knowingly or willfully advocate, abet, advise, or teach the duty, necessity, desirability, or propriety of overthrowing any government in the United States by force or violence; (ii) to attempt to commit, or to conspire to commit, any of such acts; or (iii) to become a member of any organization advocating such acts, knowing its purpose.

3) Act upheld

Dennis v. United States
341 U.S. 494 (1951).

Facts. Dennis (D) was convicted of participating in a conspiracy to organize the Communist Party in the United States. The party participated in activity prohibited by the Smith Act. D had been holding classes, giving speeches, and writing articles that advocated overthrow of the government. D appeals.

Issue. May Congress pass a law forbidding association with organizations advocating overthrow of the government?

Held. Yes. Judgment affirmed.

♦ Congress clearly has the power to protect the government from violent overthrow, and in exercising this power could properly limit any expression or utterance aimed at inciting such a result.

♦ The gravity of the evil (the possible overthrow of the government) is to be discounted by the improbability of its occurrence in order to determine whether a clear and present danger exists.

♦ In the trial court the jury is to decide whether D in fact violated the Act, and the judge is to decide the question of application of the Act to D's conduct in light of the clear and present danger test.

Concurrence (Frankfurter, J.). The First Amendment does not provide absolute immunity for all expression; some balancing of the competing interests is necessary. Congress has prime responsibility to adjust these interests; the Court merely decides whether the Constitution permits Congress to enact the Smith Act.

Concurrence (Jackson, J.). The "clear and present danger" test was designed as a rule of reason for isolated incidents. It is not a limitation on the power of Congress to deal with the threat of a conspiracy dedicated to overthrowing the government.

Dissent (Black, J.). The only way to affirm these convictions is to repudiate the clear and present danger rule. The court jettisons the rule based on fear that advocacy of Communism endangers the safety of the Republic, however, the Founders believed that the benefits of free expression are worth the risk.

Dissent (Douglas, J.). This is not a case about someone teaching methods of terror. D was organizing people to teach Marxist-Leninist doctrine found in books. These books are not outlawed so how can their use be a crime? Free speech has effectively destroyed Communism as an effective political party in this country, thus there is no clear and present danger that advocacy of Communism will succeed.

Comment. After this case upheld the Smith Act, the government brought many actions against alleged Communists. Although here the defendant was a ringleader, it was thereafter thought that all that need be shown for a conviction of any person was that she was linked with an organization that advocated overthrow as fast as possible. In all cases, of course, there had to be some connection between the advocacy and the proscribed evil, although this could be supplied by judicial notice.

---

4) Mere advocacy

The Smith Act does not prohibit "mere advocacy" or teaching of forcible overthrow as an abstract principle, apart from an effort to instigate action to that end. [Yates v. United States, 354 U.S. 298 (1957)] This is true even though such advocacy is engaged in with evil intent and uttered with the hope that it may ultimately lead to violent revolution. The urging of action for forcible overthrow is a necessary element of the proscribed advocacy.

d. Modern distinction between advocacy and incitement

Brandenburg v. Ohio
395 U.S. 444 (1969).

Facts. Brandenburg (D), a Ku Klux Klan leader, was convicted under an Ohio statute for advocating criminal terrorism and criminal syndicalism. His activities consisted of inviting television reporters to a secluded gathering where weapons were present and a speech was made. There was no threat of imminent lawless action. The state courts upheld the conviction, and D appeals.

Issue. May a state law prohibit advocacy of civil disruption without distinguishing between mere advocacy and incitement to imminent lawless action?

Held. No. Judgment reversed.

♦   The constitutional guarantees of free speech and free press do not permit a state to forbid advocacy of the use of force or of lawlessness except where such advocacy (i) is directed to inciting or producing imminent lawless action and (ii) is likely to incite or produce such action.

♦   Ohio's law fails to make the required distinction and cannot be upheld.

Concurrence (Black, J.). The Court cites the *Dennis* case, *supra,* but properly does not agree with the *Dennis* "clear and present danger" doctrine.

Concurrence (Douglas, J.). The line between permissible and impermissible acts is the line between ideas and overt acts. The "clear and present danger" test has no place under the Constitution.

Comment. Applying the incitement standard, the Court reversed a disorderly conduct conviction in *Hess v. Indiana,* 414 U.S. 105 (1973), a case involving a campus antiwar demonstration. The Court held that since the appellant's statement could be interpreted in various ways, there was no rational inference from the language that the words were intended to produce imminent disorder. The Court stated that words that only had a tendency to lead to violence could not be punished by the state.

---

e. Support of terrorist organizations

Holder v. Humanitarian Law Project
561 U.S. 1 (2010).

Facts. The Humanitarian Law Project (P) and other groups desired to provide training and expert advice to the Kurdistan Workers' Party (PKK) and the Liberation Tigers of Tamil Eelam (LTTE). The USA Patriot Act, 18 U.S.C. section 2339B, made it a federal crime to knowingly provide material support or resources to a foreign terrorist organization. Both PKK and LTTE had been designated as foreign terrorist organizations by the Secretary of State pursuant to section 2339B. P sued Holder (D), the Attorney General, in federal court, challenging section 2339B on First Amendment grounds. The District Court granted a preliminary injunction against the enforcement of the law against P regarding the bans on expert advice and training support. The Court of Appeals affirmed. The Supreme Court granted certiorari.

Issue. May Congress ban material assistance to designated foreign terrorist groups when provided in the form of training and expert advice?

Held. Yes. Judgment affirmed.

♦   The statute does not ban Ps' pure political speech; Ps can say anything about PKK and LTTE and any other topic. Congress has only prohibited "material support," which usually does not take the form of speech at all.

♦   D argues that the intermediate scrutiny of O'Brien should apply here, but more than conduct is at stake here. Section 2339B regulates speech on the basis of its content, because whether Ps can speak to these groups depends on what they say. Consequently, the rigorous scrutiny of Cohen applies here.

♦   Ps seek to provide material support to the PKK and LTTE in the form of speech. While the Government has an important interest in combating terrorism, Ps claim the support they desire to provide would advance these groups' legitimate activities, not their terrorism. However, Congress specifically found that any contribution to a designated terrorist organization facilitates that conduct and rejected the view promoted by Ps.

♦   Material support, even if intended to promote peaceable, lawful conduct, frees up other resources for these groups that can then be used for terrorism. Such aid can also confer legitimacy to these groups. Ps seek to train these groups on how to peacefully resolve disputes and petition the UN for relief, but Congress can ban such efforts because they could be used to support terrorist activities.

Dissent (Breyer, Ginsburg, Sottomayor, JJ.). The Court has concluded that the Constitution allows the Government to impose criminal liability for Ps to engage in teaching and advocacy furthering the lawful political objectives of the designated organizations. This is based on the idea that all kinds of support are fungible, but Ps' proposed support is not fungible with resources that could be used for terrorism. Ps risk prosecution for even independent advocacy because it might be deemed coordination. Now the Court is denying First Amendment protection to the peaceful teaching of international human rights law and methods of negotiating peacefully.

---

2. Speech that "Threatens"

a. Criticism of the judicial process

Bridges v. California
314 U.S. 252 (1941).

Facts. Two rival labor unions were involved in litigation. The trial judge ruled against the union headed by Bridges (D), and D published a statement criticizing the judge's ruling as "outrageous" and threatening a strike if the ruling was not overturned. As a result of this publication, D was found guilty of contempt of court. D appeals.

Issue. May comments made about the judicial process during the pendency of the case involved be punished as contempt of court?

Held. No. Judgment reversed.

- Under the *Schenck* clear and present danger rule (*supra*), utterances may be punished only when the substantive evil is extremely serious and the degree of imminence extremely high. Another consideration is the practical impact of a restriction on speech.

- In this case, the restriction on speech is significant because public interest is at its peak when the case is pending; using the contempt power to suppress this speech has a large impact on freedom of speech.

- The first substantive evil allegedly resulting from the speech is disrespect for the judiciary, but such respect cannot be won or preserved by suppressing speech. The second evil is disorderly and unfair administration of justice. While this interest may be affected by publications that interfere with pending litigation, the actual publication in this case could not have that effect. D's announcement of his intention to call a strike was nothing more than an explicit statement of what the judge must have been aware was a possibility anyway.

Dissent (Frankfurter, J., Stone, C.J., Roberts, Byrnes, JJ.). The speech used in this case was clearly intended to intimidate the judge involved. D's strike threat was an obvious attempt to secure a favorable ruling. The right to free speech does not override the right to the impartial disposition of lawsuits.

---

b. Threatening the President

The Court has upheld a federal law prohibiting the act of knowingly and willfully threatening to take the life of, or inflict bodily harm on, the President. In *Watts v. United States*, 394 U.S. 705 (1969), however, the Court held that a threat made as political hyperbole ("If they ever make me carry a rifle, the first man I want to get in my sights is L.B.J.") was not the type of threat prohibited by the statute.

c. Website enjoined as a threat

In *Planned Parenthood v. American Coalition of Life Activities*, 290 F.3d 1058 (9th Cir. 2002), the court held that a website could be enjoined as a threat. The site had put up "wanted"-type posters of known abortion providers. The names of abortion providers who had been murdered were lined out.

3. Provoking a Hostile Response

a. Basic rule

Free speech does not include the right to disrupt the community. Fighting words are not protected, but an unfavorable response by the audience is not necessarily enough to render the speech unprotected. In *Terminiello v. Chicago*, 337 U.S. 1 (1949), the Court held unconstitutional a breach of the peace statute that included a restriction on speech that stirs the public to anger, invites dispute, or causes unrest. One of the functions of free speech is the invitation to dispute; free speech is often provocative and challenging.

b. Breach of the peace

Cantwell v. Connecticut
310 U.S. 296 (1940).

Facts. Cantwell (D) played a religious phonograph record on a public street. The record attacked generally all organized religious systems and was offensive to some, who threatened D with harm. D peacefully moved up the street. D was later convicted of breaching the peace. D appeals.

Issue. May public expression, offensive to some but not personally abusive, which does not result in a clear and present danger to a substantial state interest, be punished as a breach of the peace?

Held. No. Judgment reversed.

♦   Although breach of the peace embraces a variety of conduct dangerous to public order and tranquility, including fighting words, it cannot extend to undue suppression of free communication of views, religious or otherwise. No complaints indicated that the sound of D's phonograph disturbed the public.

♦   Although D's activity aroused animosity, it was not the personal abuse that is unprotected by the First Amendment, but instead an attempt to persuade others of D's apparently unpopular views. D avoided actual confrontation. Therefore, he did not breach the peace.

----

c. Protective suppression

Feiner v. New York
340 U.S. 315 (1951).

Facts. Feiner (D) was addressing a street meeting and attracted a crowd, but there was no disorder. One man told the police officers that if they did not stop D, he would. The police asked D to stop speaking and arrested him when he refused to obey. He was convicted of disorderly conduct, and appeals.

Issue. May police act to suppress speech that in their judgment is causing a breach of the peace?

Held. Yes. Judgment affirmed.

♦   D was accorded a full, fair trial, the result of which was a determination that D was arrested and convicted not for his speech but for the reaction it caused. The police were justified in acting to preserve peace and order.

Dissent (Black, J.). The police had a duty to protect D's right to talk, even to the extent of arresting the man who threatened to interfere.

Comment. The problems of freedom of expression in public places really have two aspects—one is the idea of the content of the speech. For example, political dialogue or comment is clearly going to receive greater protection than is business advertising. The second element is that of the conduct involved. As in this case, when there is a clear and present danger that the conduct involved will lead to harmful results, greater restrictions on the speech are permitted.

----

d. Fighting words

1) Classes of speech

Chaplinsky v. New Hampshire
315 U.S. 568 (1942).

Facts. Chaplinsky (D) was on a public sidewalk distributing literature. Certain citizens complained to the City Marshall, Bowering, that D was denouncing religion as a so-called "racket." Bowering warned D of the crowd's restlessness, although he acknowledged that D's activities were legal. Later, as D was being taken to the police station following a disturbance, he encountered Bowering again. D addressed Bowering by repeating the words "You are a God damned racketeer" and "a damned Fascist." D was convicted of violating a state law that prohibited a person from addressing "any offensive, derisive, or annoying word to any other person who is lawfully in any street or public place." The lower courts upheld the conviction, and D appeals.

Issue. May a state prohibit the use of "fighting words"?

Held. Yes. Judgment affirmed.

♦ Under the Fourteenth Amendment, the right of free speech is not an absolute right. There are some well-defined and narrowly limited classes of speech that can be punished under the Constitution.

♦ Classes of speech that may be prohibited include lewd and obscene language, profanity, libel, and insulting or "fighting" words. "Fighting words" are those that "inflict injury or tend to incite an immediate breach of the peace." These classes of speech are not essential to the exposition of ideas and have only a slight social value that is outweighed by a strong social interest in order and morality.

♦ The state court interpreted the statute to apply to the limited classes of speech that include "classical fighting words." So limited, the statute is constitutional.

----

2) Balancing approach

Because categorization presents such a high risk of being overinclusive, the Court has adopted a balancing approach to most content-based restrictions on speech. Balancing presents the danger of being susceptible to manipulation by those who apply the law.

3) Current status of fighting words analysis

The *Chaplinsky* approach appears to retain validity as long as the statute involved is narrowly construed. In *Gooding v. Wilson, infra*, the Court reversed a conviction for using provocative words because the statute was overbroad. The Court apparently would uphold a statute applicable only to words that "have a direct tendency to cause acts of violence by the person to whom, individually, the remark is addressed."

4) Public vs. Private speech

Snyder v. Phelps
__ U.S. __, 131 S.Ct. 1207 (2011).

Facts. Snyder (P) was the father of a Marine killed in the line of duty in Iraq. P's son's funeral was held in a church. About a thousand feet away, on public land, Phelps (D) and other members of the Westboro Baptist Church (which D founded) picketed peacefully. They held up signs that read "God Hates the USA/Thank God for 9/11," "America is Doomed," "Thank God for IEDs,," "Fag Troops," "Semper Fi Fags," "God Hates Fags," "Thank God for Dead Soldiers," and so forth. P sued D for intentional infliction of emotional distress, intrusion upon seclusion, and civil conspiracy. The jury awarded P $2.9 million in compensatory damages and $8 million in punitive damages. The Fourth Circuit Court of Appeals reversed on First Amendment grounds. The Supreme Court granted certiorari.

Issue. May peaceful picketers on public land be held liable for intentional infliction of emotional distress based on the content of their signs?

Held. No. Judgment affirmed.

♦ The First Amendment protects speech involving public issues, but provides less rigorous protection for private speech. D's speech in this case involved the political and moral conduct of the United States and its citizens, the fate of the nation, homosexuality in the military and scandals involving the Catholic clergy, all of which are matters of public importance. Even if some of the signs could be interpreted as relating to P's son specifically, the overall theme of D's demonstration spoke to broad public issues.

♦ P claims that the context of the speech, being a funeral, made D's demonstration one of private, not public, concern. But D demonstrated on public land next to a public street, and D's choice to use the funeral, while making D's views more hurtful, does not convert its public speech into private speech.

♦ Some States and the Federal Government have restrictions on funeral picketing, but these laws are content neutral. Signs of support for P would not have been subjected to liability, so D's signs also cannot be.

♦ The jury was instructed that it could hold D liable if D's picketing was "outrageous," but this is a subjective standard that would reflect the jurors' views. The First Amendment protects even hurtful speech on public issues.

Dissent (Alito, J.). The First Amendment does not preclude liability for the intentional infliction of emotional distress by means of speech. D brutally attacked P's son to inflict injury and attract public attention. P and his son were private figures, and to the extent D targeted them, D can be held liable.

---

4. Disclosure of Confidential Information

a. Protection against prior restraint

There is a strong policy against prior restraints of media reporting of criminal proceedings. Such reporting is a means of ensuring a fair trial for the accused. On the other hand, there is a risk that media coverage could taint a trial by giving jurors evidence not properly admitted at trial or by creating an atmosphere that makes a fair trial impossible. Before an injunction against media reporting can be granted, the court must find that (i) there is a clear and present danger that pretrial publicity would (not merely could) threaten a fair trial, (ii) alternative measures are inadequate, and (iii) an injunction would effectively protect the accused.

b. Prevention of publication of sensitive government documents

New York Times Co. v. United States;
United States v. Washington Post Co.
(The Pentagon Papers Case)
403 U.S. 713 (1971).

Facts. The United States (P) sought to enjoin publication by the *New York Times* and *Washington Post* (Ds) of a classified study known as the Pentagon Papers. All federal courts involved except the court of appeals in the *New York Times* case held that P had not met its heavy burden of justification. Ds appeal the judgment of the court of appeals in its case.

Issue. May the executive branch prevent publication of items that it considers to threaten grave and irreparable injury to the public interest?

Held. No. Judgment affirmed.

♦ The United States has failed to meet its heavy burden of showing justification for the enforcement of such a prior restraint.

Concurrence (Black, Douglas, JJ.). The injunctions should have been vacated and the cases dismissed without oral argument because it would be impossible to find that the President has "inherent power" to halt the publication of news by resorting to the courts.

Concurrence (Douglas, Black, JJ.). The only possible power possessed by the government to restrict publication by the press of sensitive material arises from its inherent power to wage war successfully. Congress has not declared war, so the government cannot exercise this power.

Concurrence (Brennan, J.). Courts cannot issue temporary stays and restraining orders to accommodate the government's desire to suppress freedom of the press without adequate proof of a direct, inevitable, and immediate serious adverse effect.

Concurrence (Stewart, White, JJ.). The executive branch has the duty to protect necessary confidentiality through executive regulations. The courts are limited to construing specific regulations and applying specific laws. Since the courts were asked to do neither here, they cannot act.

Concurrence (White, Stewart, JJ.). Some circumstances might justify an injunction as requested, but not these. Congress has relied on criminal sanctions and their deterrent effect to prevent unauthorized disclosures, and the courts should not go beyond the congressional determinations.

Concurrence (Marshall, J.). The Court would violate the concept of separation of powers by using its power to prevent behavior that Congress has specifically declined to prohibit.

Dissent (Burger, C.J.). The Court has not had sufficient time to gather and analyze the facts.

Dissent (Harlan, J., Burger, C.J., Blackmun, J.). Judicial review of executive action in foreign affairs is narrow. The Court should inquire only whether the subject matter is within the President's foreign relations power and whether the head of the department concerned has personally made the determination that disclosure would irreparably impair national security.

Dissent (Blackmun, J.). The case is too important to be handled in such haste and ought to be remanded.

---

c. Injunction permitted

Distinguishing *The Pentagon Papers Case*, a federal district court enjoined a magazine from publishing technical material on hydrogen bomb design, which was available in public documents. In exercising the first instance of prior restraint against a publication, the court cited the government's showing of the likelihood of injury to the nation and the fact that the suppression of the technical portions of the article would not impede the publication in its goal of stimulating public knowledge of nuclear armament and enlightened debate on national policy. [United States v. The Progressive, Inc., 467 F. Supp. 990 (W.D. Wis. 1979)] An appeal in that case was dismissed after the government dropped its prosecution.

C. Overbreadth, Vagueness, and Prior Restraint

1. Introduction

The fact that particular speech may be constitutionally regulated does not constitute a license for any type of regulation. The courts have adopted three doctrines to control the means used to regulate speech regardless of the type of speech involved.

2. Overbreadth

Legislation that restricts or regulates speech is tested under the First Amendment on the basis of its potential applications. This approach is much broader than the normal test used in judicial review;

i.e., the application of the statute to the particular facts of the case. The overbreadth doctrine permits consideration of potential applications not before the court. In effect, this is an exception to the standing requirements because it allows litigation of the interests of persons, or even hypothetical situations, not involved in the actual facts of the case. The rationale is that persons whose expression is constitutionally protected might refrain from that expression for fear of criminal sanctions if the statute could reach their expression. There is no requirement that such persons subject themselves to sanctions to have their First Amendment rights vindicated.

a. Statute not limited to fighting words overbroad

Gooding v. Wilson
405 U.S. 518 (1972).

Facts. Georgia law defined as a misdemeanor the use of "opprobrious words or abusive language, tending to cause a breach of the peace." Gooding (D) called a police officer who was responding to an antiwar demonstration a "son of a bitch" and threatened the officer with bodily harm. D was convicted under the Georgia statute and petitioned for federal habeas corpus relief. The court of appeals granted relief and Wilson (P) appeals.

Issue. May a state forbid the use of "opprobrious words or abusive language" that tends to cause a breach of the peace?

Held. No. Judgment affirmed.

♦ Because the Georgia statute applies only to spoken words, it can be upheld if it cannot be applied to protected speech. But the states may not punish the use of words not within narrowly limited classes of speech.

♦ P claims that the Georgia statute is narrowly drawn because it applies only to fighting words, a category of speech that is not protected under *Chaplinsky v. New Hampshire, supra.* However, the words of the statute encompass much more than fighting words, and the Georgia courts have not limited the application of the statute to fighting words. In fact, the statute has been applied to punish harsh, insulting language that would not tend to incite an immediate breach of the peace. Thus the statute is overbroad.

Dissent (Burger, C.J.). D's conduct was not protected by the First Amendment. The words of the statute are sufficiently clear to constitute adequate notice.

Dissent (Blackmun, J., Burger, C.J.). I wonder what Georgia can do to proscribe this type of language. Any new statute would also be overbroad unless the legislature added words to the effect that the statute means only what the Supreme Court says it may mean and no more.

---

3. Vagueness

A statute may not be overbroad, yet it may be impermissible because it is too vague. Any law that forces persons of common intelligence to necessarily guess at its meaning and differ as to its application is considered void for vagueness. This principle applies to all statutes, but in First Amendment cases, courts frequently require a heightened degree of specificity.

4. Prior Restraint

a. Early cases

The government normally cannot regulate in advance what expressions may or may not be uttered or published, even to guard against speech or ideas that, once published, would be constitutionally unprotected and subject to state punishment, such as defamatory speech.

Individual as well as public rights are deemed sufficiently protected by the deterrent effect of such punishment. The further step of prior restraint would make the government a censor, thereby undermining the core of the First Amendment. The early cases in this area involved attempts at prior restraint through licensing requirements and court injunctions.

b. Licensing

1) Introduction

A state cannot condition the right of a person to express her views publicly on obtaining a permit to do so from local authorities if such permits are given on a purely discretionary basis. There must be some reasonable standard established on which to decide who gets a permit, when, and why.

2) Permit to distribute circulars

Lovell v. Griffin
303 U.S. 444 (1938).

Facts. The city of Griffin (P) enacted an ordinance requiring written permission from the city manager for the distribution of literature of any kind at any time, at any place, and in any manner. Lovell (D) was convicted of violating the statute by distributing religious literature without a permit. D appeals, claiming that the ordinance violates both freedom of the press and of religion.

Issue. May government prohibit all distribution of all literature without prior approval of a government agent?

Held. No. Judgment reversed.

♦ The ordinance is invalid on its face. Freedom of the press includes a right to publish without a license.

♦ The ordinance is overbroad because it prohibits distribution that does not in any way interfere with proper government functions.

---

c. Injunctions

Near v. Minnesota
283 U.S. 697 (1931).

Facts. Minnesota (P) enacted a statute that provided for the abatement, as a public nuisance, of any "malicious, scandalous and defamatory" publication. Near (D) published a periodical that criticized law enforcement officers. P brought an action seeking to suppress D's publication. The state courts granted P's request, and D appeals.

Issue. May a state grant an injunction against publication of allegedly defamatory material?

Held. No. Judgment reversed.

♦ Permitting public authorities to suppress publication of scandalous matter relating to charges of official dereliction, restrained only by the publisher's ability to satisfy the judge that the charges are true, is the essence of censorship. Liberty of the press under the Constitution has meant, principally although not exclusively, immunity from previous restraints or censorship.

♦ The only permissible restraint is the deterrent effect of actions against defamatory publications arising after publication.

Dissent (Butler, Van Devanter, McReynolds, Sutherland, JJ.). The previous restraints precluded by the First Amendment refer to subjection of the press to the arbitrary will of an administrative officer. There is no similarity between such impermissible previous restraint and the decree authorized by this statute to prevent further publication of defamatory articles, and the statute should be upheld.

D. Restrictions on "Low Value" Speech

1. False Statements of Fact (Libel)

Libelous speech is in somewhat the same category as obscenity—it receives little constitutional protection. However, the same difficult questions exist here as with obscenity; *i.e.*, what constitutes libel and what tests should be used to distinguish protected from unprotected speech?

a. Public officials and seditious libel

1) Introduction

The First Amendment clearly protects disclosure and debate on matters of public interest. On the other hand, society must protect personal reputations against injurious falsehoods. The conflict between these interests has produced some close decisions, but the Court has balanced the interests by creating a constitutional privilege for certain kinds of defamation. Thus, criticism of public officials relating to their official conduct cannot result in either criminal or civil liability for libel unless made with "actual malice." Society's interest in this type of expression is great, and public officials can normally refute false charges because they have access to the media.

2) Public officials

New York Times v. Sullivan
376 U.S. 254 (1964).

Facts. Sullivan (P) was a commissioner of the city of Montgomery, Alabama, and supervised the police department. The New York Times Company (D) carried a full-page advertisement that included several false statements about repressive police conduct in Montgomery. Although P's name was not mentioned, the accusation of the ad could be read as referring to him. P sued for damages on grounds that D libeled him. The trial court awarded damages of $500,000, which were upheld in the state courts. The controlling state rule of law dealt with libel per se, established here by merely showing that D's statement reflected upon the agency that P supervised. Once libel per se is demonstrated, the only defense is the truth. D appeals.

Issue. May a state allow a public official to recover damages for a defamatory falsehood relating to his official conduct without proof of actual malice?

Held. No. Judgment reversed.

♦ The Constitution expresses a profound commitment to uninhibited debate on public issues. This protection does not turn on the truth of the ideas or beliefs expressed, nor does concern for official reputation remove defamatory statements from the constitutional shield.

♦ The deterrent effect of damage awards—without the need for any proof of actual pecuniary loss—is so great as to severely chill public criticism, which should be openly permitted under the First Amendment.

♦ Despite First Amendment considerations, a public official may recover damages for a defamatory falsehood relating to his official conduct if he proves the statement was made with actual malice (knowledge of falsity or reckless disregard of truth). P's proof falls short.

Concurrence (Black, Douglas, JJ.). D has an absolute, unconditional privilege to criticize official conduct despite the harm that may flow from excesses and abuses.

---

3) Public figures

The Supreme Court has held that the same privilege to make statements about "public officials" exists for statements made about "public figures." In *Curtis Publishing Co. v. Butts*, 388 U.S. 130 (1967), Wally Butts, the former director of athletics at the University of Georgia, was reported to have thrown a football game while at the University. In *Associated Press v. Walker* (decided with *Butts*), the Court held that General Walker, a retired Army general, was a public figure. The *New York Times* rule was extended to both cases.

b. Private individuals and public figures

1) General rule

The *New York Times* rule applies to suits by public figures as well as by public officials. A person may become a public figure by achieving general fame or notoriety in a given community, either generally or as to particular issues. When the defamed person is neither a public figure nor a public official (or candidate for public office), "free speech" considerations are not as strong. Private individuals are more susceptible to injury because they do not usually have media access to counteract false statements published about them. Consequently, under the rules established by *Gertz v. Robert Welch, Inc., infra*, the states may impose whatever standard of defamation liability they choose, except that, for matters of public concern:

a) The factual misstatement must be such as would warn a reasonably prudent editor or broadcaster of its defamatory potential;

b) There must be a finding (by the trier of fact or the appellate court) that the publisher or broadcaster was at least negligent in publishing the misstatement (*i.e.*, liability without fault cannot be imposed); and

c) Damages must be limited to "actual injury" (which includes any out-of-pocket loss plus impairment of reputation, personal humiliation, and mental anguish). An award of "presumed" or punitive damages is permissible only if the publication was made with knowledge of its falsity or in reckless disregard for the truth (*i.e.*, actual malice).

2) Private individual involved in public issue

Gertz v. Robert Welch, Inc.
418 U.S. 323 (1974).

Facts. Gertz (P), an attorney, represented the family of a homicide victim in the family's civil suit against the police officer who had murdered him. Robert Welch (D), publisher of *American Opinion*, printed an article, concededly untrue, that discredited P's reputation and motives. P sued D for libel. After a jury awarded damages to P, the trial court reconsidered and decided that D was protected by application of the *New York Times* rule, *supra*, holding that discussion of any public issue is protected, regardless of the status of the person defamed. Because P was unable to prove that D acted with "actual malice," the court entered a judgment n.o.v. for D. The court of appeals affirmed, and P appeals.

Issue. May a member of the press who published defamatory falsehoods about a person who is neither a public official nor a public figure, but who is involved in a public issue, claim a constitutional privilege against liability for injuries?

Held. No. Judgment reversed.

♦ The need to avoid self-censorship by the news media must be balanced against the legitimate interest in permitting compensation for harm resulting from defamatory falsehoods. Defamation plaintiffs are not all in the same class, however. Public officials and public figures have more access to the media in order to counteract falsehoods than do private individuals such as P. Private individuals are also more deserving of recovery because their public exposure is not voluntary. Therefore, the rationale behind the *New York Times* rule does not extend to private individuals.

♦ Involvement in a public issue, by itself, does not bring a private individual within the class covered by the *New York Times* rule. P was not a public official or public figure. To protect defamations whenever a "public issue" was involved would introduce new uncertainties and broadly expand the scope of the *New York Times* rule.

♦ States may define their own standards of liability for defamation by a publisher or broadcaster, but may not impose liability without fault. However, states may not permit recovery of presumed or punitive damages in the absence of proof of "actual malice" (knowledge of falsity or reckless disregard for the truth). The only permissible recovery for a private defamation plaintiff who establishes liability under any standard less demanding than the *New York Times* test is compensation for actual injury.

Dissent (Douglas, J.). No "accommodation" between the law of defamation and the freedoms of speech and the press can be "proper" except those made by the Framers.

Dissent (Brennan, J.). The *New York Times* rule should apply to discussions of public issues.

Dissent (White, J.). The states should be free to impose strict liability in cases such as this.

———————————

3) Determination of public figure status

As discussed *supra*, a person may be a public figure for all purposes and in all contexts by gaining general fame or notoriety, or may become a public figure for special issues by becoming involved in a controversy. The critical element is the voluntariness of the public standing. A person is not a public figure simply because she is extremely wealthy and engaged in divorce proceedings of interest to the reading public. The fact that she files for divorce (and even holds press conferences during the proceedings) does not mean that she voluntarily chooses to publicize her married life, because going to court is the only way she can legally dissolve her marriage. [Time, Inc. v. Firestone, 424 U.S. 448 (1976)] Nor does a person become a public figure by being charged with a crime. [Wolston v. Reader's Digest Association, 443 U.S. 157 (1979)]

4) Elimination of distinction between media and nonmedia

Dun & Bradstreet v. Greenmoss Builders
472 U.S. 749 (1985).

Facts. Dun & Bradstreet, Inc. (D), a credit reporting agency, reported that Greenmoss Builders, Inc. (P) had filed for bankruptcy. The report was false and negligently prepared. P sued for defamation and recovered compensatory and punitive damages. The lower courts upheld the award. The Supreme Court granted certiorari.

Issue. May a defamed party recover presumed and punitive damages, even without proving actual malice, if the defamation is not speech on a public matter?

Held. Yes. Judgment affirmed.

♦ When defamatory statements involve no issue of public concern, the court must balance the state's interest in compensating injured parties against the First Amendment interest in protecting the expression. Speech on private matters does not merit the highest First Amendment protection; thus there are fewer constitutional limits on state libel law in this area.

---

5) Public figures and emotional distress from parody

Hustler Magazine v. Falwell
485 U.S. 46 (1988).

Facts. Hustler Magazine (D) published a parody of an advertisement in which Falwell (P), a nationally known minister, is depicted as describing a drunken incestuous rendezvous with his mother in an outhouse. The ad contained a disclaimer at the bottom. P sued for invasion of privacy, libel, and intentional infliction of emotional distress. After a directed verdict on the privacy claim, the jury found for D on the defamation claim, on the ground that it contained no assertion of fact. The jury awarded P $200,000 on the emotional distress claim, however. The court of appeals affirmed. The Supreme Court granted certiorari.

Issue. May a public figure recover damages for emotional harm caused by the publication of an offensive parody intended to inflict emotional injury, but which could not reasonably have been interpreted as stating actual facts?

Held. No. Judgment reversed.

♦ Although the First Amendment promotes political debate by protecting even vigorous criticism of public officials, not all speech about a public figure is protected. A public figure may hold a speaker liable for damages to reputation caused by publication of a defamatory falsehood if the statement was made with knowledge that it was false or with reckless disregard of whether it was false or not.

♦ P claims a different rule should apply here where the state has sought to prevent emotional distress instead of damage to reputation. While an intent to cause emotional distress may be determinative in tort law, the First Amendment disregards the speaker's intent in the area of public debate about public figures. The alternative would deter political satirism.

♦ While D's parody may be more outrageous than normal political cartoons, there is no principled standard for distinguishing between more and less outrageous expression. Speech may not be suppressed for the sole reason that it offends society.

---

2. Newsworthiness of Disclosures of Private Information

Cox Broadcasting Corp. v. Cohn
420 U.S. 469 (1975).

Facts. Cohn's (P's) daughter was the victim of a murder-rape. A reporter for Cox Broadcasting Corporation (D) obtained the name of the victim from official public court records and made the identification in a broadcast. A Georgia statute prohibited the publication or broadcast of a rape victim's identity. P sued D for invasion of privacy. D appeals state court judgments in favor of P.

Issue. May a state protect individual privacy by forbidding the publication or broadcast of sensitive personal information that is officially available to the public?

Held. No. Judgment reversed.

♦ The right of privacy has acquired increasing importance in recent years, and the information disseminated by D, although true, would clearly be offensive to a person of ordinary sensibilities. However, the law of invasion of privacy recognizes that those interests fade when the information involved appears on the public record.

♦ A rule making public records available to the media but forbidding their publication would seriously impinge on the public's right to know and would clearly violate the First and Fourteenth Amendments.

---

3. Commercial Speech

a. Introduction

Commercial speech is entitled to some degree of protection under the First Amendment, although subject to more stringent regulation than would be permissible with respect to noncommercial speech. In determining the degree of protection, the free speech interest in the contents of the speech must be weighed against the public interest served by the governmental regulation. [*See* Bigelow v. Virginia, 421 U.S. 809 (1975)—commercial speech merits some protection]

b. Scope of protection

Virginia State Board of Pharmacy v. Virginia Citizens Consumer Council
425 U.S. 748 (1976).

Facts. The Virginia State Board of Pharmacy (D) prohibited advertisement of the retail prices of prescription drugs by pharmacists. The Virginia Citizens Consumer Council (P), for itself and on behalf of users of prescription drugs, sought an injunction against the enforcement of D's rule. The three-judge district court granted the injunction. D appeals.

Issue. Is purely commercial speech wholly outside First Amendment protection?

Held. No. Judgment affirmed.

♦ First Amendment protection extends to the communication, to its source, and to its recipients. P, as a potential recipient of the advertising, has standing to bring this action.

♦ The speech in question, commercial advertising, is not disqualified from protection merely because the speaker's interest is purely economic. The particular consumer has a vital interest in the free flow of commercial information, possibly a greater interest than in current political debates, which are clearly protected.

♦ Society in general has a strong interest in the free flow of commercial information. Actually, such a free flow is essential to the proper functioning of our economic system. It is likely that no line can properly be drawn between "important," and hence protected, advertising and the opposite kind.

♦ D claims an interest in protecting the public from unscrupulous pharmacists who would use advertising to their own advantage and the public's detriment. But the choice between the dangers of suppressing information and the dangers of its misuse if it is freely available has been made by the First Amendment. Therefore, D cannot prohibit commercial advertising of the type involved here.

♦ Although commercial speech is protected, it remains subject to proper restrictions; *e.g.*, time, place, and manner restrictions, false and misleading advertising prohibitions, and prohibitions against advertising illegal transactions.

Dissent (Rehnquist, J.). The Court expands the standing requirements and extends First Amendment protection beyond what is necessary. This ruling prevents the states from protecting the public against dangers resulting from excessive promotion of drugs that should be used only with professional guidance.

Comment. The Court emphasized the importance of a free flow of information by invalidating an ordinance that prohibited the posting of "for sale" signs on real estate. The township had justified the ordinance as a means of preventing "white flight" from racially integrated neighborhoods, but this justification was inadequate. [*See* Linmark Associates v. Township of Willingboro, 431 U.S. 85 (1977)]

---

c. Four-part analysis of commercial speech

Central Hudson Gas & Electric Co. v. Public Service Commission of New York
447 U.S. 557 (1980).

Facts. The Public Service Commission (D), in response to an energy shortage, temporarily banned all advertising by electric utilities that "promote the use of electricity." Over the objections of Central Hudson Gas & Electric Company (P), D extended the ban and distinguished between promotional advertising, which was totally prohibited, and institutional and informational advertising, which D permitted. The state courts upheld D's order, and P appeals.

Issue. Does a public service commission's prohibition of promotional advertising by an electric utility violate the utility's First Amendment rights?

Held. Yes. Judgment reversed.

♦ Although D's regulation applies only to commercial speech, such speech is protected by the First Amendment because of its informational functions. Thus, a four-part analysis has developed regarding commercial speech.

♦ First, is the expression protected? If it concerns lawful activity and is not misleading, it generally is; P's speech is protected.

♦ Second, is the asserted governmental interest in regulation substantial? D based its regulation on the need for energy conservation, clearly a substantial interest.

- Third, does the regulation directly advance the governmental interest? If demand for electricity were unaffected by advertising, P would not have brought this suit. Therefore D's regulation does advance the governmental interest.

- Fourth, is the regulation more extensive than necessary? Here D's regulation fails, because it would prohibit information about electric devices or services that would not increase net energy use, although they might increase electric use; *e.g.*, use of electricity as a backup to solar heating. D's rule is overbroad, and in the absence of a showing that a more limited rule could not serve D's interest, it cannot be upheld.

Concurrence (Blackmun, Brennan, JJ.). The four-part test is inadequate in that it permits deprivation of information needed by the public to make a choice. D attempts to manipulate choices of private persons by withholding information rather than by persuasion or direct regulation. Such covert attempts are illegal regardless of their "necessity."

Dissent (Rehnquist, J.). D here is placing an essentially economic regulation on a heavily regulated state-created monopoly. Economic regulation traditionally merits virtually complete deference by the Court; D's regulation should also.

Comment. In *Bolger v. Youngs Drug Products Corp.*, 463 U.S. 60 (1983), the Court held that informational pamphlets about contraceptives were commercial speech, even though they contained discussion of important public issues, because they promoted the sponsor's products. Still, the Court invalidated a federal statute prohibiting the unsolicited mailing of the brochures, under the *Central Hudson* test.

---

d. Application of *Central Hudson* test

In *Posadas de Puerto Rico Associates v. Tourism Co. of Puerto Rico*, 478 U.S. 328 (1986), the Court upheld a Puerto Rican statute that legalized casino gambling, but prohibited advertising of casino gambling to the public. The Court held that the government had a substantial interest in preventing the seriously harmful effects of excessive casino gambling and declared that the law directly advanced that interest within the meaning of *Central Hudson, supra*. Since the government could have completely prohibited casino gambling, the Court reasoned that it could take the less intrusive step of prohibiting its advertising.

e. Ban on truthful advertising of legal activity

44 Liquormart, Inc. v. Rhode Island, 517 U.S. 484 (1996), concerned a Rhode Island statute that prohibited advertising of the retail price of alcoholic beverages, except for price tags or displays within licensed premises and not visible from the street. Rhode Island's rationale for the ban was that it advanced the state's substantial interest in promoting temperance. The Court invalidated the statute, noting that the state produced no evidence of any connection between the ban and a significant change in alcohol consumption. Also, the Court pointed out that there were several actions the state could have taken to accomplish its objective without restricting speech, such as increasing prices through higher taxation or educational campaigns. The state argued that under *Posadas, supra*, the Court should have given it particular deference because it could have, if it had chosen, banned the sale of alcoholic beverages outright. However, the Court found that *Posadas* was erroneous in applying a "greater-includes-the-lesser" approach that would allow a state that can ban activity outright to ban speech regarding the activity. The Court explained that the power to prohibit an activity is not necessarily greater than the power to suppress speech about it; under the First Amendment, it should be more difficult for the government to suppress speech than to suppress conduct. In a concurring opinion, Justice Thomas stated that where the government asserts an interest to keep legal users of a product or service ignorant in order to manipulate their choices in the marketplace, the interest should be deemed per se illegitimate.

f. Limited ban on advertising of tobacco products

In *Lorillard Tobacco Co. v. Reilly*, 533 U.S. 525 (2001), the Attorney General of Massachusetts had promulgated comprehensive regulations on the advertising and sale of tobacco products. The regulations included a prohibition on outdoor advertising within 1,000 feet of a school or playground. Tobacco manufacturers and retailers challenged the constitutionality of the regulations. The Court held that the regulations were preempted by federal law with respect to cigarettes and violated the First Amendment with respect to the advertising of cigars and smokeless tobacco products. The Court asserted that the final step of the *Central Hudson* analysis, *supra*, requires a reasonable fit between the means and ends of a regulatory scheme, but the broad sweep of the attorney general's regulations did not indicate careful calculation of the costs and benefits associated with the burden on speech imposed. The outdoor advertising regulations would not only have affected a substantial portion of the areas in the state, but would have also constituted a complete ban in some areas. The Court found that the regulations were more extensive than necessary to advance the state's compelling interest in preventing underage tobacco use.

g. Prohibition on advertising of compounded drugs

Thompson v. Western States Medical Center
535 U.S. 357 (2002).

Facts. The Food and Drug Administration Modernization Act of 1997 ("FDAMA") exempted "compounded drugs" from the Food and Drug Administration's ("FDA") standard drug approval requirements, as long as the providers of the compounded drugs refrained from advertising the drugs. Compounded drugs are created by a pharmacist by combining, mixing, or altering ingredients to create a medication adapted to the needs of an individual patient, based on a doctor's prescription. Western States Medical Center (P), a group of pharmacies that engaged in compounding drugs, sued Thompson (D), Secretary of Health and Human Services, seeking an injunction against enforcement of the advertising ban. The district court granted summary judgment for P on the ground that the restrictions did not satisfy *Central Hudson, supra*. The Ninth Circuit affirmed. The Supreme Court granted certiorari.

Issue. May the government prohibit advertising of compounded drugs?

Held. No. Judgment affirmed.

- ♦ D cites several governmental interests, including the need to draw a line between small-scale compounding and large-scale drug manufacturing, and that advertising is a fair proxy for such a line. However, D failed to show that the speech restrictions are not more extensive than is necessary to serve D's interests.

- ♦ D could rely on non-speech-related means to draw its line, including prohibiting Ps from compounding drugs in advance of receiving prescriptions or limiting the amount of compound drugs that Ps can make. Nothing in the legislative history shows why forbidding advertising was a necessary, instead of merely convenient, means to achieve D's interests.

- ♦ The government does not have a legitimate interest in preventing the dissemination of truthful commercial information to prevent members of the public from making bad decisions with the information. Beyond these problems with the FDAMA, the ban on speech would prevent pharmacists from telling doctors about alternative drugs available for their patients.

Dissent (Breyer, J., Rehnquist, C.J., Stevens, Ginsburg, JJ.). The Court undervalues the importance of D's interest in protecting the health and safety of the public. The FDAMA restricts advertising to directly advance its important safety objective—confining the sale of untested, compounded drugs to where they are medically needed. The FDAMA exempts compounded drugs from testing requirements, but this creates risks by giving untested drugs to consumers. This risk is justifiable only where the consumer has a specific medical need for a specially-tailored drug. On the other hand, consumer-oriented advertising will create a strong consumer-driven demand for the drugs, which could lead to doctors issuing prescriptions they would not otherwise issue. Congress could not have achieved its safety objective in significantly less restrictive ways.

---

4. Obscenity

a. Introduction

Obscene publications are not protected by the constitutional guarantee of freedom of speech and press. Both federal and state governments may restrict such expression. The difficulty is in defining such speech. Freedom of expression is not an end in itself. To be protected, the speech must have some content of value to society. Obscene speech has no societal value, so it is unprotected, but speech that does not descend to the level of "obscene" remains protected.

b. Difficulty of defining obscenity

Roth v. United States; Alberts v. California
354 U.S. 476 (1957).

Facts. Roth (D) was convicted of mailing obscene materials in violation of a federal obscenity statute. Alberts (D) was convicted of a similar state offense. Ds appeal their convictions.

Issue. Is obscenity presumptively without redeeming social value and therefore unprotected by the First Amendment?

Held. Yes. Judgment affirmed.

♦ The unconditional phrasing of the First Amendment was not intended to protect every utterance; *e.g.*, libel is unprotected. Obscenity is utterly without redeeming social importance. Therefore, obscenity cannot claim constitutional protection.

♦ Ds claim that their material does not create a clear and present danger to society, but merely incites impure sexual thoughts. It is true that mere portrayal of sex does not deny the material constitutional protection. But obscenity is not synonymous with sex. Obscenity deals with sex in a manner appealing to prurient interest. As such, it is unprotected.

♦ The test for obscenity is: whether, to the average person applying contemporary community standards, the dominant theme of the material taken as a whole appeals to the prurient interest.

Concurrence (Warren, C.J.). The book is not on trial, the defendants are. The government can punish persons engaged in commercial exploitation of the craving for materials with prurient effect.

Concurrence and dissent (Harlan, J.). We deal with different statutes. The states may properly regulate in this area, but federal regulation must be more narrow, since Congress has no substantive power over sexual morality.

Dissent (Douglas, Black, JJ.). The First Amendment protects all speech and precludes the courts from weighing the values of speech against silence.

Comment. After *Roth*, the Court was unable to make a majority statement on the proper standard for evaluating pornography until *Miller v. California, infra*, in 1973. In the meantime, however, the Court decided obscenity cases with plurality opinions. For example, in *Kingsley International Pictures Corp. v. Regents of New York*, 360 U.S. 684 (1959), the Court invalidated a New York motion picture licensing law that banned films portraying acts of sexual immorality or presenting such acts as proper behavioral patterns. The Court held that the concept of sexual immorality differed from the concepts of obscenity or pornography, and that the state law prevented the advocacy of an idea protected by the basic guarantee of the First Amendment.

---

c. Inability to define obscenity

In *Memoirs v. Massachusetts*, 383 U.S. 413 (1966), the state had ruled that the book *Memoirs of a Woman of Pleasure* was obscene under Massachusetts law. The Court reversed in a plurality opinion. The Court stated that under *Roth*, material is protected unless it meets three criteria: (i) the dominant theme of the material taken as a whole appeals to a prurient interest in sex; (ii) the material is patently offensive because it affronts contemporary community standards relating to the description or representation of sexual matters; and (iii) the material is utterly without redeeming social value. The Court stated that a book could have redeeming social value even if the other two parts of the test are met. An indication of the social value of the material is the manner in which it is sold. If the seller's sole emphasis is on the sexually provocative aspects of the material, a court could accept his evaluation at its face value.

d. Approach to obscenity cases

In one opinion, Justice Stewart, writing about obscenity, stated, "I cannot define it, but I know it when I see it." The Court seemed to follow this approach between 1967 and 1971, when it overturned obscenity findings in 31 cases. During this period, the Court never upheld obscenity findings when the material was textual, or when film or pictures showed only nudity. When film or pictures showed explicit sexual activity, however, it upheld obscenity findings.

e. Modern standard for defining obscene materials

Miller v. California
413 U.S. 15 (1973).

Facts. Miller (D) was convicted under a California statute of knowingly distributing obscene matter to unwilling recipients. The statute incorporated the *Memoirs* test of obscenity. D appeals the conviction.

Issue. Is the *Memoirs* test the appropriate measure of obscene expressions?

Held. No. Judgment vacated and case remanded.

♦ Obscenity is not within the area of constitutionally protected speech or press. *Roth* presumed obscenity to be "utterly without redeeming social value," but the *Memoirs* case transformed that presumption into a necessary element of proof. *Memoirs* thus requires the prosecution to prove a negative, and that test cannot be upheld.

♦ Regulation of obscene material is restricted to works that depict or describe sexual conduct, and must specifically define that conduct. The basic guidelines for the trier of fact must be:

(i) Whether the average person, applying contemporary community standards, would find that the work, taken as a whole, appeals to the prurient interest:

(ii) Whether the work depicts or describes, in a patently offensive way, sexual conduct specifically defined by the applicable state law; and

(iii) Whether the work, taken as a whole, lacks serious literary, artistic, political, or scientific value.

- Under this test, material can be regulated without a showing that it is "utterly without redeeming social value."

Dissent (Douglas, J.). The people through constitutional amendment, and not the courts, should decide what is and is not obscene.

Dissent (Brennan, Stewart, Marshall, JJ.). The challenged statute is unconstitutionally overbroad, hence invalid on its face.

---

f. Rationale for regulating obscenity

1) Possession and distribution of obscene materials

The Court reversed a conviction for possession of obscene materials found in the appellant's home in *Stanley v. Georgia*, 394 U.S. 557 (1969). In so ruling, the Court held that the First Amendment grants the right to receive information and ideas and that there is a fundamental right to be free from unwanted governmental intrusion in one's home. However, in *United States v. Reidel*, 402 U.S. 351 (1971), the Court reversed the lower court's dismissal of an indictment under the federal law prohibiting the mailing of obscene materials. The Court rejected the lower court's contention, based upon the ruling in *Stanley*, that if a person has a right to possess obscene material, then a person also has a right to deliver it. The Court held that the indictment was not an infringement of the right to freedom of mind and thought or of the right to privacy in one's home.

2) State regulation of obscene films

Paris Adult Theatre I v. Slaton
413 U.S. 49 (1973).

Facts. Slaton (P), a state district attorney, filed civil complaints against Paris Adult Theatre I (D), seeking to enjoin exhibition of films claimed to be obscene. The films were available only to "consenting adults." The trial judge dismissed the complaint, but the Georgia Supreme Court reversed, holding that the films were without First Amendment protection. D appeals.

Issue. May a state prohibit commercial exhibition of "obscene" films to consenting adults?

Held. Yes. Judgment vacated and case remanded.

- The state afforded D the best possible notice, as no restraint on exhibition was imposed until after a full judicial proceeding determined that the films were obscene and therefore subject to regulation.

- Obscene, pornographic films do not acquire constitutional immunity from state regulation merely because they are shown to consenting adults only. The states have power to make a morally neutral judgment that public exhibition of obscene material, or commerce in such material, has a tendency to injure the community as a whole, even if actual exposure is limited to a few consenting adults.

- While the right of privacy may preclude regulation of the use of obscene materials within the home, commercial ventures such as D's are not private for the purpose of civil rights litigation. Commerce in obscene material is unprotected by any constitutional doctrine of privacy.

- Incidental effects on human "utterances" or "thoughts" do not prevent state action to protect legitimate state interests where the communication is not protected by the First Amendment and where the right of privacy is not infringed. Such state action is permitted as long as it conforms to the standards of *Miller*.

Dissent (Brennan, Stewart, Marshall, JJ.). The Court's attempts to define obscenity have clearly failed. Government cannot constitutionally bar the distribution even of unprotected material to consenting adults.

---

5. Child Pornography, Animal Cruelty, and Violent Expression

a. Distribution of child pornography

New York v. Ferber
458 U.S. 747 (1982).

Facts. New York (P) enacted a statute that outlawed production and promotion (including distribution) of child pornography, regardless of whether the material was legally obscene. "Child pornography" consisted of any performance that includes sexual conduct by a child under 16 years old. Ferber (D) was convicted of selling two films of young boys masturbating. The New York Court of Appeals reversed the conviction, holding that the statute violated the First Amendment. The Supreme Court granted certiorari.

Issue. May a state prohibit distribution of all child pornography, even without requiring that it be legally obscene?

Held. Yes. Judgment reversed.

♦ Obscenity is not protected by the Constitution. States have even greater leeway in dealing with child pornography than with obscenity because of the compelling state interest in safeguarding their children's physical and psychological well-being.

♦ Distribution of child pornography is intrinsically related to sexual abuse of children because the distribution aggravates the harm to the child and because, without a market, the pornography would not be produced. Prohibiting distribution of obscene materials would not adequately promote the state's interest because the harm of abuse is unrelated to any possible literary, artistic, political, or social value of the material.

♦ Production of child pornography, of which distribution is an integral part, is illegal; the First Amendment does not protect against commission of a crime. There is no cognizable value in permitting production of child pornography.

♦ The definition used in the statute is sufficiently clear and precise. The statute is not overbroad. Even if it could conceivably extend to medical or educational material, such applications of the statute would be a tiny fraction of the materials prohibited. The cure in such instances is a case-by-case analysis of the circumstances.

Concurrence (O'Connor, J.). The compelling state interest here could allow a state to prohibit all knowing distribution of material containing sexual conduct by children, regardless of social value, because the harm to the child is unaffected by the ultimate use made of the material.

Concurrence (Brennan, Marshall, JJ.). Although the statute is not overbroad, its application to material that does have serious literary, artistic, scientific, or medical value would violate the First Amendment.

---

b. "Virtual" child pornography

Ashcroft v. The Free Speech Coalition
535 U.S. 234 (2002).

Facts. The Child Pornography Prevention Act of 1996 (CPPA) expanded the federal prohibition of child pornography to include "virtual child pornography," which is sexually explicit images that appear to depict minors but are produced without using any real children, whether by using computer imaging or by using adults made to look like children. The Free Speech Coalition (P), a trade association for the pornography, or adult-entertainment, industry, challenged the constitutionality of the CPPA. The District Court granted summary judgment for Ashcroft (D), the U.S. Attorney General. The Ninth Circuit reversed, holding that pornography can be banned only if obscene under *Miller v. California, supra,* or if it depicts actual children under *New York v. Ferber, supra.* The Supreme Court granted certiorari.

Issue. May Congress prohibit "virtual" child pornography?

Held. No. Judgment affirmed.

♦ Congress determined that children can be threatened by virtual pornography, even when they are not harmed in the production process, because pedophiles might use the materials to encourage children to participate in sexual activity. Virtual child pornography might also prompt the sexual appetites of pedophiles. But the harm Congress identified flows from the content of the images, not from the means of production.

♦ *Ferber* upheld a prohibition on the distribution and sale of child pornography, as well as its production, because these acts were "intrinsically related" to the sexual abuse of children in two ways: (i) as a permanent record of a child's abuse, the continued circulation itself would harm the child; and (ii) because the traffic in child pornography was an economic motive for its production, the state had an interest in closing the distribution network.

♦ Under *Ferber,* the creation of the child pornography was itself the crime. In the case of virtual child pornography, there is no underlying crime; virtual child pornography is not "intrinsically related" to the sexual abuse of children, as were the materials in *Ferber.*

♦ *Ferber* did not hold that child pornography is by definition without value. In fact, the Court recognized that some works in this category might have significant value and found that virtual images were an alternative and permissible means of expression. Thus, *Ferber* referred to the distinction between actual and virtual child pornography and relied on it as a reason supporting its holding.

♦ D argues that pedophiles may use virtual child pornography to seduce children. However, there are many things innocent in themselves, such as cartoons, video games, and candy, that might be used for immoral purposes, but they are not prohibited merely because they can be misused.

♦ Congress cannot prohibit speech that adults have a right to hear in an attempt to shield children from that speech. It also cannot prohibit otherwise protected speech because pedophiles might use it for illegal purposes. The tendency of speech to encourage unlawful acts is not a sufficient reason for banning it.

♦ D's argument that modern imaging technology makes it difficult to prosecute actual child pornography is an argument that protected speech may be banned as a means to ban unprotected speech. However, lawful speech may not be suppressed as the means to suppress unlawful speech. Protected speech does not become unprotected merely because it resembles unprotected speech.

Concurrence (Thomas, J.). If imaging technology develops to the point that the government cannot prove that child pornography depicts real children, it may be necessary to regulate virtual child pornography as long as there is an appropriate affirmative defense.

Concurrence and Dissent (O'Connor, J., Rehnquist, C.J., Scalia, J.). The part of the CPPA that prohibits material that "conveys the impression" that it contains pornographic images of minors is properly held unconstitutional. However, the prohibition of pornographic images that "appear to be" of a minor should be struck down only where it is applied to the class of youthful-adult pornography. D's concern about the advances in computer-graphics technology is reasonable. The CPPA is narrowly tailored if the "appears to be" language is interpreted to mean "virtually indistinguishable from."

Comment. In response to *Ashcroft*, Congress adopted the Prosecutorial Remedies and Other Tools to end the Exploitation of Children Today Act ("PROTECT Act"), which made it illegal to knowingly advertise, promote, or distribute any material in a manner that reflected the belief, or intended to cause another to believe, that the material contained a visual depiction of an actual minor engaging in sexually explicit conduct. In *United States v. Williams*, 128 S. Ct. 1830 (2008), the Court upheld the statute. The Court explained that offers to engage in illegal transactions are categorically excluded from First Amendment protection; therefore offers to provide, or requests to obtain, child pornography are not protected speech. Virtual child pornography was not prohibited by the act, and simulated child pornography could still be offered and sought, as long as it was offered and sought as such, and not as real child pornography. In a dissent, joined by Justice Ginsburg, Justice Souter asserted that a proposal to engage in a transaction involving protected materials should not be a crime.

---

c. Animal cruelty

United States v. Stevens
561 U.S. 460 (2010).

Facts. Stevens (D) was convicted of distributing videos of dogfighting. Every state outlaws dogfighting, and federal law makes it a crime to create, sell, or possess any commercial visual or auditory depiction in which a living animal is intentionally maimed, mutilated, tortured, wounded, or killed if the conduct violates federal or state law and the depiction has no serious religious, political, scientific, educational, journalistic, historical, or artistic value. The Third Circuit Court of Appeals reversed the conviction. The Supreme Court granted certiorari.

Issue. May federal law criminalize depictions of animal cruelty in commercial media?

Held. No. Judgment affirmed.

♦ There is no tradition that excludes depictions of animal cruelty from the freedom of speech protected by the First Amendment. Categories of speech to be protected are not determined by a balancing of the value of the speech against its societal costs, as the Government advocates.

♦ The Government focuses on "crush videos" that appeal to a sexual fetish by depicting torture and killing of helpless animals. Whether a statute targeting such material would be constitutional is not the question here, because this statute is overbroad.

Dissent (Alito, J.). The First Amendment does not protect violent criminal conduct. The conduct shown in crush videos is criminal throughout the country, so every crush video made in the United States records criminal acts. The law here seeks to prevent the commission of such crimes.

---

d. Violent video games

Brown v. Entertainment Merchants Ass'n
__ U.S. __, 131 S.Ct. 2729 (2011).

Facts. California law prohibited the sale or rental of violent video games to minors, and required the packaging for such games to be labeled "18." The applicable definition specified games "in which the range of options available to a player includes killing, maiming, dismembering, or sexually assaulting an image of a human being" in a depiction that "appeals to a deviant or morbid interest of minors." The game also must be "patently offensive to prevailing standards in the community as to what is suitable for minors," which "causes the game, as a whole, to lack serious literary, artistic, political, or scientific value for minors." Entertainment Merchants Ass'n (P) brought suit against Brown (D), Governor of California, to challenge the law. The District Court found the law to violate the First Amendment and enjoined its enforcement. The Ninth Circuit affirmed. The Supreme Court granted certiorari.

Issue. May a state prohibit the sale or rental of violent video games to minors?

Held. No. Judgment affirmed.

♦ Video games contain familiar literary devices that make them subjects of First Amendment protection. In Stevens, the Court held that new categories of unprotected speech may not be added on the ground that the speech is too harmful to be tolerated. That ruling applies here. D seeks to create a new category of content-based regulation that is permissible only for speech directed at children. While the State may protect children from harm, it does not have a free-floating power to restrict the ideas to which children may be exposed.

♦ D seeks to justify the law by analogy to obscenity, but speech about violence is not obscene. There is no longstanding tradition of specially restricting children's access to depictions of violence. Grimm's Fairy Tales contain many examples of gore and violence.

♦ The law does not withstand strict scrutiny because D cannot show a direct causal link between violent video games and harm to minors. D does not seek to regulate other forms of expression of violence intended for children, so the law is underinclusive.

Concurrence (Alito, J., Roberts, C.J.). There is evidence that the effects of playing violent video games is different from reading a book or viewing a movie, and the Court should recognize this. However, this particular statute used a definition of "violent video game" that is impermissibly vague.

Dissent (Thomas, J.). Freedom of speech does not include a right to speak to minors without going through the minors' parents or guardians. Our history has long recognized this and so the Framers could not have intended the First Amendment to include an unqualified right to speak to minors.

Dissent (Breyer, J.). The law is only a modest restriction on expression, supported by sufficient evidence to satisfy First Amendment concerns. The Court should defer to legislative facts and uphold the statute.

---

e. Sex discrimination and pornography

In *American Booksellers Association v. Hudnut*, 598 F. Supp. 1316 (S.D. Ind. 1984), *aff'd*, 771 F.2d 323 (7th Cir. 1985), *aff'd mem.*, 475 U.S. 1001 (1986), a federal district court held that a city may not enact an ordinance prohibiting pornography on the theory that it discriminates against women. The interest in preventing sex discrimination does not outweigh the free speech interest. The court concluded that acceptance of the civil rights approach could lead to prohibition of any speech the legislature finds unfair to a particular group.

6. Offensive Speech and Content Regulation

While the government may regulate the content of broadcasts when necessary to protect the public interest, including prohibitions against inappropriate content, such as indecent but not obscene speech [*see* FCC v. Pacifica Foundation, *infra*], the government may not prohibit discussion of public issues that lie at the heart of the First Amendment protections.

a. Offensive words

Cohen v. California
403 U.S. 15 (1971).

Facts. Cohen (D) wore a jacket bearing the words "Fuck the Draft" in a Los Angeles courthouse corridor. He was convicted of violating a state statute that prohibited disturbing the peace by offensive conduct. D appeals after the state courts upheld his conviction.

Issue. May a state prohibit as "offensive conduct" public use of an offensive word?

Held. No. Judgment reversed.

◆ Government has special power to regulate speech that is obscene, that constitutes "fighting words," or that intrudes on substantial privacy interests in an essentially intolerable manner.

◆ D's expression falls within none of these categories. D's jacket could not be considered erotic. Nor would D's jacket violently provoke the common citizen in the manner of fighting words. Persons present in the courthouse were not unwilling captives of the offensive expression; they could simply have averted their eyes. Thus there was no intrusion on privacy interests.

◆ The state's regulatory attempt must fail because it would permit the state to outlaw whatever words officials might deem improper, thus running a substantial risk of suppressing ideas. Such power would permit official censorship as a means of banning the expression of unpopular views.

Dissent (Blackmun, J., Burger, C.J., Black, J.). D's antic was mainly conduct and involved little speech. As such, it could be regulated.

---

b. Protecting unwilling audiences

Erznoznik v. Jacksonville
422 U.S. 205 (1975).

Facts. Erznoznik (D), manager of a drive-in theater, exhibited a movie containing nudity in violation of a Jacksonville (P) ordinance prohibiting such exhibitions if visible from a public street or place. The lower courts upheld the ordinance, and D appeals.

Issue. May a city prohibit exhibition of all films containing nudity by drive-in theaters whose screens are visible from a public street or place?

Held. No. Judgment reversed.

◆ By extending beyond the permissible restraints on obscenity, the ordinance applies to films protected by the First Amendment. P claims that any movie containing nudity may be suppressed as a nuisance if it is visible from a public place. However, selective restrictions based on content have been upheld only where the privacy of the home is invaded, or where the unwilling viewer cannot avoid exposure. The limited privacy interest of persons on public streets cannot justify this censorship of otherwise protected speech on the basis of its content.

♦ The ordinance is too broad to be justified as an exercise of the police power to protect children, because all nudity cannot be deemed obscene even as to minors. Nor can it be upheld as a traffic regulation, since other types of scenes might be equally distracting. The ordinance lacks the precision of drafting and clarity of purpose that are essential when First Amendment freedoms are at stake.

Dissent (Burger, C.J., Rehnquist, J.). The Court has never established such inexorable limitations upon state power in this area.

---

c. Indecent speech

FCC v. Pacifica Foundation
438 U.S. 726 (1978).

Facts. A New York radio station owned by Pacifica Foundation (D) broadcast a monologue by George Carlin that contained several indecent words. A listener complained to the FCC (P), which issued a declaratory order finding the monologue indecent as broadcast and therefore subject to regulation. The district court reversed P's determination, and P appeals.

Issue. Does the federal government have power to regulate a radio broadcast that is indecent but not obscene?

Held. Yes. Judgment reversed.

♦ The statute upon which P based its power to regulate D's broadcast (18 U.S.C. section 1464) forbids the use of any "obscene, indecent, or profane" language. Because the disjunctive is used, each word has a separate meaning, and language need not be obscene to be indecent. D's words were admittedly not obscene, but P could still properly find them indecent.

♦ Broadcasting, of all forms of communication, has the most limited First Amendment protection because of its unique ability to penetrate privacy and its accessibility to children.

♦ The First Amendment does not prohibit all governmental regulation that depends on the content of speech. Nor is P's action invalidated by its possible deterrent effect on similar broadcasts.

Concurrence (Powell, Blackmun, JJ.). While P's finding does not violate the First Amendment, the Court should not decide on the basis of content which speech is less "valuable" and hence, less deserving of protection.

Dissent (Brennan, Marshall, JJ.). The word "indecent" must be construed to prohibit only obscene speech. Since the broadcast was concededly not obscene, and since it does not fit within the other categories of speech that are totally without First Amendment protection, it should not be subject to government control. The government does not have a duty to protect its citizens from certain broadcasts merely because some citizens, even if a majority, object to the broadcast

Dissent (Stewart, Brennan, White, Marshall, JJ.). Since "indecent" properly means no more man "obscene," P had no authority to ban D's broadcast.

Comment. In *Sable Communications, Inc. v. FCC*, 492 U.S. 115 (1989), the Court held that Congress could not prohibit interstate transmission of commercial telephone messages that were indecent. The Court noted that *Pacifica* was a narrow holding that involved the unique intrusiveness of broadcasting. Telephone communications, in contrast, require a participant to take affirmative steps to receive the message. There are alternative means to protect children, and the government cannot limit the content of adult telephone conversations to what is suitable for children.

---

d. The Internet

Reno v. American Civil Liberties Union
521 U.S. 844 (1997).

Facts. Certain provisions of the Communications Decency Act of 1996 ("CDA") prohibited the knowing transmission of obscene or indecent messages to any recipient under 18 years of age and the knowing sending or displaying of patently offensive messages in a manner that is available to a person under 18 years of age. These provisions were designed to prevent Internet obscenity. The American Civil Liberties Union (P) challenged the Act. A three-judge district court enjoined enforcement of the Act, except with respect to obscenity and child pornography, on the ground that it violated freedom of speech. Reno (D), the United States Attorney General, appeals.

Issue. May Congress suppress certain types of web pages to deny minors access to potentially harmful speech?

Held. No. Judgment affirmed.

♦ *Pacifica, supra,* does not support D's position. The order in *Pacifica* was issued by an agency that had been regulating radio stations for decades, targeted a specific broadcast, applied to the timing of the broadcast, and did not involve a criminal prosecution.

♦ Broadcast media have a history of extensive government regulation, they have scarce available frequencies, and they are invasive in nature. Unlike radio or television communications that can be received passively, Internet communications require deliberate effort on the part of the recipient. There are methods to allow parents to block access to undesired web sites.

♦ The CDA contains undefined terms and different phrases for different sections, raising uncertainty about how the two standards relate to each other. It also lacks the necessary precision required by a content regulation. To deny minors access to potentially harmful speech, the CDA suppresses a large amount of speech that adults have a constitutional right to receive. Such a broad content-based restriction on adult speech is unacceptable.

♦ There are possible alternatives, such as requiring that indecent material be "tagged" to facilitate parental control and regulating some portions of the Internet differently from others. The CDA is not narrowly tailored to the goal of protecting minors from potentially harmful materials.

---

e. Restricting Internet speech to protect minors

Ashcroft v. American Civil Liberties Union, 542 U.S. 656 (2004), involved the Child Online Protection Act ("COPA"), which was enacted by Congress in response to *Reno.* COPA imposed criminal penalties of a $50,000 fine and six months in prison for knowingly posting on the World Wide Web, for commercial purposes, content that is "harmful to minors" as defined in the statute. The Court held that the government may not restrict Internet speech to protect minors if there is a less restrictive means available, such as blocking and filtering software. Justice Breyer, joined by Chief Justice Rehnquist and Justice O'Connor, dissented, arguing that COPA's burden on protected speech was modest and that it applied only to material unprotected by the First Amendment, *i.e.,* legally obscene material. He contended that COPA did not censor even that material, but merely required providers to restrict minors' access to harmful material. Justice Scalia also dissented, asserting that COPA should not have been subjected to strict scrutiny because the First Amendment allows the government to entirely ban obscene material.

f. Discrimination against "indecent" expression

Denver Area Educational Telecommunications Consortium, Inc. v. FCC, 581 U.S. 727 (1966), concerned the Cable Television Consumer Protection and Competition Act of 1992 ("Cable Act"). The Court upheld a provision of the Cable Act that authorized cable operators to prohibit "indecent" programming on leased access channels, although cable operators could not exercise any other editorial control over the content of programs. The Court invalidated a different provision that required cable operators carrying "indecent" programming to segregate such programming on a single channel, to block that channel from viewer access, and to unblock it only on a subscriber's written request. The Court reasoned that, although the protection of children is a compelling interest, the latter provision significantly differed from the former because it did not merely permit, but rather required cable operators to restrict speech.

g. Limitation of transmission to nighttime

Section 505 of the Telecommunications Act of 1996 required cable operators who provided sexually-oriented programming to either fully scramble sexually-oriented channels or to limit their transmission to between 10 p.m. and 6 a.m. The technology to fully scramble signals was so expensive that most cable operators chose the limited transmission option. When the regulation was challenged in *United States v. Playboy Entertainment Group, Inc.*, 529 U.S. 803 (2000), the Court invalidated section 505. The Court reasoned that cable television systems can block unwanted channels on a household-by-household basis, which is less restrictive than banning. The Court held that the government cannot ban speech if targeted blocking is a feasible and effective means of furthering its compelling interests.

h. Zoning ordinances

1) Proximity of adult movie theaters to similar businesses

In *Young v. American Mini Theatres, Inc.*, 427 U.S. 50 (1976), the Court upheld the constitutionality of Detroit's zoning ordinances that regulated the locations of theaters showing sexually explicit "adult" movies. The Court explained that the location of several such businesses in the same neighborhood tended to adversely affect property values, caused an increase in crime, and encouraged residents and businesses to move elsewhere. The Court noted that society's interest in protecting expression of erotic materials is wholly different, and lesser, than its interest in protecting political or philosophical discussion; although the First Amendment does not permit total suppression of erotic material, it does permit the states to use content as a basis for classification. The Court found that the line drawn by the regulation was reasonable in light of the city's valid objectives. Justice Stewart, joined by Justices Brennan, Marshall, and Blackmun, dissented, arguing that the First Amendment prohibits selective interference with protected speech, even if distasteful.

2) Proximity of adult movie theaters to residential zone, family dwelling, church, park, or school

The Court upheld a zoning ordinance that regulated adult theaters by concentrating them in certain areas in *Renton v. Playtime Theatres, Inc.*, 475 U.S. 41 (1986). The ordinance was a time, place, and manner regulation and was content-neutral since it was not directed at the film contents, but rather at the secondary effects of such theaters on the surrounding community. In a dissent joined by Justice Marshall, Justice Brennan asserted that the ordinance was clearly content-based and was designed to suppress constitutionally protected expression.

3) Concentration of adult businesses

In *City of Los Angeles v. Alameda Books, Inc.*, 535 U.S. 425 (2002), Los Angeles had determined that concentrations of adult businesses were associated with higher rates of crime. So, it adopted an ordinance that prohibited the establishment of an adult entertainment facility within 1,000 feet of another such enterprise or within 500 feet of any religious institution, school, or public park. To close a loophole in the original ordinance, the city amended the ordinance to prohibit having more than one adult entertainment business in the same building. Alameda Books operated an adult bookstore and video arcade in the same building and challenged the city's ordinance under the First Amendment. The lower court granted summary judgment to Alameda. The Supreme Court reversed the decision, noting that a content-neutral ordinance that is a time, place, and manner regulation, rather than a ban, warrants only intermediate scrutiny. Furthermore, the Court found that the ordinance served a substantial government interest. Justice Kennedy, concurring, contended that the ordinance was content-based but that it was acceptable if its purpose and effect were to reduce crime, not to reduce speech. Justice Souter, joined by Justices Stevens, Ginsburg, and Breyer, dissented, arguing that the city failed to show any causal relationship between its breakup policy and the elimination of secondary effects.

7. Hate Speech

Beauharnais v. Illinois
343 U.S. 250 (1952).

Facts. Beauharnais (D) was convicted under a state statute that made it unlawful for any person to sell or publish any publication that portrayed a class of citizens of any race, color, or creed in a derogatory manner so as to expose them to derision or to be productive of a breach of the peace. D published a leaflet calling on Chicago officials to halt the encroachment of blacks on whites' property and neighborhoods, citing the black crime rate, possible "mongrelization," etc. D appeals the conviction.

Issue. May group libel be made per se illegal, even without a showing of a clear and present danger?

Held. Yes. Judgment affirmed.

♦   Every American jurisdiction punishes libels aimed at individuals. Libel is treated much like lewd and obscene speech; punishment of these types of expression does not violate the First Amendment. Such speech is not communication of information or opinion protected by the Constitution.

♦   Because the Fourteenth Amendment does not prevent the states from enforcing libel laws to protect individuals, it should not prevent laws against group libel unless they are unrelated to a legitimate government purpose. Illinois has a history of tense race relations. The legislature could certainly conclude that group libel tends to exacerbate these problems. It could also have found that group libel directly affects individuals in the group by impugning their reputations.

♦   There is no requirement for a showing of clear and present danger because libel is not within the protection of the Constitution.

Dissent (Black, Douglas, JJ.). Restrictions of First Amendment freedoms should not be judged by the rational basis standard. Criminal libel has always been intended to protect individuals, not large groups. Additionally, the words used by D were part of a petition to the government, and part of his argument on a question of wide public importance and interest.

Dissent (Douglas, J.). This type of speech could constitutionally be punished only with a showing that it provides a clear and present danger of causing disaster.

----

8. Content of "Fighting Speech"

R.A.V. v. City of St. Paul
505 U.S. 377 (1992).

Facts. R.A.V. (D) and several other teenagers assembled a cross from broken chair legs and burned it inside the fenced yard of a black family that lived across the street from D's current residence. The city of St. Paul, Minnesota (P) charged D with disorderly conduct pursuant to an ordinance that provided: "Whoever places on public or private property a symbol, object, appellation, characterization, or graffiti, including, but not limited to, a burning cross or Nazi swastika, which one knows or has reasonable grounds to know arouses anger, alarm, or resentment in others on the basis of race, color, creed, religion, or gender commits disorderly conduct and shall be guilty of a misdemeanor." D moved to dismiss the charge on the ground that the ordinance was invalid under the First Amendment because it was overbroad and impermissibly content-based. The trial court granted D's motion, but the Minnesota Supreme Court reversed, construing the ordinance to apply only to conduct that amounts to "fighting words," *i.e.*, "conduct that itself inflicts injury or tends to incite immediate violence." The Supreme Court granted certiorari.

Issue. May the government regulate "fighting words" based on the subjects the speech addresses?

Held. No. Judgment reversed.

♦ Content-based speech regulations are presumptively invalid, but, as the Court held in *Chaplinsky v. New Hampshire, supra*, there are exceptions in a few limited areas that are "of such slight social value as a step to truth that any benefit that may be derived from them is clearly outweighed by the social interest in order and morality."

♦ Certain categories of expression are "not within the area of constitutionally protected speech" (*e.g.*, obscenity, defamation, etc.), which means that they may be regulated because of their constitutionally prescribable content. This does not mean they may be used to discriminate on the basis of content unrelated to their distinctively proscribable content; *i.e.*, the government may proscribe libel, but it cannot proscribe only libel critical of the government.

♦ The exclusion of "fighting words" from the scope of the First Amendment means that the unprotected features of the words are essentially a "nonspeech" element of communication. But there is a "content discrimination" limitation on the government's prohibition of prescribable speech; the government may not regulate use based on hostility or favoritism toward the underlying message expressed.

♦ When the basis for content discrimination consists entirely of the very reason the class of speech at issue is prescribable, there is no significant danger of idea or viewpoint discrimination. The government may prohibit only the most patently offensive obscenity, but it cannot prohibit only obscenity that includes offensive political messages. Or, the government may regulate price advertising on one industry and not in others, because the risk of fraud is greater there, but it cannot prohibit only that commercial advertising that depicts men in a demeaning fashion.

♦ The government could properly give differential treatment to even a content-defined subclass of proscribable speech if the subclass is associated with particular "secondary effects" of the speech; *e.g.*, prohibiting only those obscene live performances that involve minors. And laws against conduct instead of speech may reach speech based on content, such as sexually derogatory "fighting words" that violate Tide VII's prohibition against sexual discrimination.

The key element is that the government does not target conduct on the basis of its expressive content.

♦ In this case, P's ordinance is facially unconstitutional because it applies only to "fighting words" that insult, or provoke violence, "on the basis of race, color, creed, religion, or gender." It does not apply to abusive invectives on other topics, but singles out those speakers who express views on disfavored subjects. Instead of singling out a particularly offensive mode of expression, P has proscribed fighting words of whatever manner that communicate messages of racial, gender, or religious intolerance. This creates the possibility that P hopes to handicap the expression of certain ideas.

♦ P's content discrimination is not reasonably necessary to achieve P's compelling interests; an ordinance not limited to the favored topics would have precisely the same beneficial interest.

Concurrence (White, Blackmun, O'Connor, Stevens, JJ.).

♦ P's ordinance is overbroad because it criminalizes expression protected by the First Amendment as well as unprotected expression. The majority's rationale is a new doctrine that was not even briefed by the parties and is a departure from prior cases. The Court has long applied a categorical approach that identifies certain classifications of speech as unprotected by the First Amendment because the evil to be restricted so overwhelmingly outweighs the expressive interests, if any, at stake. The Court now holds that the First Amendment protects these categories to the extent that the government may not regulate some fighting words more strictly than others because of their content. Now, if the government decides to criminalize certain fighting words, it must criminalize all fighting words.

♦ The Court also refuses to sustain P's ordinance even though it would survive under the strict scrutiny applicable to other protected expression. In *Burson v. Freeman*, 504 U.S. 191 (1992), the Court applied the strict scrutiny standard and upheld a statute prohibiting vote solicitation and display or distribution of campaign materials within 100 feet of the entrance to a polling place, even though the statute could have been drafted in broader, content-neutral terms. Under the Court's decision today, the *Burson* law would have been found unconstitutional.

♦ Although the Court's analysis is flawed, the conclusion is correct because P's ordinance is overbroad. Even as construed by the Minnesota Supreme Court, the ordinance criminalizes a substantial amount of expression that is protected by the First Amendment. That court held that P may constitutionally prohibit expression that "by its very utterance" causes "anger, alarm or resentment," but such generalized reactions are not sufficient to strip expression of its constitutional protection.

Concurrence (Blackmun, J.). The ordinance is overbroad.

Concurrence (Stevens, J.). P's ordinance regulates conduct that has some communicative content, and it raises two questions: Is it "overbroad" because it prohibits too much speech, and, if not, is it "underbroad" because it does not prohibit enough speech? The majority and concurring opinions deal with the basic principles that (i) certain categories of expression are not protected and (ii) content-based regulations of expression are presumptively invalid. But both principles have exceptions. The majority applies the prohibition on content-based regulation to "fighting words"—speech that previously had been considered wholly "unprotected." Now, fighting words have greater protection than commercial speech, which is often regulated based on content. Assuming arguendo that the ordinance regulates only fighting words and is not overbroad, it regulates speech not on the basis of its subject matter or the viewpoint expressed, but rather on the basis of the harm the speech causes—injuries based on "race, color, creed, religion, or gender." It only bans a subcategory of the already narrow category of fighting words. It is not an unconstitutional content-based regulation of speech, and should be upheld, except that it is overbroad.

———————

9. Sentence Enhancement for Racially Motivated Crime

Wisconsin v. Mitchell
508 U.S. 476 (1993).

Facts. Mitchell (D), who is black, severely beat a white victim because of the victim's race. D was convicted of aggravated battery, which carried a maximum sentence of two years' imprisonment. The jury also found that D had intentionally selected his victim because of his race, which increased the maximum sentence to seven years under state law. D was sentenced to four years' imprisonment. The Wisconsin Supreme Court held that the enhancement statute violated the First Amendment because it punished offensive thought. The Supreme Court granted certiorari.

Issue. May a defendant's sentence for a crime be enhanced because he intentionally selected his victim on account of the victim's race?

Held. Yes. Judgment reversed.

♦   D claims that the statute violates the First Amendment by punishing his bigoted beliefs. However, motive plays the same role under the enhancement statute in this case as it does under federal and state anti-discrimination laws, which have been upheld. For example, Title VII makes it unlawful for an employer to discriminate against an employee because of the individual's race. This was cited in *R.A. V. v. City of St. Paul, supra*, as an example of a permissible content-neutral regulation of conduct. *R.A. V.* involved an ordinance directed at expression, while the enhancement statute here is directed at conduct unprotected by the First Amendment.

♦   Bias-inspired conduct is thought to inflict greater individual and societal harm, which justifies the enhanced sentence.

---

10. Statutory Inference of Intent from Conduct Not Allowed

Virginia v. Black
538 U.S. 343 (2003).

Facts. The state of Virginia prohibited the burning of a cross with "an intent to intimidate a person or group of persons." Black and others (Ds) were tried for violating the statute. At the trial, the jury was instructed that Ds' burning of the cross, by itself, was sufficient evidence from which the jury could infer the required intent to intimidate. Ds were convicted, and the court of appeals affirmed. The Virginia Supreme Court held that the cross burning statute was facially unconstitutional under the First Amendment. The Supreme Court granted certiorari.

Issue. May a criminal statute provide that the burning of a cross is prima facie evidence of an intent to intimidate when such an intention is one of the elements of the crime?

Held. No. Judgment reversed.

♦   Cross burning was originally used by Scottish tribes to signal one another in the 14th century. In the United States, however, cross burning has been closely tied to the Ku Klux Klan, which uses cross burnings to communicate threats of violence and intimidation. The Klan also uses cross burnings as symbols of shared group identity and ideology. Thus, although the cross burning does not inevitably convey a message of intimidation, when it is used to intimidate, it is a powerful message.

◆ The government may regulate categories of expression including fighting words and incitement, as well as true threats. Intimidation is a type of true threat, where the speaker directs a threat to a person with the intent of making the victim fear bodily harm or death. Some cross burnings fit within this definition of intimidating speech.

◆ The Supreme Court of Virginia held that the statute was unconstitutional because it discriminates on the basis of content and viewpoint under *R.A. V. v. City of St. Paul, supra. R.A. V.* does not hold that all forms of content-based discrimination within a prescribable area of speech are unconstitutional. The Virginia statute here, unlike the statute in *R.A. V.*, does not single out only that speech directed at one of the specified disfavored topics. The Virginia statute is aimed at burning a cross with intent to intimidate regardless of the victim's race, gender, religion, or other characteristics.

◆ Virginia may properly outlaw cross burnings done with the intent to intimidate because such activity is a particularly virulent form of intimidation, given its history as a signal of impending violence.

◆ However, the statute is unconstitutional because the prima facie evidence provision allows a conviction without proof of the very element that makes it constitutional for Virginia to ban cross burning—the intent to intimidate. Virginia could not ban cross burning alone, without the intimidation intent as an element of the offense, so it cannot simply provide that cross burning constitutes prima facie evidence of the required intent. The statute does not distinguish between cross burning with intent to intimidate and cross burning as a political statement not intended to intimidate.

Concurrence (Stevens, J.). Cross burning with an intent to intimidate is the kind of threat that is unprotected by the First Amendment.

Dissent (Thomas, J.). Whatever expressive value cross burning may have, the legislature wrote it out by banning only intimidating conduct undertaken by a particular means. The statute addressed conduct only, not speech, and should not fall within the First Amendment. Even if the statute did implicate the First Amendment, permitting a jury to draw an inference of intent to intimidate from the cross burning itself is permissible. The inference is rebuttable and the jury still has to find the existence of each element of the offense beyond a reasonable doubt. The Court values physical safety less than the right to be free from unwanted communications.

Concurrence and Dissent (Scalia, Thomas, JJ.). The prima facie evidence part of the statute is not unconstitutional, at least on a facial challenge. Only a limited class of persons, those who abstain from presenting a defense to rebut the prima facie evidence, could be wrongly convicted under that statute. Thus, the statute is not overbroad.

Concurrence and Dissent (Souter, Kennedy, Ginsburg, JJ.). The statute makes a content-based distinction within the category of punishable intimidating expression, which is unconstitutional. This content-based proscription of cross burning could be an effort to ban not only intimidation, but also the messages communicated by non-threatening cross burning. No content-based statute should survive under *R.A. V.* without a high probability that no official suppression of ideas is afoot. The statute here is not narrowly tailored, since a content-neutral statute banning intimidation would accomplish the same objective without singling out particular content.

E. Content-Neutral Restrictions

1. Introduction

The First Amendment forbids governments from regulating speech so as to favor some viewpoints at the expense of others. A viewpoint-neutral regulation may be upheld as long as:

(i) It is within the constitutional power of the government;

(ii) It furthers an important or substantial governmental interest;

(iii) The governmental interest is unrelated to the suppression of free expression; and

(iv) The incidental restriction on alleged First Amendment freedoms is no greater than is essential to the furtherance of that interest.

a. Regulation of handbill distribution

Schneider v. State
308 U.S. 147 (1939).

Facts. The state of New Jersey (P) prosecuted Schneider (D) for violating certain ordinances that prohibited all distribution of leaflets and handbills in public places. There were no provisions for licensing distribution or merely limiting distribution to a certain time, place, and manner. The Supreme Court granted certiorari. Issue. May a municipality prohibit any distribution of printed material in public places?

Held. No. Conviction reversed.

♦   Municipalities may adopt regulations to promote public safety, health, welfare, and convenience, but may not in so doing abridge the individual right to free speech. For example, a city may prohibit the stoppage of traffic by someone desiring to distribute literature or a city may prohibit littering. But an objective of keeping the streets clean and in good appearance is insufficient to justify an ordinance that prohibits a person rightfully on a public street from handing literature to one willing to receive it.

♦   If the objective is to keep streets clean, a city may punish those who actually throw papers on the street, but it cannot ban the distribution of literature. To the extent the city must clean and care for the streets as an indirect consequence of distribution of printed material, the burden on the city is a result of the constitutional protection of the freedom of speech.

---

b. Regulation of solicitors and canvassers

Martin v. City of Struthers
319 U.S. 141 (1943).

Facts. Martin (D), a Jehovah's Witness, was convicted of violating an ordinance that forbid any person from knocking on doors, ringing doorbells, or otherwise summoning to the door the occupants of a residence, for the purpose of distributing to them handbills or circulars. D appeals.

Issue. May the government impose a criminal sanction for door-to-door distribution of handbills as applied to a person distributing advertisements for a religious meeting?

Held. No. Conviction reversed.

♦   This ordinance attempts to substitute the judgment of the community for that of the householder and in so doing is an unreasonable interference with the advocate's freedom of speech and the press. Door-to-door distribution of circulars is essential to poorly financed causes. The freedom to distribute information to every citizen is so vital to preservation of a free society that it must be fully preserved, subject only to reasonable police and health regulation of time and manner.

Concurrence (Frankfurter, J.). This ordinance punishes only the distribution of literature, not all door-to-door canvassing. The Court's opinion leaves doubt as to whether a prohibition against *all* door-to-door canvassing would be permissible.

---

c. Intrusive speakers and unwilling listeners

Kovacs v. Cooper
336 U.S. 77 (1949).

Facts. Kovacs (D) was convicted of violation of an ordinance prohibiting the use on public streets of sound trucks or amplifiers that were operated so as to produce "loud and raucous noises." D appeals.

Issue. May the government impose a criminal sanction for the use of amplifying devices on public streets?

Held. Yes. Judgment affirmed.

♦ We should not enforce the right to freedom of speech in total disregard for the freedom of unwilling listeners in their homes or businesses. The ordinance does not restrict the communication of the same ideas by other means, such as the natural human voice. The need for reasonable protection of homes and businesses from distracting noises justifies the ordinance.

Concurrence (Frankfurter, J.). As long as the legislature does not prescribe which ideas may be noisily expressed, it is not for the court to supervise the limits in safeguarding the cherished right to privacy.

Dissent (Black, Douglas, Rutledge, JJ.). The statute is an impermissible flat ban. The government should be required to show actual emission of a loud and raucous noise in each case.

Comment. In *Saia v. New York*, 334 U.S. 558 (1948), the Court struck down a local ordinance that required a police permit before using a loudspeaker on public streets. The ordinance did not include any standard for granting or withholding such permits, but instead vested absolute discretion in the chief of police.

---

d. Billboard regulation

Metromedia, Inc. v. San Diego
453 U.S. 490 (1981).

Facts. Metromedia, Inc. (P) challenged a San Diego (D) ordinance that banned all outdoor advertising display signs, except for commercial on-site signs regarding the business on the premises. There were 12 additional exceptions relating to content, time, place, and manner.

Issue. May the government restrict billboards based on content?

Held. No. The ordinance is invalid.

♦ D cannot ban the billboards outright, even if the ban satisfies the four-part *Central Hudson* test (*supra*), because the law allows certain commercial signs. This gives greater protection to commercial speech than to noncommercial speech, contrary to the priority granted by the First Amendment.

Dissent (Stevens, J.). Some total prohibitions may be permissible, such as an exclusion of billboards from residential neighborhoods. Because D had a legitimate governmental interest in the regulation, it should be upheld unless the regulation is biased in favor of one point of view, or the ban precludes open communication of ideas. Neither situation existed in this case.

Dissent (Burger, C.J.). There are alternative methods of conveying a message other than billboards. It borders on frivolous to suggest that the ordinance infringes on freedom of expression.

---

e. Homeowner signs

City of Ladue v. Gilleo
512 U.S. 43 (1994).

Facts. Gilleo (P) sued the city of Ladue (D) for a permanent injunction prohibiting D from enforcing an ordinance that banned all residential signs but those falling within one of 10 exemptions. The lower courts found for P, and the Supreme Court granted certiorari.

Issue. May a city ban homeowners from displaying signs on their property?

Held. No. Judgment affirmed.

♦ D claims that the ordinance is merely a regulation of the time, place, or manner of speech, but even this type of regulation must leave room for ample alternative channels for communication. D's ordinance goes too far. Residential signs are important means of public communication and may be the only practical means for persons of modest means or limited mobility.

---

f. Disclosure of intercepted cell phone call

During contentious union negotiations between a teachers' union and the school board, the union's chief negotiator used a cell phone to talk with the union's president. An unknown person intercepted and recorded their conversation. Vopper, a radio commentator, played a tape of the intercepted conversation on his radio show. In *Bartnicki v. Vopper*, 532 U.S. 514 (2001), the Court held that Vopper could not be held liable for damages under antiwiretap laws for broadcasting the phone call. The Court acknowledged that Vopper knew or should have known that the recording was illegal. However, the Court explained that although the government has a legitimate interest in protecting privacy, it cannot suppress speech by a law-abiding possessor of information in order to deter the conduct of a non-law-abiding third party. Furthermore, the tape involved a matter of public concern, and the Court decided that, in balancing the competing interests, privacy concerns must yield to the interest in publishing matters of public importance. Chief Justice Rehnquist, joined by Justices Scalia and Thomas, dissented, arguing that the decision diminished the purposes of the First Amendment by chilling the speech of millions of Americans who rely on electronic technology to communicate.

2. The Public Forum Doctrine

While the Court has been careful to protect the rights of private property owners to prevent others from using their property for speech purposes, the Court has also protected the right of citizens to communicate in public forums. There is a distinction between streets and parks, which generally are open for speech, and other types of government property.

a. Streets and parks

Commonwealth v. Davis
39 N.E. 113 (1895), *aff'd sub nom.* Davis v. Massachusetts, 167 U.S. 43 (1897).

Facts. Davis (D), a preacher, was convicted of violating an ordinance that forbade public address on public property without a permit from the mayor. D addressed crowds on Boston Common. The Supreme Judicial Court of Massachusetts affirmed the conviction and D appeals.

Issue. May the government forbid public speaking on government-owned property?

Held. Yes. Conviction affirmed.

♦ The regulation was not directed at free speech generally, but toward the permitted uses of Boston Common. The Constitution does not allow the citizens to use public property without restriction. Instead, the government has a right to exclude all use, so it can also determine under what circumstances the property may be used.

Comments.

♦ Years after this case, in *Hague v. CIO*, 307 U.S. 496 (1939), the Court held that a state cannot require a person to obtain a permit to access public property for speech purposes where the issuance of such permits is entirely discretionary. The Court set forth a broad, guaranteed access approach to public streets and parks, based on the historical open use of public parks and streets. Such access can be regulated for the common interest, but never denied.

♦ In *Schneider v. State, supra*, the Court held that a city's interest in keeping streets clean and in good appearance was insufficient to support a prohibition on the distribution of leaflets. This approach recognizes that governments must satisfy stringent standards of justification for content-neutral restrictions that involve public forum rights.

---

b. Other publicly owned property

1) Jails

Adderley v. Florida
385 U.S. 39 (1966).

Facts. Adderley and others (Ds) were convicted of trespassing upon the premises of a county jail. Ds had entered the premises to protest the arrest of fellow students and had refused to leave after being notified that they would be arrested for trespass. Ds appeal, claiming that their convictions violated their constitutional right of assembly.

Issue. May a state use a trespass action to prohibit peaceful assembly on a special purpose public property?

Held. Yes. Judgment affirmed.

♦ The record reveals that the sheriff objected not to Ds' ideas or protests but only to their presence on that part of the jail grounds reserved for jail uses. The area occupied by Ds was not open to the general public but was reserved for those having specific jail duties. The state has power to preserve its property for the use to which it is lawfully dedicated, and the sheriff did not discriminate against these particular Ds.

♦ Ds presume that people who want to propagandize protests or views have a constitutional right to do so whenever, however, and wherever they please, but this Court has previously rejected such a concept.

Dissent (Douglas, J., Warren, C.J., Brennan, Fortas, JJ.). A prison is a seat of government and an obvious center for protest against unjust confinement. We do violence to the First Amendment by permitting this "petition for redress of grievances" to be turned into a trespass action.

Comment. The Court has upheld an ordinance prohibiting demonstrations near schools, during school hours, which materially disrupt classwork. Although school property (or adjacent property) cannot be declared "off limits" for expressive activity, such activity cannot be permitted to invade the right of students to an education. [*See* Grayned v. City of Rockford, 408 U.S. 104 (1972)]

---

2) Military installations

The Court has recognized that the military is a special environment in which First Amendment rights are subject to special restrictions because of military necessity. This includes control over nonpartisan speech. For example, in *Greer v. Spock*, 424 U.S. 828 (1976), the Court held that a military base may prohibit all outward political expression within its boundaries.

3) State fair

A state fair may restrict distribution of literature to assigned booths. [Heffron v. International Society for Krishna Consciousness, Inc., 452 U.S. 640 (1981)]

4) Letter boxes

The First Amendment does not guarantee a civic association the right to deposit literature, without payment of postage, in mail depositories authorized by the United States Postal Service. [United States Postal Service v. Council of Greenburgh Civic Associations, 453 U.S. 114 (1981)] The Postal Service's interest in efficient mail service justified this restriction, and such letter boxes are not a "public forum."

5) Utility poles

In *Los Angeles v. Taxpayers for Vincent*, 466 U.S. 789 (1984), Los Angeles prohibited the posting of signs on public property. The Court held that the city had a constitutional power to enhance its appearance that justified the ordinance. The interest was unrelated to the suppression of ideas.

6) Airports

International Society for Krishna Consciousness v. Lee
505 U.S. 672 (1992).

Facts. Members of the International Society for Krishna Consciousness (P) performed a religious ritual known as "sankirtan," which consisted of going into public places, disseminating religious literature, and soliciting funds to support the religion. P desired to perform sankirtan at the airports in the New York City area. Lee (D) was the police superintendent of the airports and was responsible for enforcing a regulation that prohibited the repetitive sale of merchandise, the solicitation of money, or the distribution of literature within the interior areas of buildings at the airport. Such activities were permitted on the sidewalks outside the terminal buildings. P challenged the regulation. The district court granted P summary judgment. The court of appeals affirmed with regard to the ban on distributing, but reversed with regard to the ban on solicitation. The Supreme Court granted certiorari.

Issue. May an airport terminal operated by a public authority prohibit solicitation in the interior of its buildings?

Held. Yes. Judgment affirmed.

♦ Solicitation is clearly a form of protected speech, but the government need not permit all forms of speech on property it owns and controls. Prior cases reflect a "forum-based" approach to assess government restrictions on the use of its property. There are three categories of government property:

(i) *Traditional public fora*—property that has traditionally been available for public expression. Regulation of speech on this type of property survives only if it is narrowly drawn to achieve a compelling state interest.

(ii) *Designated public fora*—property that the government has opened for expressive activity by part or all of the public. Regulation of speech on this type of property also survives only if it is narrowly drawn to achieve a compelling state interest.

(iii) *All remaining public property.* Regulation of speech on this type of property survives if it is reasonable, as long as the regulation is not an effort to suppress the speaker's activity due to disagreement with the speaker's views.

♦ A traditional public forum exists where the property has been immemorially held in trust for the use of the public and has been used for purposes of assembly, communicating thoughts among citizens, and discussing public questions. Examples include streets and parks. Designated public fora are areas that are intentionally dedicated for use in public discourse.

♦ Airports do not meet these requirements. For one thing, they have not been in existence for many years. For another, they have not historically been made available for speech activity, except when ordered to by the courts. Airports are not just "transportation nodes" like bus and rail terminals, but have special characteristics. The purpose of an airport is to facilitate travel and make a regulated profit, not to promote expression.

♦ Because an airport is not a public forum, D's regulations are permissible as long as they are reasonable. P's proposed solicitation has a disruptive effect on airport travelers who are typically in a hurry and for whom a delay can mean a lost flight and severe inconvenience. Face-to-face solicitation presents a risk of duress and fraud that D can properly attempt to avoid. Therefore, D's ban on solicitation is sustained.

Concurrence (O'Connor, J.). An airport is clearly not a public forum. It could be closed to everyone except those who have legitimate business there, unlike public streets and parks, but government officials make airports open to the public as a convenience. The airport does contain restaurants, shops, newsstands, and other facilities not directly related to travel, but D's regulations are reasonably related to maintaining the multipurpose environment created by D. At the same time, the ban on leafleting cannot be upheld as reasonable, since distributing literature does not present the same problems as soliciting funds.

Dissent (Rehnquist, C.J., White, Scalia, Thomas, JJ.). Airports are not public fora; both the distribution ban and the solicitation ban are reasonable. Travelers have no need to be delayed by solicitation, and leafletting may produce unsightly and hazardous litter.

---

c. The public forum—unequal access

1) Introduction

If a restriction on speech is based on the content of the speech, the Court will scrutinize it much more carefully than if the restriction is content-neutral. This analysis underlies many of the Supreme Court's cases.

2) Ban on labor picketing

Police Department of Chicago v. Mosley
408 U.S. 92 (1972).

Facts. The city of Chicago passed an ordinance prohibiting picketing, except for peaceful labor picketing, near public schools at certain times. Mosley (P), who had picketed a certain school over several months, sought declaratory and injunctive relief in order to continue his picketing. The Chicago Police Department (D) appeals a judgment in favor of P.

Issue. May a government entity regulate picketing solely on the basis of subject matter?

Held. No. Judgment affirmed.

♦ Although picketing is protected by the First Amendment, reasonable "time, place, and manner" regulations are permitted to further significant governmental interests.

♦ D's ordinance, however, invalidates certain picketing solely in terms of subject matter, while permitting other picketing of the same time, place, and manner. This cannot be permitted in the absence of a showing that the regulation is narrowly tailored to a legitimate objective.

---

3) Government regulation and captive audiences

a) Advertising space in public transportation

Lehman v. City of Shaker Heights
418 U.S. 298 (1974).

Facts. Lehman (P), a candidate for public office, sought advertising space on the cars of the rapid transit system of Shaker Heights (D). The advertising was managed by a private firm under contract with D. One provision of the contract prohibited any political advertising. P sued, claiming that public transportation is a public forum protected by the First Amendment. P appeals a state court decision in favor of D.

Issue. Is a city's transit system advertising space a public forum that cannot be foreclosed to political advertising?

Held. No. Judgment affirmed.

♦ The nature of a forum and the conflicting interests involved are important in determining the degree of First Amendment protection to be afforded.

♦ Although owned by the city, the advertising venture is essentially commercial in nature and has never been used for any political or public issue advertising.

♦ The existence of state action requires that rules relating to advertising access not be arbitrary, capricious, or invidious. D's rules are not. They advance reasonable legislative objectives of minimizing chances of abuse, the appearance of favoritism, and the risk of imposing upon a captive audience.

Concurrence (Douglas, J.). In asking us to force the system to accept his message as a vindication of his constitutional rights, P overlooks the constitutional rights of the commuters. Commuters have a right to be free from forced intrusion on their privacy.

Dissent (Brennan, Stewart, Marshall, Powell, JJ.). Having opened this forum for communication, D is barred by the First Amendment from discriminating among forum users solely on the basis of message content.

---

b) Restricted access to school district mail system

Perry Educators' Association v. Perry Local Educators' Association
460 U.S. 37 (1983).

Facts. The Perry Local Educators' Association (P) and the Perry Educators' Association (D) both represented teachers in the school district and had equal access to the interschool mail system. D challenged P's status as bargaining representative and won election as the exclusive representative of the teachers. The labor contract negotiated by D gave it the exclusive right of access to teachers' mailboxes and to use of the interschool mail delivery system. However, during a representation contest, all involved unions had equal access under state law. P brought an action for injunctive and declaratory relief, claiming the preferential access given D violated the First and Fourteenth Amendments. The district court granted D summary judgment, but the court of appeals reversed. D appeals. (The Court treats the case as a petition for a writ of certiorari.)

Issue. May a school district restrict access to its mail system to an exclusive labor bargaining representative?

Held. Yes. Judgment reversed.

♦ The existence of a right of access to public property and the type of limitations that are allowed depend on the character of the property involved. There are three basic types:

(i) Places long devoted to assembly and debate, like parks, are generally not subject to governmental restrictions of expressive activity unless narrowly drawn to achieve a compelling state interest.

(ii) Places opened for public expressive activity are usually subject to the same rules as the traditional public forum.

(iii) Public property not a public forum by tradition or designation may be protected by more comprehensive restrictions to preserve its use for its primary function.

♦ The public school mail system falls within the third category. Access may be limited as long as the restriction on speech is reasonable and not an arbitrary suppression of ideas. Exclusive use by D preserves the property for the use to which it was lawfully dedicated. P has no official need to use the system, and alternative forums are available. The legitimate state interest it furthers satisfies the equal protection claim.

Dissent (Brennan, Marshall, Powell, Stevens, JJ.). The exclusive access given to D amounts to viewpoint discrimination against P. The intent to discriminate can be inferred from the effect of the policy—which is to deny P effective communication. No substantial state interest is advanced thereby, so the restriction is unconstitutional.

---

c) Access to televised debate

The Arkansas Educational Television Commission ("AETC"), a state-owned public television broadcaster, sponsored a debate between the major party candidates for a congressional seat. When the AETC denied Forbes's request to participate, Forbes sued. In *Arkansas Educational Television Commission v. Forbes*, 523 U.S. 666 (1998), the Court held that the selective access of the debate did not create a public forum requiring strict scrutiny. Thus, applying the standard for exclusions from a nonpublic forum, the Court concluded that the decision to exclude Forbes was constitutionally permissible because it was not based on Forbes's viewpoint, but was because Forbes had not generated appreciable public support.

d. Unequal access to other forms of government property

1) Municipal theater

Southeastern Promotions v. Conrad
420 U.S. 546 (1975).

Facts. Southeastern Promotions (P) applied for permission to present the musical *Hair* at a municipal theater. The application was rejected on the grounds that the musical contains "obscenity." P sought an injunction, but was denied. The United States Supreme Court granted certiorari.

Issue. Was the denial of permission an unconstitutional prior restraint?

Held. Yes. Judgment reversed.

♦ The municipal theater is public forum. In order to deny someone access, there must be certain procedural safeguards in place to reduce the danger of suppressing constitutionally protected speech. There were no such safeguards here.

Dissent and Concurrence (Douglas, J.). The critical flaw here is not the absence of procedural safeguards, but the screening based on content.

Dissent (White, J., Burger, C.J.). *Hair* contains nudity and simulated sex acts and thus is not appropriate for children. The city may reserve its auditorium for productions suitable for all citizens, adults and children.

Dissent (Rehnquist, J.). Until now, a theater was not equated to a public street or park. As part of the business of managing a theater, the city should be able to reject a production that would offend a substantial numbers of theatergoers.

---

2) Government control over school library material

Board of Education v. Pico
457 U.S. 853 (1982).

Facts. The Board of Education (D) obtained a list of "objectionable" books and removed them from the high school library for review by board members. D appointed a committee to recommend whether the books should be retained in the library, men rejected the recommendations and returned only one of the removed books. D based its decision on the claim that the books were anti-American and that they presented moral danger to the students. Pico (P) challenged the decision in federal court. The district court granted summary judgment for D, but the court of appeals reversed and remanded for trial. D appeals.

Issue. Does the First Amendment impose limitations on a local school board's discretionary removal of books from a high school library?

Held. Yes. Judgment affirmed.

♦ This case does not involve the use of books in the classroom, but merely optional library books. Nor does it involve acquisition of books. Because of the procedural posture of the case, the judgment must be affirmed if there is any question of fact.

♦ Local school boards have discretion in managing school affairs. However, this discretion is subject to the First Amendment rights of the students. These rights may be impinged by the removal of books from a school library. D's discretion may not be exercised so as to deny students access to ideas with which the board members disagree, although they could remove books that were pervasively vulgar or educationally unsuitable.

♦ The evidence as to D's motive in removing the books is unclear. There is evidence that D acted out of disagreement with the ideas contained in the books. By disregarding the committee's recommendations, the board acted in an ad hoc manner. The case must be remanded for necessary factfindings.

Concurrence (Blackmun, J.). The state may not suppress exposure to ideas without a sufficiently compelling reason. And it may not deny access to an idea simply because state officials disapprove of or disagree with the idea. However, there is no right to receive ideas on the part of students. The determinative question is the motive of the school officials.

Dissent (Rehnquist, J., Burger, C.J., Powell, J.). D did not deprive the public generally of the ideas in the books. Education, especially short of the university level, is necessarily selective, and those charged with providing the education must be free to determine what is necessary and what is not. The First Amendment right to receive information does not apply to an institution that is necessarily selective in the ideas it may impart.

---

3) Subsidies and tax expenditures

Regan v. Taxation with Representation of Washington
461 U.S. 540 (1983).

Facts. The Internal Revenue Code grants a tax exempt status to various nonprofit organizations, including veterans' organizations and charitable organizations. Individual contributions to veterans' organizations and charitable organizations that do not participate in political lobbying are deductible from the contributor's taxable income, but contributions to charitable organizations that do lobby, such as Taxation with Representation of Washington (P), are not deductible. P challenged the deductibility provisions as a violation of its First Amendment rights. The court of appeals upheld P's claim. Regan (D), the Secretary of the Treasury, appeals.

Issue. May Congress use tax expenditures to permit some types of organizations, but not others, to lobby at taxpayer expense?

Held. Yes. Judgment reversed.

♦ Both tax exemptions and tax deductibility are government subsidies. The effect of the IRS provisions is to subsidize lobbying less than other activities undertaken by charitable organizations. Failure of Congress to subsidize P's First Amendment activities does not constitute a violation of those rights, even when veterans' organizations do receive a subsidy for lobbying. The tax code does not involve a suspect classification, nor does strict scrutiny apply whenever Congress subsidizes some, but not all, speech.

♦ A legislature's decision not to subsidize the exercise of a fundamental right does not infringe that right, so it is not subject to strict scrutiny. Although government may not place obstacles in the path of P's freedom of speech, it is not required to remove those not of its own creation.

♦ It is rational for Congress to decide to subsidize lobbying by veterans' organizations even when other groups do not receive such a subsidy. Veterans have made special contributions to the nation and can be compensated in a variety of ways.

Concurrence (Blackmun, Brennan, Marshall, JJ.). The discrimination between veteran's organizations and other charities is not based on the content of their speech. That would present a very different question.

---

4) Government subsidies to speech

Rust v. Sullivan
500 U.S. 173 (1991).

Facts. Congress enacted Title X of the Public Health Service Act, which provided federal funding for family-planning services, provided that none of the funds could be used in programs where abortion is a method of family planning. Sullivan (D), Secretary of the Department of Health and Human Services, promulgated new regulations that (i) specified that a Title X project cannot provide counseling concerning abortion or referrals for abortion; (ii) prohibited a Title X project from engaging in activities that encourage, promote, or advocate abortion as a method of family planning; and (iii) required that Title X projects be physically and financially separate from prohibited abortion activities. Rust (P) challenged the facial validity of the regulations, claiming they violated the First and Fifth Amendments. The lower courts upheld the regulations. The Supreme Court granted certiorari.

Issue. May the federal government condition the acceptance of federal funds by a particular project on the project's agreement to refrain from promoting or even discussing abortion?

Held. Yes. Judgment affirmed.

♦   D's regulations do not exceed D's authority as long as they reflect a plausible construction of the plain language of the statute and do not otherwise conflict with Congress's expressed intent. The language of the statute is ambiguous and broad enough to allow D's interpretation. Courts normally must defer to the expertise of the agency charged with administering the law. The fact that the regulations are a change from the prior regulations is justified by D's experience under the prior policy.

♦   P claims that the regulations are discrimination based on viewpoint because they promote childbirth over abortion. But D has merely chosen to fund one activity to the exclusion of the other. The government has no obligation to subsidize counterpart rights once it decides to subsidize one protected right. D's regulations do not deny anyone a benefit, but merely require that public funds be spent for the purposes for which they were authorized. And they apply to the project, not to the grantee, who is left free to perform abortions and to advocate abortion in other contexts.

♦   P also claims that D's regulations violate a woman's Fifth Amendment right to choose whether to terminate her pregnancy. But Congress's refusal to fund abortion counseling and advocacy leaves a pregnant woman with the same choices as if Congress had chosen not to fund family-planning services at all. D's regulations do not affect a doctor's ability to provide information about abortion outside the context of a Title X project.

Dissent (Blackmun, Marshall, Stevens, JJ.). D's regulations clearly constitute content-based regulation of speech aimed at suppressing "dangerous ideas." They are also viewpoint based, since they prohibit abortion advocacy but do not regulate anti-abortion advocacy. The government's interest in ensuring that federal funds are not spent for a purpose outside the scope of a program falls far short of that needed to justify the suppression of truthful information regarding constitutionally protected conduct of vital importance to the listener.

Comment. The Court noted that government funding is not always sufficient by itself to justify government control over the content of expression. For example, government ownership of real property does not justify restriction of speech in such areas if they have been traditionally open to the public for expressive activity, and government payments to universities do not justify control of speech there. In this case, D's regulations do not significantly impinge upon the doctor-patient relationship because they do not apply to post-conception medical care, and the doctor can make it clear that advice regarding abortion is beyond the scope of the Title X program.

---

5) Government support of legal services

In 1974, Congress established the Legal Services Corporation ("LSC") to distribute federal funds to eligible organizations to provide financial support for legal assistance in non-criminal proceedings. Congress prohibited LSC's funds from being used on legal representation that challenged the legality or constitutionality of existing welfare laws. In *Legal Services Corporation v. Velazquez*, 531 U.S. 533 (2001), the Court held the restriction unconstitutional. The Court noted that *Rust, supra*, involved the government's own message, which gave the government greater latitude to restrict speech. On the other hand, LSC was set up to facilitate private speech, not to promote a governmental message. The Court maintained that restricting LSC's attorneys in handling their clients' cases distorted the legal system by altering the traditional role of attorneys and would result in questions about the validity of an attorney's representation of his clients. Furthermore, if the attorney withdrew to avoid violating LSC's rules, the client would be unlikely to find alternative counsel, which meant there would be no alternative channel for the expression Congress sought to restrict.

6) Decency standards for federal spending

National Endowment for the Arts v. Finley
524 U.S. 569 (1998).

Facts. The National Endowment for the Arts (D) is funded by Congress. After D funded some controversial projects, Congress amended the statute to require D to consider "general standards of decency and respect for the diverse beliefs and values of the American people" in establishing procedures to judge the artistic merit of grant applications. Finley and other artists (Ps) applied for grants before the amendment was adopted. Ps were denied funding, and they sued, claiming D denied their First Amendment rights by rejecting their applications on political grounds. The District Court denied D's motion for judgment on the pleadings. The court granted summary judgment to Ps on their facial challenge to the amendments and enjoined D from enforcing it. The court of appeals affirmed. The Supreme Court granted certiorari.

Issue. May Congress impose decency standards on discretionary spending of federally-appropriated funds?

Held. Yes. Judgment reversed.

♦ The amendment, section 954(d)(1), does not impose a categorical requirement. It consists of advisory language only, and is aimed at reforming procedures rather than precluding speech. There is no realistic danger that the provision will compromise First Amendment values.

♦ It is also unlikely that the provision will introduce any greater element of selectivity man the determination of "artistic excellence" itself. The nature of arts funding requires content-based considerations. Some constitutionally protected expression will be rejected regardless of the criteria used.

♦ In *Rosenberger v. Rector and Visitors of University of Virginia*, 515 U.S. 819 (1995), the Court held that a school could not exclude religious student publications when it encouraged a diversity of views from private speakers. In this case, however, D is not indiscriminately encouraging a diversity of views; it is trying to make aesthetic judgments on the content of submissions.

Concurrence (Scalia, Thomas, JJ.). Section 954(d)(1) indeed establishes content-and-viewpoint-based criteria upon which D is to evaluate grant applications. However, there is a difference between "abridging" speech and funding it. The First Amendment is inapplicable to the latter.

Dissent (Souter, J.). D has failed to show why the statute should be exempted from the fundamental rule of the First Amendment that viewpoint discrimination in the exercise of public authority over expressive activity is unconstitutional. Once the government decides to subsidize expressive conduct at large, it cannot discriminate on the basis of the content.

---

7) Requiring Internet filters in government-supported libraries

After providing funding to help public libraries expand Internet access, Congress enacted the Children's Internet Protection Act ("CIPA"). CIPA prohibited libraries from receiving the federal funds unless the libraries installed filtering software to prevent minors from accessing harmful material and to block obscenity and child pornography. Although some libraries had already begun installing blocking and filtering software, a group of libraries, library patrons, and Website publishers challenged CIPA. In *United States v. American Library Association, Inc.*, 539 U.S. 194 (2003), the Court held that CIPA did not impose an unconstitutional condition on public libraries. The Court noted that libraries have never provided universal coverage, but exercise judgment in selecting material for their patrons. The Court reasoned that adding blocking and filtering software does not change the nature of a library's role because most libraries already exclude pornography from their collections. The Court also pointed out that the lack of a subsidy is not a penalty, so Congress was not penalizing libraries that chose not to install the filtering software. In his dissent, Justice Stevens described CIPA as an "overly broad restriction on adult access to protected speech." Justice Souter, joined by Justice Ginsburg, also dissented, asserting that blocking Internet access in public libraries is like denying adults access to certain books in the libraries' collections.

3. Symbolic Conduct

The protection afforded unpopular words extends to symbolic conduct that can be considered expression, *i.e.*, conduct undertaken to communicate an idea. Not all such conduct is protected, however. If regulation of the conduct has only an incidental restriction on expression, the regulation may be permitted.

a. Draft card burning

United States v. O'Brien
391 U.S. 367 (1968).

Facts. O'Brien (D) and others publicly burned their draft cards, in violation of federal law. D claims his action was intended to influence others to adopt his antiwar beliefs. D was convicted, but the court of appeals held that the statute was an unconstitutional abridgment of freedom of speech. The Supreme Court granted review.

Issue. When conduct contains both "speech" and "nonspeech" elements, may an important governmental interest in regulating the nonspeech element justify incidental limitations on First Amendment freedoms?

Held. Yes. Judgment reversed.

♦ The statute on its face does not abridge free speech, but deals with conduct having no connection with speech, *i.e.*, destruction of draft cards. It is similar to a motor vehicle law prohibiting destruction of drivers' licenses.

♦ Although freedom of expression includes certain symbolic speech, it does not include any and all conduct intended to express an idea. Even conduct that contains a protected communicative element is not absolutely immune from government regulation. A sufficiently important governmental interest in regulating the nonspeech element of conduct can justify incidental limitations on the speech element.

- A government regulation is justified if: (i) it is within constitutional authority; (ii) it furthers an important governmental interest; (iii) the interest is unrelated to the suppression of free expression; and (iv) the incidental restriction on First Amendment freedoms is no greater than is essential to the furtherance of that interest

- The draft card laws meet this test. Therefore, D may properly be prosecuted for his illegal activity.

Concurrence (Harlan, J.). This decision does not foreclose a First Amendment claim in those rare instances where a regulation would entirely prevent a speaker from lawfully conveying a message. D could have conveyed his message in many other ways.

Dissent (Douglas, J.). The underlying and basic question here is whether conscription is permissible in the absence of a declaration of war.

---

b. Flag desecration

The earlier flag cases did not reach the issue of whether flag desecration was protected speech. In a 5 to 4 decision in *Street v. New York*, 394 U.S. 576 (1969), the Court struck down a law making it a crime to publicly defile or cast contempt on an American flag. Not reaching the issue of the constitutionality of flag burning as political protest, the Court found that the law was unconstitutionally applied to the defendant as punishment for his speech, not for his conduct. In 1974, under a similar law, the Court reversed a conviction based on a flag sewn to the seat of trousers. The holding was based on a due process doctrine of vagueness. [Smith v. Goguen, 415 U.S. 566 (1974); *see also* Spence v. Washington, 418 U.S. 405 (1974)—law unconstitutional as applied to removable peace symbol attached to flag because it was a peaceful, nondestructive means of communication] In *Texas v. Johnson*, 491 U.S. 397 (1989), the Supreme Court found that flag burning constitutes expressive, overtly political conduct and thus falls under First Amendment protection. That case held that a state may not make it a criminal offense to burn the American flag. Later, the same majority that made up the majority in *Johnson* struck down a federal statute enacted by Congress in reaction to *Johnson* that was intended to prevent any mutilation, including burnings of any flag of the United States, except during proper disposal. [United States v. Eichman, 496 U.S. 310 (1990)]

c. Prohibition of nude dancing

Barnes v. Glen Theatre, Inc.
501 U.S. 560 (1991).

Facts. Glen Theatre, Inc. (P) operated a dancing establishment. P wanted to provide totally nude dancing as entertainment. Indiana had a public indecency statute that prohibited complete nudity in public places and required the wearing of pasties and G-strings. P sued Barnes (D) and other officials to enjoin enforcement of the statute. The district court held for D on the ground that P's proposed dancing is not expressive activity under the First Amendment. The court of appeals reversed, holding that non-obscene nude dancing is protected expression. The Supreme Court granted certiorari.

Issue. May a state prohibit public nudity, even if this includes nude dancing?

Held. Yes. Judgment reversed.

- Several cases suggest that nude dancing is expressive conduct, even if it is only marginally protected by the First Amendment. Under the four-part *O'Brien* test, *supra*, D's statute is justified despite its incidental limitations on some expressive activity. The public indecency statute furthers substantial governmental interests in protecting societal order and morality, and it is within the traditional police power of a state.

♦ The governmental interests are unrelated to the suppression of free expression. The statute does not proscribe nudity because of the erotic message conveyed by the dancers; erotic performances may be conducted by P as long as the performers wear a minimal amount of clothing. The law merely makes the message slightly less graphic. The state may properly prevent public nudity, even if it is combined with expressive activity.

♦ The governmental interest in prohibiting public nudity is not a means to some greater end, but an end in itself. The statute is narrowly tailored because requiring the wearing of pasties and G-strings is the bare minimum necessary to achieve the state's purposes.

Concurrence (Scalia, J.). The statute is not subject to First Amendment scrutiny at all because it is a general law that regulates conduct and is not specifically directed at expression. The dissent argues that the purpose of restricting public nudity is to protect nonconsenting parties from offense, but society may prohibit activities that are immoral, regardless of whether they harm others. Examples of such prohibited activities include bestiality, drug use, cockfighting, prostitution, and sodomy. Virtually all laws restrict conduct, and virtually any prohibited conduct can be performed for an expressive purpose, including the fact that the actor disagrees with the prohibition. The First Amendment reaches expressive conduct when the prohibition applies to the communicative attributes of the conduct, but not when the impact is merely the incidental effect of forbidding the conduct for other reasons. If the law does not directly or indirectly impede speech, the First Amendment applies only if the purpose of the law is to suppress communication.

Concurrence (Souter, J.). Performance dancing is inherently expressive, but nudity per se is not; nudity is a condition, not an activity. The voluntary assumption of the condition of nudity expresses nothing more than that the condition is somehow appropriate to the circumstances, but that is the message of every voluntary act. Calling all voluntary activity expressive would reduce the concept of expression to the point of meaninglessness. The *O'Brien* test properly applies here, and the state's interest in preventing "secondary effects" such as prostitution, sexual assault, and other criminal activity is sufficient to justify enforcement of the statute against the type of adult entertainment sought by P.

Dissent (White, Marshall, Blackmun, Stevens, JJ.). Dancing is an ancient art form that inherently embodies the expression and communication of ideas and emotions. The state's general interest in promoting societal order and morality is not sufficient justification for this statute that reaches a significant amount of expressive activity. The purpose of a ban on public nudity is to protect others from offense, but that purpose is inapplicable in P's establishment, where people pay to see the dances. With regard to P's dancers, the state is simply protecting viewers from what it believes to be a harmful message. The nudity is an expressive component of the dance, not incidental conduct, and the statute is therefore related to expressive conduct. Without a compelling state interest to support the statute, P's challenge should be upheld.

---

d. Prohibition of nudity to avoid harmful secondary effects

City of Erie v. Pap's A.M.
529 U.S. 277 (2000).

Facts. The owner of a nude dancing establishment (P) challenged an ordinance of the city of Erie (D) that banned public nudity. The purpose of the ordinance was to deter crime and other "deleterious effects" that often occur near establishments featuring live nude entertainment. The state supreme court declared the ordinance unconstitutional, and the United States Supreme Court granted certiorari.

Issue. May a state prohibit public nudity with the intent of preventing harmful secondary effects?

Held. Yes. Judgment reversed.

♦ This statute is a general prohibition, and even if it is attempting to prevent harmful secondary effects it is not related to the suppression of expression. This case is similar to *O'Brien, supra*, and satisfies the *O'Brien* test.

♦ It does not matter if the ordinance is really aimed at particular businesses. The court will not strike down an otherwise valid statute on the basis of an alleged illicit motive.

Concurrence (Scalia, Thomas, JJ.). Because this is a general law regulating conduct, not expression, it is not subject to First Amendment scrutiny.

Dissent (Stevens, Ginsburg, JJ.). For the first time the Court uses the "secondary effects" test to uphold a total ban. The purpose of this ordinance is to limit a protected form of speech, and D has admitted to allowing a production of a play that contained public nudity.

Dissent (Souter, J.). D should have to show the basis for its belief that harm is caused by public nudity and its belief that the ordinance will alleviate that harm.

---

4. Regulation of Political Solicitation, Contribution, Expenditure, and Activity

a. Campaign expenditures

Although Congress has constitutional power to regulate federal elections, it may not unreasonably interfere with First Amendment freedoms when it regulates such elections. The Court attempted to strike a balance between these competing interests when it considered the 1974 amendments to the Federal Election Campaign Act of 1971 and the Internal Revenue Code of 1954. The opinion, *Buckley v. Valeo*, below, consumed nearly 300 pages in the *United States Reports*. Basically, it held that Congress can limit the amounts individuals may contribute to federal political campaigns, but it may not limit expenditures by candidates.

b. Balancing approach to regulation of campaign financing

Buckley v. Valeo
424 U.S. 1 (1976).

Facts. Buckley and other candidates and groups (Ps) brought suit against Valeo and other federal officials (Ds), seeking a declaration that the reporting and disclosure requirements of the Federal Election Campaign Act were unconstitutional. The requirements applied to all political committees and candidates and involved detailed reporting of contributors and amounts contributed. Ps also challenged the contribution and expenditure limitations, which included the following restrictions:

(i) A limit of $1,000 on individual and group contributions to a candidate or authorized campaign committee per election;

(ii) A limit of $1,000 on expenditures relative to a clearly identified candidate;

(iii) An annual ceiling on a candidate's expenditures from personal or family resources; and

(iv) Public financing of presidential campaigns.

The court of appeals upheld the Act in its entirety. Ps appeal.

Issues.

(i) May Congress impose contribution limitations on federal elections?

(ii) May Congress impose expenditure limitations on federal elections?

(iii) May Congress impose detailed reporting and disclosure requirements on political contribution activity?

(iv) May Congress permit public financing of presidential campaigns?

Held. (i) Yes. (ii) No. (iii) Yes. (iv) Yes. Judgment affirmed in part and reversed in part.

♦ The financial limitations imposed on political campaigns cannot be considered regulation of conduct alone since exercise of free speech depends largely on the ability to finance that speech. This is especially true when the electorate depends on the mass media for so much of its information.

♦ The $1,000 limit on campaign contributions has minimal effect on freedom of association or on the extent of political discussion. On the other hand, it deals directly with the sources of political corruption, or the appearances thereof, which are the objective of the statute. It does not violate the First Amendment.

♦ Even though the expenditure limitations are content-neutral, they impose severe restrictions on freedom of political expression: Equalizing the relative ability of individuals and groups to influence elections is not a sufficient rationale to justify the infringement of First Amendment rights.

♦ The interest in avoiding the danger of candidate dependence on large contributions, which is asserted as a reason for limiting expenditures, is served by the contribution limits and disclosure requirements. It is not within the government's power to determine that spending to promote one's political views is wasteful, excessive, or unwise.

♦ The government interest in assuring the free functioning of our national institutions is served by the disclosure requirement. The electorate is provided with relevant information, thereby deterring corruption and facilitating enforcement of contribution limitations.

♦ Ps claim the requirements are overbroad as applied to minor parties and independent candidates, but Ps have failed to show any actual harm to these groups. If such harm actually occurs, courts will be available to provide appropriate remedies, but a blanket exemption is unnecessary.

♦ Public financing of presidential campaigns does not constitute invidious discrimination against minor and new parties in violation of the Fifth Amendment. Even though the scheme provides full funding only for major parties, it assists minor parties and does not limit the ability of minor party candidates to raise funds up to the applicable spending limit.

Concurrence and Dissent (Burger, C.J.). It is an improper intrusion on the First Amendment to limit contributions. Contributions and expenditures are two sides of the same coin.

Concurrence and Dissent (White, J.). The expenditure limitations do not violate the First Amendment. They reinforce the contribution limits and control corruption. The limits on the amount of money a candidate or his family may spend are also constitutional. They discourage the perception that elections are merely a function of money and encourage the less wealthy to run for office.

Concurrence and Dissent (Marshall, J.). The limits on the amount a candidate or a candidate's family may spend do not violate the First Amendment. Public office cannot appear to belong solely to the wealthy. Large contributions are the only way a less wealthy candidate can compete with a wealthy candidate.

Concurrence and Dissent (Blackmun, J.). I am not persuaded there is a principled constitutional distinction between contribution limitations and expenditure limitations.

----

c. Restrictions on "soft money" contributions and issue ads

McConnell v. Federal Election Commission
540 U.S. 93 (2003).

Facts. The Bipartisan Campaign Reform Act of 2002 ("BCRA") restricted the use of soft money and issue ads. It amended the Federal Election Campaign Act of 1971 ("FECA"), which had imposed limitations only on "hard money" contributions, or money used to influence an election for federal office. "Soft money," or money used for state or local elections and for issue ads, was unregulated under FECA. Title I of BCRA (the new section 323(a) of FECA) prohibited national party committees from soliciting, receiving, directing, or spending any soft money. Section 323(b) prevented state and local party committees from using soft money for activities that affected federal elections. Section 323(d) prohibited political parties from donating funds to tax-exempt organizations that engaged in electioneering activities. Title II imposed restrictions on corporations and labor unions to prevent them from funding "electioneering communications," defined as political broadcasts that referred to a clearly identified federal candidate that are made within 60 days before a general election (or 30 days before a primary election). Senator McConnell and others (Ps) challenged the law by suing the Federal Election Commission (D). The district court upheld part of the law and found some parts unconstitutional. Ps appeal.

Issue. May Congress limit the use of soft money contributions and impose detailed restrictions on how organizations can influence elections?

Held. Yes. Judgment affirmed in part and reversed in part.

♦ In *Buckley, supra,* this Court construed FECA's disclosure and reporting requirements and its expenditure limitations "to reach only funds used for communications that expressly advocate the election or defeat of a clearly identified candidate." Consequently, there was a bright line separating "express advocacy" from "issue advocacy." Express advocacy was subject to FECA's limitations and could be financed only using hard money, while so-called issue ads could be financed with soft money and could be aired without disclosing the identity of their sponsors. But express advertisements and issue advertisements proved functionally identical in advocating the election or defeat of federal candidates. Thus, issue ads were used to circumvent FECA's limitations.

♦ The FECA limits have a marginal impact on political speech. They limit the source and individual amount of donations, but they do not limit the total amount of money that the parties can spend.

♦ The rationale behind the contribution restrictions in section 323(a) is that contributions to a candidate's party to aid the candidate's campaign threaten to create a sense of obligation. Large soft money donations have a corrupting influence. Soft money contributions have often been much larger than the contributions of hard money that FECA permits, and the largest corporate donors have often made substantial contributions to both parties. This indicates that many corporate contributions have been motivated by a desire for access to candidates, rather than by ideological support for the candidates and parties. The best means to prevent abuses is to identify and remove the temptation; so section 323(a) is not unconstitutional.

♦ Section 323(b)'s limits on state committees are designed to prevent wholesale evasion of section 323(a). Congress determined that, without this provision, soft-money contributors would simply contribute to the state parties, which would create the same sense of obligation on the part of candidates as would contributions to the national parties. The Court must defer to Congress in this area, and the provisions are closely drawn to match the important governmental interests Congress has identified. Sections 323(d), (e), and (f) are also justified and are not unconstitutional. Title II's restrictions on funding by corporations and labor unions has been established previously, and these institutions are able to engage in express advocacy by forming separate segregated funds to pay for it. The regulation of this speech is constitutional.

Concurrence and Dissent (Scalia, J.). Today the Court, which sternly disapproves of restrictions on pornography, approves of a law that cuts to the heart of the First Amendment—the right to criticize the government. BCRA basically prohibits the criticism of members of Congress by those entities most capable of criticizing effectively—the national political parties and corporations. Even though it also prohibits criticism of those candidates challenging members of Congress, such evenhandedness is not fairness. It favors incumbents, who typically raise about three times as much hard money as challengers. Regulation of money used for disseminating speech is equivalent to regulating the speech itself.

Concurrence and Dissent (Kennedy, J., Rehnquist, C.J., Scalia, Thomas, JJ.). In *Buckley*, the Court held that only one interest justified the significant burden on the right of association involved in that case—eliminating or preventing actual corruption or the appearance of corruption resulting from contributions to candidates. Today the majority ignores constitutional bounds and replaces discrete and respected First Amendment principles with vague and unsound rules that destroy basic protections for speech.

Dissent (Thomas, Scalia, JJ.). Besides continuing the errors of *Buckley*, the Court now expands the anti-circumvention rationale beyond reason. The Court should require a showing of why bribery laws are insufficient to address the concerns asserted by Congress. The Court also continues to decrease the level of scrutiny applied to restrictions on core political speech.

---

d. Pre-election issue advocacy

Federal Election Commission v. Wisconsin Right to Life
551 U.S. 449 (2007).

Facts. Section 203 of the Bipartisan Campaign Reform Act made it illegal for any corporation to broadcast, shortly before an election, any communication that named a federal candidate for elected office and was targeted to the electorate. In *McConnell, supra*, the Court upheld section 203 against a facial challenge as long as the forbidden speech was express campaign speech or its functional equivalent. Wisconsin Right to Life (P) was a 501 (c) nonprofit advocacy organization. P planned to run broadcast ads during the election blackout period in which P encouraged voters to call Senator Feingold to protest the filibuster of judicial nominees. P filed suit against the Federal Election Commission (D), seeking declaratory relief that would permit the running of these ads. The Supreme Court granted certiorari.

Issue. May the BCRA be applied to prohibit issue advocacy that mentions a candidate for federal office but is not an appeal to vote for or against a specific candidate?

Held. No. Judgment affirmed.

♦ If P's ads are the functional equivalent of speech expressly advocating the election or defeat of a candidate, they can constitutionally be regulated. But if they are genuine issue ads, under the First Amendment, they cannot be regulated.

♦ BCRA section 203 is subject to strict scrutiny because it burdens political speech. Thus, D must prove that applying it to P's ads furthers a compelling interest and is narrowly tailored to achieve that interest. Although BCRA survived a facial challenge in *McConnell*, it is still subject to as-applied challenges.

♦ The test for an as-applied challenge does not depend on the speaker's intent. An intent-based test would chill political speech and would offer no security for free discussion. The proper standard must be objective. It must focus on the substance of the communication and must give the benefit of any doubt to protecting rather than stifling speech.

◆ An ad is the functional equivalent of express advocacy only if it is susceptible of no reasonable interpretation other than as an appeal to vote for or against a specific candidate. Under this test, P's ads are not the functional equivalent of express advocacy. They focus on a legislative issue (the filibuster), take a position on the issue, exhort the public to adopt that position, and urge the public to contact public officials regarding the issue. They do not mention an election, candidacy, political party, or challenger. They also do not take a position on a candidate's character, qualifications, or fitness for office.

◆ Section 203 may be applied to P's ads only if it is narrowly tailored to further a compelling interest. *McConnell* assumed that the governmental interest in preventing corruption in election campaigns justified regulation of express advocacy, and then extended this interest to ads that were the functional equivalent of express advocacy. But there is no basis for further extending the rationale to apply to issue advocacy ads that are not the functional equivalent of express advocacy. Section 203 is unconstitutional as applied to the advertisements at issue here.

Concurrence (Scalia, Kennedy, Thomas, JJ.). Although I agree with the Court's judgment, 1 disagree with the principal opinion's reasons. *McConnell* is unworkable because any acceptable as-applied test cannot validate the facial constitutionality of section 203 of the BCRA. That part of the Court's decision in *McConnell* that upheld section 203(a) should be overruled.

Dissent (Souter, Stevens, Ginsburg, Breyer, JJ.). The Court has effectively overruled *McConnell* without good reason. There is a tradition of campaign finance reform that responds to documented threats to electoral integrity. The line between issue ads and outright electioneering proved to be a fiction, and section 203 was Congress's response to increased spending on issue ads.

---

e. The Millionaire's Amendment and unequal financing restrictions

Davis v. Federal Election Commission
554 U.S. 724 (2008).

Facts. Federal law limited the amount of campaign contributions a candidate for the House of Representatives could receive from individuals. Section 319(a) of the Bipartisan Campaign Reform Act, the "Millionaire's Amendment," provided an exception when a candidate spent more than $350,000 in personal funds (considered to be "self-financing"), allowing the opposing candidate to receive three times the normal limits from contributors. Davis (P), a candidate for the House, sued the Federal Election Commission (D). The district court granted summary judgment for D. P appeals.

Issue. May Congress impose different campaign contribution limits on candidates competing for the same congressional seat so that a non-self-financing candidate can raise more campaign money from individuals than a self-financing candidate can?

Held. No. Judgment reversed.

◆ If section 319(a) raised the contribution level for all candidates, there would be no constitutional violation. The problem with 319(a) is that it raises the limits for only the non-self-financing candidate, and then only when the self-financing candidate's expenditures reach a threshold. The Court has never previously upheld a law that imposes different contribution limits for competing candidates.

◆ Under *Buckley v. Valeo, supra*, Congress cannot cap a candidate's expenditure of personal funds to finance his own campaign speech. While 319(a) does not cap P's expenditure of his own funds, it does impose a penalty on such expenditures by triggering discriminatory fundraising limitations. The substantial burden on the exercise of the First Amendment right to use personal funds for campaign speech must be justified by a compelling state interest in order to stand.

- There is no compelling state interest sufficient to justify this burden. The offered objective of reducing the natural advantage wealthy individuals possess in campaigning for public office is not a legitimate governmental objective. Candidates have different strengths, including celebrity or a well-known family name, in addition to wealth disparities, and Congress cannot use election laws to level electoral opportunities without making an impermissible judgment about which strengths should be allowed to contribute to the outcome of an election.

- To the extent that there is a public perception that wealthy people can buy seats in Congress, Congress could raise or eliminate campaign contribution limits. But it cannot impose different limits on different candidates.

Dissent (Stevens, Souter, Ginsburg, Breyer, JJ.). The "Millionaire's Amendment" is a reasonable response to combat the perception that congressional seats are for sale to the highest bidder. It imposes no burden on a self-financing candidate. Because it merely diminishes the unequal strength of the self-financing candidate, it does not violate the Constitution. *Buckley* was incorrect in rejecting the imposition of reasonable limitations on expenditures permitted during a campaign. Such a limitation would improve the quality of the exposition of ideas, just as it does in appellate advocacy where both sides have time limitations. Even under *Buckley*, the Millionaire's Amendment is a good-faith attempt to regulate a pernicious feature of contemporary political campaigns. It does not quiet any speech. Even if it did burden P's First Amendment rights, the burden is justified by the governmental interest in reducing both the influence of wealth on elections and the appearance that wealth alone dictates those results.

---

f. Advocacy by corporations

Citizens United v. Federal Election Commission
558 U.S. 310 (2010).

Facts. Citizens United (P) was a nonprofit corporation that released a 90-minute documentary on then-Senator Hillary Clinton titled "Hillary." The film criticized Senator Clinton and urged viewers to vote against her. P desired to run television ads promoting the film. However, the Bipartisan Campaign Reform Act (BCRA), 2 U.S.C. section 441b, prohibited corporations and unions to make independent expenditures for speech that was "electioneering communication," defined as any broadcast communication that refers to a federal candidate and is made within 30 days of an election. P sought declaratory and injunctive relief by suing the Federal Election Committee (D). The District Court gave D summary judgment. P appeals.

Issue. May Congress limit corporate independent expenditures?

Held. No. Judgment reversed.

- The Court has previously recognized that First Amendment protection extends to corporations. There is no basis for the Government to impose restrictions on certain disfavored speakers in the context of political speech. Buckley and Bellotti did not specifically address this issue, but it did stand for the principle that the First Amendment does not allow political speech restrictions based on the speaker's corporate identity.

- Austin v. Michigan Chamber of Commerce, 494 U.S. 652 (1990), bypassed Buckley and Bellotti by recognizing a governmental interest in preventing the distorting effects of aggregations of wealth through the corporate form that have little or no correlation to the public's support for the corporation's political ideas. But this rational would allow the Government to impose additional restrictions on corporate speech, such as preventing the printing of a book. It could also ban speech by media corporations. In fact, section 441b exempts media corporations, which demonstrates the invalidity of the antidistortion rationale.

- Most corporations are small, with low revenues. This fact undermines the rationale behind the regulation of corporate speech. It is not even aimed at amassed wealth.

- D claims corporate political speech can be limited to prevent corruption, but more than half the states do not restrict independent expenditures by for-profit corporations and these expenditures have not corrupted the political process in those States.

- D argues that the limit is justified by the need to protect the interest of dissenting shareholders, but this interest can be protected through the procedures of corporate democracy. If this was Congress' concern, it would not have limited the expenditures only during a short time prior to elections.

- Precedent should be respected unless it is not well reasoned. Austin was not well reasoned. Therefore it should be overruled. No sufficient governmental interest justifies limits on the political speech of nonprofit or for-profit corporations.

Concurrence (Scalia, Alito, Thomas, JJ.). The dissent correctly notes that the Bill of Rights sets forth the rights of individuals, but the right to speak includes the right to speak in association with other individuals. The First Amendment refers to speech, not speakers. There is no basis for excluding any category of speaker, individual or organizational.

Dissent (Stevens, Ginsburg, Breyer, Sotomayor, JJ.). There is no reason to overrule Austin. This case involves a time, place and manner restriction, applied in a viewpoint-neutral fashion to a narrow subset of advocacy messages made during discrete time periods through discrete channels. It is not a ban on speech. Congress developed a record of evidence when it passed BCRA that the Court should not disregard.

---

5. Other Means of Expression: Litigation, Association, and the Right Not to Speak

a. Associations for obtaining legal services

Several types of associations have been created to improve members' access to legal services. The activities of these associations have conflicted with bar rules on solicitation by attorneys and other attorney conduct. Due to the First Amendment implications, the Court has generally protected these associations against regulation.

1) Attorneys paid by organization instead of by clients

NAACP v. Button
371 U.S. 415 (1963).

Facts. The NAACP (P) followed a policy of having its lawyers represent persons in cases involving racial discrimination. The staff lawyers received compensation only from P on a per day basis. P encouraged the bringing of such suits. The state of Virginia passed a law that forbade "any agent for an individual or organization to retain a lawyer in connection with an action to which it was not a party and in which it had no pecuniary right or liability." P challenged the constitutionality of the law because it would have prevented P from compensating the staff lawyers for their work on individuals' cases. The state courts upheld the law, and P appeals.

Issue. May states restrict the right of minority groups to associate in order to obtain better legal service?

Held. No. Judgment reversed.

♦ Although "solicitation" has generally been frowned upon in the legal profession, and Virginia has a legitimate interest in regulating it, the regulation in this case impinges on P's constitutional rights. The state was applying a mere label to P's conduct in order to suppress its right to institute litigation on behalf of members of an unpopular minority group.

Dissent (Harlan, Clark, Stewart, JJ.). Virginia's regulation was reasonable. Under P's scheme, attorneys may be unable to maintain undivided allegiance to their true clients when P is paying their fees.

---

2) Union referral program

In *Brotherhood of Railroad Trainmen v. Virginia State Bar*, 377 U.S. 1 (1964), the Court held that the state could not interfere with a union's program by which it set up a system for referring union members to certain attorneys for representation in union-related matters. The Court stated that the rights of freedom of expression and association would not permit the state to regulate the conduct of the attorneys in this situation.

3) Assistance by union's attorneys

In *United Mine Workers v. Illinois Bar Association*, 389 U.S. 217 (1967), the Court struck down a state ban against a union's employment of a salaried attorney to assist with workers' compensation claims, on the grounds that the ban impaired the associational rights of the union members and was not a necessary protection of the state's interest in the high standards of legal ethics. Later, in *United Transportation Union v. State Bar of Michigan*, 401 U.S. 576 (1971), after emphasizing that collective activity to obtain meaningful access to the courts is a fundamental First Amendment right, the Court also invalidated a state injunction against a union's plan to protect members from excessive fees of incompetent attorneys in FELA actions.

b. Privacy of association's membership list

NAACP v. Alabama
357 U.S. 449 (1958).

Facts. Alabama (P) had a statute that required a foreign corporation to qualify before doing business in the state. The NAACP (D) affiliates in Alabama were required to produce records including names of its members. D refused to provide the list of names and was adjudged in contempt of court. D appeals.

Issue. May a state force production of a private association's membership lists?

Held. No. Judgment reversed.

♦ There is an important relationship between freedom to associate and privacy in one's associations. Compelled disclosure of affiliation with groups that support dissident beliefs can effectively restrain freedom of association.

♦ D has shown that, in the past, revelation of the identity of its members has exposed them to economic reprisal, loss of employment, threat of physical coercion, and other manifestations of public hostility. Thus, compelled disclosure of D's Alabama membership is likely to adversely affect D and its members and may induce members to withdraw and dissuade others from joining.

♦ P has not shown an interest in obtaining the members' names that is sufficient to justify the deterrent effect that these disclosures may have on the free exercise of the members' constitutionally protected right of association.

---

c. Protection of right to associate based on type of association

Roberts v. United States Jaycees
468 U.S. 609 (1984).

Facts. The United States Jaycees (P), an organization dedicated to developing young men for activity in civic affairs, excluded men over 35 years of age and all women from participation as regular members. These groups could participate as nonvoting, nonofficeholding associate members, however. Two local chapters of P, located in Minnesota, violated P's national bylaws and admitted women as regular members. P's national president announced an intent to revoke the local charters involved, and the local chapters filed charges of discrimination with the Minnesota Department of Human Rights. P sued Roberts and other state officials (Ds) for declaratory and injunctive relief. The district court found for Ds, but the court of appeals reversed. Ds appeal.

Issue. May a large organization that is basically unselective about membership exclude applicants solely on the basis of sex?

Held. No. Judgment reversed.

♦ "Freedom of association" comprehends two distinct types of association. There are certain intimate human relationships that the state cannot interfere with as a principle of fundamental personal liberty. There are also associations for the purpose of engaging in activities protected by the First Amendment, such as speech and religion. The degree of protection given to an association varies depending on the type of liberty involved.

♦ Personal affiliations, such as family relationships, demand the fullest possible protection. They are characterized by small numbers, a high degree of selectivity, and seclusion from others in critical aspects of the relationship. On the other hand, large business enterprises, while in a sense associations, do not involve the concerns underlying the First Amendment protection.

♦ P in this case consists of local chapters of large and basically unselective groups. The evidence indicated that members were actively recruited and applicants were never denied membership, except on the basis of sex. Women were allowed to participate in P's functions even though they were denied membership.

♦ The state statute prohibiting sex discrimination may infringe in some hypothetical way on P's freedom of expressive association, because women now are unable to vote or hold office. This interference with the internal organization, however, is justified by the state's compelling interest in eradicating discrimination against its female citizens. Besides, the impact is likely to be minimal because the state law does not change P's objective of promoting the interests of young men. The impact on P's protected speech is no greater than that necessary to accomplish the state's legitimate purpose.

---

d. Exclusive membership based on sexual orientation

Boy Scouts of America v. Dale
530 U.S. 640 (2000).

Facts. Dale (P) was an adult scoutmaster in the Boy Scouts (D). When D learned that P was an avowed homosexual and gay rights activist, D revoked P's position. P sued in state court, alleging illegal discrimination. The state courts interpreted the state's public accommodations law, which prohibits discrimination on the basis of sexual orientation, to prohibit the Boy Scouts from revoking P's position. The Supreme Court granted certiorari.

Issue. May the Boy Scouts of America prohibit participation by adult avowed homosexuals?

Held. Yes. Judgment reversed.

♦ The government may not intrude into a group's internal affairs by forcing it to accept a member it does not desire where such forced membership affects in a significant way the group's ability to advocate public or private viewpoints.

♦ Under *Roberts, supra*, freedom of expressive association is not absolute, and it must yield to regulations adopted to serve compelling state interests, unrelated to the suppression of ideas, that cannot be achieved through means significantly less restrictive of associational freedoms. To determine whether a group is protected, the courts must determine whether the group engages in "expressive association." D clearly does so when its adult leaders inculcate its youth members with its value system.

♦ The next step is to determine whether forcing D to accept P would significantly affect D's ability to advocate public or private viewpoints. D asserts that homosexual conduct is inconsistent with the values embodied in the Scout Oath and Law, particularly those represented by the terms "morally straight" and "clean," and that D does not want to promote homosexual conduct as a legitimate form of behavior. P's presence as a leader within D's organization would significantly burden D's expression of its viewpoints by interfering with D's choice to not propound a viewpoint that is contrary to its beliefs.

♦ An association's expression may be protected whenever it engages in expressive activity that could be impaired. Expression need not be its only purpose.

♦ The state interests embodied in New Jersey's public accommodations law do not justify the severe intrusion on D's freedom of expressive association that P's participation would present. The application of New Jersey's public accommodations law to require D to accept P as a leader violates D's First Amendment right of expressive association.

Dissent (Stevens, Souter, Ginsburg, Breyer, JJ.). P's participation did not send a cognizable message to D or to the world. The only rationale for this holding is that homosexuals are so different from the rest of society that their presence alone should be singled out for special First Amendment treatment.

---

e. State-permitted speech on private property

Prune Yard Shopping Center v. Robins
447 U.S. 74 (1980).

Facts. Robins (P) set up a table inside the Prune Yard Shopping Center (D) for the purpose of distributing pamphlets and seeking signatures. D had a policy to forbid such activity if not directly related to D's commercial purposes. P was asked to leave and did so. P then sued D to enjoin it from denying P access. The California Supreme Court held that the California Constitution protected P's reasonable speech, even in privately owned shopping centers. D appeals.

Issue. Does a state constitution that permits free speech on privately owned, publicly available shopping centers deny the owner's Fifth Amendment property rights or his First Amendment freedom of speech?

Held. No. Judgment affirmed.

♦ Although the United States Constitution does not grant P the right granted by the California Constitution, states may recognize more expansive rights than those existing under federal law. The limit on those rights is the extent to which they would impinge on another person's federal rights.

♦ The Fifth Amendment Takings Clause is violated when a state forces some people alone to bear public burdens that, in all fairness and justice, should be borne by the public as a whole. Here, D has realized no economic injury and retains power to establish reasonable time, place, and manner restrictions to minimize interference with its commercial function. Hence, there is no taking.

♦ D claims a right not to be forced by the state to use his property as a public forum. However, D has chosen to open his property to the public. P's message is not dictated by the state. D is free to disclaim association with P. Therefore, D's free speech rights are not impinged.

---

f. Right to refrain from speaking

The First Amendment incorporates the concept of individual freedom of mind. Thus it protects the right not to speak as well as the right to speak. In *Wooley v. Maynard*, 430 U.S. 705 (1977), the Court struck down a state law requiring display of auto license plates carrying the state motto, "Live Free or Die." The motto represented an ideological point of view that the challengers, members of Jehovah's Witnesses, found unacceptable. The Court failed to find any state interest sufficient to justify the infringement on the First Amendment right to refrain from speaking.

F. Freedom of the Press

1. Introduction

Although the First Amendment separately mentions freedom of the press, the Court has not recognized any special right for the press additional to the general freedom of speech. Yet the institutional press often faces problems different from those faced by citizens in general, which has prompted some claims that special protection is appropriate.

2. No Special Status

In considering the exact constitutional protection of the press in *First National Bank of Boston v. Bellotti*, 435 U.S. 765 (1978), an election expenditure case, the Court stated that the Press Clause did not confer a special status or institutional privilege on a limited group, and that there was no difference in the First Amendment freedom to disseminate ideas through the newspaper or through those who gave lectures that encourage publication and wide dissemination.

3. Right of Access to Gather News

a. Introduction

While reporters generally have the same right of access to sources of information as the public, they do not have any special newsgathering privilege. Hence, they may not refuse to answer relevant and material questions asked during a good faith grand jury investigation.

b. Reporter's testimonial privilege

Branzburg v. Hayes
408 U.S. 665 (1972).

Facts. Branzburg (D), a reporter, observed illegal drug transactions and featured the transactions in a news article. D was subpoenaed to appear before a grand jury. D sought prohibition and mandamus to avoid having to reveal his confidential information, but the state courts denied his petition. D appeals. (Two other cases involving two similarly situated reporters were consolidated with this appeal.)

Issue. Does the First Amendment grant a special testimonial privilege to reporters, protecting them from being forced to divulge confidential information to a grand jury's investigation?

Held. No. Judgment affirmed.

♦ D claims that forcing reporters to reveal confidences to a grand jury will deter other confidential sources of information, thus curtailing the free flow of information protected by the First Amendment. However, journalists have no constitutional right of access to several types of events (grand jury proceedings, meetings of private organizations and of official bodies gathered in executive sessions, etc.). Although these exclusions tend to hamper news gathering, they are not unconstitutional.

♦ All citizens have an obligation to respond to a grand jury subpoena and to answer questions relevant to crime investigation. The only testimonial privilege for unofficial witnesses is the Fifth Amendment; there is no necessity to create a special privilege for journalists based on the First Amendment.

♦ The public interest in pursuing and prosecuting those crimes reported to the press by informants and thus deterring future commission of those crimes is not outweighed by the public interest in possible future news about crime from undisclosed, unverified sources.

♦ A judicially created journalist's privilege would necessarily involve significant practical and conceptual problems in its administration. However, Congress and the state legislatures are not precluded from fashioning whatever standards and rules they might deem proper if they choose to create a statutory journalist's privilege.

Concurrence (Powell, J.). Journalists are not without remedy in the face of a bad faith investigation. Motions to quash and appropriate protective orders are available where the requested testimony is not within the legitimate hold of law enforcement.

Dissent (Douglas, J.). This decision will impede the dissemination of ideas that a free press protects.

Dissent (Stewart, Brennan, Marshall, JJ.). The Court undermines the independence of the press by inviting authorities to annex the journalistic provision as an investigative arm of government. Exercise of the power to compel disclosure will lead to "self-censorship" and, as a consequence, significantly impair the free flow of information to the public. To force disclosure, the government must show:

(i) Probable cause that the journalist has information clearly relevant to a specific probable violation of law;

(ii) Absence of less obtrusive means of obtaining the information; and

(iii) A compelling and overriding interest in the information.

---

c. Access to prisoners

In *Pell v. Procunier*, 417 U.S. 817 (1974), the Court held that professional journalists did not have a right to conduct face-to-face interviews of prison inmates. The Court reasoned that the government may not interfere with the free press, but the Constitution does not require the government to give the press special access to information that is generally not available to members of the public.

d. Right of access to courtroom proceedings

Richmond Newspapers v. Virginia
448 U.S. 555 (1980).

Facts. Early in the fourth criminal trial of the same defendant, the trial judge granted an uncontested closure motion made by the defendant. Later, reporters for Richmond Newspapers (P) sought a hearing on a motion to vacate the closure order; the hearing was granted, but the public was excluded from the hearing. At the hearing, the court denied the motion, considering the defendant's interest paramount. The defendant was acquitted in the closed trial. P appealed from the trial court's closure order, but the state courts affirmed. P appeals.

Issue. Is the right of the public and press to attend criminal trials guaranteed by the Constitution?

Held. Yes. Judgment reversed.

♦ In *Gannett Co. v. DePasquale*, 443 U.S. 368 (1979), this Court held that neither the public nor the press has an enforceable right of access to a pretrial suppression hearing.

♦ Throughout the evolution of the trial procedure, the trial has been open to all who cared to observe. However, the Constitution contains no explicit provisions protecting the public from exclusion.

♦ The First Amendment protects freedom of speech and press, including expression regarding events at trials. These guaranteed rights would be meaningless if access to the trial could be foreclosed arbitrarily. Other constitutional rights, not explicitly established, have been recognized as implied. Clearly, the public interest in judicial functions and in freedom of speech requires open trials.

♦ In some circumstances, where an overriding interest is articulated in findings, a criminal trial may be closed to the public, but only where the common alternatives are insufficient (*e.g.*, jury sequestration, witness sequestration, etc.).

Concurrence (Brennan, Marshall, JJ.). Publicity is an important means of assuring the right to a fair trial. What happens in a courtroom is public property. The First Amendment requires open access, and agreement between the judge and the parties cannot override the First Amendment.

Concurrence (Stewart, J.). The First and Fourteenth Amendments give the press and the public a right of access to civil and criminal trials. A courtroom is a public place, even more so than city streets and parks. The right is not absolute, but in this case the judge gave no recognition to the right of the press and the public to be present.

Dissent (Rehnquist, J.). There are no provisions in the Constitution that prohibit a state from denying public access to a trial when both the prosecution and the defense consent to the closure order.

---

e. Mandatory closure for minor victims not permissible

Globe Newspaper Co. v. Superior Court
457 U.S. 596 (1982).

Facts. A state law required trial judges to exclude the general public from the courtroom during the testimony of minor victims of sex crimes. The trial judge closed the entire trial in a rape case, and Globe Newspaper Co. (P) sought injunctive relief. The state supreme court upheld the statute because of its narrow scope. The United States Supreme Court granted certiorari.

Issue. May a state require closure of criminal trials in narrowly defined cases?

Held. No. Judgment reversed.

♦ As stated in *Richmond Newspapers, supra*, criminal trials have historically been open to the public, and this right of access is important to the proper functioning of the judicial system. This constitutional interest is not absolute, however.

♦ The state may deny access in order to inhibit disclosure of sensitive information if the denial is narrowly tailored to serve a compelling state interest. The state interests in protecting minor victims from further trauma and encouraging them to testify are compelling. But a mandatory closure rule is not narrowly tailored. Instead, the determination to close must be made on a case-by-case basis.

Dissent (Burger, C.J., Rehnquist, J.). The verbatim transcript is available after trial, so there is no denial of public access to information. Thus, the minimal impact on the First Amendment is justified here.

---

4. Differential Treatment of the Press

Minneapolis Star & Tribune v. Minnesota Commissioner of Revenue
460 U.S. 575 (1983).

Facts. Minnesota imposed a general sales tax and a related use tax for items on which no sales tax had been paid. Publications were exempt from these taxes until 1971, when the state imposed a use tax on the cost of paper and ink products consumed in producing a publication. Three years later, the state exempted the first $100,000 of paper and ink used. As a result, the Minneapolis Star (P), one of eleven newspapers (out of 388 in the state) that had to pay a use tax, paid nearly two-thirds of all the use tax collected. P sued the Minnesota Commissioner of Revenue (D) for a refund. The state courts upheld the tax, and P appeals.

Issue. May the states single out the press for special tax treatment?

Held. No. Judgment reversed.

♦ Other than the structure of the tax itself, there is no indication that the state imposed the tax with an impermissible or censorial motive. This case therefore differs from *Grosjean v. American Press Co.*, 297 U.S. 233 (1936), in which a publishing tax was held invalid because of improper government motive.

♦ Differential taxation of the press, unrelated to any special characteristic that requires such treatment, is unconstitutional. Such treatment suggests suppression of expression, a presumptively unconstitutional goal. In the absence of a compelling counterbalancing interest, differential taxation may not be allowed.

♦ D has no adequate justification for the tax. Even though the tax burden may be lighter than it would be under general application of the regular sales tax, differential treatment of any kind opens the door for more burdensome treatment.

♦ The tax also targets a small group of large newspapers, presenting an impermissible potential for abuse.

Dissent (Rehnquist, J.). This tax favors newspapers. It does not abridge the freedom of the press. D's scheme is rational because the large volume of inexpensive items involved (newspapers) makes the regular sales tax impractical.

---

5. Regulation Intended to Improve the Idea Marketplace

a. Access to the mass media

The mass media presents difficult First Amendment problems because of its pervasiveness and the barriers to entry. There are a limited number of frequencies to be used by radio and television, and the government allocates these frequencies according to established procedures. Those who are permitted to broadcast have a special privilege. Government therefore also imposes a special responsibility to provide a range of programs that are in the public interest. Newspapers, which are also part of the mass media, of course do not operate on allocable frequencies. Yet some argue that the expense of establishing a significant newspaper is such that government should also regulate to some extent the content of newspapers, or at least assist the general public in gaining access to newspapers.

1) Access by statute

In response to the problems of access to the media, some states and Congress itself have provided rights of access by statute. In assessing such statutes, the Court looks to the nature of the media involved. In this context, the First Amendment acts as a protection against government interference.

2) Access to newspapers

Miami Herald Publishing Co. v. Tornillo
418 U.S. 241 (1974).

Facts. Tornillo (P) was a candidate for the Florida state legislature. The Miami Herald Publishing Company (D), a newspaper publisher, printed editorials critical of P's candidacy. P sued to force D to publish P's response under a Florida "right of reply" statute. The state supreme court reversed the lower court and held the statute constitutional. D appeals.

Issue. May the state require a newspaper to publish a candidate's reply to criticism made by the newspaper?

Held. No. Judgment reversed.

♦ P demonstrates the consolidation of control over the public media, and argues that an enforceable right of access is a necessary remedy to assure open public debate. However, such a right requires some mechanism, either governmental or consensual. If governmental, as here, the First Amendment protections are invoked.

♦ Although a responsible press is desirable, it is not mandated by the Constitution and, like many other virtues, cannot be legislated. P would use governmental coercion to compel D to publish material that D deems improper for publication. Such interference with editorial decisionmaking exceeds constitutional bounds.

♦ To uphold the state law would encourage editors to avoid controversial subjects, to the detriment of public discussion.

---

b. The "fairness doctrine"

Red Lion Broadcasting Co. v. FCC
395 U.S. 367 (1969).

Facts. The "fairness doctrine" was adopted by the FCC (D) early in the history of broadcasting. It required radio and television broadcasters to present discussion of public issues on broadcast stations and to provide fair coverage on each side of those issues. D also adopted regulations that required broadcasters to give any person who is personally attacked notice, a transcript of the attack, and a reasonable opportunity to respond. A broadcaster who chose to endorse or oppose a political candidate must also notify the opposition and allow them a reasonable opportunity to reply. Red Lion Broadcasting Company (P) challenged these rules.

Issue. May the government impose a fairness doctrine on licensed broadcasters?

Held. Yes. Judgment affirmed.

♦ First Amendment protections apply to broadcasting, but the characteristics of broadcasting require special First Amendment standards. The physical realities of broadcasting limit its availability to a select few. Those who are unable to obtain licenses are barred from the airwaves. The First Amendment may not be construed to prohibit the government from restricting access to airwaves; otherwise, no one could effectively use radio or television broadcasting.

♦ The First Amendment does not protect licensees more man nonlicensees. A licensee has no constitutional right to monopolize a radio frequency. The government may therefore require a licensee to act as a proxy or fiduciary with obligations to present views and voices representative of the public that would otherwise be barred from the airwaves.

♦ Under the First Amendment, the right of broadcast viewers and listeners is paramount to the right of broadcasters.

♦ To the extent that the fairness doctrine may prompt broadcasters to eliminate coverage of controversial issues, the doctrine may need to be reexamined, but so far it has not had such an effect.

Comment. In 1987, the FCC repealed the fairness doctrine on grounds that it "chilled" broadcasters' First Amendment rights.

---

c. Other regulation of media content

1) Right of access

The First Amendment does not require a government-regulated broadcaster to sell broadcast time to responsible parties for comment on public issues. In *Columbia Broadcasting System v. Democratic National Committee*, 412 U.S. 94 (1973), a radio station had refused to sell air time to individuals and groups who wished to express views on controversial issues. The Court held that the fairness doctrine required broadcast licensees to provide full and fair coverage of public issues, and that Congress and the FCC could appropriately give licensees the responsibility for editing.

2) Publicly funded broadcasting

Congress cannot prohibit editorializing on the air by television and radio stations that accept federal subsidies. The Public Broadcasting Act of 1967 prohibited noncommercial educational stations that receive a grant from the Corporation for Public Broadcasting to "engage in editorializing." In *FCC v. League of Women Voters*, 468 U.S. 364 (1984), the Court held that provision unconstitutional. The government's interest in safeguarding the public's right to a balanced presentation of public issues, which justified the fairness doctrine in *Red Lion, supra*, was insufficient to justify the substantial abridgement of important journalistic freedoms that the ban imposed.

3) Cable television and "must carry" provisions

Turner Broadcasting System Inc. v. FCC
512 U.S. 622 (1994) (Turner I).

Facts. The Cable Television Consumer Protection and Competition Act of 1992 required cable television operators to carry, free of charge, the transmission of local broadcast television stations. The purpose of the Act was to counter the concentration of economic power in the cable industry, which Congress found was endangering the availability of free over-the-air broadcast television, especially for those consumers who did not have cable. Turner Broadcasting System Inc. and other cable television system operators and programmers (Ps) brought an action against the FCC (D) challenging the "must carry" provisions. The lower court found for D and the Supreme Court granted certiorari.

Issue. Should the regulation of cable television be governed by the same relaxed level of scrutiny as regulation of the broadcast industry?

Held. No. Judgment vacated and case remanded.

♦ Because cable systems do not share the physical limitations of the broadcast industry, the relaxed *Red Lion, supra*, standard should not apply.

♦ The "must carry provisions" might affect the editorial discretion of cable owners, but only based on their channel capacity, not the content of the programming. The provisions do not force cable operators to alter their own messages. Thus, the appropriate level of scrutiny is the intermediate level applicable to content-neutral restrictions that impose an incidental burden on speech. [O'Brien, *supra*]

♦ Under this standard, the case must be remanded for further factfinding as to whether the provisions are truly necessary to protect the viability of broadcast television.

Concurrence (Stevens, J.). No remand is necessary; I would defer to Congress's factfindings.

Concurrence and dissent (O'Connor, Scalia, Thomas, Ginsburg, JJ.). The provisions are content-based because they are based on a determination that broadcast television should be preferred over cable programmers, whose access to cable channels would be reduced by the application of the "must carry" provisions.

Comment. After remand for additional factfinding, the Court affirmed the prior result on the ground that Congress had substantial evidence for making *the* judgment it did and that the rules were substantially related to the important government interest in competition and diversity in programming. [Turner Broadcasting System, Inc. v. FCC, 520 U.S. 180 (1997) (Turner II)]

Chapter IX

The Constitution and Religion

The First Amendment provides that "Congress shall make no law respecting an establishment of religion, or prohibiting the free exercise thereof." These two clauses, the Establishment Clause and the Free Exercise Clause, have provided considerable grounds for litigation. One other reference to religion is found in the Constitution. Article VI provides that "no religious test shall ever be required as a qualification to any office or public trust under the United States."

A. Historical and Analytical Overview

1. Introduction

The central purpose of the Establishment Clause is to ensure governmental neutrality in matters of religion. "When government activities touch on the religious sphere, they must be secular in purpose, evenhanded in operation, and neutral in primary impact." [Gillette v. United States, 401 U.S. 437 (1971)] Many cases arising under the Establishment Clause have involved schools. As applied to schools, the clause prevents governments from enacting laws that further the religious training or doctrine of any sect.

2. Alternative Approaches to Establishment Clause Problems

a. No-aid theory

This view requires the government to do nothing that involves governmental support of religion or that is favorable to the cultivation of religious interests. It leaves open the problem of the constitutionality of legislation having incidental impact on religion.

b. Neutrality theory

This view requires the government to be neutral with respect to religious matters, doing nothing to either favor or hinder religion. This combines the no-aid test with a no-hinder test.

c. Balancing test

This view assumes that it is impossible for the government to preclude all aid to religion, or to observe absolute neutrality. Governmental action must take into account the free exercise guarantee. In some situations, the government must, and in others, may, accommodate its policies and laws to further religious freedom. This is the most prevalent view.

3. Application: Transportation to Parochial Schools

Everson v. Board of Education
330 U.S. 1 (1947).

Facts. A local New Jersey board of education (D) authorized reimbursement to parents of the costs of using the public transportation system to send their children to school, whether public or parochial. Everson (P) challenged the scheme as an unconstitutional exercise of state power to support church schools. P appeals adverse lower court decisions.

Issue. May a state use public funds to assist student transportation to parochial, as well as public, schools?

Held. Yes. Judgment affirmed.

◆ The Establishment Clause was intended to erect a wall between church and state. It does not prohibit a state from extending its general benefits to all its citizens without regard to their religious belief.

◆ Reimbursement of transportation is intended solely to help children arrive safely at school, regardless of their religion. It does not support any schools, parochial or public. To invalidate D's system would handicap religion, which is no more permissible than favoring religion.

B. The Establishment Clause

1. The *Lemon* Test

As applied to schools, the freedom of religion guarantee means that the state may not enact laws that either further the religious training or doctrines of any sect, or prevent any sect from carrying out its own religious training programs. The court has established a three-part test for determining the validity of statutes granting financial aid to church-related schools. [See Lemon v. Kurtzman, 403 U.S. 602 (1971)] To be upheld under the Establishment Clause, the law in question must:

   a.   Reflect a clearly secular purpose;

   b.   Have a primary effect that neither advances nor inhibits religion; and

   c.   Avoid excessive government entanglement with religion.

2. The Anticoercion Principle: Prayer at Graduation Ceremonies

Lee v. Weisman
505 U.S. 577 (1992).

Facts. Lee (D), the principal of a middle school, invited a rabbi to deliver prayers at a graduation exercise. He gave the rabbi a pamphlet containing guidelines that recommended public prayers be composed with "inclusiveness and sensitivity," and advised the rabbi that the prayers should be nonsectarian. Weisman (P), one of the students, objected to the prayers' being part of the graduation ceremonies. The rabbi offered the prayers, which were nondenominational but did refer to and acknowledge God. P sued to enjoin school officials from inviting clergy members to deliver prayers at future graduations. The district court held that D's inclusion of prayers violated the Establishment Clause and granted the injunction because it violated the second *Lemon* test, *supra; i.e.*, it did not have a primary effect that neither advances nor inhibits religion. The court of appeals affirmed, and the Supreme Court granted certiorari.

Issue. May a public school invite members of the clergy to offer prayers at graduation ceremonies?

Held. No. Judgment affirmed.

♦ At a minimum, the Constitution guarantees that government may not coerce anyone to support or participate in religion or its exercise. In this case, D, as a public official, directed the performance of a formal religious exercise at a graduation ceremony for a public secondary school. Although attendance is not a condition for receipt of the diploma, students' attendance and participation is in a fair and real sense obligatory, even for students who object to the religious exercise. Including the prayer thus violated the Constitution.

♦ The government not only decided to include a prayer and chose the clergyman, but advised the rabbi about the content of the prayer. This means that D directed and controlled the content of the prayer. But the Establishment Clause does not allow the government to compose official prayers to be recited as part of a religious program carried on by the government. The fact that D acted in good faith does not make its participation in the content of the prayer permissible.

♦ Religious beliefs and religious expression are too precious to be either proscribed or prescribed by the government. The government cannot choose to compose a nonsectarian prayer, even if it were possible to devise one that would be acceptable to members of all faiths.

♦ The First Amendment protects speech and religion differently. Speech is protected by insuring its full expression even when the government participates, since some of the most important speech is directed at the government, but in religious debate or expression, the government is not a prime participant. The Free Exercise Clause is similar to the Free Speech Clause, but the Establishment Clause prevents the government from intervening in religious affairs, a prohibition with no counterpart in the speech provisions.

♦ Prayer exercises in public schools carry a particular risk of indirect coercion, particularly in the elementary and secondary public schools. Even at the graduation ceremony, there is pressure to stand and remain silent during the prayer, signifying a degree of adherence or assent. The government may not exact religious conformity from a student as the price of attending her own school graduation.

Concurrence (Blackmun, Stevens, O'Connor, JJ.). Under the Establishment Clause, the government may neither promote nor affiliate itself with any religious doctrine or organization, nor intrude into the internal affairs of any religious institution. In *Engel* v. *Vitale*, 370 U.S. 421 (1962), the Court held for the first time that a prayer selected by school officials could not be recited in a public school, even though it was "denominationally neutral." In *Abington School District v. Schempp*, 374 U.S. 203 (1963), the Court held unconstitutional a public school's opening exercises that consisted of a reading from the Bible or a recitation of the Lord's Prayer. The prayers offered at the graduation ceremonies in this case are likewise prohibited by the Constitution. Even if no one is forced to participate, mixing government and religion threatens free government because it conveys a message of exclusion to all who do not adhere to the favored belief.

Dissent (Scalia, J., Rehnquist, C.J., White, Thomas, JJ.). The meaning of the Establishment Clause must be determined by reference to historical practices and understandings. Yet the majority ignores history in its holding. The tradition of invocations and benedictions at graduation ceremonies is as old as the ceremonies themselves. Even the Declaration of Independence appeals to "the Supreme Judge of the world," and relies on the "protection of divine Providence." Presidents, beginning with George Washington, have included prayer in their official acts. The Court's test of psychological coercion is boundless and boundlessly manipulable, and is based on facts that are not true in any relevant sense. Even if students were coerced to stand, which they were not, such an act does not establish a "participation" in a religious exercise, any more than standing for the Pledge of Allegiance moments earlier constituted coerced approval of the political message it contains. The Establishment Clause was aimed at coercion of religious orthodoxy and financial support by force of law and threat of penalty, but P in this case faced no threat of penalty or discipline. This situation is entirely different from daily prayers in classroom settings where parents are not present, which could raise concerns about state interference with the liberty of parents to direct the religious upbringing of their children. The Court has replaced the unfortunate *Lemon* test with its psycho-coercion test, which is not at all grounded in our people's historical practice. The Constitution must have deep foundations in the historical practices of our people, not the changeable philosophical predilections of the Justices of the Court.

---

3. The Nonendorsement Principle: Government Sponsorship of Christmas Display

Lynch v. Donnelly
465 U.S. 668 (1984).

Facts. The city of Pawtucket, Rhode Island, annually erects a Christmas display that includes Santa Claus and related figures, colored lights, and a crèche, or nativity scene, containing the infant Jesus, Mary, Joseph, and other traditional figures. Donnelly (P) and other citizens brought suit in federal court against Lynch and other city officials (Ds) to have the crèche removed. The district court enjoined Ds from including the crèche in the display, and the court of appeals affirmed. The Supreme Court granted certiorari.

Issue. May a city include a nativity scene in its annual Christmas display?

Held. Yes. Judgment reversed.

♦ The First Amendment is intended to prevent the intrusion of either the church or the state upon the other, but total separation is not possible. Some relationship between the two must exist. The Constitution requires accommodation of all religions.

♦ The same week that Congress approved the Establishment Clause as part of the Bill of Rights, it provided for itself paid chaplains. The role of religion in American life has been officially acknowledged in numerous ways. For example, the government subsidizes holidays with religious significance, such as Christmas and Thanksgiving, by giving its employees paid time off.

♦ Under *Lemon v. Kurtzman (supra)*, the display of the crèche has a valid secular purpose—to celebrate the holiday and depict its origins. Its inclusion in Ds' display has less effect on advancing religion than do other types of government accommodation of religion, including providing textbooks to religion-sponsored schools and tax exemptions for church properties. Nor does the minimal cost cause excessive entanglement between religion and government.

Concurrence (O'Connor, J.). The Establishment Clause prohibits government from making adherence to a religion relevant to a person's standing in *the* political community. Excessive entanglement with religious institutions and government endorsement or disapproval of religion violates this principle. Ds' crèche display falls within neither category of government activity.

Dissent (Brennan, Marshall, Blackmun, Stevens, JJ.). Ds' display constitutes an impermissible governmental endorsement of a particular faith. The display does not satisfy the *Lemon* test. It excludes non-Christians on religious grounds. Christmas has both secular and religious aspects, and the government should not emphasize the religious aspects.

---

4. De Facto Establishment

a. Sunday closing laws

In *McGowan v. Maryland*, 366 U.S. 420 (1961), the Court upheld a state law that required most retail stores to close on Sundays. It found that such laws do not involve the "establishment" of religion in that they do not directly aid or inhibit any religion, but merely set aside a uniform day of rest, which is a proper exercise of the police power to promote the public welfare. This is true even though the laws also incidentally accomplish another purpose (aiding church attendance), which by itself would be improper.

b. State-employed chaplains

In *Marsh v. Chambers*, 463 U.S. 783 (1983), the Court upheld the practice of the Nebraska legislature of opening each day with a prayer by a chaplain paid by the state. The Court noted that the colonies, federal courts, and Continental Congress itself followed such a practice. As deeply imbedded in history and tradition as such prayer is, it cannot be held to violate the First Amendment. The dissenting Justices noted that the practice does not pass any of the *Lemon v. Kurtzman* tests (*supra*).

5. Restrictions on Teaching Particular Subjects

While the state undoubtedly has the right to prescribe curriculum for the public schools, it does not have the right to forbid the teaching of any scientific theory, doctrine, or other subject merely because it may be contrary to some religious doctrine. The Court held that an Arkansas statute that forbade the teaching of evolution in public schools violated the freedom of religion under the First and Fourteenth Amendments. The statute was not "religiously neutral"; it was aimed at one doctrine (evolution) that was offensive to certain fundamentalist religions. [*See* Epperson v. Arkansas, 393 U.S. 97 (1968)] In another case, Louisiana enacted a law requiring "balanced treatment" of the theories of creation and evolution if the subject of the origin of man, life, Earth, or the universe is dealt with in public schools. The lower courts, including a sharply divided Fifth Circuit, held that the law was unconstitutional because the theory of creation is a religious belief. The Supreme Court affirmed, holding that the law was motivated primarily by religious purposes. [Edwards v. Aguillard, 482 U.S. 578 (1987)]

6. Financial Aid to Religion

a. Basic test

The Court has promulgated three guidelines for determining the validity of state statutes granting financial aid to church-related schools. Recall that under the *Lemon* test, to be valid, a statute must: (i) reflect a clearly secular purpose; (ii) have a primary effect that neither advances nor inhibits religion; and (iii) avoid "excessive government entanglement" with religion. [Lemon v. Kurtzman, *supra*] The wall of separation between church and state works both ways. It prevents religion from seeping into the functions of government, and it also prevents government from encroaching on matters of religion.

b. Use of state university's facilities

The three-part test of *Lemon* was successfully used to invalidate a state university's ban against religious groups using its buildings. The university opened its facilities to student groups in general, except for religious groups. The Court held that this violated the First Amendment rights of the religious groups; a fully open forum policy would satisfy the three-part test because it would have a secular purpose, would avoid entanglement, and would not have a primary effect of advancing religion. [Widmar v. Vincent, 454 U.S. 263(1981)]

c. Tax deduction for tuition

Mueller v. Allen
463 U.S. 388 (1983).

Facts. Minnesota allowed citizens paying state income tax to deduct the cost of their children's tuition, physical education clothing, supplies, and other items. The deduction applied whether the school was public or private. Most private schools in the state were sectarian. Allen (P) challenged the statute under the Establishment Clause. The state courts upheld the deduction. The Supreme Court granted certiorari.

Issue. May a state permit parents to deduct from their income tax the cost of their children's education, including tuition paid to private sectarian schools?

Held. Yes. Judgment affirmed.

♦ The deduction is limited to actual expenses incurred for the tuition, textbooks, and transportation of dependents attending elementary or secondary schools. The validity of the deduction depends on application of the three-part *Lemon* test (*supra*).

♦ The tax deduction has a secular purpose because it promotes education in all types of schools. The statute does not have the primary effect of advancing the sectarian aims of nonpublic schools because it is part of a broader scheme of tax deductions, it is available to all parents, and whatever aid it provides to parochial schools is available only through the decisions of individual parents. Thus, there is no imprimatur of state approval.

♦ The statute does not excessively entangle the state in religion, because the only state involvement is the determination as to which textbooks qualify for a deduction (the cost of religious books is not deductible).

Dissent (Marshall, Brennan, Blackmun, Stevens, JJ.). The Establishment Clause prohibits state subsidies to sectarian schools, including deductions for tuition payments. Aid to sectarian schools must be restricted so it is not used to further the religious mission of those schools. This tax education scheme is not so restricted, so it is unconstitutional.

Comment. In *Aguilar v. Felton*, 473 U.S. 402 (1985), the Court struck down a federal plan for educationally deprived children from low-income families that permitted payment of federal funds to public school employees for remedial and guidance services provided in parochial school classrooms. The plan included a system for monitoring the religious content of the services. The Court held that this supervisory surveillance resulted in excessive entanglement of church and state.

---

d. Publicly financed school choice

Zelman v. Simmons-Harris
536 U.S. 639 (2002).

Facts. The state of Ohio adopted a pilot program that gave financial assistance to families living in any Ohio school district that was under a federal court order to be supervised by the state education superintendent, Zelman (D). The Cleveland City School District was the only district in that category. The children in the Cleveland district were mostly from low-income and minority families. The pilot program provided tuition aid for students to attend a participating public or private school chosen by their parents instead of the one they would otherwise be assigned to. Both religious and nonreligious schools could participate in the program, but 96% of the students who participated in the program attended the religious schools. Simmons-Harris and other taxpayers (Ps) sought an injunction against the program. The district court granted Ps summary judgment. The court of appeals affirmed. The Supreme Court granted certiorari.

Issue. May a state provide tuition vouchers that enable students who would otherwise attend public schools to attend private religious schools?

Held. Yes. Judgment reversed.

♦ The state had a valid secular purpose for adopting the program—to provide educational assistance to poor children in a demonstrably failing public school system. The program would violate the Establishment Clause only if it had the forbidden effect of advancing or inhibiting religion.

♦ There is a clear distinction between government programs that provide aid directly to religious schools and programs that allow, through the exercise of true private choice, for government aid going to religious schools. In previous cases, the Court has upheld neutral government programs that provided aid directly to individuals who, through their own choice, directed the aid to religious schools.

♦ Funding programs based on choice might lead to the incidental advancement of a religious message, but that advancement is attributable to the individual recipient who makes the choice, not to the government. Ohio's program does not give rise to any reasonable inference that the government is endorsing religious schools in general.

♦ The program in this case actually gives more aid to participating public schools than it gives to private schools. Families who send their children to private schools must co-pay a portion of the school's tuition.

♦ The dissent notes that 96% of the children in private schools are enrolled in religious schools, but when all children enrolled in nontraditional schools are counted, that percentage drops to 20%.

Dissent (Souter, Stevens, Ginsburg, Breyer, JJ.). Under Ohio's pilot program, students are eligible to receive tuition vouchers transferable to religious schools, but regular public schools can get no voucher payments. The voucher provisions were written in a way that benefits religious schools.

C.   The Free Exercise Clause

The Free Exercise Clause is designed to protect against governmental compulsion in regard to religious matters. It bars governmental acts that would regulate religious beliefs as such or interfere with the dissemination thereof, impede the observance of religious practices, or discriminate in favor of one religion over another, where such acts are not otherwise justifiable in terms of valid governmental aims.

1. Conflict with State Regulation

a.   Introduction

Although the Free Exercise Clause prohibits any infringement of the freedom to believe, it does not constitute an absolute protection of all activity undertaken pursuant to religious beliefs. Such activity may be regulated or prohibited by the government if there is an important or compelling state interest that prevails when balanced against the infringement of religious freedoms.

b. Development of belief-action distinction

The belief-action distinction arose in *Reynolds v. United States*, 98 U.S. 145 (1879), which upheld a law against bigamy aimed at stopping the practice of polygamy by Mormons. The Mormons practiced polygamy as a religious belief. The Court held that because polygamy was traditionally condemned, the practice could be outlawed. In *Cantwell v. Connecticut*, *supra*, an action involving fund solicitation by a Jehovah's Witness, the Court abandoned the *Reynolds* ruling that conduct was outside the protection of the First Amendment. The Court found that the freedom to act under the Free Exercise Clause, although not absolute like the freedom to believe, could only be regulated without undue infringement of the freedom to believe.

c. Flag cases

In *West Virginia State Board of Education v. Barnette*, 319 U.S. 624 (1943), the Court overruled its previous decision in *Minersville School District v. Gobitis*, 310 U.S. 586 (1940), which had sustained another flag salute public school regulation that had been challenged on religious grounds by Jehovah's Witnesses. Characterizing *Barnette* as a freedom of expression, rather than free exercise, action, the Court held that there is no power to make a salute a legal duty, that such a compulsory rite infringes an individual's constitutional liberty, and that under the Bill of Rights, orthodoxy in politics cannot be prescribed.

d. Day of worship

1) Introduction

Sunday closing laws have been upheld against attack by Sabbatarians (*e.g.*, Orthodox Jews). Such laws do not promote or discourage any religious beliefs, but simply make the practice of certain beliefs more expensive. [*See* Braunfeld v. Brown, *below*] However, the state may not punish a person for worshipping on a day other than Sunday. [*See* Sherbert v. Verner, *infra*] On the other hand, a state may not establish an obligation to give a day off to the employees choosing to worship. [*See* Estate of Thornton v. Caldor, Inc., 472 U.S. 703 (1985)]

2) Sunday closing laws affecting non-Christians

Braunfeld v. Brown
366 U.S. 599 (1961).

Facts. Braunfeld (P) was a Philadelphia merchant and a member of the Orthodox Jewish faith, so he closed his store from Friday night to Saturday night. Pennsylvania had a Sunday closing law. As a result, P lost two days of business. P sought a declaration that the Sunday closing law would prohibit the free exercise of his religion because of the economic loss. The lower courts upheld the law, and P appeals.

Issue. May a state require all businesses to close on Sunday even when a particular merchant recognizes another day of the week as his Sabbath?

Held. Yes. Judgment affirmed.

♦   The freedom to act according to one's religious convictions is not totally free from legislative restrictions. If the religious practice conflicts with the public interest, it may be regulated or prohibited. Such cases require delicate balancing. This case, however, does not make unlawful any of P's religious practices; it just makes observance more expensive.

♦   All laws that indirectly burden religion are not invalid. If the purpose or effect of a law is to impede the observance of one or all religions or to discriminate invidiously between religions, the law is invalid even though the burden is indirect. But if a general law with a secular purpose indirectly affects religion, it is valid unless the state could attain its purpose without imposing such a burden.

♦ The state is not required to exempt from its laws those whose religious convictions require observance of a different Sabbath. The state's goal of providing a day of elimination of commercial noise and activity is best attained by making a uniform day of rest.

Dissent (Brennan, J.). The Court has exalted administrative convenience to a level high enough to justify making one religion economically disadvantageous.

Dissent (Stewart, J.). The law forces an Orthodox Jew to choose between his religious faith and economic survival. This is not a choice that the government can constitutionally demand.

---

3) Disqualification for public benefits

Sherbert v. Verner
374 U.S. 398 (1963).

Facts. South Carolina (through Verner (D)) denied unemployment compensation benefits to workers who failed to accept offered employment without good cause. Sherbert (P) was denied benefits because she failed to accept a job that required Saturday work. Her basis for refusal was her membership in the Seventh Day Adventist Church, which recognized Saturday as the Sabbath day. The state courts upheld the denial of benefits. P appeals.

Issue. May a state deny benefits to otherwise eligible recipients whose failure to meet all the requirements is based on a religious belief?

Held. No. Judgment reversed.

♦ Conditioning the availability of benefits upon P's willingness to violate a cardinal principle of her religious faith effectively penalizes the free exercise of her constitutional liberties, and can only be justified by a compelling state interest.

♦ The only state interest lies in discouraging spurious claims, but D has failed to show that this possibility is significant or that no alternative, less damaging regulation exists.

♦ The result here reflects merely the governmental obligation of neutrality in the face of religious differences and does not promote or favor one religion over the other.

Concurrence (Stewart, J.). The Establishment Clause as previously construed by this Court requires denial of P's claim. Otherwise, the government would be establishing P's religion by granting her benefits because of her beliefs, while others, not of P's faith, are denied benefits. The decision proves that the Court has incorrectly construed that clause in prior cases. *Braunfeld v. Brown, supra,* should be specifically overruled.

Dissent (Harlan, White, JJ.). The Court actually overrules *Braunfeld*, since the secular purpose of the statute here is even clearer than the one in that case. The Court goes too far in holding that a state must furnish unemployment benefits to one who is unavailable for work whenever the unavailability arises from the exercise of religious convictions.

---

e. Compulsory education

Wisconsin v. Yoder
406 U.S. 205 (1972).

Facts. Yoder and other Amish parents (Ds) refused to send their children to school beyond the eighth grade despite a Wisconsin (P) law requiring attendance until age 16. Ds claimed that further education would violate their religious beliefs because the values taught in public high schools contrasted with the Amish values and way of life. Ds were convicted, but the conviction was reversed by the Wisconsin Supreme Court. P appeals.

Issue. Must a state make provision in its compulsory education laws for students whose religious beliefs prevent them from attending secondary schools?

Held. Yes. Judgment affirmed.

♦ The values of parental direction of the religious upbringing and education of their children in their formative years have a high place in our society. Only essential state interests not otherwise served can prevail over legitimate claims to the free exercise of religion.

♦ The Amish way of life is an essential part of their religious beliefs and practices. Elementary education, given locally, did not subject Ds' children to adverse influences, and is not challenged. Ds have adequately shown, however, that secondary education would tend to severely infringe on Ds' religious beliefs.

♦ P's interest in assuring education is substantially achieved in the elementary grades. Ds' children continue their education through parent-supervised agricultural vocational training. The children are thus fully prepared for responsibility. Because the state's interest in requiring the one or two extra years of education is minimal compared with Ds' religious interests, Ds' interests must prevail.

Dissent (Douglas, J.). We ought to reverse the judgment as to the parents of those students who have not affirmatively indicated a desire not to attend public high school.

---

f. Other cases

1) Social Security payments

An employer may be required to pay Social Security on his employees' wages despite objections based on religious belief. [United States v. Lee, 455 U.S. 252 (1982)]

2) Conscientious objection

The Selective Service Act permitted exemption from the draft for those who, by reasons of religious belief, are conscientiously opposed to war in any form. This has been construed to apply only to persons opposed to all wars, not just to particular wars in which the United States is involved, such as the Vietnam War. [Gillette v. United States, *supra*]

3) Tax-exempt status

The IRS may deny tax-exempt status to religious schools that practice racial discrimination. [Bob Jones University v. United States, 461 U.S. 574 (1983)]

4) Veterans' preferences

The Court has upheld a federal law that grants educational benefits to veterans while denying the same benefits to conscientious objectors, even though the conscientious objectors performed the alternate civilian service required by the draft laws. The distinction was considered at most an incidental burden of the free exercise of religion and was justified by the need to raise and support armies. [Johnson v. Robison, 415 U.S. 361 (1974)]

5) Exclusion of clergy from public office

In *McDaniel v. Paty*, 435 U.S. 618 (1978), the Court overturned a state constitutional provision that prohibited ministers from serving as state legislators. The Court noted that experience had shown that ministers were not less faithful to their oaths of civil office than unordained legislators, and that, applying a balancing test, the restriction violated the Free Exercise Clause.

2. Limitation on Required Accommodation

Employment Division, Department of Human Resources of Oregon v. Smith
494 U.S. 872 (1990).

Facts. The state of Oregon made it a crime to use peyote. Smith (P) was dismissed from his job for using peyote as part of his religious ritual as a member of the Native American Church. P was denied unemployment benefits because his dismissal was due to misconduct. P sued the Employment Division, Department of Human Resources (D), claiming that his use of peyote was inspired by religion and therefore was protected under the Free Exercise Clause of the First Amendment. The Oregon Supreme Court reversed, holding that the criminal sanction was unconstitutional as applied to the religious use of peyote, and ruled that P was entitled to unemployment benefits. The Supreme Court granted certiorari.

Issue. May a state make criminal certain conduct that is part of a religious organization's ritual?

Held. Yes. Judgment reversed.

♦ P relies on *Sherbert v. Verner, supra*, which held that a state could not condition the availability of unemployment insurance on an applicant's willingness to forgo conduct required by his religion. In that case, however, the conduct was not prohibited by law; in this case, peyote use was prohibited by law.

♦ The states cannot ban acts or abstentions only when they are engaged in for religious reasons, or only because of the religious belief they display, because this would constitute a prohibition on the free exercise of religion. This does not mean that a religious motivation for illegal conduct exempts the actor from the law. If prohibiting the exercise of religion is merely an incidental effect of a generally applicable and otherwise valid law, the First Amendment is not implicated.

♦ In some cases, such as *Wisconsin v. Yoder, supra*, the First Amendment may prevent application of a neutral, generally applicable law to religiously motivated action, but these cases involve the Free Exercise Clause in connection with other constitutional protections, such as parents' right to direct the education of their children.

♦ P argues that the *Sherbert* test should be applied, but this test has never invalidated governmental action except the denial of unemployment compensation, and should not be extended beyond that field to require exemptions from a generally applicable criminal law. In unemployment cases, the test is applied to prevent a state from refusing to extend religious hardship cases to a system of individual exemptions.

♦ If the compelling interest requirement were applied to religion cases such as this, many laws would not satisfy the test, and the result would approach anarchy, particularly in a society such as ours that contains a diversity of religious beliefs. This alternative would raise a presumption of invalidity, as applied to the religious objector, of every regulation of conduct that does not protect an interest of the highest order. The states are free, as many have, to exempt from their drug laws the use of peyote in sacramental services, but the states are not constitutionally required to do so.

Concurrence (O'Connor, Brennan, Marshall, Blackmun, JJ.). A law that prohibits religiously motivated conduct implicates First Amendment concerns, even if it is generally applicable. The First Amendment does not distinguish between laws that are generally applicable and laws that target particular religious practices; it applies to generally applicable laws that have the effect of significantly burdening a religious practice. The balance between the First Amendment and the government's legitimate interest in regulating conduct is struck by applying the compelling interest test. To be sustained, a law that burdens the free exercise of religion must either be essential to accomplish an overriding governmental interest or represent the least restrictive means of achieving some compelling state interest. In this case, the prohibition on use of peyote does satisfy the compelling state interest test.

Dissent (Blackmun, Brennan, Marshall, JJ.). The state's broad interest in fighting the war on drugs is not the interest involved in this case; the interest is the state's refusal to make an exception for the religious, ceremonial use of peyote. There is no evidence that the religious use of peyote ever harmed anyone, and 23 other states have adopted exemptions for the religious use of peyote. The assertion that requiring the state to make an exemption in this case would open the government to anarchy is speculative; such a danger is addressed through the compelling interest test.

D. Permissible Accommodation

1. Employment on the Basis of Religion

Corporation of Presiding Bishop of the Church of Jesus Christ of Latter-Day Saints v. Amos
483 U.S. 327 (1987).

Facts. The Corporation of Presiding Bishop of the Church of Jesus Christ of Latter-Day Saints (D) operated the nonprofit Deseret Gymnasium. Amos (P) was a janitor at the gym. P did not qualify for a temple recommend (a certificate that a person is a member of the church), which required observance of D's standards including church attendance, tithing, and abstinence from coffee, tea, alcohol, and tobacco. P was fired. Section 702 of the Civil Rights Act of 1964 [42 U.S.C. §2000e-1] exempts religious organizations such as D from the general prohibition against employment discrimination on the basis of religion. P sued, claiming that the exemption should not apply to secular nonprofit activities of religious organizations. The district court and court of appeals upheld P's claim, and D appeals.

Issue. May Congress accommodate religious practices by permitting religious organizations to discriminate in employment on the basis of religion even in secular nonprofit activities?

Held. Yes. Judgment reversed.

♦ Governmental accommodation of religious practices does not necessarily violate the Establishment Clause. Such benevolent neutrality permits free exercise of religion without either sponsorship or interference.

♦ The three-part *Lemon* analysis may be applied to accommodation cases. [Lemon v. Kurtzman, *supra*] The first requirement, that the challenged law serve a secular legislative purpose, is intended to prevent Congress from abandoning neutrality and acting to promote a particular point of view in religious matters. A legislative purpose to alleviate significant governmental interference with a religious group's ability to exercise its religion is a permissible purpose.

- Congress amended the Civil Rights Act to extend the exemption to secular nonprofit activities of religious organizations because the exemption previously applied only to religious activities. The exemption acted to minimize governmental interference with the decisionmaking process in religious groups, which is a permitted purpose.

- The second *Lemon* requirement is that the law have a principal effect that neither advances nor inhibits religion. A law may permit churches to advance religion; the prohibition is only against governmental advancement, through its own activities and influence, of religion. Any advancement of religion that D might achieve through its gymnasium cannot be fairly attributed to the government, as opposed to D.

- The third requirement is that Congress must have chosen a rational classification to further a legitimate end. Section 702 is rationally related to the legitimate purpose of alleviating significant governmental interference with the ability of religious organizations to define and carry out their religious missions.

Concurrence (Brennan, Marshall, JJ.). The exemption from Title VII's prohibition of religious discrimination burdens the religious liberty of employees such as P. However, religious organizations such as D have an interest in autonomy in ordering their internal affairs, including defining the religious community. While individual interests in religious freedom would only permit an exemption for religious activities, a case-by-case determination of which nonprofit activities are religious and which are not would involve unacceptable entanglement with religion and a chill on religious expression, and the balance between these interests must fall in favor of the broader exception relied on by D.

Concurrence (O'Connor, J.). Judicial deference to all legislation that purports to facilitate the free exercise of religion would vitiate the Establishment Clause. The Court suggests that the "effects" prong of the *Lemon* test is not implicated if the government action merely "allows" religious organizations to advance religion. A better approach is to recognize that by exempting religious organizations from a generally applicable regulatory burden, the government does advance religion; it only remains to be determined whether the benefit accommodates free exercise or unjustifiably awards assistance to religion. The probability that a nonprofit activity is involved in the organization's religious mission is sufficient to justify a conclusion that the government action exempting such activities is an accommodation of religion, not a government endorsement of religion.

---

2. Impermissible Tax Exemption

Texas Monthly v. Bullock
489 U.S. 1 (1989).

Facts. The state of Texas exempted the sale of religious periodicals by religious organizations from its sales tax. A publisher of a nonreligious publication challenged the statute. The trial court found the exemption unconstitutional, but the court of appeals reversed. The case is before the United States Supreme Court.

Issue. May a state exempt religious publications from state sales tax?

Held. No. Judgment reversed.

- The exemption has insufficient breadth of coverage; it applies only to religious publications and does not apply to nonreligious publications that contribute to the community's cultural, intellectual, and moral betterment. Hence, it constitutes an unjustifiable award of assistance to religious organizations and conveys a message of endorsement

Dissent (Scalia, J., Rehnquist, C.J., Kennedy, J.). Breadth of coverage is not relevant unless the state asserts purely secular grounds for the exemption. When religion is singled out, particularly for an exemption from a tax that could be construed as an unconstitutional burden on religion, the exemption should be construed as an accommodation.

Concurrence (Blackmun, O'Connor, JJ.). The exemption is unconstitutional because it is limited to the sale of religious literature by religious organizations.

---

3. Impermissible Establishment

Board of Education of Kiryas Joel Village School District v. Grumet

512 U.S. 687 (1994).

Facts. The New York state legislature created the Kiryas Joel Village School District and authorized its board of education (D) to open and close schools, hire teachers, etc. D's jurisdiction was limited to the Village of Kiryas Joel, which had been founded by, and was inhabited exclusively by, Satmar Hasidim, practitioners of a strict form of Judaism. The Satmars sought to avoid assimilation into the modern world and educated their children in private religious schools. These schools did not provide any distinctive services to handicapped children; such services were provided by the public school district that included the village, until the Court decided in *Aguilar v. Felton, supra*, that such arrangements were unconstitutional. D's only program was a special education program for handicapped children, but it did provide transportation and health and welfare services for the parochial schools. Grumet and others (Ps) successfully challenged the constitutionality of the creation of D, and the Supreme Court granted certiorari.

Issue. May a state create a separate school district, the boundaries of which are determined by the boundaries of a village inhabited exclusively by a distinct religious group?

Held. No. Judgment affirmed.

♦ Pursuant to the Establishment Clause, the government may not demonstrate a preference to one religion over another one. In this case, we have no assurance "that the next similarly situated group seeking a school district of its own will receive one." While the government in certain cases may take steps to alleviate certain burdens on a religious group, *the* creation of D "singles out a particular religious sect for special treatment" and thereby violates the idea that "neutrality as among religions must be honored."

Concurrence (Stevens, Blackmun, Ginsburg, JJ.). The state could have addressed the fears of the Satmar children by teaching other school children to have tolerance and respect for the Satmar customs. The type of affirmative state action in aid of religious segregation displayed in this case constitutes establishment, not accommodation, of religion.

Concurrence (Kennedy, J.). The real problem with D is that the state created it "by drawing political boundaries on the basis of religion." Such religious gerrymandering violates the First Amendment.

Concurrence (O'Connor, J.). The government may accommodate religion through neutral laws. The creation of D, rather than accommodating the Satmars, singles them out for favorable treatment. **Dissent** (Scalia, J., Rehnquist, C.J., Thomas, J.). "[T]he Court's 'no guarantee of neutrality' argument is an assertion of this Court's inability to control the New York Legislature's future denial of comparable accommodation. [Most] efforts at accommodation seek to solve a problem that applies to members of only one or a few religions. . . . [The Court should not require] some 'up front' legislative guarantee of equal treatment for [other religious] sects."

---

4. Unusual Religious Beliefs and Practices

The definition of "religion" for purposes of the First Amendment has not yet been definitively determined. However, the Court has set forth certain parameters.

a. Inquiry into truth of religious precepts forbidden

In *United States v. Ballard*, 322 U.S. 78 (1944), the Court articulated its position that under the First Amendment, submission to a jury of the truth of a party's religious beliefs is barred because of the subjective nature of such proof. "Men may believe what they cannot prove," so the truth or reasonableness of a belief cannot be questioned by a court.

b. Belief in God

Belief in God may not be used as an essential qualification for office. When Maryland denied a commission as a notary public to an otherwise qualified appointee because he refused to declare his belief in the existence of God (as required by the Maryland Constitution for those who seek to qualify for "any office or profit or trust"), the Court held that such a "religious test for public office" imposed a burden on the applicant's freedom of belief and religion. [Torcaso v. Watkins, 367 U.S. 488 (1961)]

c. Draft-exemption definition

In a draft case turning on whether a person was exempt as a conscientious objector by virtue of his "religious training and belief (a requirement of the Selective Service Act, not a constitutional issue), the Court held:

1) "Religious" belief is something more than essentially sociological, philosophical, economic, or political views.

2) It does not require belief in any particular dogma, or in any supernatural force or Supreme Being.

3) It must, however, be sincere and meaningful and occupy a place in the life of its possessor parallel to that filled by the orthodox belief in God of those who are customarily regarded as "religious" persons. [United States v. Seeger, 380 U.S. 163 (1965)]

Chapter X

The Constitution and State vs. Private Action

A. Introduction to the State Action Doctrine

1. Basic Issue

Both the Fourteenth and Fifteenth Amendments prohibit certain "state action" as opposed to private, nongovernmental action. The determinative question is whether any particular conduct is state action. The response to that question has changed over the years. Early cases held that these amendments did not apply to private acts of discrimination. Distinguishing between public and private conduct became increasingly difficult as government became more intimately involved in regulating and even participating in the private sector, as will be seen in the more modern cases.

2. Nineteenth Century Approach

The Civil Rights Cases
109 U.S. 3 (1883).

Facts. The Civil Rights Act of 1875 made it unlawful for anyone to deny a person the enjoyment of accommodations at inns, on public transportation, etc., on the basis of race. Certain blacks (Ps) were excluded from inns, theaters, and a railroad in five separate states. The cases were consolidated before the Supreme Court.

Issue. May Congress prohibit private discriminatory actions by facilities generally open to the public?

Held. No. The Civil Rights Act is unconstitutional.

♦ The Fourteenth Amendment permits Congress to take corrective action only against state laws or acts done under state authority. The Civil Rights Act is directed toward acts by individuals and cannot be upheld under the Fourteenth Amendment.

♦ The Thirteenth Amendment permits direct as opposed to merely corrective legislation, but it only covers slavery or involuntary servitude, or the lingering badges of such. Refusing accommodation to a black does not impose any badge of slavery or servitude. Mere racial discrimination is not a badge of slavery.

♦ Congress has no power to pass the Civil Rights Act, and Ps must seek a remedy in state law for any cause of action against private individuals or corporations that are discriminating.

Dissent (Harlan, J.). The Court has ignored the substance and spirit of these Amendments. Freedom includes immunity from and protection against racial discrimination, especially in the use of public, albeit privately owned, accommodations and facilities licensed by the state.

Comment. The common law of all states at the time of the Civil Rights Act of 1875 held that it was unlawful to deny the facilities of inns and carriers to any person. Therefore, Ps did have a remedy in state law. However, this case illustrates the approach to state action that permitted individuals to discriminate freely if they wanted.

B. Government Inaction

1. Introduction

State action exists whenever a state has affirmatively facilitated, encouraged, or authorized acts of discrimination by its citizens. States are not required to outlaw discrimination, but they cannot do anything to encourage it. The mere fact that the government permits certain commercial activity does not make that activity state action. But if enforcement of commercial rights, such as contract rights, becomes necessary, the government may decline to take action if the commercial activity is unconstitutional.

2. Government's Failure to Act

DeShaney v. Winnebago County Department of Social Services
489 U.S. 189 (1989).

Facts. DeShaney (P), a two-year-old child, had been the victim of child abuse by his father. The incidents were reported to the Winnebago Department of Social Services (D), which investigated but took no action. One year later, after P was treated at a hospital for further abuse, D required P's father to undergo counseling and to have his girlfriend move out, but the father never fully complied with these requirements. During the next year, D's caseworker recorded additional incidents of abuse, but took no action. P's father finally beat P so badly that he suffered permanent brain damage. P sued D, claiming D had deprived him of his liberty without due process of law. The lower courts granted judgment for D, and the Supreme Court granted certiorari.

Issue. May the government's failure to protect a child from his parent's abuse constitute a violation of substantive due process?

Held. No. Judgment affirmed.

♦ Nothing in the Due Process Clause requires the state to protect the life, liberty, and property of citizens against invasion by private actors. The clause protects people from the state; it does not require the state to protect citizens from each other.

♦ The Due Process Clause does not confer an affirmative right to governmental aid, even when necessary to secure life, liberty, or property interests. Because the clause does not impose such an obligation, the state cannot be held liable under the clause for injuries that could have been avoided had the state assumed the obligation. There is no special relationship between P and D that arose merely because D knew P was in danger. If any such relationship is desired, the people may, through their legislatures, adopt a tort law remedy.

Dissent (Brennan, Marshall, Blackmun, JJ.). D in effect cut off private sources of help by preempting them. When D refused to help, it should not be permitted to avoid responsibility for the harm that resulted from its refusal.

---

3. Commercial Rights and Remedies

Flagg Brothers v. Brooks
436 U.S. 149 (1978).

Facts. Brooks (P) was evicted and her possessions stored by Flagg Brothers (D). When P failed to pay storage charges, D threatened to sell P's possessions, pursuant to procedures established by the New York Uniform Commercial Code ("U.C.C."). P brought an action seeking damages, an injunction, and declaratory relief that the U.C.C. provision was unconstitutional. The district court dismissed the complaint, but the court of appeals reversed, finding state involvement in D's action sufficient to invoke constitutional protections. D appeals.

Issue. Does a warehouseman's sale of goods entrusted to him for storage constitute state action because it is permitted by state law?

Held. No. Judgment reversed.

♦ P claims that the state delegated to D a power traditionally held only by the state. While many functions have been traditionally performed by governments, very few have been exclusively reserved to the states. The settlement of disputes between debtors and creditors is not traditionally an exclusive public function, so D's action is not state action.

♦ P also claims that D's action is state action because the state has authorized and encouraged it by enacting the U.C.C. While private action compelled by a state is properly attributable to the state, mere acquiescence by the state is insufficient. The state here has merely refused to provide P a remedy for D's private deprivation of P's property. Therefore, D's action is not a state action.

Dissent (Stevens, White, Marshall, JJ.). The question is whether a state statute that authorizes a private party to deprive a person of his property without his consent must satisfy due process requirements. Clearly, it should. Permitting only state delegation of exclusively sovereign functions to bring private action within constitutional bounds is inconsistent with prior decisions. P should be permitted to challenge the state procedure permitted by state law.

---

4. Writ of Attachment

Lugar v. Edmondson Oil Co.
457 U.S. 922 (1982).

Facts. Edmondson Oil Co. (P) sued Lugar (D) in state court for debts. Using state law, P filed an ex parte petition for prejudgment attachment of some of D's property, which was granted and executed by the county sheriff. D later prevailed. D men brought this action in federal court and alleged that P deprived him of his property without due process of law.

Issue. Does the prejudgment attachment procedure deprive a debtor of his property through state action?

Held. Yes.

♦ Private use of state procedures with the help of state officials constitutes state action for purposes of the Fourteenth Amendment.

♦ The applicable framework for state action analysis is as follows. First, the court must ask whether the claimed constitutional deprivation resulted from the exercise of a right or privilege having its source in state authority. If so, the court then must determine whether the private party charged with the deprivation could be described in all fairness as a state actor.

Dissent (Powell, Rehnquist, O'Connor, JJ.). P is a private individual who did nothing more than commence a legal action. This does not make P a state actor. D could have sued the state officials but did not.

---

5. Enforcement of Private Contracts

Shelley v. Kraemer
334 U.S. 1 (1948).

Facts. Shelley (D), a black person, purchased residential property that, unknown to D, was encumbered by a restrictive agreement that prevented ownership or occupancy of the property by non-Caucasians. Kraemer (P), a neighbor and owner of other property subject to the restriction, brought suit to restrain D from possessing the property and to divest title out of D. The trial court denied relief, but the Missouri Supreme Court reversed. D appeals.

Issue. Does the Fourteenth Amendment Equal Protection Clause prohibit judicial enforcement by state courts of restrictive covenants based on race or color?

Held. Yes. Judgment reversed.

♦ Property rights clearly are among those civil rights protected from discriminatory state action by the Fourteenth Amendment. Early decisions invalidated any government restrictions on residency based on race. Here the restrictions are purely private and, standing alone, are not precluded by the Fourteenth Amendment.

♦ Actions of state courts are state actions within the meaning of the Fourteenth Amendment. Judicial enforcement of these private racial restrictions constitutes state discrimination contrary to the Fourteenth Amendment, and denies D equal protection.

Comment. *Shelley* and other cases indicate that what is essentially a private act of discrimination may become illegal state action if the state or its officers are in any way involved in carrying out the private action. Possibly any private action that gets into court may then amount to state action.

---

6. Additional Cases

a. Civil damages

In *Barrows v. Jackson*, 346 U.S. 249 (1953), a case involving a damages action against a co-covenantor, the Court applied the *Shelley, supra,* reasoning to block enforcement of the restrictive covenant. The Court stated that it would not require a state to coerce a covenantor to respond in damages for failure to observe a covenant that the state would have no right to enforce.

b. Will provisions

In *Pennsylvania v. Board of Directors of City Trusts,* 353 U.S. 230 (1957), the Supreme Court held that a will that had discriminatory provisions might be infused with state action when enforced by a state court. There, a private citizen willed his property to be used for a school for poor white orphan children, the city council to serve as the board of trustees.

c. Trespass

In a three-to-three decision rendered in a case involving a restaurant sit-in, the Court reversed a trespass conviction on the basis of *Shelley, supra.* The Court stated that the discrimination was done for business reasons and the property was associated with serving the public. The dissent, construing Section 1 of the Fourteenth Amendment more narrowly, argued that without cooperative state action, no property owner was forbidden from banning people from his premises, even if the owner was acting with racial prejudice. [Bell v. Maryland, 378 U.S. 226 (1964)]

C. State Subsidization, Approval, and Encouragement

1. Introduction

Private activity may also be treated as state action when the government requires, significantly encourages, or profits from the activity. This does not mean that the government's mere failure to forbid private discrimination is a constitutional violation, but if the government is closely involved in private discrimination in some way, the private discrimination is state action.

2. Private Use of Government Property

Burton v. Wilmington Parking Authority
365 U.S. 715 (1961).

Facts. Burton (P), a black man, was denied service at a private restaurant (the Eagle) located within a building owned and operated by the Wilmington Parking Authority (D), a state agency. D had leased out some of its space, including the lease to the Eagle, to assist in its financing. P sued, claiming that although the Eagle was private, it had sufficient nexus to D to make its discrimination a state action. The trial court granted summary judgment for P, and the Delaware Supreme Court reversed on the basis of a state law assuring restaurants of the right to refuse service to any person whose reception would injure the business. P appeals.

Issue. Is a private lessee of state property required to comply with the Fourteenth Amendment if the lease furthers state interests and forms an integral part of a state operation?

Held. Yes. Judgment reversed.

♦ Although private conduct abridging individual rights does not violate the Equal Protection Clause, if any significant state action is involved, the discrimination is unconstitutional. D is so closely involved with the Eagle that it is a joint participant, and the Eagle is not so purely private as to fall beyond the scope of the Fourteenth Amendment. The government has a symbiotic relationship with the Eagle and is profiting from the invidious discrimination.

♦ D clearly could have required the Eagle to agree to a binding covenant not to discriminate, but its failure to do so does not permit D to abdicate its responsibilities to prevent discrimination. D has, by its inaction, become a party to the discrimination. Lessee Eagle must therefore comply with the Fourteenth Amendment.

Concurrence (Stewart, J.). There is no evidence that P as an individual was a person whose reception would injure the business.

Dissent (Harlan, Whittaker, JJ.). It is unclear what it is in the record that is "state action."

Comment. Following the particularized approach set forth in *Burton*, the Court remanded *Gilmore v. City of Montgomery*, 417 U.S. 556 (1974), an action involving a federal injunction barring a city from permitting private segregated school groups and racially discriminatory nonschool groups to use its recreational facilities. The Court held that although exclusive temporary use interfered with a school desegregation order, the lower court's ruling against nonexclusive use by the groups, especially the private nonschool groups, was invalid without a proper finding of state action.

---

3. Publicly Funded Private School

Rendell-Baker v. Kohn
457 U.S. 830 (1982).

Facts. Rendell-Baker and five teachers (Ps) were employed at a private school that specialized in assisting students who could not complete public high school. The school was funded primarily by the state and was subject to various state administrative regulations, including mandatory written job descriptions and personnel standards and procedures. The state used the school to fulfill a statutory requirement to assist students needing special help. Ps were discharged by the school for supporting certain student grievances of school policies. Ps sued but were denied relief. The Supreme Court granted certiorari.

Issue. Does action taken by a private school used by the state to fulfill a legislative requirement constitute state action?

Held. No. Judgment affirmed.

♦ The fact that the school depended on government funds to operate is not determinative, for all private contractors that perform government contracts depend on public funds.

♦ The school was subject to government regulation in some areas, but its decision to discharge Ps was not compelled or even influenced by state regulation. Even though a government committee approved hirees, the decision to discharge Ps was made solely by private management.

♦ Operation of a school is not an exclusive public function. Service to the public interest does not render private activity state action. Nor is there a symbiotic relationship because the government does not profit from the school's activity any more than it does from any contractor's performance of a public contract.

Dissent (Marshall, Brennan, JJ.). The school's very survival depends on the state, and the state depends on the school to perform its statutory duty. A closer relationship between government and private enterprise is difficult to imagine.

---

4. Exclusive Use of Term

San Francisco Arts & Athletics, Inc. v. United States Olympic Committee
843 U.S. 522 (1987).

Facts. Congress gave the United States Olympic Committee (P) the exclusive right to use the term "Olympic." On occasion, P had permitted other groups to use the word "Olympic." San Francisco Arts

& Athletics, Inc. (D) organized and promoted the "Gay Olympic Games." P sued to enjoin D from using the word "Olympic." D argued that P was discriminating against it in violation of equal protection. The lower courts found for P and the Supreme Court granted certiorari.

Issue. Does P's allegedly discriminatory conduct constitute state action?

Held. No. Judgment affirmed.

♦ All corporations receive charters granted by the government, P is no different.

♦ Furthermore, the right to exclusive use of the word "Olympic" is comparable to standard trademark rights created by the federal government. The government did not decide how P would use the right.

Dissent (Brennan, Marshall, JJ.). There is a sufficient nexus between P and the government to find state action. P has been given the authority that no other private organization has ever held. The public also sees P as connected to the federal government. It would be ironic if P were financed by the government to represent the virtues of our political system, but were free to use government-created economic leverage to prohibit political speech.

---

5. Supervision and Investigation by Government

Public Utilities Commission v. Pollak
343 U.S. 451 (1952).

Facts. Capital Transit Company ("Capital"), a private corporation acting under a franchise from Congress, operated buses and streetcars in the District of Columbia. Capital installed and used radio receivers on the streetcars and buses as part of a "music as you ride" program. On its own motion, the Public Utilities Commission of the District of Columbia ("the Commission") began an investigation into whether the use of the radios was consistent with public convenience, comfort, and safety. The Commission determined that the program was permissible and dismissed its investigation. Pollak and some other passengers (Ps) appealed, and the court of appeals reversed finding that the program deprived passengers of liberty without due process of law. The Supreme Court granted certiorari.

Issue. Does the program amount to state action?

Held. Yes, but the broadcasts are not unconstitutional. Judgment reversed.

♦ In order to find state action is involved, it is not enough that Capital operates a public utility or that Capital enjoys a substantial monopoly thanks to the federal government. What is important is that the Commission, an agency authorized by Congress, supervised Capital and ordered an investigation of the program, held public hearings, and ultimately drew its own conclusion about the program and had the investigation dismissed.

---

6. State Licensing

Moose Lodge No. 107 v. Irvis
407 U.S. 163 (1972).

Facts. Irvis (P), a black person, was refused service by Moose Lodge No. 107 (D). P claimed that D's action was a state action because D was licensed by the state liquor board to sell alcoholic beverages. A three-judge district court held for P on the merits, and D appeals.

Issue. Does state alcoholic licensing of a private club constitute sufficient state action to require that the club observe Fourteenth Amendment prohibitions against discrimination?

Held. No. Judgment reversed.

♦ A private entity is not covered by the Fourteenth Amendment when it merely receives any sort of benefit or service at all from the state, or if subject to any state regulation. Otherwise the distinction between private and public would be meaningless. If the impetus for the discrimination is private, state involvement must be significant to implicate constitutional standards.

♦ Here, the state's liquor regulation in no way fostered or encouraged racial discrimination. However, those regulations did require that licensed clubs must adhere to their own constitutions and bylaws. States may not use sanctions to enforce segregative rules, and P is entitled to an injunction against the enforcement of the state regulation that would require D to enforce its own discriminatory rules.

Dissent (Marshall, Douglas, JJ.). The state's licensing scheme includes a complex quota system. The quota in D's area has been full for many years; no more club licenses may be issued in the city. Since private clubs are the only places that serve liquor for significant portions of each week, the state has restricted access by blacks to liquor by granting a license to D instead of to a nondiscriminatory club.

Dissent (Brennan, Marshall, JJ.). The state has become an active participant in the operation of D's bar through its detailed regulatory scheme, and D should be required to observe Fourteenth Amendment standards.

---

7. Business Regulation

Jackson v. Metropolitan Edison Co.
419 U.S. 345 (1974).

Facts. Metropolitan Edison Company (D), a private utility regulated by the state, terminated Jackson's (P's) electric service for nonpayment before affording P notice, hearing, and an opportunity to pay. P sued, contending that D's action constituted state action depriving her of property without due process of law. The lower courts dismissed P's complaint, and P appeals.

Issue. Does termination of service by a heavily regulated private utility, using procedures permitted by state law, constitute state action?

Held. No. Judgment affirmed.

♦ State regulation of a private business, even if extensive and detailed, does not by itself convert private action into state action for Fourteenth Amendment purposes. There must be a close nexus between the state and the actual activity of the regulated entity. D's monopoly status, by itself, fails to show such a nexus. Nor is D's service a public function, since the state has no obligation to furnish such service. The limited notion that businesses "affected with a public interest" are state actors cannot be expanded to include private utilities.

♦ The state concededly approved D's termination procedures, but not upon consideration of a specific case. The state's approval amounts merely to a finding that the procedures are permissible under state law. For these reasons, D's actions cannot be considered to be state actions.

Dissent (Marshall, J.). The essential nature of D's service requires that D be subject to the same standards as other governmental entities. The interests of diversity and flexibility that favor protection of private entities from constitutional standards are irrelevant in monopoly situations like

D's. Finally, the majority's opinion would appear to apply to a broad range of claimed constitutional violations by the company, including racial discrimination.

D. The Public Function Doctrine

1. Introduction

Some activity undertaken by private individuals or organizations replaces traditionally exclusive prerogatives of the state. In these situations, the private activity may be treated as state action on the grounds that it is a public or government function. The Supreme Court's approach to the public function doctrine has varied through the years. The basic competing interests are the need for "private space" free from governmental control and the risk that private action will undermine constitutional values.

2. Private Company Towns

Marsh v. Alabama
326 U.S. 501 (1946).

Facts. The town of Chickasaw was entirely owned by the Gulf Shipbuilding Corporation. The town consisted of homes, streets, a sewage plant, and a business district, which was accessible from a public highway. A notice posted in the stores stated that they were private property and that no solicitation was allowed without written permission. Marsh (D), a Jehovah's Witness, began distributing religious literature outside the post office. She refused to leave after being warned that she needed permission to distribute the literature and that no permit would be issued. D was arrested and convicted of trespassing, and D appeals.

Issue. May a company town forbid the distribution of religious literature in its streets?

Held. No. Judgment reversed.

♦ A company town's power over its inhabitants is not the same as a homeowner's right to regulate his guests. Ownership does not always mean absolute dominion. The more a private owner extends the use of his property to the public, the more his rights must yield to the rights of those who use his property.

♦ The company cannot curtail the First Amendment rights of the people as it has done here, and any state action to enforce such a curtailment, such as prosecuting D, violates the First and Fourteenth Amendments. The constitutional rights of freedom of press and religion outweigh the constitutional rights of property owners who open their property to the public.

Dissent (Reed, J.). This decision allows one to remain on private property against the will of the owner as long as she is there to spread her religious views.

Comments.

♦ At one time, many workers lived in houses owned by their employers, including about one-half of the miners in the United States.

♦ The Court has held that the "company town" rational of *Marsh* does not extend to the passageways in a privately owned shopping center. [Hudgens v. NLRB, 424 U.S. 507 (1976)]

3. The Conduct of Elections

Through a series of cases called the *White Primary Cases*, the Court has held that the conduct of elections is an exclusively public function. Therefore, state attempts to vest in private boards or political parties any effective control over the selection of candidates or the exercise of voting rights are not valid. The Court has invalidated such state action as:

a. Giving authority to a political party to determine who can vote in primary elections from which the party nominee for the general election is chosen [Smith v. Allwright, 321 U.S. 649 (1944)]; and

b. Structuring the state's electoral apparatus to vest in a political party the power to hold a primary from which blacks are excluded, or to determine who shall run in the party primary in which blacks are permitted to participate. [Terry v. Adams, 345 U.S. 461 (1953)]

4. Public Utilities

Jackson v. Metropolitan Edison Co.
supra.

Facts. See supra.

Issue. Does the doctrine of public function include all businesses that are affected with the public interest?

Held. No.

♦ The phrase "affected with a public interest" is not susceptible of definition and therefore cannot form a satisfactory test. Doctors, lawyers, and even a grocery selling regulated milk all arguably provide essential goods and services "affected with a public interest." That status, by itself, is insufficient to convert their actions into the actions of the state.

Dissent (Douglas, J.). The utility is a monopoly and provides electricity, without which a home is likely to become unlivable.

Dissent (Marshall, J.). In many communities, the government does provide electricity, so that utility service is traditionally identified with the state.

---

5. Shopping Centers

At one time, the Court held that the *Marsh* principle applied to shopping centers. [Amalgamated Food Employees Union v. Logan Valley Plaza, 391 U.S. 308 (1968)] That holding was subsequently limited in *Lloyd Corp. v. Tanner*, 407 U.S. 551 (1972), and ultimately abandoned in *Hudgens v. NLRB*, 424 U.S. 507 (1976), which held that the free speech guarantees do not apply to expression in private shopping centers.

6. Other Locations

The Court has held that other private entities do not convert their actions into state action merely because they perform a function that serves the public. This includes private schools [Rendell-Baker v. Kohn, *supra*], nursing homes [Blum v. Yaretsky, *supra*], and amateur sports [San Francisco Arts & Athletics, Inc. v. United States Olympic Committee, *supra*].

E. Unconstitutional Conditions

1. Introduction

The government often imposes conditions to the receipt of government benefits, such as housing, licenses, money, and employment. These conditions may raise constitutional questions.

2. Policy-Based Funding

In *Rust v. Sullivan*, 500 U.S. 173 (1991), a federal statute provided that federal funds could not be used for family service programs in which abortion was a method of family planning. The Court held that the government may selectively fund a program to encourage programs that it finds to be in the public interest, without violating the Constitution. Such activity is not discrimination, but merely a policy choice to fund one activity and not the other. The Court noted that the government was not denying a benefit to anyone, but merely requiring that public funds be spent for authorized purposes. The Court distinguished cases in which the government places a condition on the recipient of the subsidy rather than on a particular program or service.

3. Selective Funding

In *Maher v. Roe*, 432 U.S. 464 (1977), the Court held that a state may allow Medicaid benefits for childbirth while denying benefits for nontherapeutic abortions. [Maher v. Roe, 432 U.S. 464 (1977)] The regulation did not discriminate against a suspect class. It did not place an obstacle in the way of pregnant women getting an abortion. The state merely made childbirth a more attractive option than it otherwise might have been.

4. Selective Withholding of Funds

In *South Dakota v. Dole*, 483 U.S. 203 (1987), the Court held that the federal government may withhold funds from states that do not prohibit 21-year-olds from purchasing alcohol. The Court noted that Congress might offer a financial inducement that is so coercive as to become compulsion instead of pressure, but the provision in this case was a relatively mild encouragement. However, as discussed supra, in National Federation of Independent Business v. Sebelius, 132 S.Ct. 2566 (2012), the Court held that the Medicaid expansion was unconstitutional because States not agreeing to the expansion would lose all their pre-existing Medicaid funding. When "pressure turns into compulsion" legislation runs contrary to the constitutional system of federalism.

5. Condition Requiring Forfeiture of Property

In *Nollan v. California Coastal Commission*, 483 U.S. 825 (1987), the Court held that a state could not condition the grant of a building permit on the owners' agreement to grant the public an easement across their property to the beach. The right to build on one's property is not a "government benefit." Under the Fourteenth Amendment, the state could not require an uncompensated conveyance, so it could not make such a conveyance a condition for approval of a building permit.

Table of Cases